P9-ARD-771

Early Childhood
ART

• • • • • • • • • • •

Fifth Edition

Barbara Herberholz
California State University, Sacramento

Lee Hanson
Palo Alto Unified School District, Palo Alto, CA

Boston, Massachusetts   Burr Ridge, Illinios   Dubuque, Iowa
Madison, Wisconsin   New York, New York   San Francisco, California   St. Louis, Missouri

McGraw·Hill

A Division of The **McGraw·Hill** *Companies*

Book Team

Associate Publisher *Rosemary Bradley*
Developmental Editor *Deborah Daniel Reinbold*
Production Editor *Karen A. Pluemer*
Art Editor *Brenda Ernzen*
Photo Editor *Shirley Lanners*
Production Manager *Beth Kundert*
Visuals/Design Freelance Specialist *Mary L. Christianson*

Executive Vice President/General Manager *Thomas E. Doran*
Vice President/Editor in Chief *Edgar J. Laube*
Vice President/Marketing and Sales Systems *Eric Ziegler*
Vice President/Production *Vickie Putman*
Director of Custom and Electronic Publishing *Chris Rogers*
National Sales Manager *Bob McLaughlin*

President and Chief Executive Officer *G. Franklin Lewis*
Senior Vice President, Operations *James H. Higby*
Corporate Senior Vice President and President of Manufacturing *Roger Meyer*
Corporate Senior Vice President and Chief Financial Officer *Robert Chesterman*

Cover and interior designs by Terri W. Ellerbach

Cover photo © Stephen Simpson/FPG International

Copyedited by Karen Dorman

**Copyright © 1974, 1979, 1985, 1990, 1995 by The McGraw-Hill
Companies, Inc. All rights reserved**

Library of Congress Catalog Card Number: 93–74955

ISBN 0–697–12524–6

No part of this publication may be reproduced, stored in a retrieval
system, or transmitted, in any form or by any means, electronic,
mechanical, photocopying, recording, or otherwise, without the
prior written permission of the publisher.

Printed in the United States of America

10 9 8 7 6 5 4

Contents

Part 1

3 Accessing Artworks 52

4 Artistic Development in the Early Years 74

5 Motivating and Evaluating Children's Art 95

6 The Teacher as Facilitator 118

7 Artistic Talent and Special Needs 134

Part 2

8 Drawing and Painting 156

9 Cutting, Tearing, and Pasting 184

10 Printmaking 205

11 Modeling and Constructing 218

12 Puppets and Masks 244

13 Fabric and Fiber 261

14 Celebrations 286

Color Gallery

"To see the world through the eyes of children is, perhaps, one of the greatest rewards for the adult in charge of structuring and facilitating the child's artistic encounters. This book urges teachers to experience again, with the children under their direction, the delight of visual discovery, ideation, aesthetic involvement and emotional response to the world of art. This ongoing, never-ending, very human process of self-awareness and fulfillment in creative expression renews us and keeps us all `young in art.'"

—*Audrey A. Welch,*
Art Consultant, Founding Member and Past President,
California Art Education Association

Introduction

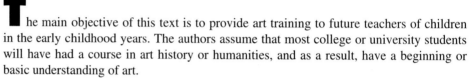

The main objective of this text is to provide art training to future teachers of children in the early childhood years. The authors assume that most college or university students will have had a course in art history or humanities, and as a result, have a beginning or basic understanding of art.

The term *early childhood* encompasses preschool through the third grade. This is a crucial time in the child's total growth and development. The art tasks and aesthetic dialogues described in this text are aimed at assisting children to discover creative solutions as they work with art materials and to make informed responses by heightening their aesthetic awareness; that is, how they see and what they feel and know about their visual world and the world of art. The chapters on the various media have a conceptual base and encourage divergent thinking and individual art expression.

The National Art Education Association and discipline-based art education both support the point of view that art as a subject has a well-defined content, and elementary teachers must be familiar with the four areas or components of art. These areas, as stated by the National Art Education Association in its publication *Quality Art Education,*[1] are explained and explored in detail in Chapter 1 and are reflected throughout the remainder of the book. The four content areas are

a. **Art production** as an activity in which students work creatively in the various appropriate art media, expressing their individual thoughts, feelings, and perceptions.
b. **Aesthetics** as a branch of thinking and philosophy that relates to the child's perceptual development and to the nature and meaning of art. It involves a refinement of all the senses as a basic component for all things the child will learn.
c. **Art criticism** as a way for children to learn how to look at and understand artworks and how to put into words their own descriptions, analyses, interpretations, and judgments.
d. **Art history** as a way of developing children's understanding of the important place that art has and continues to have in all cultures throughout all times.

A great deal of learning in the early years concentrates on convergent thinking skills—knowing the one right solution—to compute answers in arithmetic or to spell words correctly. Through the four content areas of art, children also develop divergent thinking because intuitive as well as rational thought processes are encouraged. This textbook takes the approach that art may be treated either as a separate discipline or integrated in other areas of the curriculum.

The college or university student who is preparing to teach young children needs to be very familiar with these four content areas of art. These areas have been well established nationwide during the past decade and are repeatedly stated in individual school district and state curriculum guides. Children's art textbooks and packaged programs are geared for this kind of balanced and encompassing approach to teaching art.

Specific objectives of this book are to prepare the future teacher

a. To be familiar with how children develop in their artwork during these early years in order to motivate them and to be able to apply age-appropriate methods of instruction.
b. To be knowledgeable in looking at and understanding art. The appropriate language as it relates to the elements and principles of art is a basic communication component.
c. To be comfortable and conversant in investigating strategies that will help children develop critical thinking skills about art.
d. To gain personal skills in using both two- and three-dimensional art media that are standard commodities in early childhood classrooms.
e. To be aware of the content of art and of the major role that art has played in all cultures throughout history. (For a complete and comprehensive view of world art and art history, the student will need to seek additional resources elsewhere.)

"Nicky," Rebekah Patterson, Northern Lights ABC School, Anchorage, Alaska, Kindergarten, age 5.
Courtesy © 1991–92 Crayola® Dream Makers™

The Color Gallery in this book provides material for students to use in discussing various aspects of art. The color reproductions are especially useful in Chapter 2 in responding to questions that refer to specific works of art.

"Topics for Discussion"—A short list of pertinent questions found at the end of each chapter—may be used to analyze and interpret the points made in the text. Students will be required to review chapter contents using critical thinking skills. In addition, the questions assist students in developing ways to actually use the material that they have read.

Part I is made up of seven chapters. The first chapter, "Art Education in the Early Years," begins with some thoughts on the developmental needs of young children and a list of ten characteristics of creative people, characteristics that are nurtured by creative art experiences. The National Art Education Association's Art Program of Quality is explained along with the newly developed "National Standards for Visual Arts Education." A chart shows Content Standards and Achievement Standards for kindergarten through grade four, first for creating and performing, then for perceiving and analyzing, and finally for understanding cultural and historical contexts. Following this, the four content areas of art are explained in detail beginning with "Art Production," in which the student learns the educational significance and importance of having a broad range of both two- and three-dimensional creative experiences. The second content area, "Aesthetic Perception: Seeing in a Special Way," leads the student to differentiate between "aesthetics," "aesthetic perception," and "aesthetic judgment." The third content area, "Art Criticism," assists students in learning how to see and describe the visual world of art and to talk about their feelings and emotional responses. The fourth content area, "Art History," gives different reasons why artists have made artworks throughout all cultures and all times.

Chapter 2, "Responding to Artworks," introduces students to the language of art as each of the elements and principles of art is described in detail. Following each section on an element or principle, students will find two levels of questions directing them to look at the reproductions in the Color Gallery. First they will encounter questions to ask themselves as adults, questions that will enhance their own understanding of that element or principle. These are followed by examples of questioning strategies to use with young children.

In Chapter 3, "Accessing Artworks," students learn many ways of providing their students visual encounters with artworks and artists. These consist of utilizing such community resources as museums and galleries, artmobiles, art-in-a-trunk, and local artists. Folk art items from many world cultures are readily available for actual see-and-touch experiences. The chapter offers an example of an art docent presentation in which large art reproductions are utilized. On a smaller scale, suggestions are made on how to use postcards or small reproductions mounted on stand-up panels, along with a few questions to help children describe what they see in this miniexhibit. The chapter concludes with descriptions of how to make and play a number of art games that sharpen the children's perception and introduce them to great artworks.

Chapter 4, "Artistic Development in the Early Years," provides students with knowledge of how children develop in their artwork and gives them age-appropriate methods of motivation. Children all over the world begin their artistic development with scribbling, moving from irregular to controlled to named scribbling. The chapter suggests remarks and responses for the adult to make in dealing with the scribbling child. The second significant stage in a child's artistic development occurs when the schema, or symbol, emerges. At this stage, the adult needs to provide topics and motivations for drawing that will expand the child's perceptual growth, cognitive powers, and emotional responses. The child soon arrives at rather definite symbols for "mother," "dad," "dog," "tree," "myself," for example, and the student is given suggestions to help the child remain fluent and flexible by deviating from his or her established schema. At this time the use of a baseline is seen in children's drawings and deviations from it are presented in topical form. The chapter concludes with some thoughts on the characteristics of the schematic years and with a chart showing achievement expectations at the completion of grade three.

Chapter 5, "Motivating and Evaluating Children's Art," stresses the importance of providing opportunities for children to become more aware of their environment and to reflect on their feelings as subject matter for their artwork. The vital part that perceptual observation plays in these activities is emphasized. A variety of motivational techniques challenge children to make choices and decisions as they create personal expressions. Seven different motivational techniques are described and examples given of each. The chapter closes with an explanation of ways to evaluate children's artistic progress.

The role of the teacher is defined in Chapter 6, "The Teacher as Facilitator." The chapter explains how the teacher sets the stage for learning, and how to communicate with parents on the importance of participating in and fostering the child's artistic development. Suitable and safe art materials and effective use of classroom space is covered in a practical manner. Text and photographs show examples of art learning stations.

Chapter 7, "Identifying Talent and Special Needs," offers the future teacher means for identifying and challenging the artistically and exceptionally talented child and offers suggestions for providing the appropriate creative environment for these children. The rest of the chapter provides help for the future teacher to deal with children who have special needs. Appropriate art activities and examples are presented, along with suggestions of adaptive tools and aids.

The chapters in Part II focus on art production and emphasize the importance of diversified and repeated experiences in both two- and three-dimensional media. Some of the art production activities are highly structured; others are more open-ended. The authors hope that each future teacher will gain an understanding of the art concepts and skills presented, and that when using them in their classrooms as part of a sequentially planned art program, will recognize each student's individuality and need for self-expression.

Many of the art production activities presented here can be coupled with the other three content areas of art at any of the grade levels in early childhood. Each aspect of Part I—the child's growth in art, the child's aesthetic judgment, and art history—can be intertwined with art production to aid each child in self-discovery and in finding his or her own way to creative fulfillment in art and life.

The college or university student will experience these art production techniques on an adult level. The authors suggest that students explore their own cultural backgrounds in relation to many of the art production activities: banners and sculpture of Africa, masks and pottery of Mexico and Native America, and festivals and celebrations unique to their own particular culture, as well as national American holidays.

"The Safe Forest," Quinn Beerwilder, Sacramento Country Day School, Sacramento, California, Grade 3, age 9.
Courtesy © 1991–92 Crayola® Dream Makers™

In Chapter 8, "Drawing and Painting," the students learn that drawing is basic to art production; many avenues are explored. Practical suggestions for setting up the classroom and distributing materials are given. The chapter describes unique and exciting approaches to drawing and painting, illustrated with children's examples.

Chapter 9, "Cutting, Tearing, and Pasting," presents activities that include both two- and three-dimensional products made from paper. These include collage projects, paper crowns and medals, assembled murals, and stand-up animals.

In Chapter 10, "Printmaking," students learn to make multiple prints using potatoes and simple gadgets, and using more sophisticated media such as polystyrene and erasers.

Chapter 11, "Modeling and Constructing," deals with clay, salt ceramic, and baker's clay. Innovative edible art projects include bread sculpture, candy clay, and fruit and vegetable puppets. Papier mâché creatures, constructions with boxes and cardboard, wood scraps, and glue provide children with endless opportunities to express creative ideas.

Puppets and masks have been used in many cultures throughout the world and in Chapter 12, students are provided with suggestions for quickly making simple and usable puppets. Materials include paper plates, folded paper, socks, papier mâché, and salt ceramic. The chapter suggests ways to use the puppets. Methods to make simple masks are explained along with ideas for dramatic play in the classroom.

Chapter 13, "Fabric and Fiber," explains the use of banners and flags in various cultures and times. Examples of wall hangings, both banners and murals made of "stuffed stuff," are given. The chapter illustrates basic beginning stitches to use with yarn, needle, and burlap. Several types of weaving are described, including paper and yarn on simple cardboard looms, and soda-straw weaving. Two group weaving projects are presented: one uses a large frame loom, and the other uses a latch hook and canvas mesh.

The final chapter takes a creative look at "Celebrations." Emphasis is placed on noting special days by participating in creative rather than stereotyped activities and on explaining to the children the background and origin of the holiday or event. Festivals, parades, and special days occur in every culture throughout the world, and teachers have many options for classroom celebrations. Children can celebrate by making creative gifts and cards or by making murals, puppets, kites, masks, costumes, hats, flags, and banners. The chapter includes a list of special days that might be used for minicelebrations.

The book concludes with a list of Resources for Art Education, a Glossary, a Bibliography, and an Index.

The authors hope that this text shows future teachers how to convey to children the content and joy of art, and that teachers will be able to introduce students to the freedom, creativity, and feelings of self-esteem that are vital to an art experience.

The Reviewers for the Fifth Edition

Susan Carlisle Bell   Gardner-Webb College
Sally James, Retired   Bemidji State University
Virginia Sadler   Abilene Christian University

Notes

1. National Art Education Association, *Quality Art Education, Goals for Schools, An Interpretation* (Reston, Va.: National Art Education Association, 1986).

Art projects can make connections to other parts of the curriculum. Nathan is attaching scales, gills, and fins to the fish he is making as part of an art project. At the same time, he is learning some scientific facts about the use of the fish symbol in a Japanese holiday. Learning enriched by art forms an important part of quality educational experiences, particularly in the primary grades.

"Bug Buddies," Zachary Dangerfield, Kimberly Elementary School, Kimberly, Idaho, Kindergarten, age 5.
Courtesy © 1991–92 Crayola® Dream Makers™

Part 1

1

Art Education in the Early Years

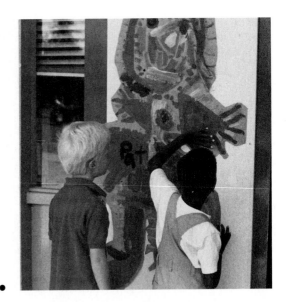

● ●

In a society becoming more technological, complex, and mass-oriented, art education has the responsibility to foster and preserve an individual's human identity and self-esteem. Young children reflect the experience of beauty, so when they engage in art production and view works of art and the world around them, they better understand themselves and others. The many diverse cultures in America today, cultures whose roots are grounded in countries around the world, have made educators more aware of the need for programs in the schools that are inclusive and broad. As Jesse Jackson said in a recent magazine article, "America is not like a blanket—one piece of unbroken cloth, the same color, the same texture, the same size. America is more like a quilt—many pieces, many colors, many sizes, all woven and held together by a common thread."[1] The main objective of art education should be to bring children in contact with and give them a better understanding of their visual environment and culture.

Education in art is essential and is designed to enrich students' lives by increasing their capacity to use their senses and minds joyfully and confidently in experiencing their environment. Such aesthetic encounters are for all children, and are best provided by schools, the institutions that provide for personal development and the transmission of cultural heritage. Art education should enable students to make personal life choices and to be responsible for what they reject or prize in our society.[2]

The American Association of School Administrators has taken the position that

> It is important that pupils, as a part of general education, learn to appreciate, to understand, to create, and to criticize with discrimination those products of the mind, the voice, the hand, and the body which give dignity to the person and exalt the spirit of man.

Boys and girls in the awakening, formative years of early childhood have special developmental needs. These include perceptual, emotional, artistic, and creative implications that can best be fostered through an art program that incorporates four principal content areas as listed by the National Art Education Association.[3] These are art production, aesthetics, art criticism, and art history.

A school art program that has depth and meaning and that is dynamic must include all these components. They are not separate entities; rather, they are interrelated, and knowledge of and experience with each of them enriches and nourishes the others. For early childhood, a sequential and developmental art program that is based on these content areas recognizes that not every child is destined to become an adult artist but that art can enrich the present and future lives of all children by giving them satisfaction and joy.

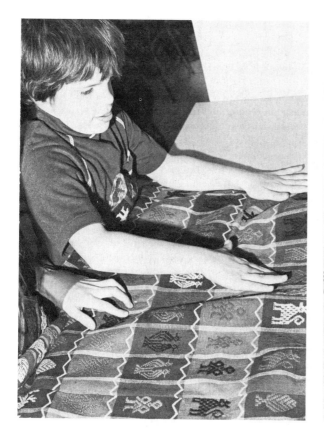

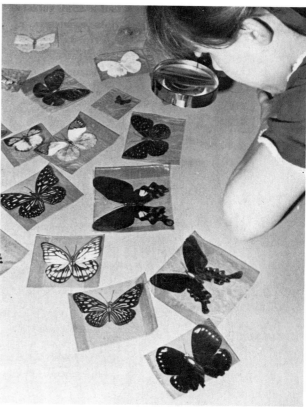

The child's visual language expands if he or she is surrounded with materials and an encouraging and many-faceted atmosphere. "Come touch, come see" should be bywords in the early years.

Creative people become totally absorbed in activities that are challenging and require originality.

A personal involvement in art develops positive attitudes, stimulates an appreciation for and an understanding and enjoyment of art, and promotes thought and creative self-expression.

CHARACTERISTICS OF CREATIVE PEOPLE

Except for differences in terminology, researchers generally agree on basic characteristics of the creative person. Charles Schaefer lists the following ten characteristics of the creative child and states that these characteristics are evident from the earliest years:

1. A sense of wonder and heightened awareness of the world

2. Openness to inner feelings and emotions

3. Curious, exploratory, adventuresome spirit

4. Imagination, the power of forming mental images of what is not actually present to the senses or of creating new images by combining previously unrelated ideas

5. Intuitive thinking, the solving of problems without logical reasoning

6. Independent thinking, the desire to find things out for oneself rather than accepting them on authority

7. Personal involvement in work, total absorption in meaningful activities

8. Divergent thinking, thought patterns that seek variety and originality, that propose several possibilities rather than seeking one right answer

9. Predisposition to create rather than considering how things are supposed to be or always have been expressed

10. Tendency to play with ideas, to mentally toy with the possibilities and implications of an idea[4]

Paul Torrance also states that the creative behavior of preprimary children is characterized by a spirit of wonder and magic; most healthy young children have this spirit unless they have been victims of neglect, harshness, lack of love, coercive punishment, or sensory deprivation.[5] It is natural for children to be creative, and the characteristics of creativity can be kept alive as children mature if the children are regularly involved in quality art experiences. These experiences, when based on the content areas and interrelated through meaningful, sequential instruction, stimulate attitudes and awareness that are the foundation of both the creative thought process and the quality art program. Creative people are perceptually very aware of their environment. They are visually observant of the world, and they are curious to know how things feel to the touch. They listen to sounds and are sensitive to the ways things smell and taste. They are able to take in information without prejudging it; they delay structuring the information until after they have had a chance to look at things from several points of view.[6] Imagination relies on this perception for recharging and enhancement.

The relationship between creativity and art production is shown in the chart on page 6, which was developed by Ronald Silverman and printed in the newsletter of the California Art Education Association.[7] This chart points out that interpretive skills and creative skills are equally important in the production of a work of art and that each relates directly to the goals and objectives of a program in visual art education.

AN ART PROGRAM OF QUALITY

The National Art Education Association (NAEA) states that art is one of the most revealing of human activities, as well as one of the richest sources for understanding cultures, since the earliest things we know of ourselves are recorded in visual forms and images.[8] People throughout history have made and used art to communicate and express ideas and to convey hopes and feelings. Art is a way of giving form to our imagination, of defining our surroundings, and of expressing our hopes and aspirations for the future. A quality art education integrates a number of opportunities: making beautiful things; learning to look at artworks with pleasure, sensitivity, and appreciation; using creative and imaginative ways to solve problems; integrating art in all subjects; finding outlets for feelings and emotions; and increasing perceptual sensitivity.

The NAEA goals for a quality art education mandate that students complete a sequential program of instruction in art that integrates the study of art production, aesthetics, art criticism, and art history. NAEA states that through a quality art education program, students learn to develop, express, and evaluate ideas. They produce, read, and interpret visual images in an increasingly visually oriented world. They recognize and understand the artistic achievements and expectations of diverse societies.

The content of art is significant. Its educational value and expressive power demand sequential instruction in a quality art education program. Sequential lessons provide continuity and build on the skills, concepts, themes, and knowledge that students have encountered previously, moving from simple to complex and demanding. Each art activity is related to the next so that what is learned today can be used and expanded on tomorrow. Sequential lessons provide students with a chance to grow, sharpen their perceptions, practice skills, and make connections with what they have already learned. A stimulating program of logically sequenced lessons in art provides the structure that gives students access to visual literacy. A large number of school districts provide art textbooks, packaged programs,[9] or a printed curriculum with sequential lesson plans that take into consideration a balance of media, themes, and skills as well as the developmental

Table 1.1 Interpretive Skill and Creative Skill in Producing Art

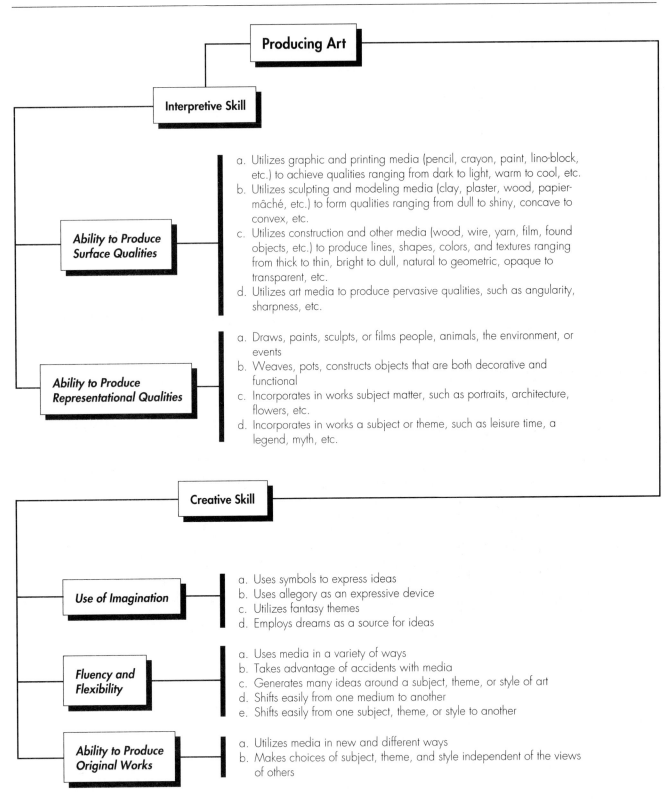

A quality art program integrates the study of aesthetics, art history, and criticism with creative production. This student is working on whimsical line drawings that are the result of an art activity motivated by a discussion on Joan Miró.

Children paint what they know and see around them. The entire length of the playground in this San Francisco school is bright with paneled murals painted by the children in the primary grades.

needs of different grade levels. Some districts provide leadership in the form of an art specialist who assists teachers in planning a sequential program.

In defining a sequential quality art program more clearly, NAEA states that making art is central to the art education of all pupils and that, in the early grades, it is the primary mode through which students can fluently tell stories, relate experiences, fantasize, convey messages, express feelings, and give ideas concrete form. In so doing, children learn to observe, recall, find relationships, make choices, accept or reject alternatives, respond, value, and make decisions.

NAEA has recently developed both content and achievement standards for children in kindergarten through grade four. These standards expand the original statements about content and form a part of the newly developed "National Standards for Visual Arts Education."[10]

"Artists in their studio" is an enjoyable activity for these kindergarten students. They have viewed and discussed works that show well-known artists such as Marc Chagall, Pablo Picasso, and Jacob Lawrence painting portraits in their studio spaces. Here a young artist works on a double portrait while his two models sit patiently. All are in the "studio" space they constructed from blocks.

The content of art instruction as specified by the NAEA goals must be an integration of art production, aesthetics, art criticism, and art history, but the view is taken that art production has always been and probably will continue to be central to the art education of students because it is an "activity that comes naturally to the young and can continue to be a rewarding experience throughout life."[11] When students make drawings, paintings, or other artworks, they are challenged to observe in the same way that artists perceive—with clarity, precision, and discrimination—those things that are significant in their artwork. Students remember and recall experiences, places, events, people, and objects. They explore their feelings, emotions, and attitudes toward the subject or theme with which they are dealing. They make decisions relative to the composition, working within the format of the paper and the limitations or special characteristics of the medium. They make aesthetic judgments about the colors and space and lines they will use to best show their ideas.

The branch of philosophy known as aesthetics provides complex structures for interpreting the meaning of art and beauty. Its complicated ideas about the responses of human beings to nature and artworks provide a means for analyzing and interpreting some of the deepest of human emotions. The *California Visual and Performing Arts Framework* perceives aesthetic perception as designating a specific aspect of perception, learning to see the world metaphorically as well as directly: ". . . a tree may be viewed as a symbol which expresses majesty or somberness in contrast to a source of wood for building a structure."[12]

Aesthetic considerations in early childhood begin with the easiest and most understandable basis possible. Questions deal with students' responses to artworks as well as to beautiful things they see in the natural world. Students explore the differences between nature and art. They begin to ask themselves why they feel a special way when they look at a particular painting, how they may feel differently when they look at a tree and then at a painting of a tree, how they would make a picture that shows a lot of movement and action, how they would choose colors to express their feelings to another person. NAEA states that attention to aesthetics is important in a quality art education in that

> It causes students to question, weigh evidence and information, examine intuitive reactions, and come to tentative conclusions about their experience. It begins with simple concrete experience in thinking and discussing art at the very earliest elementary grades.[13]

Laura Chapman has stated that aesthetic perception is not simply learning to decode symbols with fixed meanings.[14] She believes that aesthetics pertains to perception based on feeling and sensation and is not generalized for all instances. For this reason, she affirms that the perceptual skills that children normally learn from reading, science, and mathematics must be complemented with experiences that stimulate multisensory awareness and that promote a sensitivity to expressive meanings and to contexts.

When children find reasons for selecting one artwork to be more interesting than another, they are engaging in art criticism. When they have good reasons for liking one artwork more than another, they are making aesthetic judgments. In position papers, NAEA states that there is an important difference between ". . . because I like it," and "I like it because. . . ." From their first guided encounters with art, young children progress in making careful, sensitive observations and thoughtful interpretations. In practicing techniques of art criticism, they begin making comparisons that are based on their increased viewing of artworks. Early practice in art criticism begins an individual's lifelong habit of arriving at judgments about the value and intent of visual images, reasoned judgments that are based on the person's knowledge and visual sensitivity.

NAEA further states that knowledge of art history must be fully integrated with the other parts of a quality art program to help students understand how people throughout time have recorded experiences and events and expressed ideas and feelings. Art history provides an enriched source of inspiration for today and connects us with our artistic roots.

Discipline-based art education (DBAE) is an approach to teaching art in which ideas and skills from the four disciplines are integrated into a cumulative curriculum. Discipline-based art education does not require equal time and attention to each discipline: The amount devoted to each is likely to depend on the different forms that DBAE curricula will take and students being taught. In elementary schools, art production probably receives a major share of attention because of the developmental capacities of students.[15]

Many state and local school district curriculum guides agree that art production, or studio art, is a central feature. So does the National Art Education Association's Quality Goals Statement. Discipline-based art education does not wish to replace art-making with talking about art, but does wish to reinforce the totality of the visual arts through a variety of learning modes.[16]

In summarizing the effects of a sequential quality art program, NAEA lists the following visual literacies needed by students to understand and respond to the many visual materials they will encounter during the rest of their lives:

1. An understanding of and the ability to apply their own intellectual and creative potential to situations they will encounter

2. An appreciation for the magnificence of the creative power of others as encountered in architecture, painting, sculpture, and other visual arts

3. An ability to make informed choices related to the many visual options available to them, choices based on intellectually and emotionally valid criteria

4. A sensitivity to the environment and to the impact individuals have on nature, architecture, city planning, monuments, and so on

5. An understanding of the past and its artistic triumphs and tragedies

6. An appreciation for and understanding of the cultural values of different peoples of different times and places

7. A reinforcement of their own beliefs and values by being awakened to achievements and contributions of visually creative people

NAEA emphasizes in its conclusion that quality art education, presented consistently and regularly throughout each student's education, can contribute to society's need for "well-rounded, intelligent, informed, sensitive, self-confident, and contributing people."[17]

Art production has always been central to art education largely because it comes naturally to the young and continues to be a rewarding experience throughout life.

"My Snowman", Ellen Murphy, Huffman Elementary School, Anchorage, Alaska, Kindergarten, age 5. Courtesy © 1991–92 Crayola® Dream Makers™

ART PRODUCTION:
Making Art

Art production is a creative process for the child; it is an avenue through which experiences are expressed nonverbally as well as verbally. Involvement with art tasks provides experiences for young children that can be derived in no other way. When very young children pick up a crayon or brush, they have taken the first step in the creative act: that of selecting and making a decision. As they mature, they develop meaningful artistic expressions involving their personal feelings, their cognitive awareness, and their sensory impressions, and they use these expressions to communicate with others. If the environment is warm, supportive, and receptive, children enjoy and freely incorporate moods and original concepts in all sorts of subject matter and use many kinds of art materials.

Art production provides the skill and power to show clearly what one is thinking, feeling, or perceiving in a unique and individual way. Preceding production is perceiving, searching, discriminating, selecting, and enjoying the visual world. Art production is a way of expressing individual uniqueness.

Two specialists—commenting on Piaget, an authority on the general intellectual development of children—believe that the leading argument for teaching Piaget's theory is that young children learn best from concrete activities.[18] Since Piaget believes that it is advisable to permit children to absorb experiences in their own ways and at their own rates, teachers must provide a rich environment that permits a maximum number of concrete activities. And they must keep to a minimum those situations in which children are shown exactly how to structure their responses.

Situations in which children are unable to fall back on preconceived ideas and in which they explore previously undiscovered areas have educational value. The early childhood art program should promote children's own personal production of concepts and should develop their skills in painting, drawing, cutting, pasting, modeling, constructing, weaving, printmaking, and so on. Art productions in both two and three dimensions are important and reinforce each other.

Paul Torrance lists three fundamental attributes of learning activities that facilitate creative behavior and motivate learning: (1) the incompleteness or openness of the learning experience, (2) the requirement to produce something and utilize it, and (3) the use of children's questions (the "wanting to know") to capture the excitement of learning.[19] Creative expression in art also originates in open-ended problem-solving activities in which

Close-up photographs of cactus, leaves, flowers, metal, and such are made into puzzles by cutting a circle from the center of each and attaching a bead for a handle. The child must whirl the circle in the empty space until he or she matches the correct position.

the child's creation is not predetermined by adult dictates. The adult's role in the art production arena is to motivate in ways that stimulate perceptions, thoughts, and feelings and to provide instruction in any necessary media skills.

Very young children need exceedingly little stimulation to begin art production. They are eager to respond to the visual attraction of brightly colored paint and paper and to the tactile appeal of modeling or collage materials. They delight in cutting paper for the sake of cutting and in pounding and squeezing pliable materials for the kinesthetic enjoyment it gives them. They may not always choose to recount an experience, but in the exploration of materials, they develop the skills that they will need when they do wish to communicate an idea or tell a story about something important to them.

Art production activities make especially meaningful connections when students view artworks by famous artists and see the artworks as having such commonalities as similar themes or emotions, universal subject matter, or familiar styles or media.

The educational significance of art production is that children use a broad range of cognitive and affective learnings:

1. They must form a concept of what it is they want to draw, paint, or make.

2. They must call on feelings and emotions related to what it is they want to draw or make.

3. They must use memory of events and objects as well as perceptual intake of the environment to help them record and interpret things in their artworks.

4. They must develop skills in different media to achieve the effects they desire.

5. They must order and arrange the composition through the use of color, line, shape, and so on, so that the end result is satisfying to them.

6. They must decide when the work is finished and what they feel is right and good about it.

7. They become acquainted with how artists in other times and places expressed and communicated their observations, thoughts, and feelings.

a

a. A rock polisher produces smooth, sculpturelike forms from ordinary pebbles. The colors, patterns, shapes and surface qualities invite the child to examine them.

b. Early childhood is a time for many intake experiences, and art is a means of activating the child's sensibilities.

b

As Frederick Spratt of San Jose State University once said, "It is through art production that we 'reaffirm discovery' in the students, as in each young artist we witness the reinvention of art."[20]

AESTHETIC PERCEPTION: Seeing in a Special Way

What we know of the world, we take in through our senses. The refinement and sharpening of these senses, then, becomes paramount in the development of the student. Education of the senses in early childhood is crucial for later life. It forms the basis for judging artworks and valuing the things we see in our environment. While *aesthetics* is a noun and deals with extremely complex issues that are more suitable for college classes and philosophy courses than primary school, the phrases *aesthetic perception* and *aesthetic judgment*—using the word as an adjective—are applicable in early childhood art programs.[21] Aesthetics is a rather complex branch of philosophy concerned with giving meaning to artworks and is somewhat different from the experiences of aesthetic perception and aesthetic judgment that very young children encounter. Also, some answers to aesthetic inquiries are best found in discussions that combine art criticism and art history.

Young children are enthusiastic, curious, and eager participators, interested in exploring everything around them. The quality and quantity of that exploration must not be left solely to chance. Rather, the teacher should lead, guide, and direct children's perceptual experiences to help them to better recognize and discriminate art elements in both the natural world and in objects of human origin. Through these experiences, the child becomes more skillful in recalling observations and better able to understand, describe, and make use of colors, textures, lines, and shapes. Design is found everywhere in the world, but it may go unnoticed until the individual becomes aware of it.

French artist Henri Matisse was a keen and sensitive observer of the world. He still had a rich "library of images" in his head when he became bedridden at age seventy-one.

This felt-covered bulletin board in preschool invites small children to touch and feel a variety of appealing objects. Small, round mirrors catch the children's reflections.

He had observed nature all his life and had drawn and painted the world around him so many times that he felt that these images now belonged to him. He was able to represent them using his own language of shapes and colors.

If perception is basic to all learning, if selective viewing is a desirable kind of behavior, and if conceptualization comes after sensory experiences, then it becomes imperative that teachers provide paths for numerous visual and tactile explorations and experiences so as to keep all the child's senses alive and active. If left to their own devices, children are not as apt to discover these aesthetic learnings by themselves.

Art gives children new ways of seeing and knowing. Through looking at nature and artworks and through discussions—whether in the form of a motivational dialogue before they draw or paint or whether after they have completed making art—their ways of seeing are expanded. Discussions may revolve around such concepts as close-up, magnified, transparent, bird's eye view, worm's eye view, silhouette, larger or smaller, thick or thin, rough or smooth. Visual factors can involve movement as well and can be experienced by exploring such concepts as spirals, curving, straight, zigzags, backward, forward, swing, spin, burst, and kinesthetic flow.

As children mature, they become more aware of spatial relationships and have more detailed perceptions of objects. They understand more about overlapping shapes, dark colors in contrast to light colors, and bright versus dull. They perceive things from above and below, inside and out.

Through heightened perceptual experiences, the child often discovers in both new and familiar things a beauty and uniqueness otherwise dismissed or overlooked. Sensory encounters give wings to children's imaginations and at the same time enable them to relate and react to the real world around them and to think in terms of visual images. Personal involvement in quality art activities develops children's increasing perceptual powers and provides the mental images needed for creative thinking and problem solving. According to Paul Torrance, a child must have a rich store of imagery to go very far in developing creative powers. This quality is essential in the scientific discoverer, inventor, and creative writer as well as in the artist.[22]

ART CRITICISM AND AESTHETIC JUDGMENT:
Informed Responses

Werner von Braun has reflected on the idea that we would all have dead souls if we had no aesthetic values. Children early in life need to recognize and become familiar with different kinds of art. They will respond in their own way, often having different feelings toward art than adults. Sequential programs—where the artworks of painters, architects, craftspeople, and sculptors play an important role—build and expand on the child's knowledge and judgment of the roles that art plays in everyday life, government, religion, and business.

Knowledge and visual sensitivity are necessary when engaging in art criticism. There is an important difference between ". . . because I like it" and "I like it because . . . ."

When art criticism is introduced in early childhood classrooms, children are given the opportunity to learn to see and describe the visual world in a special way. Instead of using their eyes only in a practical way—to identify things, recognize them, categorize them, and keep from bumping into them—children learn to take a contemplative, reflective look and expand their perceptual skills. They learn to direct their attention to the aesthetic aspects of artworks as well as of their surroundings.

Children need repeated and regular opportunities to describe what they see in an artwork. They may notice how one artist used thick paint and made curving brushstrokes and how another applied the paint in broad, thin washes of color. These are the technical properties of an artwork. Children can use words to describe the elements of art that they see in the artwork: colors, lines, shapes/forms, textures, value, and space. They can look for how these elements are arranged and ordered within the composition: the principles of art. They can seek out the emphasis of an artwork and describe how their eyes are led to this focal point. They can try to discern how the artist balanced the dark and light places or how the artist repeated a shape to make a patterned area. They can find ways that the artist provided variety and yet achieved a unified look of completeness and harmony.

Children react to artworks with their own feelings and emotions, perhaps empathizing with the subject matter and projecting their own feelings. They give studied thought as to how successful the artist was in making an extremely real and lifelike artwork, or one that expresses a strong feeling, or one that makes use of colors, lines, and shapes (perhaps without relying on any real subject matter at all), or one that represents dreams and fantasy. They may come to the conclusion that artists sometimes combine two of these different ways of making art.

Looking, thinking, and talking are involved when art criticism and aesthetic judgment are aspects of the art program. In large or small groups, or on an individual basis, the teacher can guide the children in learning to describe, analyze, select, interpret, appraise, and evaluate. Children can begin to name and describe the art elements and principles and to recognize different media and individual artist's works, as well as an artwork's technical properties. Vocabulary development is important because words are needed to discuss, identify, compare, contrast, and interpret artworks—either their own,

Students are eager to discuss the reproduction of a painting by Ben Shahn as the teacher directs questions about line and shape.

those of their peers, or those of adult artists. The children can begin to recognize some artistic styles, cultural expressions, movements in art, and different kinds of art, such as realistic, abstract, expressive, and surrealistic.

If children do not experience art, both through response and production activities, they are culturally disabled. Becoming literate is one of the main goals of education. If children are encouraged to speak of their attitudes, feelings, and perceptions about a work of art, their educational years will contain enriching ideas related to the artistic contributions of human beings. Acquiring and using art terminology with fluency is an important part of children's visual learning. They respond to each art encounter with attitudes, judgment, and nonverbal feelings, and words can help to sharpen and direct their perceptions about their own work and the works of others.

Elliot Eisner distinguishes between aesthetic judgment and preference, with judgment being the process whereby an individual not only appraises the importance, significance, and quality of something, but also has some basis for justifying that judgment.[23] On the other hand, one's preference is a simple statement of like or dislike, approval or disapproval. Therefore, aesthetic judgment involves evaluating and judging what is artistically excellent, rather than making statements of what we may like or not like.

Aesthetics pertains to the sense of the beautiful; the word has its roots in the Greek word *aisthetikos,* pertaining to sense perception. Its opposite is *anesthetic,* which has to do with the loss of the senses. Aesthetics is defined as a branch of philosophy that provides a theory of the beautiful and of the fine arts. It was first used to mean "the science of the beautiful." For early childhood, we may think of aesthetics as trying to understand those things that we find attractive and interesting to our senses. We usually qualify it as being a philosophical discipline that is primarily concerned with artworks, and as such it poses complex questions that have to do with the nature of art, how art provides knowledge, and appropriate ways for appraising quality in art. It is an arena in which students reflect and make judgments on the quality of artworks as well as on the qualities they see in the world around them.

When children encounter a new work of art, verbalizing about it with familiar words can make for a nonthreatening starting point. Preschool and kindergarten children can begin to use elementary art terms and add to their basic vocabulary every time they

The main objective of art education is to give children a better understanding of their visual environment and culture.

handle art materials or look closely at natural objects or works by famous artists. They can talk about how the colors, lines, and images evoke in them feelings of happiness or sadness. Very young children are able to look at reproductions of art created by such artists as Pablo Picasso, Georgia O'Keeffe, Fritz Scholder, Jacob Lawrence, Henri Matisse, and Frida Kahlo and discuss such concepts as real and not real, curved and straight, big and small, bright and dull. They can point out paintings that look like dreams and paintings that exaggerate and distort what is real, as well as enjoy patterns and colors for their own sake.

Preprimary children can become aware of art that shows pleasing relationships, harmonious organizations, rich textures, and such. Through handling art materials and seeing original and reproduced items of art, they can come to identify a variety of art forms, such as paintings, sculpture, ceramics, woven works, and architecture.

Aesthetic judgment involves an awareness of our environment. The humanities stress this relationship and the relevance of art to society. We are concerned not only with clean air and water, green spaces, and protecting nature's balance, but also with guarding against visual pollutants. A visually literate populace demands an aesthetically pleasing environment, which means good design qualities in homes and home furnishings, schools, office buildings, city planning, transportation, television, and films. Early childhood is the time for these critical beginnings and aesthetic foundations.

ART HISTORY: Art from Past Ages

Our history as human beings is vividly portrayed through art, and thus we can better understand ourselves by understanding our ancestors and their cultures. Different places and different times have always been expressed through art. In looking at primitive cultures, we realize that art cannot be separated from the everyday life of the tribe, a people in tune with nature and natural laws. Art has been valued by people from the very beginning of recorded history. Today, painters, sculptors, craftspeople of all kinds, photographers, filmmakers, industrial designers, fashion designers, architects, graphic artists, and city planners all influence the quality of our lives.

Boys and girls in the awakening formative years of early childhood have creative, emotional, and artistic needs.

When young children view different kinds of art, they learn the different purposes that art has served and the different reasons why artists have produced art, including the following:

1. Artists record historical events in their artworks and make visual images about myths and great pieces of literature. Narrative art tells stories about people, places, and events.

2. Artists show us how people and places looked during various periods of time.

3. Artists have made artworks to inspire people to take social action. Some have used their art to promote their political ideals, to spread propaganda, and to show the horrors of war.

4. Artists have created artworks to inspire, persuade, and inform people about religion.

5. Some artists express their feelings about the world they see around them through images such as landscapes, the city, people, still-life subjects, and animals.

6. Some artists show us a dreamlike world of fantasy and imagination.

7. Some artists explore and invent new ways to use art materials and to make artworks.

8. Some artists choose little if any subject matter from the real world but concentrate on portraying the pure impact of colors, shapes, textures, and lines.

9. Some artists design or make usable objects: buildings, furniture, dishes, jewelry, clothing, containers, and so on.

In their early years, children can begin to learn that art and culture interact. The culture determines its art. The needs of culture are met by the artist. Artists are influenced by the events and world around them, as well as by what other artists are doing. They are influenced by what has gone before them, and, in turn, they influence artists who follow them.

Young children can come to know that art has changed over the years and that artworks in different places and different periods of history may be quite different. Artists have been limited by the art materials and technology of the time in which they lived. Renaissance artists, for instance, made much use of egg tempera and fresco, whereas artists today may choose from a broader range of media.

Young children are not expected to achieve a keen understanding of the chronological aspects of art history; dates and sequencing of art come later in their school years. Rather, it is better to focus on the different purposes that art has served and the many ways that art has interacted with and reflected culture throughout time. Very young children profit from viewing thematic groups of artworks. Such a grouping may emphasize the commonalities of subject matter. Portraits made centuries apart and created in vastly different styles, for instance, introduce children to the idea that some artists choose to record likenesses, others choose to focus on showing character and personality, and still others choose to use imagination and take delight in working with colors, lines, and shapes.

TOPICS FOR DISCUSSION

1. In what ways does art enrich the lives of students?

2. What are the characteristics of creative people? How does art reinforce these characteristics?

3. How does the National Art Education Association define art in school, and what are the characteristics of a quality art program, as described by the NAEA?

4. What is discipline-based art education, and how does it align with the components of art education as described by the NAEA?

5. In your own words, describe visual literacies and the areas of learning reinforced by a sequential quality art program.

6. What is aesthetic perception, and how can it be nurtured in young children?

7. What is the educational significance of art production activities?

8. List some of the characteristics you would expect to observe in an activity focused on art criticism and aesthetic judgment. How is a teacher able to guide students in this process?

9. What are the purposes of art? How do these influence culture, and how does culture reflect the work of artists?

10. Describe a theoretical concept from this chapter that you believe to be particularly significant in the development of your own views about art education.

NOTES

1. Jesse Jackson, *Modern Maturity,* June–July 1992, 23.
2. Aesthetic Education Program, *Aesthetic Education: A Social and Individual Need* (St. Louis, Mo.: CEMREL, 1973), 4–5.
3. National Art Education Association, *Quality Art Education, Goals for Schools, An Interpretation* (Reston, Va.: National Art Education Association, 1986).
4. Charles E. Schaefer, *Developing Creativity in Children* (Buffalo, N.Y.: D.O.K. Publishers, 1973), 162.
5. Paul E. Torrance, *Creativity* (San Rafael, Calif.: Dimensions Publishers, 1973), 1.
6. Donald W. Herberholz and Kay Alexander, *Developing Artistic and Perceptual Awareness,* 5th ed. (Dubuque, Iowa: Wm. C. Brown Publishers, 1985), 7–8.
7. Ronald Silverman, "Curriculum Corral," *The Painted Monkey* 8 (February 1983):2.
8. National Art Education Association, *Quality Art Education,* 1.
9. Kay Alexander, *Clear* (Wilton, Conn.: Communicad, 1987).
   Kay Alexander, *Spectra Program* (Menlo Park, Calif.: Dale Seymour Publications, 1987).
   Art Works (Austin, Tex.: Holt, Rinehart and Winston, 1989), grades 1–6.
   Monique Briere, *Art Image* (Champlain, N.Y.: Art Image Publications, 1989), grades 1–6.
   Rebecca Brooks et al., *Through Their Eyes, Primary Level—A Sequentially Developed Art Program for Grades 1–3* (Austin, Tex.: W. S. Benson, 1989).
   Laura Chapman, *Discover Art* (Worcester, Mass.: Davis, 1985), grades 1–6.
   Laura Chapman, *Teaching Art 1–3* (Austin, Tex.: Henrick-Long Publishing, 1989).
   Lee Hanson, *Creative Expressions: An Art Curriculum* (Menlo Park, Calif.: Dale Seymour Publications, in press), grades K–8.
   Barbara Herberholz, *Art Docent Program* (Gold River, Calif.: Art Media, Etc., 1990).
   Guy Hubbard, *Art in Action* (Austin, Tex.: Holt, Rinehart and Winston, 1987), grades 1–8.
10. Draft: July 1, 1993 version, *NAEA News* 35(4) (August 1993) 2–3.
11. National Art Education Association, *Quality Art Education,* 11.
12. *Visual and Performing Arts Framework, Kindergarden through Grade Twelve* (Sacramento, Calif.: State Department of Education, 1989), 5–7.
13. National Art Education Association, *Quality Art Education.*
14. Laura Chapman, *Approaches to Art in Education* (New York: Harcourt Brace Jovanovich, 1978), 172–73.
15. Ralph A. Smith, ed., *The Journal of Aesthetic Education* 21 (2) (Summer 1987): 171–72.
16. Ibid.
17. National Art Education Association, *Quality Art Education,* 27–28.
18. Herbert Ginsburg and Sylvia Opper, *Piaget's Theory of Intellectual Development: An Introduction* (Englewood Cliffs, N.J.: Prentice-Hall, 1969) .
19. Torrance, *Creativity,* 43.
20. Frederick Spratt, *Discipline-Based Art Education: What Form Will It Take?* (Los Angeles: The Getty Center for Education in the Arts, 1987), 23.
21. Mary Erickson, "Teaching Aesthetics K–12," in *Research Readings for Discipline-Based Art Education: A Journey Beyond Creating* (Reston, Va.: National Art Education Association, 1988), 148–61.
22. Torrance, *Creativity,* 40.
23. Elliot Eisner, *Instructional Monographs: Ideas to Provoke the Thoughts and Actions of Education* (Sacramento, Calif.: Sacramento County Superintendent of Schools Office, 1968), 32.

2

Responding to Artworks

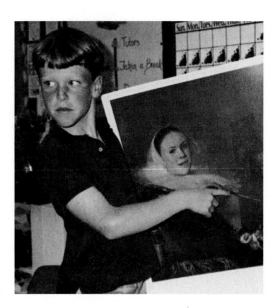

●●●●●●●●●●●●●●●●●●●●●●●●●●●●●●●

Children respond to looking at artworks and to making art with a natural enthusiasm and can readily acquire, with appropriate guidance and visual materials, an introduction to understanding art.

Works of art can be likened to people: Getting to know them often takes time and effort. When a new student enrolls in class, teachers encourage the other students to be friendly, to find out what the new person is like rather than forming a quick impression and judgment. Often, a person that we tend to dislike at first becomes a good friend when we get to know him or her better. In fact, the person we find more difficult to become acquainted with often turns out to be a more interesting friend in the long run. The same is true with a painting or a work of art.

Which works of art by adult artists appeal to the very young? Generally speaking, children like to see things that have something in common with their own world and lives. They love to see paintings and sculptures of children (both those who lived long ago and contemporary children), animals, people doing things, narrative art, fantasy and imaginative themes, landscapes and seascapes—perhaps showing action and adventure—and works of art in which they can identify with the artist's love of colors, paints, lines, and textures. Large reproductions, filmstrips, videos, and, of course, textbooks showing works of art all facilitate bringing a "museum into the classroom."

Through viewing a thematic grouping of reproductions, students arrive at the important understanding that different artists express the same theme or subject matter in vastly different ways and, therefore, that there is no one correct or best solution in making visual images. Exposing children to a variety of art teaches them that people express themselves in many ways. Encounters that compare and contrast art can free young artists to create expressive and imaginative images that reflect their own unique personalities.

Although art galleries and museums are ideal places to view original art, visits are usually limited by finances or availability. Therefore, large reproductions can help students become acquainted with artworks and can prepare them for seeing original artworks at a later time. The artworks can be presented one at a time or thematically, in portfolio groups, by the teacher or by trained volunteers called docents.

THE LANGUAGE OF ART

To carry on a meaningful dialogue about art, both teachers and children need to become acquainted with and understand the vocabulary of art: the verbal tools that will help them identify, describe, analyze, and react to an artwork, whether it is their own production or one created by a well-known artist. The basic components that all artists use—whether they are making a painting or piece of sculpture, planning a building, designing fabric, clothing, furniture, jewelry, and such—are the elements of art. They can be thought of as the ingredients of both two- and three-dimensional art. Color, value, line, shape/form, texture, and space are the elements of art.

The principles of art are the ways that artists organize and arrange these elements to create the painting, building, or craft object. The artist strives for a harmonious use of these art elements. The principles of art are: balance, emphasis, proportion, movement, rhythm/repetition/pattern, variety, and unity.

Elements of Art

Color

Color can be used in a realistic manner, in a decorative manner, or in an expressive or emotional way. It also can be used symbolically. A color wheel makes it easy to understand about different colors and to learn how to mix and use them in producing artworks. Plate 1 in the Color Gallery features a color wheel.

The three primary colors are placed equidistant apart on the wheel, and the secondary colors are placed between them. The primary colors are red, yellow, and blue. Mixing any two of these produces the secondary colors: orange, green, and violet (red + yellow = orange; yellow + blue = green; blue + red = violet). The intermediate colors are between each of these colors. They are: red-orange, yellow-orange, yellow-green, blue-green, blue-violet, and red-violet. Two colors that are opposite each other on the color wheel are called complementary colors. Complementary colors contrast strongly with each other. In addition, when a small amount of one complementary color is mixed with its opposite, it tends to dull the other color slightly. A pair of complementary colors mixed together in somewhat equal amounts results in a dull gray; green, for instance, may be dulled slightly by mixing it with a little bit of red. A monochromatic group of colors is made by selecting one color and mixing a variety of its tints and shades. Tints are made by adding white to a color; shades are made by adding a small amount of black to a color. Neutrals are black, white, and gray. Though they are not on the color wheel, they are usually thought of as colors and are used as colors.

Colors can be grouped in several ways. Red, orange, and yellow are thought of as warm colors in that they remind us of fire and heat. Blue, green, and violet are called cool colors because they make us think of water, cool grass, and icy snow.

A challenging motivation is to use a limited palette to make an entire painting. For instance, students may be given their choice of one of the pairs of complementary colors, plus black and white. The focus another time might be on mixing tints and shades of one color and creating a composition with this monochromatic color scheme. Another focus might be on making a picture with only warm or cool colors.

The Color Gallery can help us identify and describe ways that artists have used color. There may be several different answers to the queries that follow. Discuss the reasons for your answers.

The book *Color Seems* illustrates concepts such as *warm* and *cool,* and *bright* and *dull* and can be shared and discussed by teacher and children.

1. In his artwork *I Am Always Thinking about Animals,* Tookoome used primary colors. Find an artwork that is made up of both primary and secondary colors.

2. Which artwork has only the secondary colors along with neutrals?

3. What sort of mood or emotion does Tamayo create by using mostly warm colors in his painting *Animals?* Do you think the animals may be guarding their owner against an intruder?

4. Select an artwork that has one or more small areas of red in it. Try to decide why the artist used red in that manner.

5. Find an artwork that uses colors in (a) a very realistic way, (b) a decorative or imaginative way, and (c) an expressive way.

6. Find an artwork that is mostly cool colors, and describe its mood. Do the same with an artwork that is mostly warm colors.

7. Find an artwork with (a) bright colors, (b) soft colors, (c) dull colors, (d) complementary colors, (e) monochromatic colors.

Discussing Color in the Classroom   These four art reproductions in the Color Gallery can help young children to identify and describe some ways that artists have used color: Mary Cassatt, *The Bath;* Simon Tookoome, *I Am Always Thinking about Animals;* André Derain, *London Bridge;* and Andy Warhol, *A Set of Six Self-Portraits.*

Questions for Preschool-Age Children
Which artwork has faces of all different colors? (Warhol's) Do the faces look real? Why or why not?

Are there colors in the other pictures that make you feel happy? Why or why not?

Some colors make us feel warm—like we're sitting in sunshine. Can you find colors like that in any of these paintings? Which ones? Where?

There are two pictures with water in them. Can you point out the water?

Which one uses cool colors that remind us of cool water? (Cassatt's)

Which one uses a warm color in the water? (Derain's)

A six-year-old used warm colors to make this painting of a summer sun.

Questions for Early School-Age Children

Which picture is mostly blue? (Cassatt's) Some blues are light and some are dark. Can you find a light blue in this painting? Can you find a dark blue?

What colors did Warhol use in his self-portraits? Which one does your eye go to first? Why?

What artist used three primary colors (red, yellow, blue)? (Tookoome)

Find the three primary colors in Derain's painting. What other colors did he use?

What time of day is it in Derain's painting? How do colors help set a time of day?

Questions for Upper Primary-Age Children

Which artist painted a picture that looks real but with colors that are unreal? (Derain)

Which artist created a picture with colors that look most real? Why did you pick that one?

Colors that are across from one another (opposites) on the color wheel are called complements. Can you find colors in these paintings that are complements? (red/green, blue/orange, yellow/violet)

Can you find places in the pictures where the artist used complementary colors right next to one another? (Warhol's, Derain's, and minimally in Cassatt's)

Two of the artworks are paintings and two are prints. Can you point out where there are colors that look flat? (Warhol's and Tookoome's—the prints) Can you point out areas where the colors look as if they were painted in?

Colors help to create a mood. What is the mood of each painting? Can you tell me a word that describes how the colors in each artwork make you feel?

Before going on to the next section, look at other artworks in the Color Gallery and formulate questions about color that you might use with young children. Georges Seurat's *A Sunday on La Grande Jatte,* Franz Marc's *Yellow Cow,* and Jacob Lawrence's *Cabinet Makers* are particularly suitable for a dialogue focused on color concepts.

a

b

a. Colored, wooden shapes to fit and arrange in a box frame give children experiences in color and space.

b. A set of plastic bracelets can be a teaching toy. Bracelets are graded in value, and the child must stack them on a round, wooden post in a light to dark arrangement.

Value

Value has to do with the lightness or darkness of a color in an artwork. Light colors, to which white has been added, are called tints. Dark colors, to which black has been added, are called shades. A value scale shows a gradual transition from a very light tint to a very dark shade. If an artwork is made up of lights and darks of one color, we say that it has a monochromatic color scheme, and this can contribute a great deal to the artwork's mood or emotion.

Some artworks, including pen and ink, charcoal, and pencil drawings, black and white photographs, and various forms of printmaking, depend greatly on the use of value alone and not on color.

With a gradual, blended transition from light to dark values in an artwork, artists can create the illusion of three-dimensional form. Sharp changes in value are seen on angular surfaces of buildings, and this helps us to see the buildings as three-dimensional. A strong directional light creates a great contrast in light and darks, which results in dramatic and expressive impact.

Changes in value can be achieved by shading techniques called hatching (many parallel lines), cross-hatching (crossed parallel lines), stippling (dots), or blending (smooth transition from dark to light).

The Color Gallery can help us identify and describe ways that artists have used value. There may be several different answers to the queries that follow. Discuss the reasons for your answers.

1. Picasso has used light and dark values of two colors in his painting *Family of Saltimbanques.* How would the mood of the artwork change if he had used five or six different colors instead?

2. Compare the use of value in Kahlo's *Fulang-Chang and Me* and O'Keeffe's *Cow's Skull with Calico Roses.*

3. Do you feel that the sharp contrast of lights and darks in Picasso's *Still Life* are harmonious with the harsh geometric shapes?

4. In Kandinsky's *Painting No. 198,* we see a strong contrast of dark and light. How does this contribute to the feeling of movement and restlessness? Compare this same quality in Lawrence's *Cabinet Makers.*

5. Select an artwork that has a dramatic impact due to the use of value, and explain the reasons for your choice.

A limited palette of one color plus black and white encouraged this kindergartner to mix colors to complete a tempera self-portrait.

6. Notice the dark and light areas created by the light striking the three-dimensional form of Modigliani's sculpture. Is the change of value gradual or sharp?

7. Find two artworks that use a gradual blend of a light to a dark color to show three-dimensional form.

Discussing Value in the Classroom   These three art reproductions in the Color Gallery can help young children identify and describe ways that artists have used value: Pablo Picasso, *Family of Saltimbanques;* Grant Wood, *American Gothic;* and Georges Seurat, *A Sunday on La Grande Jatte.* (Note: Sometimes value is more evident if the viewer squints while looking at the artwork.)

Questions for Preschool-Age Children
Which artwork has dark places? Can you show me some dark places?
Which artwork has light places? Can you show me some light places?
Which artworks have light and dark places right next to one another?
Can you find a picture where people are standing in the shade? (Seurat's) What do
   you think is making the shade? Show me the light parts of the picture.
Which picture makes you feel happy? Why?

Questions for Early School-Age Children
When an artist mixes white with color, he or she makes a tint. Can you show me some
   places in these paintings where there are tints?
When an artist mixes black with a color, a shade is created. Can you show me some
   places in these paintings where there are shades?
Can you find some places where there are black and white or shades and tints right
   next to each other? Artists call this contrast.
Help me find some shadows in the pictures. Can you trace the shadows with your
   finger? How do you think the artist made the shadows?

Questions for Upper Primary-Age Children

Which artwork has lights and darks but only uses two colors? (Picasso's)

Which painting is mostly light on the top and mostly dark on the bottom? (Wood's)

Some artists blend light and dark so that things look rounded. Can you find places in these artworks where this has been done? (heads, hands, bodies of people)

Can you show me some places where there are shadows on the people's faces?

Some artists made shadows by adding black, but other artists used color to make shadows. Can you find any colors in the shadows?

Where are the areas of greatest contrast (lightest and darkest areas next to one another)? Can you find places where there is little or no contrast?

Before going on to the next section, look at other artworks in the Color Gallery and formulate questions about value that you might use with young children. Picasso's *Still Life* and O'Keeffe's *Cow's Skull with Calico Roses* are particularly suitable for a dialogue focused on value concepts.

Line

Line is thought of as a continuous mark or stroke made on a surface by a point of a moving tool, such as a pencil, crayon, or pen. It is usually associated with two-dimensional artworks, but it can also be an important part of three-dimensional art. We usually think of line in relation to edges or contours. Where one object stops and meets another, even if it is the air, an edge is formed. Some artists make definite outlines around the objects they draw or paint; others separate the shapes by different colors or textures.

Lines can be implied; that is, a line begins and may be interrupted, but its direction sends our eye on its journey through the composition anyway, filling in what is missing. The tool that the artist uses somewhat controls the line quality; a line made with a crayon is quite different from a line made with a pen or one made with a brush and ink. Likewise, the surface of paper lends different characteristics to line. Lines made on rough paper are quite different from those made on smooth paper, even if the drawing tool is the same.

Lines have direction—horizontal, vertical, diagonal—each evoking different feelings and responses. Strength, stability, and dignity are communicated when artists use vertical lines. Horizontal lines, on the other hand, tend to remind us of restful, quiet, calm, peaceful things. When artists want to create tension or movement or an illusion of action, they use diagonal lines. Such lines lead our eyes in slanting directions, upward, downward, or forward.

Other characteristics of line include whether the line is straight or curving, long or short, thick or thin, blurred and uneven or sharp and clear-edged. If a line changes as it moves along and goes from thick to thin, it is a gradated line. Lines may meander, be continuous, or be broken. Lines may be repeated in a regular or random manner to create a pattern or to lend a feeling of rhythm to an artwork.

The Color Gallery can help us identify and describe ways that artists have used line. There may be several different answers to the queries that follow. Discuss the reasons for your answers.

1. Simon Tookoome used black contour lines in *I Am Always Thinking about Animals.* Find more artworks in which the artist used lines to separate shapes. Find several artworks in which no lines were used to separate the shapes.

2. What kind of feeling do all the straight, vertical lines give you in the *Empress Theodora and Retinue?* Contrast the lines in this artwork with the diagonal lines in Lawrence's *Cabinet Makers.*

3. Marc used curving and diagonal lines in his *Yellow Cow.* How would the use of only vertical and horizontal lines change the mood of the picture?

Notice the amount of detail in this artwork after a discussion of the elements of line and shape.

4. Find important diagonal lines in the artworks by Degas, van Gogh, Derain, and Seurat.

5. Find artworks that have lines that could be described as (a) graceful, (b) bold, (c) angular, (d) smooth, and (e) thick.

Discussing Line in the Classroom   These four art reproductions in the Color Gallery can help young children identify and describe ways that artists have used line: Piet Mondrian, *Composition*; Li-Anzhong, *Shrike and Bamboo;* Jacob Lawrence, *Cabinet Makers*; and Pablo Picasso, *Still Life.*

Questions for Preschool-Age Children
Can you find some lines that go up and down—the way we do when we stand up straight and tall? Where?
Can you find some lines that look as if they are lying down? Where?
Which artwork has lines that are very straight? (Mondrian's)
Where did the artists use curved lines? Straight lines? Wavy lines?
Where are some thin lines? Where are some thick lines?
Where did the artist use both thick lines and thin lines in the same picture?

Questions for Early School-Age Children
Lines can go in many directions. Can you find vertical (up and down) lines? Can you find horizontal lines (ones that go across the picture)?
Which lines separate two areas of color? (several places, but especially the black lines in Mondrian's *Composition*)
Can you find some places where lines cross one another? (many places, but especially the black lines in Mondrian's *Composition*)
Lines have color. Where in the artworks can you find colored lines?
Which artwork uses lines to show the edges of things?

Questions for Upper Primary-Age Children

Lines that go from one corner across a picture are called diagonals. Which painting has the most diagonals? Can you show me some?

Some lines come together at a point and make an angle. Can you find one? (there are some in all the paintings)

Lines that are repeated over and over again and go in the same direction form a pattern called stripes. Which artwork uses striped patterns? (Lawrence's) In which direction do the stripes go? (the wood—vertical)

Lines that go around a shape are called outlines or contour lines. Can you point out some outlines?

Point out some lines in each of the artworks. What words would you use to describe these lines? (busy, heavy, sharp, wavy, swirling, moving)

Before going on to the next section, look at other artworks in the Color Gallery and formulate questions about line that you might use with young children. Simon Tookoome's *I Am Always Thinking about Animals* and Vasily Kandinsky's *Painting No. 198* are particularly suitable for a dialogue focused on line concepts.

Shape/Form

Shape is an enclosed space on a two-dimensional surface. When a line moves around and comes back and meets where it began, it creates a shape. Shapes may be determined either by a definite contour line (outline) or by a change in color or texture. Shapes may be flat, like a silhouette, or they may be shaded to give the illusion of being a solid three-dimensional form in the real world. Shapes may overlap to give this illusion also. Form has to do with three-dimensional artworks—sculpture, architecture, and craft objects.

Shapes can be described in many ways. They can be large or small in size. They can have hard, crisp edges or soft, blurred contours. When the same shapes are repeated many times, they create a pattern. Shapes can be described as geometric when they remind us of squares, rectangles, triangles, and circles. They can be organic or free form when they remind us of natural objects. When a number of similar shapes are close together in an artwork, they give us a feeling of closeness, unity, and compactness.

A shape that is realistic represents something we recognize in the real world, but sometimes artists simplify, distort, and change the shapes they see. This is called abstraction. A positive shape in a composition is the object itself; the space that surrounds it is called the negative shape. Artists always want to make both of these shapes relate to each other harmoniously.

The Color Gallery can help us identify and describe ways that artists have used shape and form. There may be several different answers to the queries that follow. Discuss the reasons for your answers.

1. Mondrian used all flat geometric shapes in his *Composition.* Describe the shapes Matisse used in *The Wild Poppies.*

2. Grant Wood has used realistic shapes in *American Gothic.* Find two other artworks that use realistic shapes. Now compare them with the elongated shape of the face in Modigliani's *Head of a Woman.* How do distortion and elongation contribute to the mood of this sculpture?

3. What shapes are repeated to create an irregular pattern in Li-Anzhong's *Shrike and Bamboo?*

4. How did Warhol vary the same shapes in *A Set of Six Self-Portraits?*

5. Observe the variety of hard-edged geometric shapes in Chagall's *Green Violinist.* Then look for artworks in which the shapes are defined in a softer blurred manner by a change in color or texture.

The seven-piece tangram puzzle originated in China in the 1800s and involves arranging a square, a parallelogram, and five triangles into silhouettes of people, animals, and objects. Manipulations aid the child in developing concepts of size, shape, symmetry, and similarity.

6. Shapes that are larger seem closer to us. Notice the two chairs in van Gogh's *The Bedroom at Arles.* Make similar observations about the shapes in Derain's *London Bridge* and Seurat's *A Sunday on La Grande Jatte.*

7. The repetition of what shape in Degas's *The Millinery Shop* contributes to a feeling of unity?

8. Discuss the variety and relationship of positive shapes and negative spaces in Moore's sculpture *Reclining Figure.*

Discussing Shape/Form in the Classroom   These six art reproductions in the Color Gallery can help young children identify and describe ways that artists have used shape and form: Pablo Picasso, *Still Life;* Vasily Kandinsky, *Painting No. 198;* Henri Matisse, *The Wild Poppies;* Franz Marc, *Yellow Cow;* Henry Moore, *Reclining Figure;* and Amedeo Modigliani, *Head of a Woman.*

Questions for Preschool-Age Children
Where do you see a big blue shape? Can you find a little blue shape in the same picture? (Matisse's)

Can you find a shape that reminds you of a leaf? Of a butterfly?

Which artwork has the shape of a big animal? What is the animal? Can you find some little animal shapes in the picture, too? (Marc's)

Which artwork has many wiggly shapes? (Kandinsky's)

Which artwork has shapes that do not touch? (Matisse's)

Which artworks look like people? (Modigliani's and Moore's)

Show me a place where there is a shape inside a shape.

Which artworks look very round? Which ones look very flat?

Questions for Early School-Age Children
When a line comes around and meets where it began, it makes a shape. Find a line that makes a shape in Kandinsky's *Painting No. 198.* How many can you find?

Which artwork has many squares, rectangles, triangles, and circles? (Picasso's) Can you find some other shapes, too?

Do any of the artworks have shapes with hard edges? Soft edges? (Kandinsky's painting has a wide variety)

Which artwork looks as if it has shapes cut from paper? (Matisse's)

Which artwork looks very, very long? (Modigliani's)

Which artworks are flat? (the four paintings)

Which artworks are *not* flat? (the two sculptures)

This felt-covered bulletin board stimulates both visual and tactile perception in young viewers. Designed by Nancy and Wally Remington for a preschool classroom at Inverness Day School, Carmichael, California.

Questions for Upper Primary-Age Children

The curving shape of Marc's *Yellow Cow* gives us a feeling of movement and action. Which other artwork has curved shapes? Does it seem as if it has action, too?

The two sculptures have forms that remind us of something familiar. What are they? (people)

In the photographs of the two sculptures, can you find forms that look like heads?

Which artist used lines and shapes to make a painting that does not look like anything? (Kandinsky) How would you describe the shapes in his artwork?

In Matisse's *The Wild Poppies,* find an interesting shape in the space between the colored shapes.

Find an artwork that has distorted shapes. (Picasso's *Still Life* is a particularly good example)

In Picasso's *Still Life,* what shapes remind you of things in the real world? (some are recognizable as a vase, guitar, table) These are called abstractions.

Before going on to the next section, look at other artworks in the Color Gallery and formulate questions about shape and form that you might use with young children. The mosaic of *Empress Theodora and Retinue,* for example, is particularly suitable for a dialogue focused on concepts about shape and form.

Texture

Texture refers to how things feel when touched or to the illusion of how something would feel. An object's tactile quality is appealing. Through our sense of touch, we learn about the world. Some of the words we use to describe texture include soft, furry, rough, fluffy, smooth, bumpy, grainy, slick, and hard.

Actual textures are those surfaces that we can really feel. Sculpture, architecture, and craft objects often rely on actual texture as one of their main elements. The smoothly polished surface of marble or wood, the woolly feel of a woven tapestry, the shiny or rough feel of metal are all vital parts of such artworks. We like variety in texture and choose different fabrics for our clothing and home furnishings. Some painters apply the paint to their canvases in such a way as to create an impasto effect; that is, thick paint applied in broad strokes or swirls creates a real texture.

Texture forms a significant part of this kindergarten painting. Colored paints are spread and sponged into place, creating a rich surface for the final artwork.

Another kind of texture is visual or simulated. This kind is created by artists in two-dimensional artworks to give the illusion of real texture. Our eye is attracted to texture, so artists often include several contrasting textured areas or use an interesting texture to direct our attention to a focal point.

The Color Gallery can help us identify and describe ways that artists have used texture. There may be several different answers to the queries that follow. Discuss the reasons for your answers.

1. Compare the actual textural differences between Modigliani's *Head of a Woman* and Moore's *Reclining Figure.* How do the materials the artists used (stone and wood) contribute to textural qualities?

2. Discuss the variety of simulated textures in Kahlo's *Fulang-Chang and Me.*

3. The mosaic *Empress Theodora and Retinue* is made up of thousands of very small pieces of glass or stone set in plaster. How do you think its texture contributes to its feeling of dignity and richness?

4. Compare the actual textures of the paint on the canvas in works by Derain, van Gogh, and Seurat. In which do you see brushstrokes? Which is made up of many tiny dots of color that give it a grainy texture?

5. Find two paintings that show highly realistic simulated textures.

6. Find two paintings in which the artists relied on textural qualities of brushstrokes and thick paint.

Discussing Texture in the Classroom   These four art reproductions in the Color Gallery can help young children identify and describe ways that artists have used texture: Amedeo Modigliani, *Head of A Woman;* Frida Kahlo's *Fulang-Chang and Me;* the mosaic *Empress Theodora and Retinue;* Vincent van Gogh, *The Bedroom at Arles.*

Questions for Preschool-Age Children
Which picture shows something that is soft and fuzzy? (Kahlo's)
Which artwork would you like to touch? Why?

Actual texture is incorporated into this self-portrait by a third-grade student. Using yarn in the drawing helps students to keep the image large and bold.

Touch something in the room that feels the way part of the artwork looks.

Which artworks would feel very hard if you could touch them? (Modigliani's and the mosaic)

Find the brushstrokes in van Gogh's painting, and imagine how the painting would feel if you could touch it.

Questions for Early School-Age Children

Where in the artworks are there both rough and smooth parts?

Which artwork looks as if the artist used very thick paint to make texture? (van Gogh's)

How would you describe the textures of the hair, fur, and plants in Kahlo's *Fulang-Chang and Me?*

In which artwork can you see the artist's brushstrokes?

In the mosaic, we can see different kinds of textured clothing. If you could touch the mosaic, how do you think it would really feel?

Questions for Upper Primary-Age Children

If the real artworks were here, which ones do you think would feel smooth?

Which artwork has a great deal of visual texture but is probably fairly smooth? (Kahlo's)

Which artwork has actual textures created by brushstrokes? Which artworks have a surface texture because of the way they are made?

Compare the visual textures in Kahlo's *Fulang-Chang and Me* and van Gogh's *Bedroom at Arles.*

Which artwork looks rather rough and is probably also rough to the touch?

Which artwork shows the most variety of textures? Explain your choice.

Before going on to the next section, look at other artworks in the Color Gallery and formulate questions about texture that you might use with young children. Pablo

Actual "found textures" are combined in this scarecrow to create an inviting piece of sculpture. A nature-walk search for a variety of textured objects can lead to increased student awareness of tactile qualities and can expand children's vocabularies.

Picasso's *Still Life,* Henry Moore's *Reclining Figure,* and Georgia O'Keeffe's *Cow's Skull with Calico Roses* are particularly suitable for a dialogue focused on texture concepts.

Space

Three-dimensional space is all around us, and such artworks as architecture, sculpture, and crafts are concerned with both functional and artistic ways of creating forms that have height, width, and depth. Artists who draw and paint on two-dimensional surfaces also deal with spatial concepts because they fit the objects and shapes they are creating into the format and limitations of the surface on which they are working.

Through the ages, artists have found many ways to create the illusion of three-dimensional space on a flat two-dimensional surface. The easiest way to create this illusion of space is by overlapping. When one object covers part of a second object, the one in front seems closer. When artists make compositions with only a few overlapped objects to create depth, we say the composition has a shallow or flat space. The sizes of various shapes are important in showing space. Larger shapes seem closer to us; smaller shapes seem farther away. Placement of shapes also contributes to the illusion of depth: Those objects closer to the bottom of the composition are seen as closer than those higher up. This works in reverse for objects in the sky: Clouds or birds at the top of the picture seem closer to us than those nearer the horizon. Details, colors, and textures of figures and objects that are close to us are more distinct, bright, and clear than those objects deeper in space. This is often called atmospheric or aerial perspective. Another way that artists are able to make objects look as if they exist in space is through the use of directional lighting. This gives the illusion of modeled form to three-dimensional objects in that the objects are shaded gradually from light to dark. Converging lines that are used in perspective also lead our eyes into the spatial depths of a picture. Renaissance artists learned that lines that we perceive in nature as being horizontal and parallel to each other tend to meet at a point on an eye-level line called the vanishing point.

The Color Gallery can help us identify and describe ways that artists have used space. There may be several different answers to the queries that follow. Discuss the reasons for your answers.

1. Observe the flat use of space in Mondrian's *Composition* and Matisse's *The Wild Poppies.* Do any other artworks show flatness? Would you describe the space in Picasso's *Still Life* as shallow, flat, or deep? Find several artworks that show depth (deep space).

2. In *Yellow Cow,* Marc used overlapping to show space. Which ways of showing depth did he *not* use?

3. Measure the closest, tallest figures in the foreground of Seurat's *A Sunday on La Grande Jatte.* Then measure a figure a little higher up in the middle ground; then a figure still higher up in the background. What does this tell you about the use of size and placement to show depth?

4. What repeated shapes and colors lead your eyes from the foreground to the background in Lawrence's *Cabinet Makers?*

5. Find an artwork in which directional lighting shows the modeled forms of figures.

6. Where are the converging lines and vanishing points that create an illusion of deep space in van Gogh's *The Bedroom at Arles* and Derain's *London Bridge?*

Discussing Space in the Classroom   These four art reproductions in the Color Gallery can help young children identify and describe ways that artists have used space: Marc Chagall, *Green Violinist;* Edgar Degas, *The Millinery Shop;* Vincent van Gogh, *The Bedroom at Arles;* and Henry Moore, *Reclining Figure.*

Questions for Preschool-Age Children

Find the picture that looks as if people are walking on air. (Chagall's) Why does it look that way?

Which person in Chagall's artwork looks closest to us? Why? (size)

Which artworks show an inside place? (Degas's and van Gogh's) How do you know it is inside?

Which artwork looks as if it has holes in it? (Moore's)

How do you think the sculpture would look without the holes—heavier or lighter? More like a person or less like a person?

Questions for Early School-Age Children

Look at the two chairs in van Gogh's bedroom. Which one looks closer? Why? (bigger)

Identify all the things that are in front of the girl in *The Millinery Shop.* (counter, hats)

Is your bedroom bigger or smaller than van Gogh's? What makes you think so?

Two of the paintings have people in them. Which of the people look farthest away? Why? (small figures in Chagall's painting because of size and placement higher in the picture)

What words would you use to describe Henry Moore's sculpture that would tell us about its size and weight? Can you point out some spaces inside the artwork?

Questions for Upper Primary-Age Children

Which artist has used space so that the painting looks like a dream? (Chagall) What is dreamlike about the space in the picture?

Which hat in *The Millinery Shop* looks farthest away? (the one with red trim) Why? (it is the smallest, highest, and dullest in color of the hats; it is also overlapped by others)

What has van Gogh done with the edges of the floor, bed, and other furniture to give the feeling of space? (the edges seem to come together as they approach the back wall of the bedroom)

Which artwork seems to have the most depth? Why?

"Battle," drawn by a six-year-old, includes a variety of details that indicate a growing awareness of the complexities of space.

Sculptors use space in their artwork, too. Find space around and inside Moore's *Reclining Figure.* How would you describe this space?

Before going on to the next section, look at other artworks in the Color Gallery and formulate questions about space that you might use with young children. Rufino Tamayo's *Animals,* Georgia O'Keeffe's *Cow's Skull with Calico Roses,* and Georges Seurat's *A Sunday on La Grande Jatte* are particularly suitable for dialogue focused on space concepts.

Principles of Art

Balance

Balance has to do with a visual feeling of weight that we see and feel when we look at an artwork. There are two kinds of balance: formal and informal. Formal, or symmetrical balance, is when one side of an artwork is exactly like the other side—a mirror image. If architects wish to design a building in which serious, dignified activities take place, one in which a feeling of formality and stability is to be achieved, they may choose this sort of balance. Many government buildings and churches show formal balance. Balance that is almost symmetrical is called approximate balance.

Symmetrical balance is evident in this head-on drawing of a fox. Placement of the head in the center of the paper accentuates the symmetry.

"The Peaceful Fox," Meri Clare, O'Malley Elementary School, Anchorage, Alaska, Grade 3, age 8. Courtesy © 1991–92 Crayola® Dream Makers™

Informal, or asymmetrical balance, on the other hand, creates a sense of equilibrium, even though both sides of the artwork are different. Artists usually use informal balance in making paintings, and they find many different ways of achieving it: They may balance one large shape against several small shapes, or a small, roughly textured, or patterned area with a large, smooth, or plain one. A dark value of a color seems heavier than a light color. Bright colors attract our attention more than do low-intensity colors. Warm colors appear heavier than cool colors. More-complicated shapes catch our eye and thus appear heavier than those with simpler contours.

The Color Gallery can help us analyze ways that artists have used balance. There may be several different answers to the queries that follow. Discuss the reasons for your answers.

1. What kind of feeling does the symmetrical balance of Modigliani's *Head of a Woman* create?

2. Compare the ways in which balance was achieved in *I Am Always Thinking about Animals* and in *Prince Riding an Elephant.*

3. Find the shapes in Marc's *Yellow Cow* that create a comfortable feeling of informal balance.

4. Look at Kandinsky's *Painting No. 198* upside down and sideways, and discuss how he achieved balance. Does this create a calm feeling?

5. Is the feeling of balance comfortable or uncomfortable in Picasso's *Family of Saltimbanques?* Why?

6. In Chagall's *Green Violinist,* the figure is in the center. How did Chagall achieve a feeling of balance in the top and bottom of the picture?

7. How do shapes and their repetition contribute to balance in Seurat's *A Sunday on La Grande Jatte* and Degas's *The Millinery Shop?*

A parent docent helps young students identify ways that Picasso created emphasis in his painting, *Three Musicians*.

Emphasis

Artists have many ways to emphasize what they want us to see within an artwork. The center of interest, or focal point, is the main part of the composition and usually the part that we see first when we look at an artwork. This area dominates the other parts of the composition. Normally, we are drawn immediately to the center of a picture, but most artworks do not have the focal point in this position because it is rather static and sometimes makes for an uninteresting arrangement. Most artists place the emphasis to the right or left of center and use various means to establish a feeling of balance.

The subject matter of an artwork is what usually catches our eye first. As human beings, we are drawn to images of other human beings, especially their faces, and most especially their eyes. So this is often a focal point. If the subject matter is unusual or at least treated in an unusual, surprising, or even shocking manner, that area becomes dominant. Contrasting elements can catch our eye, too. The lighting in the composition can create strong contrasts of lights and darks that arrest our attention. Likewise, an intricately textured or patterned area can create an emphasis. Some artworks use the color red to focus attention on a special area. Many artworks use pointers such as someone's uplifted arm or lines that take our eye in a given direction. Even someone's eyes within the composition, if looking in a particular direction, make our eyes follow them in the same direction. Converging lines created by the illusion of perspective direct our path of vision to a focal point as well. Isolated elements, perhaps a figure or object set apart from the other parts of the composition, also tend to attract our attention.

The Color Gallery can help us analyze ways that artists have created an emphasis. There may be several different answers to the queries that follow. Discuss the reasons for your answers.

1. In Cassatt's *The Bath,* notice the heads of the woman and the child. They are the darkest areas, and they are looking down to the pan of water. What other devices direct your eyes to a focal point?

2. Can you discover ways in which Kahlo created a center of interest in her self-portrait *Fulang-Chang and Me?*

3. What do you perceive as the focal point in Kandinsky's *Painting No. 198?* What directs your attention to it?

4. Are there any directional pointers in Chagall's *Green Violinist?*

5. What is the focal point in Degas's *The Millinery Shop?* How is it achieved?

6. Can you find any artworks that achieve emphasis through isolation?

7. Find two artworks that show emphasis through contrast.

8. Can you find any artwork in which the center of attention is in the center of the composition?

Proportion

Proportion involves the relationship of one part to another. Long ago, people in ancient Greece sought a perfect proportion that would establish a rule, a mathematical formula to compare sizes, that could be used for perfect results in whatever artworks they created. The ratio they developed was called the Golden Section. Artists today are free to use it or not, but generally it results in a harmonious relationship of the various parts of an artwork.

A figure or face has realistic proportions when it closely resembles what we see. The proportion of the average adult is about seven and a half heads high. Children are about five or six heads tall, and a baby is three heads long. When artists depict the human figure, they may choose to use realistic proportions or to change them to suit their needs. If artists wish to be expressive and communicate a feeling, mood, or emotion, they often distort, exaggerate, or elongate the proportions.

The proportions of the face likewise follow certain guidelines for a realistic portrayal. The eyes are halfway between the chin and top of the head. The eyes are an eye-width apart. The nose is about an eye-width long. If lines are extended downward from the middle of the eyes, they establish the corners of the mouth. The ears are on a line with the top and bottom of the nose. Once again, artists change, distort, elongate, and exaggerate the size and location of the features in many different ways.

The Color Gallery can help us analyze ways that artists have used proportion. There may be several different answers to the queries that follow. Discuss the reasons for your answers.

1. Find some figures that seem to have realistic proportions. Check to see if the figures are about seven and a half heads high.

2. If Modigliani had used realistic proportions in his *Head of a Woman,* where would he have placed the eyes in his sculpture? How would that have changed the feeling of his work?

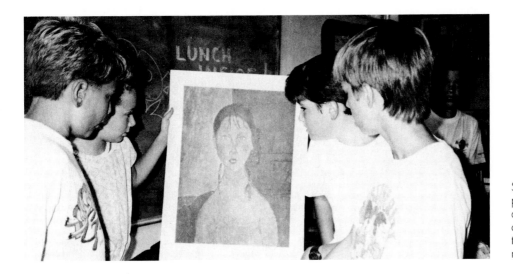

Students respond to Modigliani's painting by describing and analyzing the lines, shapes, and colors to determine what part they played in establishing the mood of the artwork.

3. Do the proportions of the figures in Picasso's *Family of Saltimbanques* appear to be realistic or elongated? Does this contribute to the mood?

4. Which figure in the mosaic *Empress Theodora and Retinue* is the tallest? Why do you think the artist made this figure taller than the others?

Movement

When we speak of movement in an artwork, we generally refer either to the illusion of movement or to how our eyes move around the composition, because the only artworks that have actual movement are mobiles and motion pictures.

Simulated movement creates in the viewer the feeling of action and can be accomplished in a number of ways. Artists can create paintings or sculptures that show figures running or jumping, and the effect can be rather static and stiff, or quite realistic. Shapes and lines can be repeated in a flowing, sweeping, swinging manner. A progressive arrangement of shapes moving from large to small can create a restful, relaxing feeling of movement or a jerking, mechanical one. Diagonal lines can contribute to a downward, upward, or powerful movement. Even though the subject matter itself may not be one that suggests action, artists can combine different elements that cause our eyes to move or sweep over the composition, directing our eyes from one point to another.

The Color Gallery can help us analyze ways that artists have used movement. There may be several different answers to the queries that follow. Discuss the reasons for your answers.

1. Choose an artwork that suggests actual movement and describe how the artist depicted it.

2. Lawrence used lines, shapes, and colors to make our eyes move through *Cabinet Makers*. Analyze the way your eyes move through this artwork and then compare the path your eyes take with a classmate's path.

3. What contributes to the feeling of movement in Marc's *Yellow Cow?*

4. How is the feeling of movement achieved in *Prince Riding an Elephant?*

5. How do the round shapes and vertical lines move your eye around Degas's *The Millinery Shop?*

"Batman," by a six-year-old,
shows movement and action.

6. Let your eyes follow the curving shapes in Moore's *Reclining Figure* and describe how the positive and negative shapes guide the ways your eyes move.

7. What makes the water seem to be moving in Derain's *London Bridge?*

Rhythm/Repetition/Pattern

Rhythm refers to a regular or harmonious pattern that is created by the repetition of a line, shape, or color. The unit that is repeated is called a motif, and it creates a decorative allover pattern. Patterns can be regular or irregular, even random, depending on the manner in which the motif is repeated. They can also be gradated, going from a large motif to a small one. A pattern can consist of alternating motifs and colors. Patterns can flow and lead our eyes around a composition. Patterns provide decorative effects and surface enhancement. They attract our eyes. Some patterned areas simulate texture, and sometimes, surface patterns create the illusion of a form beneath them.

The Color Gallery can help us analyze ways that artists have used pattern. There may be several different answers to the queries that follow. Discuss the reasons for your answers.

1. Find two different areas of pattern in *Prince Riding an Elephant.*

2. Look at Cassatt's *The Bath* and Chagall's *Green Violinist.* In which one does the pattern of the clothing reveal the form of the figure underneath?

3. Why do you think that O'Keeffe repeated the white rose in her composition?

4. The mosaic *Empress Theodora and Retinue* is rich in patterned areas. Look for four different motifs that are repeated.

5. A random pattern created by the repetition of a tree shape is found in which artwork?

6. What effect do the repeated yellow brushstrokes in the water have in Derain's *London Bridge?* What about the repeated arch shapes of the bridge itself and the repetition of the buildings?

A student creates both pattern and rhythm by repeating shapes in this detailed drawing.

"King Matthew," Matthew Saffer, Grace Christian School, Medford, Oregon, Grade 2, age 7. Photo Courtesy © 1991–92 Crayola® Dream Makers™

7. Describe how Warhol varied his motif and created a pattern in *A Set of Six Self-Portraits*.

8. Look carefully at Grant Wood's *American Gothic* and find places where he repeated the lines of the pitchfork.

Variety and Unity

Variety is concerned with differences and contrasts, such as differences in sizes of shapes or contrasting lights and darks of a color. Lines can show variety by being thick or thin, straight or curving. An artwork is boring if it has too much sameness, yet too much variety creates a chaotic effect.

Unity is the feeling the artwork gives us when we look at it and know that nothing should be added, taken away, or changed. All the different parts seem to belong together. Colors do not jar us; they harmonize. Nothing seems out of place or superfluous. The technique or style of the artist is harmonious with the subject matter, theme, or mood. Sometimes an artist repeats the same shape, color, line, or texture throughout the composition to achieve unity since our eyes like to move from one color or shape to a similar color or shape. Limiting the number of colors or the different kinds of shapes also helps an artist achieve unity, as does grouping similar shapes closely together, letting them overlap and cluster.

The Color Gallery can help us analyze ways that artists have used variety and unity. There may be several different answers to the queries that follow. Discuss the reasons for your answers.

1. Tamayo limited the number of colors that he used in *Animals*. Discuss how the unified effect would have changed had he used seven or eight different colors.

2. Similar shapes are repeated and the colors are limited throughout Lawrence's *Cabinet Makers*. Find another painting in which the artist used similar shapes to contribute to the feeling of unity.

3. Look closely at the figures in Seurat's *A Sunday on La Grande Jatte*. How is each one varied? With so much variety, how did the artist achieve unity?

4. What if Chagall had used the same bright colors for his background that he used for the violinist in *Green Violinist* instead of having the bright colors contrast with the neutral ones? Would he have achieved more unity or less unity?

5. How do the brushstrokes contribute to the feeling of unity in van Gogh's *The Bedroom at Arles?*

6. Are the colors and shapes that Marc used in painting the *Yellow Cow* in harmony with his theme? Compare with the colors in O'Keeffe's *Cow's Skull with Calico Roses*. What if O'Keeffe had used the bright colors that Marc used?

7. Picasso used a variety of different values of orange and blue for his group portrait of a family. Does his choice seem in harmony with the mood of the subject matter? Compare it with the colors in Chagall's *Green Violinist*.

Discussing the Principles of Art in the Classroom

Young children are able to understand some of the complexities involved in how artists organize the elements of art in their works. Simple questions that direct their attention and thoughts in early childhood form the foundation for informed judgments in later years. Select works from the Color Gallery and use some of the questions in the following list. The questions in parentheses are for older children. As you match questions to artworks, try to think of other questions that are appropriate for young children.

Balance   What is in the middle of the artwork? What do you see at the top? What do you see at the bottom? What did the artist put at the sides? Does one side of the picture seem heavy? (If the artwork were a teeter-totter, would both sides be equal? Where is all the weight in the picture/sculpture/print? Is there any part that looks like a wheel or the sun with all the rays coming out?)

Emphasis   Where does your eye go first? Is there some part that you looked at right away? Why do you think you looked there first? What makes this part stand out? What is the focal point? (Is there more than one focal point? What did the artist do to draw your eye to this place?)

Proportion   Does this artwork look like something you would see around you? Does this look like a photograph? Is some part bigger or smaller than something you might see? (Is some part of it bigger/longer or smaller/shorter than you think it should be? Did the artist change the size or shape of some of the things in the artwork? Which things look real and which ones look unreal?)

Movement   Do you see anything in the artwork that looks very still? Do you see something that looks as if it is moving? (Do you see something or someone that looks like it is caught in the middle of some action? What makes the artwork look as if there is motion in it? Can you find places where there are repeated shapes? Or where there are blurred edges?)

Rhythm/Repetition/Pattern   Do you see something—color, line, shape—more than once in the artwork? Do you see something over and over again? (Can you find a place where shapes, lines, or colors are repeated over and over again to make a pattern? Can you use your hands to clap out the rhythm or pattern that you see?)

Variety   Are there any surprises in the artwork? Can you find two things in the artwork that are alike? Two that are different? Can you find something that is big next to something that is little? Can you find something bright next to something dull? Light next to dark? These things create contrast. (Can you find two things that are both alike and different? Can you find things that are used and then changed when they are used again? Can you find places where things are changed as they are repeated? Can you find things that are opposite one another? Why do you think the artist used opposites?)

Unity   Do you like the way the artist put all the parts of the artwork together? (Does it look as if all the parts of the artwork go together? Find color/lines/shapes/textures that look as if they belong together. Use a word that describes the way you feel when you look at the artwork. How did the artist organize the artwork so all the parts seem to go together?)

GETTING ACQUAINTED WITH ARTWORKS

Commentary and questions that help us understand artworks involve art criticism and art history. When we look at an artwork in terms of art criticism, all the information is contained within the painting, drawing, or piece of sculpture. However, we need to turn to outside sources, such as books or informed persons, to find information relative to art history. These strategies, when intermingled, enrich and reinforce our comprehension of any artwork. Both art criticism and art history commentary encompasses:

1. description
2. analysis
3. interpretation
4. judgment [1]

Description

Art criticism asks us to look carefully and thoughtfully at the artwork and describe the subject matter. We may note where the figures or objects are placed. We state if the artwork is a landscape, portrait, still life, or abstraction, and we study its technical properties (broad sweeps of watercolor washes, thick application of brushstrokes, chisel marks in the wood, and so on). We also identify and describe the elements of art.

Art history describes the work by telling us when, where, and by whom the work was done. If we are looking at a small reproduction, it is helpful to know the size of the original and perhaps where it is located. We should know if the medium was oil, pastels, watercolor, wood, stone, etc.

A replica of a 4,000-year-old Egyptian ceramic hippo gives children both tactile and visual experiences as first steps to aesthetic awareness.

Third graders at Sacramento Country Day School gain an understanding of the art of Henri Rousseau through a careful study of the plants and animals that he painted in his detailed and highly patterned jungle scenes.

Looking at the way an artwork is organized and put together is one way to respond to visual images. Variety and unity are particularly appropriate concepts to discuss in this drawing by an eight-year-old.

"The Candyhouse Delight," Justin Anderson, Gladys Wood Elementary School, Anchorage, Alaska, Grade 2, age 8. Photo Courtesy © 1991–92 Crayola® Dream Makers™

Analysis

Art criticism asks us to respond to the artwork by perceiving how it is organized and put together. Here, we focus on how the principles of art have been used to arrange the elements of art.

Art history tells us what is special about the artwork, compared to and contrasted with those features found in other artworks. This helps us determine the work's artistic style.

Interpretation

Art criticism asks us to react to the emotions, feelings, moods, and ideas communicated by the artwork. This is a highly personal reflection and is influenced by many factors. We endeavor to understand what it is within the artwork that elicits a particular response—the colors or lines, the brushwork, the sense of chaos or movement achieved, the subject matter itself, as well as our own background and previous experiences.

Art history tells us how artists were influenced by the world around them. When and where they lived and the events, values, and attitudes of their immediate culture influenced the direction of their artwork. Information about an artist's background, friends, personality, and outlook on life helps us understand why the artist created in the way he or she did. Art history tells us why the artwork was created and why the artist chose to work in a particular manner. We can better interpret an artwork if we know these things, especially if the artwork was created for narrative, religious, or political reasons and for a culture other than the ones with which we are familiar.

Students respond to the feelings, moods, and ideas communicated in visual images. For two decades, the "Learning through the Arts Project" in New York City has created and implemented curriculum designed to stimulate learning for students who are academically performing below grade level. The program is an outgrowth of a pilot initiated at the Guggenheim Museum and stresses perception and interpretation. Year after year, nationally normed tests indicate that the majority of participating students demonstrate a dramatic increase in test scores at each grade level.

Judgment

Art criticism asks us not to merely express a personal preference for an artwork but to make a decision regarding the artwork's artistic merit. To make an appropriate judgment of an apple, we do not taste it and state that it is not a good apple because it does not taste like pumpkin pie; it is not pumpkin pie and must be judged instead on its "appleness" qualities. The same thinking applies when judging an artwork in relation to artistic styles, and our final evaluation should be in the spirit of stating, "I like it (or don't like it) because . . ." rather than ". . . because I like it (or don't like it)."

Art history helps us understand why an artwork is considered important. A particular artwork may be significant because the artist was the first to create art in that particular manner, or the artist has many followers, or a particular artwork had a powerful effect on religion or political life, and so on. We learn from art history what influenced a particular artist and how that artist, in turn, influenced other artists.

Four styles of art are often referred to in this regard:

1. **Representationalism or realism:** Artists strive to achieve a literal imitation of the subject matter before them. An artwork is successful if it looks like and reminds us of what we see in the world around us.

2. **Expressionism/emotionalism:** Artists feel that their most important objective is to communicate moods, feelings, and ideas in vivid and powerful ways. To do this, they often distort and exaggerate shapes and use unrealistic colors.

3. **Abstraction/formalism:** Artists strive to effectively organize the elements of art through the principles of art. Their compositions may or may not include any real people or objects.

4. **Surrealism/fantasy and dreams:** Artists endeavor to show us the world of the imagination, even the subconscious, often basing their images on realistic objects but presenting them in unlikely situations, combinations, and connections.[2]

We may use the qualities inherent in each of these four styles of art to judge an artwork. We often find that the artwork has qualities from more than one category. For instance, in looking at Grant Wood's *American Gothic,* we would agree that the two figures and the background are very skillfully painted and are quite realistic in color, shape, proportion, and so on. However, expressive qualities are also quite evident in the expressions and directions of the eyes in both figures, in the stark depictions of their clothing, and in the fine details of the house. He achieved these qualities without distortion or exaggeration. As we judge the artwork using the third category, that of abstraction/formalism, we would decide that Wood organized the colors and shapes and so on in a unified way, creating a pleasing and balanced arrangement. If we look for evidence of surrealism or fantasy and dreams, we would see nothing to suggest these qualities; it was not Wood's intent to do so. When making a judgment of Kandinsky's *Painting No. 198,* we would not use the first style of art—realism—because the painting is totally nonobjective, that is, it has no recognizable objects in it. In evaluating its expressive qualities, we would say that the explosive energies and rapid brushstrokes contribute to a restless feeling of movement and excitement. Kandinsky is credited with being the first artist to completely abandon the use of realistic subject matter and rely totally on the arrangement of colors, lines, and shapes to create the mood and to make up the composition. We would not judge this artwork in the fourth category because surrealism and dreams were not the reason or purpose that Kandinsky had in painting this artwork.

INTERMINGLING ART CRITICISM AND ART HISTORY COMMENTARY

Let us use Marc Chagall's *Green Violinist* in the Color Gallery to model our commentaries for art criticism and art history.

Description

"This oil painting, by the Russian artist Marc Chagall (1887–1985), is quite large: 78 × 42¾ inches. It was painted in 1923–1924 and is in the Guggenheim Museum in New York. We see a man sitting down and playing a violin. He takes up most of the space in the picture and his head is tipped to one side. There are some small houses behind his head, some clouds, and a floating figure. Beneath his feet are some more houses, a tree, ladder, bird, and a dog with its paws on the rooftop. There is another small figure at his side. The most important colors are purple, orange, and green—the secondary colors. The background and smaller figures are in light neutrals. The purple coat has dark and light values of purple in somewhat triangular shapes. The man's face and one hand are green and the violin is orange. There are very few outlines around the shapes. Small, square shapes are repeated in his pant legs and in the windows of the house. We can't see any brushstrokes; the colors seem to be blended smoothly."

Analysis

"The center of interest or emphasis is the violinist himself with his green face and one green hand. Our eyes go directly to him because of his central location and size. We especially see his face because it contrasts strongly with the other colors and is bright green instead of a realistic flesh color. The strong, bright colors contrast with the lighter, neutral colors. The black lines on the violin also lead our eyes to his face. The repeated triangular shapes in his coat make our eyes dance upward in a rhythmical manner to his face and hand. The roundish shapes of the clouds are a pleasing contrast to the blocky shapes of the buildings. The houses and objects in the lower portion balance those at the top. The proportion of the houses and small figures to the violinist himself are unrealistic but add to the feeling of fantasy and dreams. This artwork is quite different from a number of other artworks in that it relies on fantasy and imagination and has strange and unusual things happening that make us wonder what is going on—for example, the floating figure, the strange relationships of sizes, the positions of figures, houses, the dog, and so on."

Interpretation

"We wonder what we would hear if we could 'walk into this picture.' We would probably hear some happy, vibrant music. We would most likely hear the dog barking to the beat of the tune. The light-hearted happy feeling in the picture makes us feel that we could fly ourselves. Chagall was born to a poor Jewish family in a tiny village in Russia. He referred to his childhood as being both sad and happy. His family saw to it that he had art lessons. When he grew up, he always painted in a very personal style, using bright colors and taking his subject matter from his childhood memories of folk tales and fantasy. His paintings often tell of a dream world where delightful fairy tales come true and the laws of gravity are overturned. His art is a happy mixture of reality, dreams, nostalgia for his childhood, and fantasy. He delighted in nature and in music."

Judgment

"This painting seems to be quite successful, especially in its expressive content. The artwork communicates a lilting poetic feeling of fantasy by not being painted in a highly realistic manner, but in a more abstract style. We feel that Chagall created a fine balance and harmonious relationship in his limited use of colors and shapes. He was mostly concerned with fantasy and with the way he was organizing the colors and shapes that he used. We enjoy looking at it again and again, pondering and delighting in its mood. We can pretend that we hear the violin music as our eyes move from shape to shape and follow the lines in the composition. Chagall has been called a magic surrealist, and his colors and use of fantasy influenced other painters considerably, especially postwar German artists. He had a genuine love of humanity. He designed painted ceilings for the opera houses in Paris and New York. He has made paintings and stained glass artworks for the United Nations and the Jerusalem Synagogue."

Activities for Eliciting Student Responses to Artworks

When responding to artworks—whether the artworks are originals being viewed in a museum or are reproductions—children need to be as close as possible to the artworks to see details and to prevent them from becoming distracted. Small children are often comfortable seated on the floor near the artworks. The following activities are very successful during a presentation of several artworks:

1. With a "magic paintbrush" for a pointer, the teacher or the children can point to different details in an artwork, such as all the places the artist used red, all the curving shapes, and so on. The magic paintbrush can also be used to show how technical properties were achieved—how the brush left a path called a brushstroke and how some brushstrokes overlap and swirl. The magic paintbrush is also useful for tapping children's shoulders to let them take turns at having "magic artist eyes" and telling something that they see that no one else has yet mentioned. A magic paintbrush is made by covering the handle of the brush with glue and sprinkling it

Children observe the construction techniques of slab, coil, pinch pot, and texturing by examining ceramic animals and figures from folk cultures.

with glitter. Children who have the opportunity to use the magic paintbrush frequently notice that some of the magic is left on their hands after they have used the brush. A long "super brush" can also be used effectively as a pointer. It is made by attaching about two or three feet of dowel stick to the ferrule of a brush.

2. One aspect of reading readiness is developing the ability to sequence: what happened first, what happened next, and so on. The teacher can start a story about an artwork and have students add on to the story after they are tapped on the shoulder with the magic paintbrush. Another aspect of reading has students grasping the main idea of a paragraph or story. Thinking in terms of "the big idea" or important concept can also be visual when students are asked to name an artwork before they are told the actual name that the artist gave it. Or they can be encouraged to rename the artwork. Conversely, the teacher may tell the children the name of one of the artworks in the group and ask them to identify which one it is.

3. Visual memory skills can be developed by asking the students to sit very quietly for fifteen or twenty seconds and memorize an artwork. Then the artwork can be turned around and the students asked to describe it, or they may enjoy making up questions about it to ask their friends.

4. The teacher can ask students to tell how two artworks are alike and then to find ways in which they are different. The students may find differences and similarities in subject matter, the elements and principles of art, the mood or feeling of the paintings, the artist's technique and style, the degree of realism, and so on. Unusual responses and fluency should be encouraged.

5. The students can be asked to enter a painting with their "magic artist eyes" and "take a walk," using the magic paintbrush as a pointer. The path will be the direction their eyes follow, going from one shape, line, or color to another in the

composition. Different children will take different "walks." "Magic artist eyes" do not need to have legs to walk; they can climb trees and leap across clouds if that is the way the artist has related the lines and shapes in a composition.

6. Students can be asked to imitate a pose or a facial expression in an artwork. Several students can imitate a group pose. This involves the students kinesthetically and helps them to identify emotionally with the figures and scene. Other kinesthetic activities include having children point a finger and swing their arms as they follow sweeping curving lines in a painting such as Marc's *Yellow Cow* in the Color Gallery.

7. After students have viewed a number of artworks and have had sufficient time to understand and respond to them, they can take turns "selling" an artwork to the rest of the class, with a time limit of twenty or thirty seconds. Students should base their sales pitch on the way the artist was able to show movement, express a feeling of excitement or loneliness, show fantasy or imagination, show realistic textures, and so on.

8. At the conclusion of a discussion about an artwork, the students can take turns using a word or short phrase to describe the artwork. The first child may say "bright colors." The second child might say "bright colors and black outlines." The third child repeats what the first and second children said and adds another word or phrase.

9. The teacher can cover an art reproduction with a piece of butcher paper and cut several small openings that reveal details of the painting. If only an eye is showing, students should guess what the rest of the person looks like. The artwork should remain covered a day or two. Before the teacher removes the butcher paper, the students can use crayons and draw on the butcher paper what they think might be beneath it.

10. For upper grade primary children, the teacher may prepare small cards and on each, write one of the following terms (or similar ones): lonely feeling, lots of movement, strong lines, cool colors, geometric shapes, and so on. When the students have finished looking at a group of three or four prints, the teacher holds up one card, reads it, and asks the class to vote on which painting should receive that descriptive card.

11. The teacher may use a pretend microphone and let children ask or respond to questions by talking into it. Or the teacher may use a hand puppet to initiate a conversation about a painting, with the puppet asking questions or the child asking questions to the puppet. These improvisational situations with puppets can provide children with a stimulating way to participate in the discussion.

12. Use a toy telephone and let one of the children play the following role: You have just found an artwork (one of the reproductions being viewed) in your attic. You wonder if it might be an important artwork, so you call a museum curator and describe it. The child must remember that the curator on the telephone can't see the picture, so the child will describe its subject matter, colors, shapes, lines, focal point, and so on, as well as its emotion or mood and artistic style. You or another student will respond with comments and questions. Or use the toy telephone for this scenario: You have just successfully bid on a painting at an art auction. As you are going home with your purchase, you are robbed. When you call the police, you are asked to describe the painting. Tell the detective its subject matter, describe its colors, lines, and so on, as well as its emotional content and artistic style.

13. Ask for a volunteer student to pretend that he or she is on a ship taking three or four paintings to Paris for an art exhibit. The ship is sinking, and after everyone is safely on the lifeboat you remember the valuable artworks, but the captain says there is only room on the lifeboat for one painting. The child must decide which one to save and why, basing those reasons on things that were observed and discussed during the presentation of the reproductions.

14. A sheet of clear vinyl may be placed over the reproduction to cover it entirely. Then, with a black, water-soluble marking pen, the teacher or the students can draw over all occurrences of, for example, contour lines, diagonal lines, negative areas, oval heads, and so on. Pen marks can be wiped off with a damp paper towel.

15. For figure and portrait paintings, ask students what they think the person would write in his or her diary that night. Or let one child ask questions of the person in the picture and have another student stand behind the reproduction and answer questions.

TOPICS FOR DISCUSSION

1. Using a large reproduction of an artwork, discuss the elements of art and how the artist used them.

2. What is the difference between shape and form? Study both two-dimensional and three-dimensional art reproductions, and discuss the characteristics of positive and negative space in each.

3. In each of the sections that list sample questions to ask young children about works of art, formulate at least one additional question of your own.

4. Use the Color Gallery to formulate questions for very young children that would concentrate on the principles of art.

5. What are the four components of commentary that emphasize both art criticism and art history? Using the art reproductions from questions 1 and 2, list possible vocabulary and questions that might be suitable for very young children.

6. What is the difference between art criticism and art preference?

7. Use the Color Gallery to find examples of the four styles of art.

8. Select one artwork from the Color Gallery, and formulate questions that might be useful in guiding a discussion with young children. Concentrate on description, analysis, interpretation, and judgment.

9. Plan a new motivational strategy that would utilize sequencing.

10. Describe a concept or activity introduced in this chapter that is completely new to you and that you perceive as being particularly useful as you interact with young children.

NOTES

1. Gene A. Mittler, *Art in Focus* (Mission Hills, Calif.: Glencoe, 1989).
2. Edmund B. Feldman, *Varieties of Visual Experience,* 4th ed. (New York: Harry N. Abrams, 1992).

3

Accessing Artworks

•••••••••••••••••••••••••••••••••••••

It is through early contact with art and artists that children's attitudes and concepts form. Young children are ready to find and enjoy art in their community. This discovery can be facilitated in several ways.

MUSEUMS AND GALLERIES

Most of the larger cities and towns in the United States have small galleries and a museum or two that offer exciting viewing potential for field trips. Some museums have specially designed rooms, galleries, or exhibits for elementary schoolchildren. Visits to museums and galleries, when begun early, can become a lifelong habit and a source of enjoyment.

Most museums are able to supply the teacher with pertinent information that will help them plan for and schedule a field trip. They may send the teacher some written information or slides to use in preparing the children for the trip. When the children arrive, the museum may provide a volunteer docent who is trained in talking with children about the museum and about the artworks they will be seeing. Most museums are enormous places, and it is advisable to check ahead of time and request a short viewing of perhaps only one gallery so as not to lose the children's interest and attention before their energy is depleted.

Young children should be in small groups and briefed on museum manners before they go. They need to understand that they may only "touch" the artwork with their eyes, since the paintings and sculptures are very valuable and could be damaged by people's hands. The museum may have a special studio for children to visit after walking through the exhibit, where they can have a hands-on opportunity to make art that has some relationship to the theme or perhaps the media of the exhibit they have just seen. Many museums provide simple printed materials, including pamphlets and gamelike "search sheets," to help children be specific in their viewing.

After the children have viewed the exhibit, a brief stop in the museum shop allows each student a chance to buy a postcard reproduction of a favorite piece of art that they have just seen—an early start on becoming an art collector! Some museums have a rental room where students can browse and collectively vote on which artwork they would like to borrow for the classroom for a month or two.

These students look for the artist's name on this sculpture by Miró in the Sculpture Garden of the San Diego Museum of Art.

Preschoolers visit an art gallery and study the swirling, contrasting patterns that the ceramist created on these pots.

ARTMOBILES

In some parts of the country, museum-sponsored artmobiles or vans travel to areas somewhat distant from a museum or to school districts whose budgets for field trips are inadequate. Proper planning ensures that both teachers and children are prepared for their sojourn in the traveling unit, that they are escorted through the exhibit in small groups with a guide who is well-versed in talking with young children, and that adequate follow-up activities are provided.

Crocker Art Museum, Sacramento, sends the ART ARK for a week's visit to schools. The mobile unit is staffed by an artist who talks with small groups of children as they tour its interior and see original works of art.

Courtesy of Crocker Art Museum, 1983/Chad Chadwick, photographer.

"Birds and Beasts" is the theme for this art trunk that contains the multimedia materials required for teaching the four components of art: history, criticism, aesthetics, and production.

ART TRUNKS AND BOXES

A similar concept to the artmobiles, but on a much smaller scale, is the Art-in-a-Trunk. Museums, community groups, civic clubs, leagues, and businesses often cooperate with an art educator in sponsoring these art trunks. Footlockers may be equipped with shelving, compartments, and wheels, and the interiors transformed into a multimedia milieu for teaching art in kindergarten through the sixth grade. On loan to elementary schools, the art trunks each have a theme. Some encompass multicultures, such as "Arte de México," "African Art," "Native American Art," or "American Heritage." Other trunks are cross-cultural and contain items related to weaving, puppetry, toys, art in music, design, birds and beasts in art, or jewelry.

These students explore an art box that contains items from India, including puppets, costumed dolls, and fabrics.

The contents of each art trunk can be structured around the following general categories:

1. *Minimuseum:* Replicas, originals, or folk art from many cultures, countries, and periods, and incorporating a variety of materials.

2. *Bulletin board visuals:* Photographs from books, magazines, etc., mounted on colored poster board and laminated. Holes are prepunched for attaching with pins to a bulletin board.

3. *Stand-up visuals:* Zigzag fold-up display materials made of pages from books, magazines, calendars, etc., mounted on 9 × 12 inch colored poster board, laminated, and taped at the sides. Also, plastic cubes with photos mounted on five sides.

4. *Videos and cassettes:* These may be purchased from commercial sources, or produced locally from slides taken from private collections, local museums, and other sources.

5. *Books:* Both children's and teachers' reference books, how-to books, related storybooks, descriptive books, historical books, detailed books, etc.

6. *Games and puzzles:* Crosswords, word matches, word-a-grams, acrostics, etc., for vocabulary and general concept development; manipulative puzzles and games, commercially purchased or created by committee members; postcard puzzles, mounted on colored poster board, cut, and placed in vinyl fold-up envelopes.

7. *Project cards:* Written and visualized descriptions, directions, how-to's, etc., on 8½ × 11 inch paper, mounted on colored poster board, and laminated. Originals are kept in files to guard against loss. Schools are encouraged to copy these so that they can make ongoing use of the ideas inspired by the visit of the trunk.

8. *Examples to accompany the project cards:* Mounted, laminated, and placed in a vinyl packet with the project card.

9. *Tools for projects:* Brayers, looms, magnifying glasses, clay tools, and others.

a

b

a. This young boy experiences the ancient task of carding wool.

b. Preschoolers examine several kinds of fleece used for spinning yarn on the wheel.

10. *Tape cassettes or videos that introduce the child to the trunk:* Descriptive, explanatory, motivating. Also, cassettes with stories, legends, and folk tales related to the theme of the trunk and made by members of the committee.

11. *Reproductions:* Sets of small prints or postcards, laminated, and placed in colored vinyl packets.

Smaller than the art trunks but highly concentrated and practical are art boxes. Filled with items relating to such themes as Japanese art, masks around the world, or the art of India, the boxes stimulate development of a unit. The boxes may contain such hands-on items as folk art, a video or tape cassette, brayers, games, puzzle sheets, or sets of reproductions, and are an open-ended tool to establish, implement, and nourish art projects related to the four components. Art boxes are easy to store, an exciting challenge to compile and assemble, and a joy for the creative and inventive teacher to use. Any single idea or concept can be embodied in an art box and can be geared to any age level and used repeatedly in many different ways.

CONTACTS WITH ARTISTS

A visit to the studio of a working artist offers much to young children. They come into contact with an adult whose life is devoted to his or her art, and they see the artist at work—producing paintings, sculpture, prints, or crafts in an art studio. They observe the artist using fascinating equipment, and they listen and watch as the artist explains the steps to complete an object. Most artists' studios abound in finished objects as well as works in the making, and they are intriguing places for students to visit. The students can come to know and identify art as a natural and vital part of adult endeavor and of a community's life. A unit on the "Community and Its Helpers" often includes visits to fire stations, post offices, and factories. What better time than this to arrange a visit to the studio of an artist? To see a potter throwing a pot on a fast-spinning wheel, to watch a sculptor chisel a block of stone or wood into a beautiful form, to see a craftsperson create jewelry with metal and heat, to watch a weaver make a shuttle fly back and forth on a loom, or to observe a printmaker work on a silk screen—all are inspiring experiences for the young child.

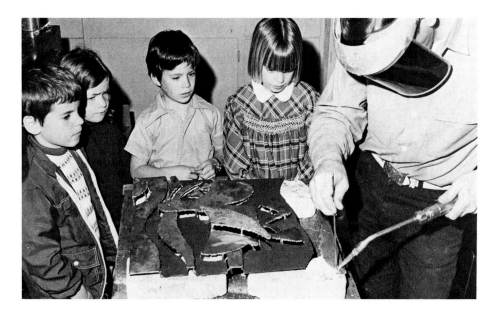

On a trip to a metal sculptor's studio, these children discover the beauty inherent in steel, copper, and brass when these materials are touched by the torch of a skilled and sensitive craftsperson.

Many shopping centers hold art fairs with dozens of artists and craftspeople not only exhibiting their work but participating in an art-in-action performance. These occasions offer opportunities for children to see sculptors welding, jewelers setting stones, wood carvers polishing sculpture, and potters throwing on a wheel.

Besides taking children to art galleries and artists' studios, it is also highly recommended that artists be invited to the school. Teachers can enlist the help of guilds, leagues, museums, galleries, local arts councils, and artist-in-the-schools programs to recruit resource people to visit classrooms. In one case, a woman from the Weaver's Guild brought her spindle, fleece, and spinning wheel to a preschool and not only demonstrated her skill but let the children work at carding wool and try their hand at spinning. They watched with keen attention as she showed them how yarn can be spun on such a simple device as a stick inserted in an onion. She told them of the many sources of fleece and brought along samples from a number of animals for them to touch. In a similar manner, an enamelist, linoleum block printer, painter, jewelry maker, or other artist could touch the children's lives in a memorable way through a classroom visit.

FOLK ART: A Multicultural Emphasis

Above the entrance to the International Museum of Folk Art in Santa Fe, New Mexico, are inscribed the words: "The art of the craftsman is a bond between the peoples of the world." Folk art comes to us from many ethnic and cultural groups. The people who have produced it were and are the common people of a nation or region. They modeled, constructed, carved, wove, stitched, and otherwise made objects for both utilitarian and nonutilitarian purposes. Folk art embodies the values and beliefs of different cultures. By examining folk art, children can begin to have a feeling of the past as well as of the present. They can learn something of their origins and of themselves. Folk art celebrates the creative spirit of a people and preserves cultural traditions. Alexander Girard, in speaking about the Collection of Folk Art from the Girard Foundation, makes a plea for the present-day evolution of customs and the shaping, in our own way, of contemporary objects of equivalent value, using new methods and materials. Folk art, he believes, should not be sentimentally imitated, but its creative spirit should nourish the human productive attitude of the present.[1]

Very young children can be introduced to the artistic heritage of many countries, peoples, and times by seeing items with origins in diverse ethnic and cultural groups. They can learn that art has always been an important and significant aspect of life for

Here, Mexican and Indian figures, both human and animal, are modeled from clay. These six-year-old children are fascinated with the figures' simplicity and tactile appeal. Folk art in the classroom inspires, stimulates, and conveys historical and cultural concepts.

American folk artist Howard Finster makes wood sculpture, applies paint in decorative patterns, and then adds words to emphasize his message.
Collection of the author.

young and old alike. Folk literature, folk music, folk dance, and folk costumes have long been meaningful areas of exploration in the educational program. Children respond readily to the directness and simplicity of folk art and to its sometimes humorous, whimsical notes. In the early childhood classroom, folk art can motivate an art production, be the focal point for a discussion of aesthetic considerations, or provide information about the way of life of another people.

Though the roots of various cultures differ widely, there is a pervasive similarity in most folk art, and at the same time much similarity to child art. The materials and subject matter of folk art are often familiar to children. Carved and modeled figures (both human and animal), masks, baskets, pots, dolls, toys, jewelry, textiles, and metal pieces usually

Volunteer docents are an important part of this school's art program. Here a parent and a kindergarten class discuss "Artists paint portraits." Students look at the many ways an artist can show people in artworks.

portray an individual craftperson's response to a need. Throughout time, cultures around the world have given a high priority to fine artistry and good design in all sorts of objects—whether for everyday use, for religious or ceremonial purposes, or even for play.

Almost all art of ethnic origin uses overall decoration, whether it is applied to a fabric, carved on an animal, painted on a clay pot, or hammered on a tin mask. Although the motif is usually uncomplicated, it is often repeated over and over because the folk artist delights in rhythmic design rather than natural appearance. Many folk groups use their own legends, stories, religions, and everyday events as a basis for their craft work. In a similar manner, children model and construct characters from their favorite tales and from their immediate environment. Folk artists everywhere love to carve, model, and make small figures of both humans and animals, and children respond instinctively to this sort of sculpture with delight and interest.

Although industrial growth and the emergence of city life have brought about a decline in folk art, recent years have witnessed new and revitalized interest. It appears from this trend that the need for being involved in craft and art production, as well as for owning handmade objects, is a very natural and human one. The need can be fostered and nourished by introducing folk art in the early childhood educational program.

REPRODUCTIONS IN THE CLASSROOM: Docent Presentations

Regular presentations of artworks, either by classroom teachers or by trained parent volunteer docents, can enhance and supplement the classroom art program. A docent can bring a portfolio or miniexhibit of great artworks into the classroom. Such a portfolio contains a thematic group of three to six large reproductions. The usual length for a docent's visit is about thirty to forty-five minutes, during which time the children respond to the docent's comments and questions. Reproductions of many famous paintings and drawings are available at reasonable prices from several sources.[2]

Students examine George Catlin's portrait of *White Cloud, Head Chief of the Iowas,* to identify visual textures and details of his clothing. Catlin's portrayal of this early 19th century tribal leader reflects the Native American's nobility and dignity.

A successful docent program in northern California features eight different portfolios for each grade level and covers a variety of subjects and themes. Each portfolio presentation is followed by a hands-on art activity that involves one or more concepts emphasized in the presentation. The hands-on activities for the year's program for each grade level cover many media and media skills.

Following is a sample set of subjects for portfolios, and a sample lesson titled "People of the Old West."

Kindergarten
Artists Paint Stories
Artists Paint Animals
Artists Paint People of the Old West
Artists Paint Parents and Children

Grade 1
Artists Paint Flowers and Plants
Artists Paint People Doing Things
Artists Paint the Circus
Artists Paint Self-Portraits

Grade 2
Artists Paint Birds
Artists Paint Kings and Queens
Artists Paint Winter and Summer
Artists Use Lines

Grade 3
Artists Paint Still Lifes
Artists Paint Trains
Artists Paint Portraits
Artists Paint Landscapes

The following artworks focus on a favorite theme of several American artists, "The Old West." A portfolio presentation by a docent or teacher can show how these artists have chronicled the adventures and lives of cowpunchers and Native Americans and have told us through their pictures how these individuals dressed and what they did. The reproductions discussed in the paragraphs that follow are from the *Art in Action Enrichment Program*[3] and can be presented to the children using art criticism, art history commentary, and questioning strategies, and can relate the theme of "The Old West" to the children's own art productions. (Allowing the children to copy or imitate any of the paintings is to be firmly avoided.)

White Cloud, Head Chief of the Iowas by George Catlin "This proud leader of the Iowa tribe of Native Americans is depicted by artist George Catlin as being strong, confident, and brave. Catlin said that White Cloud was humane and noble and was worthy

Frederic Remington's painting *The Fall of the Cowboy* tells children about an important change in the western frontier of the United States in the late nineteenth century. Students can identify the mood of the painting by describing the colors and other compositional components.

of being chief. The picture was painted more than 150 years ago. Describe what White Cloud is wearing (eagle quill headdress of war and special paint on his face; grizzly bear claws strung around his neck; skin of a white wolf hangs from shoulders). Catlin was very skilled in painting a variety of textures; we can almost feel the soft, white fur and the sharply pointed feathers. The repeated curves of his necklace make a pattern. Can you find any other patterns? We see White Cloud in three-quarter view. His face is oval shaped. Catlin was a lawyer who decided to spend the rest of his life observing and painting Native Americans, making a visual record of how they looked, dressed, and lived. He collected Native American relics, and today his artworks and collections can be seen in the Smithsonian Institution in Washington, D.C."

The Fall of the Cowboy by Frederic Remington "This painting was made almost one hundred years ago and, like Catlin's painting, is a visual record. Frederic Remington loved the Old American West and knew that times were changing fast, with more and more people settling there. He thought that the 'wild riders and vacant lands' were about to vanish and wanted to capture the spirit and vigor of life on the frontier. He named this painting *The Fall of the Cowboy* because he sensed an end to the time when cowboys could roam freely, herding cattle and camping out with the chuck wagons. Farmers were moving in and building fences. Describe what you see in this painting (one cowboy at the gate, his horse waiting for him; another cowboy on a horse; fence going way back into the distance). Notice how cold it looks, how there are no trees or bushes, just a lot of snow and gray skies. We get a lonely feeling when we look at this picture; even the horses hang their heads sadly, almost as if they know that their time to gallop across the open plains is nearing an end. Notice how the cowboys are dressed and what they have on their heads. Remington worked as a ranch cook, shepherd, and cowpuncher. He painted many pictures of the West so that people would know what life in this part of America was like in the 1800s."

Indian Portrait with Tomahawk by Fritz Scholder "Fritz Scholder is the artist who made this lithographic print (a print made from the flat surface of a stone), and he is still living today. Scholder has shown us a full figure of a Native American in profile. The many, many feathers cascading down his back make a strong, repeated pattern. His head seems very small in proportion to his body; perhaps the artist did this to make him look very strong and powerful, like a statue of a hero. Can you see details on his face, as you did in Catlin's painting? Scholder was painting the idea of many Native Americans rather than a specific one, as Catlin did. This Native American is a symbol of stature and dignity. The colors we see are mostly red, white, and blue with a little soft, mustard yellow. The spots and splashes of red in the artwork make our eyes continually move over the

Students respond to a contemporary artwork—*Indian Portrait with Tomahawk* by Fritz Scholder—and describe the full figure with feathered headdress. They compare this painting to Catlin's portrait of White Cloud, identifying similarities and differences, in color, texture, and proportion. Their observations help them decide which portrait represents a realistic image and which is a symbolic rendering.

A first grade class used potato prints to make face shapes. A class member, dressed in a blanket and feather headdress, modeled while the rest of the class used oil pastels to complete their drawings.

surface. We see a yellow stripe going up the trouser leg, and this leads our eyes to the tomahawk, a horizontal element in the composition. The background is a warm, neutral color."

After a discussion of this group of paintings on "The Old West," the children are ready to make visual statements of their own about how these individuals lived and how they dressed. A follow-up lesson could involve the following:

What kinds of work did cowpunchers do, and what kinds of adventures did they have? (herded cattle, lassoed strays, branded cattle, rode horses, made camp fires, cooked meals at the chuck wagon, and so on.) What did Native Americans do? (rode horses, hunted animals such as buffalo, herded sheep, shot bows and arrows, carried babies, gathered and prepared food, made clothing from animal hides, made objects from beads, wove on looms, made pottery, acted as scouts, and so on.)

Live models with simple costumes and props help students include details in their oil pastel drawings.

Describe in detail the clothing of men and women of the Old West and of Native Americans, both male and female, that you have seen in books or on television. Describe their headgear and footwear. What did they carry?

Children can make their own pictures about the people of the Old West. As preparation, the teacher can cut a potato in half and drain the flat, cut side on paper toweling to absorb moisture. The potato half is an oval shape and can serve as the faces for the children's drawings of people of the Old West. The children brush the cut potato surface with watercolor paint or diluted tempera and make one or several prints on manila paper. After the prints are dry, two or three students, perhaps from an upper-grade classroom, can dress up in western costumes and model for the children. With two or three models, all the students can be close enough for good observation. Costumes might include a western hat, kerchief, boots, lasso, saddle, feather headdress, necklace, blanket, tomahawk, or moccasins. The children can use crayons or oil pastels to draw the facial features, body, and clothing. The teacher's comments can encourage the children to include clothing and facial details and to show what their characters are doing and where they are. The children might want to include a horse, buffalo, wagon, trees, rocks, and so on. The pictures may show upper bodies only, as Catlin did in his portrait of White Cloud, or they may show full figures, as Scholder and Remington did.

CLASSROOM GALLERY OF ART: Postcard Reproductions

A Classroom Gallery of Art can easily be assembled by the teacher and used by children for quiet and reflective enjoyment in the classroom. This little gallery is made of two pieces of mat board that are hinged vertically with tape and placed in a convenient and comfortable spot, perhaps on a counter, tabletop, or bulletin board. Children can take a leisurely "walk" through the gallery and look at great artworks in miniature form: postcard reproductions. Different sets of themes or subject-related postcards with adhesive-backed Velcro allow the exhibit to be changed easily.

"Classroom Gallery of Art" brings a minimuseum with changeable theme exhibits to students. Comments and questions on cards provide a springboard for discussion. Spaces on panels allow students to make their own theme-related drawings and to attach them in the frames with Velcro.

The Classroom Gallery of Art shown in the photograph was based on a set of thirty postcards called ARTPACK, produced by the Museum of Fine Arts, Boston.[4] The thirty cards are divided into five theme-related sets, with six postcards in each set. The themes are: "Portraits," "Everyday Scenes," "Modern Art," "Landscapes and Seascapes," and "Still Lifes." Postcard reproductions are also available in museum shops and could be grouped in a similar manner.

A Classroom Gallery of Art requires two pieces of mat board, 16×20 inches each. A black or metallic marking pen is used to draw ten frames, 4×6 inches, on the mat boards. Five of the frames should be horizontal and five vertical in format. Half-inch squares of adhesive-backed Velcro tape are attached to the back of each postcard and inside each frame. The two pieces of mat board are hinged together with filament tape so that the gallery stands up by itself and folds flat for storage. Six of the ten frames are used for the postcards, two are used for study questions, and two are used for the students' artwork.

Two study-question cards can be made to accompany each theme-related set of prints. The cards should be the same size as the postcards and have Velcro on the back so that they can be attached inside one of the frames. For example, for "Landscapes and Seascapes," one card might say: "Artists make paintings to show us how places look—fields, lakes, mountains, rivers, city streets, and the ocean. Which place would you like to visit? What sounds might you hear? What would you do there? Choose two pictures and compare them. Make a picture of a place you have been, and put it in an empty frame. Think about the weather and the skies."

The second card might say: "DESCRIBE: the weather, the light, the brushstrokes, figures, and animals. FIND: foreground, middle ground, background, horizons, different kinds of skies. THINK ABOUT: the path that your eyes follow, things that overlap, distant objects smaller and higher up, the mood of each picture, which picture is most real, which picture is least real." Some blank tagboard cards of the same size and with Velcro on the back should be provided so that students can fit their own artwork in the two remaining empty frames.

ART GAMES

Games have long been used as a teaching device. Friedrich Froebel used the game technique in 1896 when he developed his gifts, which consisted of blocks, triangles, straws, and other materials.[5] The game approach can be especially useful for teaching art concepts. The competitiveness factor is minimal in the games described here. These games can be an excellent activity for an individual child or for cooperative learning activities with small groups. They are easy enough so that most children can play them independently, thereby minimizing the teacher's role.

The games that follow are examples of play activities designed to sharpen children's perception, familiarize them with great works of art, and contribute to their visual and verbal knowledge about the elements and principles of art. The directions for the games described here are open-ended and flexible. It is hoped that the ideas presented will stimulate teachers to become involved in creating other art games, too. The teacher needs to collect a number of small postcard reproductions and other prints of great artworks, as well as photographs showing patterns, colors, textures, and close-ups of natural objects. Calendars, museum catalogs and flyers, advertisements, and magazines often provide good visual materials for the game maker. Game cards that are laminated or covered with clear adhesive last longer. Plastic file boxes are excellent storage containers. Also, colored vinyl from yardage shops can be stitched into envelopes on a sewing machine and the flaps secured with an inch of Velcro.

Artcentration

Twelve pairs (or more) of mounted reproductions are needed for the game. One pair consists of two prints by the same artist, either the same painting or different paintings. Or the pairs can be landscapes, still lifes, figures, abstractions, seascapes, architecture, ceramics, sculpture, or jewelry. Or the pairs can be matching textures, shapes, lines, or colors. To play the game, the children mix the cards and place them all facedown on the table. The first child turns one card over and tries to find its mate by turning over one more card. If successful, the child keeps the pair and tries again. If unsuccessful, both cards are placed back in the same position, facedown, and the next child turns one card over and then tries to find the mate. With very small children, the teacher will want to start with four pairs of cards and increase the number of pairs as the children become familiar with the artworks and the artists' names.

Art Squares

The teacher cuts five-inch squares of colored poster board, and cuts small art reproductions in half diagonally into two triangular pieces. All the blank squares are placed on a table, and each matching pair of triangles is arranged so that each triangle is on a different square (see page 66); all pieces are then glued. A number—1, 2, 3, or 4—is placed on one of each pair of triangles. To play the game, children place all the cards in a stack, facedown. The first player draws the top card and places it in the middle of the table. He or she then draws again and places the second card along one of the sides of the first card. If this first player is able to match a pair, he or she scores the number printed on the matching set. If no triangles match up, the card must be played anyway, along a mismatched side. The second player continues, drawing the top card and adding it to the already-placed squares. Players are not allowed to move any squares after the squares have been put in place. Blank sides can be placed anywhere, but no score is given. Plays in which a player is forced to place a card in a nonmatching position do not score. After the last card is played, players add up their scores. Variation: Art Squares can be played as a jigsaw puzzle, with one or more players putting all the squares together, matching all sides.

"Art Squares" can be played in several ways. Two triangles match to complete each picture.

"Arty Knows," a form of dominoes, is made with small reproductions cut in half and mounted on poster board.

Art Words

From photographs of zoo, farm, or jungle animals, one child secretly chooses a photo and describes the animal to the group in terms of the animal's color, shape of its ears, size of its feet, placement of its nose, and so on. This causes the child to look carefully at the animal and to select its significant and characteristic details. He may then say, "I have four thick legs. My skin is wrinkled and rough. My ears are flat and roundish. Which animal am I?"

Arty Knows

Small reproductions are cut in half and mounted, domino-style, on small rectangles of poster board. Two different colors of beads are used to keep score. Each child should have a notebook ring to hold the beads as he or she scores. Eighteen half-dominoes, fifteen double

A bag of pairs of diverse textures challenges children to discriminate and select the disc inside the bag that matches the disc on the table beside them.

dominoes, and four blank dominoes are needed for the game. All the beads are placed on a large notebook ring serving as the bank. All the Arty Knows cards are placed facedown on the table and this becomes the gallery. Each player selects four cards from the gallery. Play begins when the first player chooses one card from the gallery and places it faceup in the center of the table. She then tries to play one of her cards in a matching position. If she plays a double card, she takes a black bead from the bank; if she plays a half card, she takes an orange bead. She draws another card from the gallery and play passes to the left. If a player cannot play at all, she passes to the second player and retains her four cards. Blank ends of half cards may be joined to other blank ends, but no beads are collected from the bank. A perpendicular joint may be made with a blank card where two blanks have joined. When the gallery is empty and no more plays can be made, the player with the highest score wins. Orange beads equal one point; black beads equal two points.

Bag of Textures

Discs, two each of a variety of textures such as leather, vinyl, sheet plastic, cork, corduroy, velvet, and sandpaper, are placed in a cloth bag. The child reaches into the cloth bag without looking and tries to find matching pairs by touch. The child may be asked to describe the texture. Or one disc of each texture can be placed on the table and the child is asked to reach in the bag and find each disc's mate.

Circle-in-a-Picture

Close-up texture photos from a magazine or color photos that you have taken yourself of flowers, tree bark, seed pods, shells, tires, and pebbles are needed for the game. Each photo should be mounted on a piece of poster board and a round hole cut in the center of each one. A small bead is glued to the cut-out circle for a handle. The picture minus the circle is then glued to another piece of poster board. Children gently twirl the discs in the center holes to find the correct locations. This game may also be done with fine art reproductions.

"Match the Paintings" game challenges children to find similar styles from a mixed assortment of small prints.

Match-It

Two or three different small reproductions from each of five to ten artists are needed for the game. The reproductions should be mixed up and placed in a box or a fabric drawstring bag. The child takes the cards out and spreads them on a table. Then he pairs up or matches the two or three that are by the same artist. Two van Goghs have similar characteristics, colors, and style, and the child should be able to separate and differentiate them from two Rembrandts, two Gauguins, and so on.

Matching Halves

Small reproductions or postcards are cut in half and mounted on pieces of poster board to make a number of very simple puzzles. For younger children, start with three or four prints mixed up and placed in a small box. The child takes out the pieces and puts them together, matching the top half with the bottom half.

Match the Paintings

For this game, the child needs a playboard with five or six rows drawn across it. Each row contains a single picture by a different artist mounted on the left, followed by four blank squares to the right of the picture. Four additional pictures by each artist are then mounted on small squares of poster board. To play the game the child must perceive similarities and differences in various artists' styles and techniques by grouping all the paintings by one artist on the blank squares to the right of the example. A color dot on the reverse side of the cards matches a color dot by the picture to provide for a self-checking device.

Multi-Game Cards

Four works of art by one artist are mounted on four pieces of poster board. (Variations: Four different textures, landscapes, portraits, sculptures, or sets of four values of one color.) Twelve sets are made in this manner for a total of forty-eight cards.

Game 1—Museum: The cards are shuffled, and seven cards are dealt to each of four players. The remaining cards are placed in a center pile, called the Museum. The first player asks another player to look for all the cards that he has by one artist (or all landscapes or textures). If this player has any, he must give them to the first player, who then asks the same player for more cards of a set. If this player has none, the first player draws a card from the Museum. If the first player draws the card he asked for, he may ask a second player for cards. The next player repeats play as described. When a player collects a set of four cards, she places the set in front of her. The winner is the one who has the most sets of cards when play is over.

Game 2—Great Master: This game requires one additional card, one that reads Great Master. The cards are shuffled and dealt out to four players. The dealer places on the table all the matching sets in her hand, if she has any. She then takes a card from the hand of the player to her right. If the card she chooses matches cards in her hand, she puts the set on the table. The player to her left then does the same, and the game proceeds until all the cards are matched, leaving the Great Master card in the winning player's hand.

Game 3—Paintbrush: Any number can play this game, but one set of four matching cards is needed per player. In the center of the playing area is placed one paintbrush for each player, minus one. Four cards are dealt to each player. The object of the game is to collect four cards of one set. Each player selects one card he does not need and places it facedown next to the player to his left. When all of the players have done this, the players pick up the cards on their right. Play is repeated until one player has a set of four. That player quickly grabs a paintbrush from the center, and then each player grabs one. The player who does not get a brush loses.

Perceptual Recall

The child looks for a few minutes at a tray with several objects. The tray is then covered and the child names the objects he or she can remember. The task is varied by asking the child to name all the brown objects, or all the hard objects, or all the round ones. Or one or two objects can be secretly removed to see if the child can remember which ones are missing. Just a few objects should be used at the beginning and the number increased as the child becomes more skilled.

Postcard Puzzles

Postcards that show fine art reproductions are mounted on lightweight poster board and then cut in four, six, eight, or nine pieces. For each puzzle, an identical postcard should be mounted on poster board, with some interesting information about the artwork and the artist on the back. A convenient storage pouch can be made from colored vinyl and a pocket stitched for each set of pieces.

See, Touch, and Tell

A natural object such as a seed pod, flower, or shell is passed from one child to another in a circle, with each child adding a word or phrase to describe it. A seashell, for instance, might be called "big" by the first child, "big and bumpy" by the second, "big, bumpy, and pink" by the third, "big, bumpy, pink, and curving" by the fourth, and so on. This causes the child to observe and feel the object carefully, to use a word to describe it, and to remember the other descriptive words that have been used.

"Great Master" and several other games require a pack of cards containing sets of four works by each artist.

Secret Guessing

A small object is passed around a circle with everyone blindfolded or with everyone facing in and holding their hands behind them. Each child, in turn, feels the object and silently guesses what it is. When all the children have examined the object, the teacher calls on the children to see how many guessed correctly.

Tactile Dominoes

Each half of a regular domino is covered with different bits of textured materials. For example, the ones can be covered with sandpaper, twos with vinyl, threes with cork, fours with suede, fives with felt, sixes with calico, and blanks with wood stripping. The dominoes are placed facedown on the table, and each child draws five and stands them up in front of him or her. The first player places one domino in the center of the table, and the second player matches one of the ends with one of his dominoes. If he does not have a domino that matches, he draws from the pile until he can play. After he has played, the third player has a turn. Play continues until a player has used all of his or her dominoes and becomes the winner.

Tell About It

A number of reproductions of fine paintings, drawings, or pieces of sculpture are needed for this game. The teacher asks three children to leave the room and the rest of the class chooses a secret picture. The first child to return is told which is the secret picture. She then must describe it to the second child, when he returns, using art words that do not refer to the picture's subject matter. The second child must remember what he has been told and repeat the description to the third child, who was waiting outside the room and who must try to guess which is the secret picture. This game can be modified in many ways, according to the number and kind of reproductions available, and the interest and maturity of the children.

Three-Dimensional Jigsaw Puzzles

All six sides of nine wood cubes are used for mounting six or nine different reproductions that have been cut into six or nine squares to fit the square sides of the cubes. The children then try to piece together these three-dimensional jigsaw puzzles.

The game "Tactile Dominoes" enables children to see and feel differences and similarities in texture.

Sets of Tint and Shade Cards challenge the child to arrange each set from dark to light. Each set consists of five cards of different color values for one color.

Tint and Shade Cards

With chips of paint samples from the paint store, the child arranges each color from light to dark.

Touch and Guess

Players sit in a circle, with one child blindfolded in the center. The other children take turns selecting an object from a tray for the child in the center to hold and guess what it is. Objects should include such things as a feather, a piece of sandpaper, a cube, a cylinder of wood, a nail, a bit of fur, a scrap of soft satin, a button, a paintbrush, a rock, and a wooden spoon. If the blindfolded child guesses correctly on the first attempt, the child who selected the item gets to take a turn in the center.

Game A

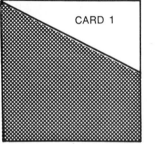

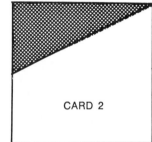

Game B

A set of "Visual Perception" cards, made with two contrasting colors, allows children to make designs by matching sides of the cards.

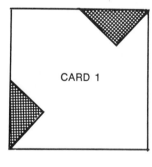

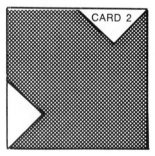

Verbal/Visual Match-It

A set of cards with small reproductions glued onto them is needed for this game. Another set of cards contains short written descriptions of these reproductions. Children may play at matching up the visual image with the written description. Or the cards can be distributed to the children to see how quickly they can find their verbal/visual mate. For children who have not yet learned to read, the teacher may distribute the visual cards and then read the written cards, with the children listening to see if the description matches the card they are holding.

Visual Perception Game

Twelve 3-inch squares each for Cards 1 and 2 for Game A and twelve 3-inch squares each for Cards 1 and 2 for Game B are needed. (See diagrams.) Two contrasting colors should be used. Cards are the same on the back and front sides. The children play at matching and making configurations and forms. This game helps with figure-ground differentiations, visual closure, positioning, synthesizing, and visual memory.

TOPICS FOR DISCUSSION

1. How is it possible to provide opportunities for young children to see original works of art? List places in your community where that could happen.

2. What kind of items would you expect to find in an art trunk, and how are art trunks designed for classroom use?

3. How does folk art reflect the culture where it originates?

4. What are the similarities and differences to be found in folk art that originates in different times and places?

5. How can a classroom teacher facilitate children's exploration of art in their community? List at least six specific resources that could be used in your local area.

6. Formulate at least one theme for art lessons at each of the following levels: preschool, kindergarten, grade 1, grade 2, and grade 3.

7. Select artworks from the Color Gallery that relate to a theme. Discuss thematic questions that might be appropriate to ask young children.

8. Which of the art games described (a) are most likely to strengthen visual perception? (b) utilize reproductions of contemporary or historical art? (c) require verbal responses? (d) reinforce concepts discussed in Chapter 2?

9. Collect postcards that show artwork related to a theme. Assemble the postcards in a minigallery as described in the section "Classroom Gallery of Art: Postcard Reproductions."

10. Select a specific work of art that is in your community. What kind of background information is appropriate to provide for young children? What guiding questions can be formulated that will increase students' understanding and appreciation of the work when they see the original?

NOTES

1. Alexander Girard, *The Magic of a People* (New York: Viking Press, 1968), Introduction.
2. See "Resources for Art Education" on page 315.
3. Barbara Herberholz, *Art in Action Enrichment Program,* Levels I and II (Orlando, Fla.: Harcourt Brace Jovanovich, 1987).
4. Museum of Fine Arts, Boston, P.O. Box 74, Back Bay Annex, Boston, Mass., 02117.
5. Friedrich Froebel, *Education of Man* (New York: D. Appleton, 1896).

4

Artistic Development in the Early Years

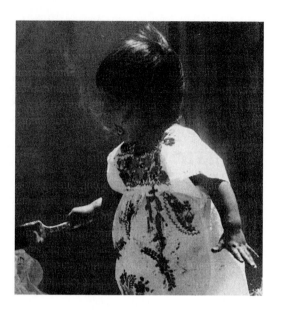

Children all over the world begin at an early age to reveal certain developmental characteristics in their art products. General stages of growth appear to be universal and identifiable. The adult's task is to provide an environment for maximum growth, that is, the means through which the child's motor, affective, perceptual, cognitive, and aesthetic development can reach its fullest potential.[1]

Two points of view regarding artistic development in children have been prevalent. One holds that the child manifests changes in his or her artwork, with the teacher merely providing the materials. The other maintains that the unfolding of the child's artistic self can be aided and abetted by direction and training. Howard Gardner insists that a deeper understanding of both views can emerge and benefit from a developmental perspective.[2] He notes that, by age seven or eight, perhaps earlier, children have an initial grasp of the major symbolic media of our culture. They are incipient artists because they now have the raw materials involved in the artistic process, ideas of how symbols work in an aggregation of symbolic media, and some knowledge of how to construct works themselves.

The school curriculum in early childhood should provide a qualitative developmental sequence of art experiences. The result should be that during the later realism stage (about eight or nine years of age when children are very self-critical), they will have developed skills at a sufficiently high level that they will not dismiss their artistic abilities. In addition, they will have a store of ideas and feelings they wish to express. A developmental program in art is based on experiences the children have had at earlier levels and helps the children to recall visually and verbally and to perceive, organize, define, clarify, and reinforce their thoughts and feelings. It provides the foundation for the realism stage that follows.

The early childhood years are marked by children's eagerness to participate in art with enthusiasm and naturalness. They enjoy creating their own art. They like looking at pictures and reproductions of works of art, and visiting galleries and museums. Their art expression progresses from scribbles into more organized forms and symbols and is an important means of nonverbal communication. Art is a first language for all children, according to the National Art Education Association, which states that

> The first language of humans was the creation of images on cave walls, just as the first language of a child is drawing. Art is a universal and basic language. The inclination to express oneself visually begins early. Its subsequent development is fundamental for every person and essential for our society.[3]

At seventeen months, the scribbling child enjoys making random movements with a marker.

In grades 1 to 3, children become even more responsive and curious in reacting to visual/tactile experiences than they were in earlier years. They are able to handle a greater variety of materials and tools—they can construct, model, paint, stitch, weave, and make prints. They can begin to talk about the art of others, make choices and express preferences, and understand the relationship of art to literature, social studies, mathematics, and music. It is a time for learning about diverse cultures and times.

Children who have had paper, marking pens, crayons, scissors, paint, and modeling materials available at home come to preschool or kindergarten more advanced in their artistic development than those who have not. Mental, emotional, and physical handicaps as well as social and cultural influences also have a bearing on a child's development of visual images. Some children pass quickly through the stages of growth in art, but the characteristic pattern of their artistic behavior remains very similar.

Repeated downward strokes with brush and paint show a growing awareness of controlled lines in this work by a 2½-year-old scribbler.

It is of paramount importance that this early period of development be fostered to its fullest to set the stage for future growth and development. Without basic and supportive experiences with art materials, children tend to be hampered in their artistic expression. They do not acquire a language of nonverbal symbols that enables them to express their personalized images of the world in artistic forms. If at this time adults encourage children to do copy work and to use coloring books and if they forbid children's spontaneous scribbling, the child's development in learning as well as in art may be harmed.[4]

Children derive pleasure not only from handling materials but from experiencing the thrill of discovery and the intense satisfaction of mastery. Through early manipulative and exploratory experiences, children develop concepts of searching, investigating, recording, selecting, building, and determining. From relatively simple, limited, and direct use of materials, young children advance to more complex, sophisticated involvement.

These manipulative experiences, which begin in preschool, may not seem of great significance as the adult views the final product. Yet the children are establishing

Children at 2½ enjoy covering the surface of the paper by using newly developed skills in controlling the brush or marking implement.

beginnings—in using the elements of art; in planning, executing, and completing an artwork; in judging the wholeness or completeness of a composition; in correlating visual expression with other forms of expression; and in demonstrating originality, self-confidence, and competency. The adult's attitude when these early expressions begin has much to do with the children's later ability to communicate ideas, images, symbols, and feelings in their own unique and original way.

For children, as for the adult artist, art is more than a factual recording of an object. They are coming to grips with their thoughts, feelings, and perceptions, and these may involve fantasy, dreams, suspense, surprises, thrills, sorrow, fear, delight, wonder, anger, pleasure, joy, or hate.

IRREGULAR SCRIBBLING

The first marks the child makes, usually between the first and second year, are random scribbles and are most likely derived from the kinesthetic enjoyment of moving the arm and hand. At this stage, children do not realize that they can control these marks. They show variation in these random marks in both length and direction. They may show some repetitive movements as they swing the arm back and forth, but the main principle involved is kinesthetic. Accidental results occur. The line quality varies. The crayon or drawing implements may be held in various ways, and the size of the marks and movements are in relation to the size of the child's arm.

There is no intent by children at this time to make representational symbols; rather, their work shows a somewhat random, haphazard grouping of marks. They enjoy scribbling,

The developmental stages from symbolic scribbling to fully evolved schema are shown in these four drawings by Mia at ages three, four, five, and six. The looped fingers and outstretched arms were repeated without variation for some time during the later stage.

and they need to have the time, materials, and space to engage in it. Chalk and chalkboard, crayons, marking pens, pencils with strong, blunt points that do not break easily—all are vehicles for the child to use for this kinesthetic activity.

CONTROLLED SCRIBBLING

Usually about six months after children begin to scribble, they develop some control and discover that they can make the marks do what they want. They become consciously aware of scribbling. While an adult may detect no difference between these scribbles and those of the previous disordered stage, this marks an important step in children's artistic growth. The children begin to vary their motions. They repeat some lines that give them particular satisfaction and spend a longer time at this activity. They make circular and longitudinal scribbles. They are mainly interested in the kinesthetic sensation and in mastering their movements.

NAMING OF SCRIBBLING

At about three and a half years of age, most children begin to name their scribbles, which is a landmark in their development because the child's thought process has now changed from thinking kinesthetically to thinking imaginatively. Until now, the children were principally involved in motions; now, they have connected their motions to the world around them. Although the actual drawings may appear much like those of the previous stage, the children's intent is different. They may start a drawing and say, "This is Daddy," or at least have some idea of what they are going to draw. They may call it something else when they are finished.

At this stage, young children may talk the entire time that they are drawing, or they may announce what it is when they are finished. The next day, looking back at their drawing, they may possibly call it something else, but they have established a visual relationship to the world with their drawings. They may revert back to manipulation of the medium if they have a new tool. If given baker's clay, salt ceramic, or clay, their thought processes are the same as with drawing and painting in that they first manipulate it—pound it, roll it, pinch it. Their movements gradually become more controlled until the naming stage evolves and they begin squeezing little blobs of the modeling material and giving their creations names.

Since scribbling mainly involves muscular activity, gaining control, and then establishing a relationship with the outside world, color does not play a very important role at this time. Children begin learning the names of colors. The colors that children choose are those they happen to like and not those that are related to the visual world. What is most important is that children have an art medium that enables them to gain control of their lines. Therefore, crayon, chalk, marking pens, or paint should be of a color that contrasts with the paper on which the children are working so that they can see clearly what they are doing.

Joseph and Marilyn Sparling focus on meaningful dialogues with scribblers, on positive approaches to increasing communication skills.[5] They suggest that these beginners in art need (1) encouragement in the form of verbal approval and respect, (2) to be aware of their own creative process and product, and (3) to perceive their own thoughts and feelings. When children gain new names or labels for things, they have a way of reusing and recalling experiences. Skills in forming concepts have been shown to be linked to the acquisition of language, especially labeling.

In talking with the beginning scribbler, the adult could mention the child's movements, since the child at this stage is more fascinated with the kinesthetic process than by the marks he or she is making. These comments make the child more aware of his or her own movements, and motor coordination is an important task. The adult might comment on how fast the child's hand is moving back and forth, or on how hard the child is pressing on the crayon, or on how big the child's movements are. If comments are directed toward how the child's work looks, the child becomes more aware of the things that he or she has created spontaneously. The adult could describe some of the child's marks—such as long, curving lines, or where the marks were placed on the page, or the colors used. At some point the adult may want to touch or trace some of the lines with his or her finger to reinforce the comments.

The adult can find clues to the child's feelings in the child's facial and body expressions and preferences. Comments on what a long period of time a child has been working and how he or she must have enjoyed it help the child to know that the adult understands and values what the child is feeling.

In the controlled stage of scribbling, comments should be directed toward the child's increased motor control and ability to devise a variety of movements. Because the child at this time is better able to repeat certain movements, comments on how the child's hand is going around and around would be appropriate. Conversation directed at the way the scribble looks helps children to realize that they have made a particular mark many times or that they have made a number of closed shapes and lines. The adult might call their attention to how they drew a small circle inside a big one and how hard that is to do. The adult might also refer to contrasting colors and values, describe different lines or shapes, and note how these marks relate to each other. Since scribblers feel great satisfaction in being able to control their marks, remarks about their feelings should focus on this new accomplishment and how exciting it is.

When children begin to name their scribbles, a much richer opportunity for communication exists. Since the actual marks may not differ much from those done earlier, and since children frequently change their ideas and meanings by the time they complete a scribble, it is unwise for the adult to try to guess or name an object in a child's artwork. Instead, the adult should listen to the child's comments and extend the child's frame of reference based on what he or she has said. That is, the adult should pick up on the clue and ask questions relating to both the composition and to the child's personal ideas. A child's comment about a drawing of "my Daddy" could be countered with questions not

A typical exaggerated size of one body part is seen in this five-year-old's drawing of the figure. Note use of geometric shapes.

only about the shapes and colors, but also about what Daddy is doing. These comments concentrate the children's thinking in the direction they have begun and have more meaning for them.

If children are hesitant to talk about their work, the Sparlings suggest encouraging conversation by commenting on how much fun the children seem to be having and asking them whether they would like to tell about some of the things they have made. If the child does not respond, he or she may be at an earlier stage of scribbling or may just be unwilling to converse. A positive or reassuring comment could be made about the "nice lines going around the paper" or about how glad the adult is that the child is having fun. Children should not be forced to comment, but with continued support, they will gradually want to converse about their work.

The Sparlings suggest remedial techniques to use with children who are reluctant to scribble. The adult may sit down with the child, use a crayon along with the child, and comment on how he or she is letting the crayon move all around the paper and how good it feels to do so, even with his or her eyes closed. Then the adult can suggest that they try doing it together. The smallest efforts should be praised and attempts made each day, because it takes time for children's confidence to be built up if they have had an unhappy experience or are frightened of new encounters.

Some children enjoy humming and making other noises as they work. Other children stare into space while they are engaged in scribbling. It is best not to interrupt when the child is fully involved. When the child puts the crayon or brush down, or takes a moment to stop work, the time is good for communicating. The adult should use the child's name and sit at the child's level. The child should not be asked what he or she is drawing or whether an object is a house or a dog, since these questions put the child "on the spot" and leave no room for creativity and further exploration. A comment might be directed at an especially bright color the child has used and the child asked if he or she would like to tell about something special in the drawing.

a

b   **c**

a. The circle as a symbol for a face can be seen in Bradley's early drawing (age three). Although the scribbles representing the hair and one ear are detached from the circle, details have been added to form a recognizable symbol for the human face.

b. Bradley's later drawing (age four) uses a rectangular shape for the body, with two lines extending from the rectangle to form legs. Notice how scribbled circles are repeated to form symbols for eyes, the nose, buttons, and knees. Radial lines have been added for hair.

c. A third drawing shows a complex ensemble of figures—a clown, two trapeze artists, and a tightrope walker. Drawn when Bradley was five years old, the picture represents his experiences and interests.

Sensitive and thoughtful comments directed to the scribbler help children become more enthusiastic about expressing themselves through art. They become more motivated to continue and expand their artwork, while the general awareness that has been built up through language enables them to translate their art experiences into art concepts. This sort of awareness is needed when children reach later stages in their development and are required to use aesthetic concepts to evaluate their work and the works of others.

THE SCHEMA (SYMBOL) EMERGES

It sometimes seems as though the scribbling stage is endless. Then, at a specific point in the child's development, scribble lines evolve into rudimentary shapes of people, animals, and objects. The child's early visual schemas, or symbols, for figures and objects may not appear realistic to adult eyes because children relate their ideas in a less complex fashion, using their own interpretations. However, these symbols represent the child's understanding of the world as he or she experiences it and are indicative of giant steps in cognitive thinking.

The Early Symbol Stage

Usually during the fourth or fifth year, children make the remarkable discovery that they can make a closed, round shape and repeat it at will. This circle, a direct outgrowth of the child's former scribbling, becomes the basis for the child's schema or symbol system. In this drawn circle, children recognize a symbol that they can use to represent a number of objects that are of emotional significance to them in their world. They can add two lines, and the circle becomes "mommy." This new configuration—usually referred to as the "head-feet" or "polliwog" symbol—is used to communicate about experiences that have some important conceptual or emotional meaning to the young child. These first head-feet representations may not be easily recognized without the child's naming them.

These two drawings of a girl, drawn by the same child, show the development that occurs between the ages of three and six. The development of a definite schema is evident in the later drawing.

When children first begin drawing the head-feet symbol, their concepts of space have not developed beyond that of representing objects in a random floating array. A symbol for "mommy" may be placed high on the page, the child's kitten may be positioned lower, and perhaps a house may be placed off to the side. The objects are not related to one another in position or size; nor are they related to the ground. It is satisfaction enough for children to be aware that they have created a symbol that is recognizable as a person, animal, or house.

The Later Symbol Stage

At some point, children will begin to experiment—modifying the head-feet symbol—making it more elaborate and detailed by adding eyes, mouth, ears, and so on. They may add a number of radial lines and call it "the sun," or four legs and a tail and make it a "dog." Eventually children draw a connecting line near the lower part of the two lines that are extending from the circle, making it into a body, from which they may extend two more lines for arms and two for legs. The body is sometimes in a triangular shape, or sometimes it is another circle or an oval, with the legs and arms represented by lines or shapes.

As children continue to mature, their schemas show more variations and details until, by age six, the drawings are fairly elaborate. A child may draw things differently each time, depending on the experience or feelings at that moment. Often children are more interested in relating the drawing to the object than they are in relating the color to the object, and thus they may draw themselves with green hair or make a red tree. Visual depiction of relative sizes and proportion is not a major concern at this time. Rather, children have an honest sense of logic that is naive and obvious, and perhaps quite realistic in the true sense of the word: a long strong arm is needed to pull a wagon; hence, that arm appears longer in the picture. To depict oneself with a newly lost tooth requires drawing a huge mouth. A stubbed toe feels larger than it looks and may be drawn that way. *Exaggerations, changes of shape, concentration of details, and omissions* are all healthy and to be expected during the schematic period. When children want to express something that a person is doing or experiencing, not only do they often exaggerate the bodily part involved in the activity, but they may enrich it with many details. Or children may change the shape they ordinarily give to a symbol for a bodily part. If a child who usually draws a circle to represent a hand is given a new ring or has fingernail polish applied, the circle often disappears, to be replaced by a much more elaborate and detailed drawing of a hand. This indicates that the child is maintaining a degree of flexibility and is able to change his or her schemas to meet the needs of what it is he or she wants to represent.

These two drawings, both done by children in the same kindergarten class, show differing stages of development. Although the faces in the first drawing are detailed, the legs and feet are the only parts of the body represented. A body, arms, and fingers appear in the second drawing; the child clearly has the concept of "many fingers," but an exact number has not been determined. Both drawings depict the children's families.

By the time children are six or seven years old, they usually have developed definite schemas—a symbol for a person, a house, a dog, a tree, and objects important to them. They will repeat these symbols without variation unless some motivation or experience causes them to deviate. To prevent these symbols from becoming locked in and stereotyped, the teacher should endeavor to keep children flexible in their thinking and, thus, in their depictions. By structuring appropriate motivations and experiences, the teacher can help make children more aware of visual details related to the figures and to objects, thus causing them to deviate from and enrich their schemas.

The way that people and objects are depicted by children is related to several factors: the degree to which the child's passive knowledge has been activated by remembering or engaging in an experience, by the keenness of his or her perception and overall

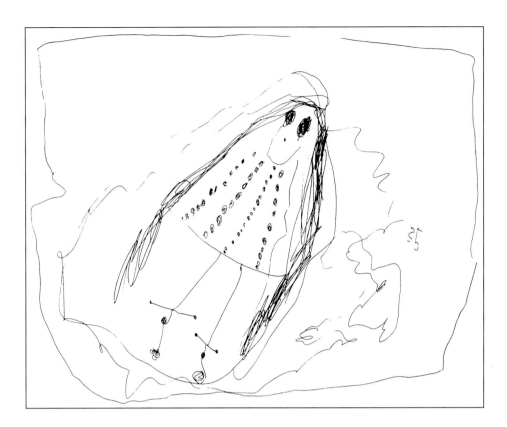

Accuracy isn't essential in this whimsical drawing of an "ice skater with thirty-five buttons." Notice the number "35" on the right side of the drawing. The four-year-old artist has allowed long, wandering lines to enclose the figure in a box.

awareness, his or her possible intellectual capacity since a large number of details in a drawing often indicates a higher intelligence, and in general, to more highly developed personality characteristics.

Concepts regarding space become obvious during the later symbol stage. A greater awareness of how to deal with spatial ideas is probably the most notable achievement at this stage of development. Children begin to include the baseline, a line drawn across the paper and upon which objects are placed. This signifies that the child is now aware that there are other objects in the world and that they have a definite place on the ground and in relation to other people and objects. Girls and boys often put a line across the top of the picture for the sky, with "air" in the middle.

An adult should never "correct" children's drawings, show them "how to draw," or ask them to copy another person's artwork. Such interference is meaningless and is damaging to children's self-esteem as well as to their artistic growth, and to their development of an independent and creative personality. Such interference makes them dependent on an adult at a time when they need to be building confidence in their own visual language and learning to reach out, explore, and communicate their own thoughts. When adults interfere by teaching children a cliché of a stick figure or a house, children usually cling to that particular form and it becomes a stereotyped repetition that is locked in, halting artistic growth. It is equally harmful for an adult to criticize children's color choices as "not right" for an object; children will discover the relationship themselves as their work merges into a later stage of development. The adult should find ample opportunity, however, to develop and encourage this awareness through art games (see Chapter 3) and motivations (see Chapter 5), and in impromptu informal chats: for example, "What a bright red shirt Kim is wearing today" or "Maria's dog is as brown as a chocolate bar."

At all stages, communication with the young artist should be geared to the child's developmental level. Comments should relate specifically to what the child has done. Generalized comments and stereotyped phrases that show that the adult has not

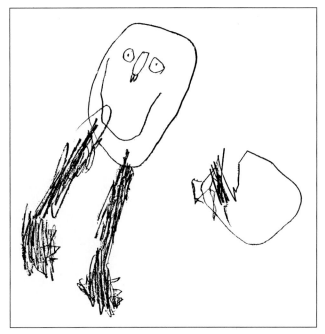

really looked carefully at the child's work and taken the time to discuss it with the child convey a message of lack of interest and a low regard for the importance of the artwork.

Although this is a time for verbal skill development, Lowenfeld feels that there is no substantial reason for attempting to teach children of this age to read, because they are not able to relate letters to form words and words to form sentences—skills learned later when they have established a baseline concept that is symptomatic of a higher level of

These three drawings illustrate Nina's development at ages four, five, and six.

This tempera painting by a six-year-old fills the format of the picture with bold and happy colors.

seeing and understanding spatial relationships.[6] Furthermore, if children begin their reading instruction later, they will learn to read more quickly and with less struggle, and the resulting attitude toward reading and learning in general will be positive and eager.

TOPICS FOR DRAWING

If motivational topics are sensitively structured and are discussed regularly, children's awareness is awakened and incorporated into their drawings. The symbols children use become richer, more detailed, and more unified, and they are able to use, change, and enrich these symbols to depict all manner of experiences and ideas.

Children of four, five, and six years of age are self-centered, and the names they give their drawings usually have in them the words *I, my,* and *me.* Topics for drawing, therefore, should focus on extending the child's field of awareness and expression in this direction. Productive topics are those that have to do with the body: "I have a new pair of dark glasses," "I have a stomachache," "I am pulling my wagon," "I am jumping rope," or "I am blowing soap bubbles."

Each motivational topic of this type emphasizes one body part, a part that at that particular moment is charged with emotional and/or kinesthetic impact. The adult can use these moments to ask such questions as: "How do your dark glasses feel? What holds them up? Did you look at yourself in the mirror with them on?" Or "Where is your stomach hurting?" Or "Where are your arms when you jump rope? Do you bend your knees?" Or "Show me how you blow bubbles. Do you puff your cheeks out? How do you hold the pipe?" Children often become so involved in depicting an experience or idea that they may omit a body part that at that particular time is unimportant. Ears may be left off a figure who is jumping rope. However, a subsequent motivational topic might emphasize the ear by asking the children to draw "when I had an earache," or "my new pierced ears," or "whispering a secret in my ear."

At seven years, the child has established a spatial order as seen here in a drawing of "I am playing with my dog."

Topics with more emotional significance can also be used as motivators for helping children identify their own feelings: "when my kitten died," "saying goodbye to Grandma at the airport," "my new baby brother," or "I am eating birthday cake." The adult may extend the child's idea by asking questions after the child has initiated an idea for drawing, or the adult may suggest drawing topics that are tuned into the child's experiences and recent happenings.

Such discussion of topics can expand the child's perceptual growth, cognitive powers, and emotional responses, and all discussions at this time relative to drawing, painting, and modeling should incorporate several questions or points related to the important three areas of *perceiving, thinking,* and *feeling.* Appropriate motivational topics can help children become more aware of things in their world; help them develop flexible personalities; assist them in thinking with imagination, originality, and fluency; and increase their ability to face new situations and to recognize and express both pleasant and unpleasant feelings in an acceptable manner.

An insecure or inflexible child may respond to a new experience by drawing the same schema over and over or by responding to a motivational concept such as "Playing Ball" by stating "I can't draw myself throwing a ball." In this case, rather than drawing for the student when she states that she can't draw herself playing ball, it is advisable to have the child actually throw a ball while the adult makes her aware of how she moved her arms and body. The child might also observe the stance and movement of another child throwing a ball.

Child-centered topics for motivations can also include questions and comments that assist children in making judgments, such as considering where they will place objects on their paper, what shapes they will use, and which colors will be best. During this stage, children begin to discover and use colors that are related to objects. Hair is no longer purple and noses green. They are eager to classify and categorize things, to feel that they have a tangible hold on the world. Children's attention can be directed to warm, happy

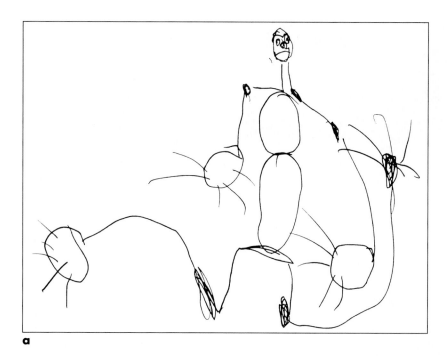

a

b

a. The exaggerated legs of a running figure dominate this drawing by Max at age four. Children often become so involved with their experiences or ideas that they emphasize the parts involved in the activity and minimize or eliminate those parts not being used.

b. Four years later, Max's drawing of a robot indicates increased concern with detail and proportion.

colors in their environment, such as red, orange, yellow, and pink, and what things these colors make them think of. They can also be introduced to cool, calm colors, and encouraged to think of images that these tones of green, blue, and purple evoke. They should have ample opportunity to practice mixing different colors together, adding a bit of one color to white to make tints and a bit of black to a color to darken it and make a shade. As they become more deeply involved in picture making and see the manner in which red

"My trip to the circus" is the title of this drawing by a seven-year-old. Lines no longer just delineate shape but are used to indicate mass and pattern. Some shapes have been filled in solid. A growing awareness of the entire picture area is indicated.

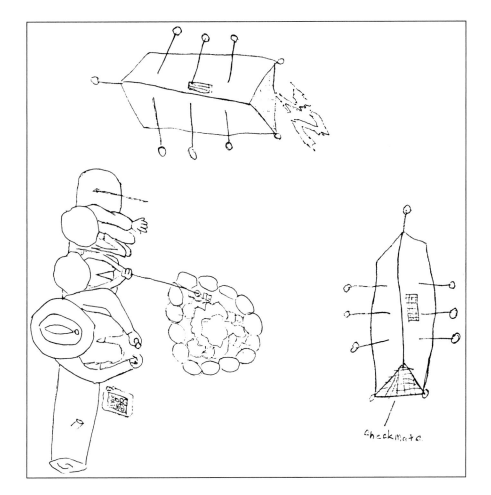

checkmate

Occasionally, this student draws pictures looking down on people. Roasting marshmallows, sleeping, and playing chess seem to be the activities in this Boy Scout camp-out. Jeff, age nine, has a remarkable ability to manipulate space in his mind's eye. This ability appeared at the age of six, when he completed a picture of a baseball game, again looking from above.

89

This drawing by a five-year-old shows a keen perceptive awareness of spatial concepts. Notice the multiple baselines.

vibrates next to green or the effect that a great deal of a dull color has next to a single bright spot of orange, children acquire the skills needed to mix and blend their own colors to suit their needs.

As children become more aware of spatial concepts, the use of baselines should be encouraged. Because children of this age are also developing social awareness, motivational topics should extend outward to include where and with whom the action took place.

Again, it is very important to make sure that the spatial schema does not become a rigid concept. Many ideas and experiences are unfolding at this time and the child will often find that the baseline will not suffice to show his or her idea clearly. Therefore, motivations that encourage baseline deviations are appropriate. Such deviations along with appropriate topics might include

Bent or curved baseline: We are climbing a mountain; We are going skiing.
Multiple baselines: Horses racing on tracks; Booths at the carnival; We are picking cherries in an orchard.
Elevated baseline (*placed near the top of the paper*): Inside an ant hill; Under the sea; Animals that burrow beneath the ground.
Mixed plane and elevation (part of the objects are drawn as if we are looking down on them, and others are drawn as if we are looking at them at eye level): We are floating down the river on rafts; A parade on a street with buildings on both sides; We are playing rummy.

Reproductions of famous artworks whose subject matter is the same or similar to the children's can assist students in making relevant connections at this time: for example, the works by Cassatt, Chagall, and Lawrence in the Color Gallery. They can become aware of the many ways in which artists depict the same subject matter, and they can understand that there is no one right or wrong way to make art.

Children in these schematic years are eager participants in group projects, such as making assembled murals, creating puppets, and constructing with large boxes. They like to explore new materials and processes, such as printmaking, stitchery, weaving, puppetry, and modeling techniques and gain skills in repeating the use of each new material. By the end of the third grade, children should be able to express their own ideas creatively and confidently, using a wide variety of art materials.

THE REALISTIC STAGE

At the end of the early childhood years children become interested in a more representational approach to art. However, girls and boys who are considered talented in art will reach the realistic stage earlier, so the characteristics of this developmental stage are noted here. The beginning of the realistic stage in art reflects the child's maturation and is generally thought of as the last outpost for childlike symbols and schemas. It is a time of great adjustments. Children between the ages of eight and twelve are undergoing enormous physical changes; they are alive and bursting with a new awareness about themselves and their world. They no longer consider the conceptual symbols that they used in their earlier artworks as satisfactory. They desire a more representational approach to figures, with a greater emphasis on realistic proportions and less exaggeration and distortions. At this time there may be attempts by children to shade objects, to draw shadows, to include more details, patterns, and textures, and in general to depict things more carefully.

Children at this time are overlapping objects in order to create a sense of visual space. They may also make distant objects smaller and place them higher on their paper to make them seem farther away. These signs mark their beginning stages in understanding and using perspective.

As some children reach this stage in their artistic development, they often become critical of their own work and are dissatisfied when something does not look just as they want it to look. This is especially true if students have not had numerous perceptual encounters, if they have not experimented with a variety of art materials, and if their artistic growth has been interfered with by the use of coloring books and other highly directed projects.

Teachers need to have children draw from direct observation—focusing their attention on shapes and outlines, angles, sizes, colors, patterns, details, and relationships. Teachers can also help by stressing the importance of originality and the personal expression of ideas and feelings. Children need the opportunity to experiment, explore, and discover what they can create using a variety of materials. As in the previous stages, children need appropriate motivational activities and directed visual encounters so that they will be able to express their own observations, thoughts, and emotions with creativity and confidence.

It is helpful and informative for both the teacher and child if the child's drawings are collected, if possible, over a period of time—from initial scribbles through the realistic stage. Children often talk while they are drawing—recalling, reorganizing, and fantasizing about an experience—and the child's comments as well as the date should be noted on the back of each piece of artwork. Since different children progress through the various artistic stages at different rates, it is also revealing to collect drawings from an entire classroom of children to see the wide range of artistic development.

a

b

c

It is informative to collect drawings from one child over a period of time. These drawings, collected over a seven-year period, show the developmental characteristics of a young artist:

a. Irregular or uncontrolled scribbling (age 2½)

b. Rhythmic or controlled scribbling—longitudinal (age 3)

c. Identified scribbling—"a dog" (age 3½)

d. Early symbol stage—"Momma" (age 4)

e. Later symbol stage (age 6)

f. Beginning of realistic stage (age 8)

d

e

f

Chart 4.1 Achievement Expectations—Completion of Grade 3

Aesthetic Perception	Aesthetic perception enables individuals to recognize beauty, its character and conditions. Heightened perception sensitizes students to the world about them, enabling them to see, feel, and react with greater responsiveness. Art develops aesthetic perception by providing sensory experiences and heightening responsiveness to aesthetic qualities in the environment.	By the end of the third grade, a student should be able to: Perceive differences and similarities among groups of lines, shapes/forms, textures, colors, values, and internal and external spaces. Classify lines, shapes/forms, textures, colors, and values into families or groups. Verbalize an expanding awareness of the elements, line, shape/form, texture, color, value, space. Manipulate space in two-and three-dimensional works to create personal art forms. Demonstrate understanding of the principles of design (balance, unity, emphasis, rhythm) by expressing simple concepts in his or her own words. Demonstrate increased ability to arrange elements to achieve emphasis, unity, and rhythm in both two-and three-dimensional works of art. Describe ideas and feelings when observing works of art, nature, events, and objects.
Creative Expression	Visual expression results when the urge to communicate is linked with originality and with knowledge of the structure and language of art. Art enables students to express their own creativity through a nonverbal form of communication that embodies their personal symbols, images, feelings, ideas, and spirit. Involvement in quality art experiences enables students to realize moments of satisfaction, accomplishment, and joy.	By the end of the third grade, a student should be able to: Express personal ideas and feelings through drawing, painting, printmaking, modeling, constructing, ceramics, filmmaking, graphics, textiles, and so on. Interpret a single subject or theme in a variety of ways, using a variety of skills and materials. Produce with confidence in several art media. Create varying types of art (portraits, self-portraits, landscape, still life, collage, rubbings and prints, torn and cut paper, sculpture and constructions, ceramics, and so on). Apply simple concepts learned about line, shape/form, texture, color, value, and space in personal artwork. Create a balanced composition in both two-and three-dimensional works. Demonstrate originality in selection and arrangement of images in personal artwork. Utilize varying sources of inspiration in own environment to create original works of art. Utilize simple perspective techniques of overlapping, placement, size variation. Express both fantasy and perceptions of the real world through imaginative application of two-and three-dimensional media.
Art Heritage (Historical/Cultural)	Opportunities to see and study a rich variety of artworks develop understandings of artists and works of art as well as their evolution and functions, both today and in the past. Awareness of artistic accomplishments of various cultures of the world enables pupils to see the place of art in relation to those cultures and in their own lives. Consequently, art serves to connect students to their cultural heritage as well as to increase their appreciation of the artistic contributions of other cultures.	By the end of the third grade, a student should be able to: Recognize similarities and differences among works of art produced in varying cultures. Distinguish the ways that people (past and present) use art to express (ideas, emotions), celebrate (events), embellish (everyday items), enrich (personal life), and intensify (spiritual beliefs) the human experience. Make associations with own artwork and the work of professional artists in the past and present as well as artists working in other cultures. Verbalize in own words ways that people everywhere use art to record ideas, feelings, and events. Recognize the purpose of museums as places where artwork is cared for and displayed (actual museum experience is recommended). Point out ways that art has been used to decorate and enhance daily life. Identify at least three well-known artists from examples or reproductions of their work.
Aesthetic Valuing	As students learn to recognize, discuss, and work with art, they come to understand it and to build a foundation for making judgments about its form, content, technique, and purpose. Discussion, critical analysis, reading, and observation of both original art and reproductions are requisite to develop criteria for arriving at personal preferences and opinions. Art develops and refines students' sensibilities, providing bases for understanding, enjoying, and appreciating art and its contributions to life.	By the end of the third grade, a student should be able to: Select personal favorites of well-known works of art and briefly describe reasons for choice. Identify broad categories of artworks by subject matter (for example, portrait, still life, landscape, abstract, and so on) as well as form (for example, painting, print, sculpture, drawing, fiber, ceramic, construction, photography). Recognize the ways that artists organize the elements of design (line, shape/form, texture, color, value, space) by using principles (such as balance, unity, emphasis, and rhythm). Use appropriate new terms in discussing visual art forms. Recognize the role of professional artists (such as architects, industrial designers, ceramists, illustrators, muralists, fabric and wallpaper designers) in our everyday life. Compare and critique differences and similarities in works of art (their own, their peers, professional artists living in the present and past, artists of other cultures). Compare environments and describe the qualities that make them aesthetically similar and different.

Reprinted with permission of the California Art Education Association (from the "Scope of Sequence").

TOPICS FOR DISCUSSION

1. What influences have a bearing on a child's development of visual images?

2. What is the importance of manipulative experiences in the early years?

3. Outline or list the characteristics of the sequential levels of artistic development, from irregular scribbling through the realistic period.

4. What are the characteristics of drawings of four- and five-year-old children? How can the children's interests be used to motivate expression and development?

5. At what point in the child's development does the head-feet symbol emerge? What would be the implications of observing this symbol in drawings by a seven-year-old child?

6. What are suitable motivational strategies for art at the various developmental stages?

7. In what ways can an adult respond and communicate with children about their art so that the dialogue helps children be enthusiastic and confident?

8. How might an adult encourage a child who either draws the same schemas over and over or who just says "I can't" during art experiences?

9. How would the use of art reproductions help the child's growth and development?

10. Summarize the achievement expectations at the end of the third grade.

NOTES

1. National Art Education Association, *Art for the Preprimary Child* (Washington, D.C.: National Art Education Association, 1972), 59–73.
2. Howard Gardner, "Unfolding or Teaching: On the Optimal Training of Artistic Skills," in *The Arts, Human Development, and Education,* Elliot W. Eisner, ed. (Berkeley, Calif.: McCutchan, 1976), 154.
3. National Art Education Association, poster, 1988.
4. Rhoda Kellogg, *Analyzing Children's Art* (Palo Alto, Calif.: National Press Books, 1969), 100.
5. Joseph Sparling and Marilyn Sparling, "How to Talk to a Scribbler," *Young Children* 28 (Aug. 1973): 333–41.
6. Viktor Lowenfeld and Lambert W. Brittain, *Creative and Mental Growth,* 6th ed. (New York: Macmillan, 1975), 208.

5

Motivating and Evaluating Children's Art

●●●●●●●●●●●●●●●●●●●●●●●●●●●●●●●●●●●●●●

Art education practices are firmly founded on the fundamental philosophy that children have the innate capacity to transform their primary means of knowing—the experiences of feeling, thinking, and perceiving—into their own unique art forms. In attempting to retain and foster the precious human gift of discovery through art, leading art educators have emphasized the importance and basic value of motivations as the primary method of evoking art responses in the child.

Any motivation that precedes an art production experience should engage children in a visual analysis that also includes both emotional and cognitive functions. Children should learn that every object, whether it is natural or of human origin, has a form and characteristics that distinguish it from other objects. For example, the overall shape of a lion is different from that of a peacock, and the parts of the lion can be analyzed as to thickness, thinness, relative sizes, and positions. Attention can be directed toward distinguishing lines in a bird or animal, such as pointed tail feathers or sharp, jutting antlers. Appropriate terminology can be used to describe the object's visual and tactile qualities: rough, shaggy, shiny, bumpy, and so on. The gesture or bearing of the object can be noted—it may be restful, tense, ready to jump, or running. The position of the figure or creature should be perceived. Are the arms stretched to catch a ball? Is the cowboy seated on a horse? Is the beak of the toucan higher or lower than its body when it sits on the branch? The brightness or dullness of colors can be observed, along with which color is dominant. Children can become aware of the pattern of bricks in a building and stripes on a zebra. They can note contrasts between dark and light, large and small, and plain versus patterned.

Providing many visual and tactile experiences and directing the child's observation is necessary to attain the high levels of perception required for creative and imaginative art production. Frequently children are expected to draw or paint pictures without making any observations. When this happens, children rely on their memories, and the result is as good, or as poor, as the images stored in their minds. If the child wants to draw an elephant, for example, the child's memory may include a long trunk, but all the other visual characteristics—the large ears, wrinkled skin, thick legs—may be lost in the finished work of art. Direct observation of objects in the real world—or carefully looking at photographs of real-world objects—provides experiences that can be stored and used later. Drawing or painting by careful observation is a way to increase perception and to store visual information that can be recalled. The development of fantasy creatures and environments is based on observation and recall. In this case, the imaginary creatures and objects are combinations, variations, and distortions of those observed in the real world.

Students asked to draw what they remember must call upon a large bank of stored visual images.

PROVIDING MOTIVATIONS

Motivations can help children **think, feel,** and **perceive** with more intensity and depth about the subject they are going to draw or paint. Motivations that incorporate these three factors, through questions and comments from the teacher, extend and abet children's enthusiasm, and help them sort out pertinent details, eliminate unnecessary elements, and establish harmonious relationships within their work.

Most three- and four-year-olds need no more motivation for drawing and painting than the excitement and pleasure they gain from using crayons, markers, or paint. Manipulating the material, learning to control lines, making shapes, and so on are highly stimulating factors in themselves. As children reach the schematic stage and discover the baseline, they think more about the placement or environment of the subject or idea they are portraying. Six- and seven-year-old children are ready to experience different art materials and to explore more challenging and intricate processes. They are eager to develop their skills in manipulating all sorts of materials, and the teacher should not underestimate their capabilities. These children tend to be less spontaneous and fluent, so the teacher should use many motivational channels to stimulate their art production. Second and third graders are ready to preplan their pictures—that is, think of a point of view and decide where the objects will be placed on the paper ("Will I draw it from the front, side, or back? From below or above? From close up or far away?"). Children should be encouraged to verbally describe the object they are going to draw or paint, striving to note as many of the aforementioned factors as possible. With practice and perseverance, the child's skill in learning to look and looking to learn substantially increases.

A variety of motivational techniques[1] provides opportunities for the adult to ask leading questions that stimulate the child to look, feel, remember, and engage in art production. The child's artwork subsequently may be evaluated for evidence of behavioral change and artistic growth. Motivations set up by the teacher provide artistic problems for children to solve. During the production period that follows, children need to develop a critical eye and conscious judgment. The aesthetic choices and decisions made during the work process ultimately result in a higher level of visual literacy, and the teacher/child verbal interchange can better bring this about.

a

b

A dialogue on "What I Like to Do on the Playground" led to the line drawing on the right. "It shows how my stomach feels when I go down the slide," reported the six-year-old artist.

DIALOGUES AS MOTIVATORS

A dialogue between the teacher and children involves a lively verbal interchange during which the child remembers an experience from which new relationships and fresh feelings are generated. Sometimes children form silent responses, which allow each child to form a different and unique answer or idea. If a dialogue is considered a group brainstorming session and is enlivened with challenging colorful questions, action-packed phrases, and provocative ideas, it opens a new world of awareness that will help the child rediscover a particular happening or situation. When memory patterns are triggered, the child is free to unify and invent new symbols for his or her art products. Such verbal interchanges as the following will prove to be stimulating triggers for motivating children's artwork: "Picking fruit," "My birthday party," "My friends and I are climbing a mountain," "We are in a treehouse," "I get a hair cut," "I am feeding the ducks," "When I went to the dentist," "We are swimming," "I am skating," "I am fishing."

This sample dialogue, "What I like to do on the playground," includes questions related to thinking, feeling, and perceiving:

We all like to play on the playground. We have some play equipment here at school, and perhaps you have visited parks and playgrounds. What do you like to play best of all? Some boys and girls like to swing very high. How do you hold your hands when you swing? How do you hold your feet? Do you stand or sit on the swing? If you go high, does your stomach tickle? How do your feet help you pump yourself higher and higher? Does someone push you?

Some boys and girls like to climb and hang on the bars and on jungle gyms. Can you swing by your knees upside down? How does the world look that way? Where are your arms when you hang by your knees? Do your knees get tired? How many children are usually on the bars or jungle gym at one time? How do you sit when you go down a slide? Where are your legs, knees, and arms? Do you go fast? How do you land? How do you climb up the

Photo files organized by subject are useful to motivate drawing lessons and to refresh mental images. After looking at many photographs from the "jungle animals" file, children made drawings to be used on notecards and as illustrations for calendars.

ladder? Where do your hands go? Did you ever fall off the ladder? Or did you land too hard when you slid down? When you were quite young, were you frightened when you first played on a slide? Did you ever go down any other kind of slide than a straight one? Some slides even land in a swimming pool for a big splash.

Did you ever swing across the parallel rings? How many rings are there? How large are they? Does it make your arms tired to swing across? Where are your feet and what are your legs doing as you swing across? Do you look up or down as you go? Do you find yourself short of breath? Who likes the teeter totter the best? How do you sit on it? Do you play on it alone? How is the teeter totter shaped? How do you use your feet and where do you hold your hands? Do you like to go up high? Did you ever bounce hard when your end of the board went down fast? Think of all the things you do on the playground and then draw a picture about what you like to do the best.

PHOTOGRAPHIC MATERIALS AS MOTIVATORS

Visual materials such as photographs, videos, slides, and filmstrips provide rich material for precise observations. Field trips to places all over the world can be brought directly into the classroom. Such visual aids not only provide visual information and stimulation, but also present opportunities for language development as the children look, question, discuss, compare, contrast, and note specific shapes, colors, lines, patterns, and size relationships.

Photographs can be collected from magazines such as *Junior World, Your Big Backyard,* or *Ranger Rick,* or from calendars and books that deal with a single theme or subject. The teacher should trim the photos and mount them on railroad board with spray adhesive. Spray adhesive, in addition to being quick and easy to apply, keeps the photos flat and neat on the boards and avoids the wrinkles and stains that sometimes occur when paste or glue is used. One large piece of railroad board can be cut into four or more small panels. Photographs can be grouped by subject and stored in envelopes. The following subjects are suggested: birds, fish, reptiles, animals, butterflies, trees, flowers, insects, portraits, people at play, people at work, sports and action, buildings, trains, cars, cities, landscapes, seascapes, and skies. A photo file on birds, for instance, would include closeup views of feathers, wings, beaks, and such, as well as birds in flight, on a nest, sitting on a branch—the many varieties of birds and their environments.

Studying photographs that deal with birds, for example, prior to an art activity about birds can increase children's perceptual skills through directed observation. The discussion helps the children note the different shapes of beaks and how different birds make use of their beaks, the lengths of different legs and necks, different sizes and shapes of bodies, the relative size of a bird's head to the size of its body, details that relate to the placement of the eyes and to the position of the wings at rest and in flight, the different kinds of claws and tails, and so on. The children should pretend that they are birds, swooping, feeding, pecking, roosting, and nesting, thereby ensuring that different modes of sensory awareness—visual, auditory, and kinesthetic—are open to them.

The importance of this approach, which ensures that children's strongest modes of learning are addressed, has been demonstrated by a study that found that 33 percent of individuals learn primarily in the visual mode, 24 percent are auditory learners, 14 percent are kinesthetic learners, and 29 percent learn in mixed modes.[2] In other words, some individuals learn best when the input is mostly taken in through the eyes. Others tend to listen and take in more information through their ears. The small but significant minority are those who need to move and go through the motions to take in data. Almost one-third of us learn best through a mixture of these modes of sensory awareness.

If the teacher, in initiating a drawing or painting activity, only tells the child to draw a bird and provides no visual information, no directed observational opportunities, and no kinesthetic activity, the drawing that is produced is usually symbolic, generalized,

Children prepare for an art activity about birds by observing photographs of birds and discussing the different sizes and shapes of their bodies, beaks, wings, legs, and tails. The result of directed observation is reflected in the details included in the children's paintings.

and lacking in any degree of emotion or self-identification. The child is content to present a symbol to stand for "bird," using only small bits of remembered information. By using and discussing photographs during a motivation, a teacher calls on the child to analyze birds in a logical manner, to use words to name, define, and describe birds step by step and part by part. Students are challenged to synthesize or put a bird together as they draw and paint, focusing on the likenesses between things, seeing where the different parts are in relation to other parts, and how different parts go together. If the motivation is open-ended and encourages fluency of response, children are free to make metaphorical relationships, arriving at divergent conclusions based on intuitive insight, hunches, feelings, and visual images.

Such observational skills involving the child's thoughts, feelings, and perceptions can be increased through frequent, short encounters with visual materials. These input skills establish a perceptual learning pattern or base that can be transferred to other media and other occasions—for example, when the students look at photographs on a variety of subjects and when they observe real-life objects that are either brought into the classroom or seen on field trips. These encounters build up within children's minds visual image "banks" in which their imagination may find rich resources for expression. Students can review, recall, and visualize ideas, feelings, and experiences in their subsequent art production.

A student sits in a real saddle, wears oversized boots, and rides a make-believe horse while the class observes and draws or paints. Live models with simple costumes and props assist in schema development by providing visual clues and emotional identification with real-life experience.

ACTUAL OBJECTS AS MOTIVATORS

Using actual objects that intrigue and interest the children is a motivational strategy that is challenging and open-ended. A bugle, a drum, a bicycle, a toy truck, a favorite doll, or a pet rabbit brought into the classroom can all trigger immediate enthusiasm and responses. For example, through interaction with a saddle during a motivation, children could

1. Enjoy sitting on the saddle

2. Act out or pretend to ride horseback

3. Observe other children's body positions when they are sitting on the saddle and verbalize as to the placement of arms, legs, and so on

4. Discuss various situations and environments where people ride horses

5. Think of items of clothing they might be wearing when they ride and what sort of hat and boots they might have

6. Observe the shape of the saddle and the length of the stirrups

7. Imagine their drawings on paper, thinking of where they would place the different parts and what background and which details they would use

8. Close their eyes and feel the texture of the leather, stitching, and metal

9. Draw or paint themselves or another person riding a horse

These considerations stir the individual's creativity and do not preordain or control the child's response; they do not specify how the child must draw or paint. The motivation or stimulus is provided, with the main focus being on perception, motor and cognitive awareness, and affective involvement, along with some preproduction planning.

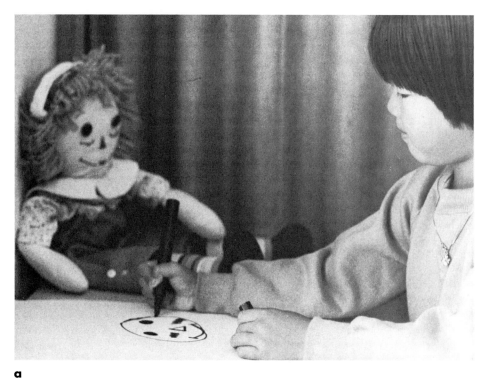

a

b   **c**   **d**

a. Students use dolls, stuffed toys, and other everyday objects in this draw-from-the-real-world lesson.

b, c, and **d.** These three drawings, all done by first-grade students in the same class, show the wide variety of creative expression possible, even when the subject matter is the same.

The school playground is a source of images for young artists.

"Having Fun," Logan Holland, Abbott Loop Elementary School, Anchorage, Alaska, Grade 2, age 9. Courtesy © 1991–92 Crayola® Dream Makers™

Rachel's drawing captures the experience of "jumping rope at Walter Hays School." Notice the child who jumped so high that only her feet are visible. This drawing was among the nine selected by The California Art Education Association for their annual notecard collection.

Rachel Knowles, Grade 1, Palo Alto School District. Courtesy of the California Art Education Association

ACTING-IT-OUT ACTIVITIES AS MOTIVATORS

In addition to verbal involvement, the actual physical reenactment of a past experience will refresh the children's memories and help them to retrieve kinesthetic sensations. The acting-it-out technique provides a warm-up period in which the children are able to feel as well as to see which body parts are moved in the action being discussed and described. This is accomplished in two ways: First, one or two children go through the motions while the class watches so that they might see how the body moves in the performance, and second, the entire class acts out the movements, thus enabling each child to remember how it feels kinesthetically and to identify what his or her own muscles are doing.

The accompanying dialogue sets the stage for the integration of the child's thoughts, feelings, and perceptions. Such questions might include where the action took place, how the participants were dressed, what the weather was like, and what size relationships, colors, textures, and shapes were observed.

A sample, "We jump rope together," follows:

Jumping rope is a game that we are able to do alone or with friends. Jumping rope has been a favorite of children for many years. People once believed that the higher they could jump rope, the higher their crops would grow, and every spring, they had a jumping contest. Now we usually sing a rhyme as we jump; it may tell a fortune such as how many children we'll have. Some jingles tell a story. Do you know any jump rope jingles? Do you know what "peppers" or "hot" means? (turn rope rapidly) Who can show us how to jump rope alone by turning the rope over your head? Can you jump on one foot? How many times have you jumped without missing?

Jumping rope can be done with your friends, too, with one holding each end of the rope and one or more children jumping in the middle. Who will show us how it is done? (While children are demonstrating . . .) Are they swinging the rope with one arm or both? See how high their arms must go to make the rope go all around. How do they place their feet? Can you run into the rope while it is turning and begin jumping? Where do the children who are jumping put their hands? Do they bend their knees or jump straight up and down? Do they jump on one foot or two? Sometimes the rope is turned back and forth in an arc and isn't turned all the way over the head of the jumper. Draw a picture about jumping rope. (The teacher may want to give each child a piece of string to paste on his paper to serve as a jump rope.)

Some acting-it-out motivations require the child to identify with another person or object; questions are prefaced with "If you were a helicopter pilot (or a scarecrow, or a balloon seller, or a robot). . . ." These motivations call for children to project their thoughts, feelings, and perceptions into another being or object, placing themselves in that being or object's position and imagining how they would feel, what they would see, and what they would think and do. For example, students can be asked where they have seen balloon sellers and if they themselves have ever let go of the string on a balloon and watched the balloon vanish in the distant sky. Other questions could include "Would you like to sell balloons? What colors would the balloons be? How many shapes of balloons have you seen? How many balloons could you hold if you were selling them at a fair? Would your balloons be on sticks or strings? Would you need one hand or two to hold all of them? Where would you put the money you are collecting? What kind of clothing would you wear? Would you get tired? How would you like to look up and see about twenty balloons over your head?" Children might then cut out a large number of circles from colored paper, paste them onto a piece of drawing paper, and finish the drawing with their crayons.

Pretending to become a grasshopper for a few minutes before drawing these insects challenges the children to imagine how it would feel to be on a leaf hiding from a big, hungry bird. Questions to ask the children could include "What shape is your body? What do you like to eat? Where do you hide from your enemies? Do you know that grasshoppers are musicians and that they rub their legs and wings together to make music? How would it feel to have three pairs of legs? What if a grasshopper wore shoes and had to tie shoestrings on all of them? What position are your legs in when you hop? (The children should crouch down, elbows bent upward, to simulate grasshopper legs.) Hop! Hop! Now crawl along a juicy leaf and take a bite of it."

WORD IMAGES AS MOTIVATORS

Children produce highly imaginative artistic responses when they are presented with humorous image-evoking songs, stories, or poems. The students can be asked to close their eyes while listening to the song or poem and to pretend that they have a television set "inside their heads" on which to "see" what the words are describing.

"Our street is us and we are it. Our street is where we like to be, and it looks like all our dreams." Mr. Plumbean's neighborhood is drastically changed in Daniel Pinkwater's book, *The Big Orange Splot.* Children produce highly imaginative artistic responses when presented with image-evoking stories. Here we see young artists painting "dream houses" that are colorful and unique.

The song "The Big Black Hat" by Rolf Harris describes a man who is dressed in a very strange way. The rhythm and melody are lively and easy to remember. After listening to the song, the children are asked to call on their visual memory and to tell whether they would be frightened, curious, or amused to meet a man dressed in the manner described. Questions that the teacher might ask the students include "Can you remember how the man was dressed, starting with what he wore on his head? What sort of brim did the hat have? What kind of band? How do you imagine the man's mustache was shaped? What sort of glasses were on his nose? What was around his neck, and what was attached to it and dragging on the ground? What is a sunshade? What color was the man's sunshade, and where did he hold it? What sort of coat and shirt and trousers do you suppose he might have worn? Do you imagine that this strange man was tall or short, fat or thin? Do you think he had large feet or small? Do you think he wore boots, shoes, or sandals?"

Edward Lear, who lived during the nineteenth century in England, was a master of limericks—five-lined, often humorous poems that are always rich in visual images. The people and other creatures in the limericks are often connected in odd and unexpected ways. Children generally create many different illustrations after listening to the following limericks:

> There was an old man in a tree,
> Whose whiskers were lovely to see:
> But the birds of the air,
> Pluk'd them perfectly bare,
> To make themselves nests in that tree.

Language and art can be combined in meaningful ways for young students. Here are three booklets that celebrate the writings and artwork of students throughout the Chula Vista City School District in California.

There was a young lady whose bonnet,
Came untied when the birds sat upon it;
But she said, "I don't care!
All the birds in the air
Are welcome to sit on my bonnet."

There was an old man of Dunrose,
A parrot seized hold of his nose.
When he grew melancholy,
They said, "His name's Polly,"
Which soothed that old man of Dunrose.

There was an old man with a beard,
Who said, "It is just as I feared!
Two owls and a hen,
Four larks and a wren,
Have all built their nests in my beard!"

Mother Goose rhymes, Aesop's fables, and numerous books of poems for children contain descriptive accounts of people, real and imaginary animals, places, and events. The teacher should avoid showing the children any illustrations that may accompany a poem until after the children have completed their drawings.

Most children enjoy the illustrations in books as well as the stories. Books can also motivate art activities through both the words and the pictures. Children can be asked to extend the story by drawing or painting an additional picture for the book. For example, *The Big Orange Splot* by Daniel Manus Pinkwater tells about a street where everyone's house looked the same. Mr. Plumbean makes some drastic changes, and a chain of events leads to a neighborhood where every house is unique and colorful. After listening to the story, the children are asked to remember and describe what they found humorous in the book.

Fantasy is an appealing focus point for motivation that sparks the young artist's imagination and leads to new perceptions and images.

"Outerspace Cat," Marguerite Lauri, Chugiak Elementary School, Chugiak, Alaska, Grade 3, age 9. Courtesy © 1991–92 Crayola® Dream Makers™

Questions that the teacher might ask include "Can you remember Mr. Plumbean's house? What did it look like? What caused Mr. Plumbean to change his house? What is your favorite house in the story? What did it look like? What colors were used? How was it different from the other houses?" Children then use their imaginations to describe and create a picture that shows the house they would build if they lived in Mr. Plumbean's neighborhood.

FANTASY AND HUMOR AS MOTIVATORS

Fantasy and humor are also appealing focus points for a motivation that charges children's mental batteries and aids them in pushing forward in their artistic production. Fantasy themes can be fanciful, unreal, absurd, and dreamlike. Humorous topics deal with whimsy, wit, jests, jokes, and just plain funny situations. Examples might include: "The Mixed-Up Animal I Saw in My Backyard," "What I Think I Look Like Inside," "Inside Our TV Set," "Magic Flowers," "Underground Tunnels for Alligators," "What If Cars Could Walk?" "What If Elephants Could Fly?" "What If Insects Became Giants?" "What If Fish Had Legs and Animals Had Wheels?" and "What If Cities Were Built in Jungles?" Pretend and make-believe, weird visual connections, old ideas placed in fresh surroundings, and silly, absurd situations help children grow creatively and explore new visual connections in individual and inventive ways.

As an alternative to the usual size and shape of drawing paper, children will enjoy using blank white postcards (3¾ × 6 inches) and drawing a picture of something they imagined in the "Land of Pretend." They may choose to use colored markers or colored pencils. They may want to first draw a border or frame around the sides before illustrating their messages. Following are ideas to stimulate visual images and imaginative responses for postcard messages:

"I saw two mountain peaks with flowers growing on them. A rainbow arched from one to the other. Animals walked on the rainbow bridge."
"I went snorkeling in the blue water and saw fish—round fish, long fish, and seahorses—of many colors swimming among the plants."

"I saw a garden of many flowers that reminded me of different kinds of candy-striped
   stems and lollipops."
"I went to the zoo and saw a creature I never saw before. It had the head of a . . . , the
   body of a . . ., the tail and legs of a . . ."
"I went on a ride to a faraway planet in a spaceship. This is what the spaceship looked
   like."
"We landed on a faraway planet and everything there was different—the buildings,
   people, plants, and animals. This is what I saw."
"When I want to fly, I sit on my magic carpet. This is what it looks like. I like the
   bright colors and pretty patterns."
"I rode in an airplane. I looked down and saw a river, fields, orchards, highways, cars,
   barns, animals in the field . . ." or "I looked down and saw a beach, boats, and
   people playing on the sand and in the water."
"I went to the zoo. All the animals were acrobats. A rooster stood on the back of a
   lion. A lion stood on the back of an elephant. It was funny."

GROUPS OF SUBJECT-RELATED ARTWORKS AS MOTIVATORS

A group of related artworks by well-known artists, all dealing with the same subject or
theme, can motivate students to make art that has the same or similar subject matter. By
viewing several large reproductions by different artists, students begin to understand art's
diversity and how each artist can use the same subject in a different way. Reproductions
are available from a number of suppliers (see Resources for Art Education on page 315).
A set of subject-related reproductions may be selected and presented as a portfolio.

   The motivation should encourage students to deal with the theme in their own individual ways. Children should first be actively engaged in describing, analyzing, and interpreting the artworks and then presented with a similar topic and appropriate materials.
Portfolio subjects and themes could include: "Portraits," "Animals," "Sports and Games,"
"Flowers," "The Sea," "Families," and "The Circus." A sample lesson for a portfolio follows; the artworks discussed are found in the Color Gallery.

"Artists Paint People Doing Things"

"Do you like to make pictures about things you do with your friends and family? Many
artists have used this as a favorite theme. Perhaps more than any other subject, artists
have chosen people to draw and paint, often showing us exactly how the people looked
and dressed and what they were doing. Sometimes, they show us just one person, and
sometimes they tell us about what two people are doing, and sometimes they show us
whole groups of people. They show people at work and play, indoors and out. Often, they
paint ordinary people doing everyday activities. When they do this, they usually include
many details and textures that make their pictures look very real. Sometimes artists try
new ways to paint people; they aren't concerned with making the figures look exactly
like someone we may know. These artists enjoy working with shapes and lines and colors
and expressing a certain feeling more than showing us the subject in a very real manner.
If you could be a person in one of these pictures, which would you choose?"

A Sunday on La Grande Jatte
by Georges Seurat

"What do you see? I see a large number of people near the water, enjoying the sun and
shade. They are wearing clothing in a style that was popular a little more than one hundred
years ago when this picture was painted. How would you dress for a day at a lake or near a
river? An artist named Georges Seurat made this oil painting about a place near where he
lived. Do you think it is warm or cool here? Why? Choose a figure, and describe what that
person is doing. Stand or sit in the same position. Which figures are painted the largest?
They are in the foreground and appear closer to us. Which are somewhat smaller? They

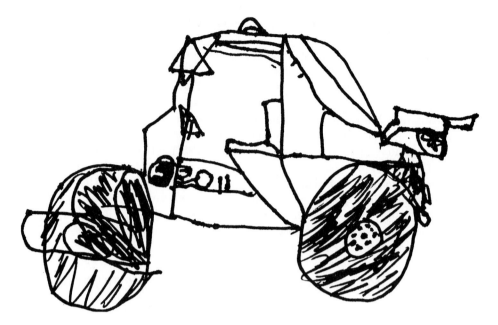

Some teachers considered the construction at Punahou School in Hawaii to be an irritating distraction, while others welcomed the opportunity for their students to observe machines and workers in action. This drawing illustrates one kindergartner's observational skills and involvement.

are farther away, in the middle ground and background. Our eyes are led to the background by the diagonal shoreline. What kinds of animals do you see? What are they doing? Can you find shadows?"

"What colors do you see? Can you find some dark greens, light greens, yellow-greens? The artist used a red-orange to contrast with all the greens and blues. Our eyes seem to go from one red shape to another. There are many curving shapes in this picture. The curving shape of the umbrellas is repeated, and we see the same curving shape in the sailboat and even in the tails of the dog and monkey. Look at the many shapes of hats. What would you hear if you were in this picture? Would it be quiet or noisy? The many vertical shapes of the trees and figures give us a feeling that nothing much is moving. If we could see the original of this painting, we would discover how large it is. It is $81 \times 120\frac{3}{8}$ inches. Can you see the grainy texture over the entire surface? Seurat invented a new way to paint. He made many tiny dots of color placed very close together. He wanted your eyes to mix the colors when you viewed his artwork. Instead of mixing a yellow-green, he would put tiny dots of yellow and green together. This is called pointillism. Do you think it took him a long time to make this picture? He was very skilled at this technique. He has shown us quite a realistic scene in which people seem to be posed stiffly and very formally, almost like statues. Can you find a painting in this group that shows people who are posed more naturally?"

The Bath by Mary Cassatt

"In this painting, we see a woman helping a little girl wash her feet in a bowl of water. Have you ever sat on your mom or dad's lap while they helped you wash your feet or put on a new pair of shoes? Perhaps the little girl has been outdoors playing and is getting ready for a nap. The little girl is seated on the woman's lap, and they are both looking down. Their shapes take up most of the picture space. They are probably in a bedroom because we see the repeated pattern of the carpet on the floor and more patterns of furniture and wallpaper behind them. Can you find any other patterns? Their two heads are the darkest areas of the picture, and we tend to see them first. Where do your eyes go next?

Perhaps down the long lines on the mother's sleeve to her hand, around the bowl, and back up, following the line along the little girl's leg and up to her bent arm and back to her head. Find all the round shapes in the picture. See how the pattern of lavender, gray, and white stripes on the mother's garment curves and shows the form of her body. Mary Cassatt painted this picture about one hundred years ago. She often painted women and children. She was an American but spent most of her life in Paris, painting with other artists. Can you find another picture that shows people engaged in an ordinary everyday activity?"

Cabinet Makers by Jacob Lawrence

"This painting is called *Cabinet Makers.* This means that people are making cabinets to use in a home or store. There are places called shops where things are made from wood. In this cabinet shop, five men dressed in blue overalls and shirts are working hard. Four are placed in each corner of the composition and one man is in the center. See how they are leaning, pushing, and reaching. Their bodies form strong lines and shapes that go across the picture from one corner to the other. The man whose face is in the center is like the place where lines cross to make an X. Can you find shapes that go up and down? Can you find lines and shapes that go from side to side? See how some lines meet to make corners and angles. The workers are using different tools. Does anyone in your family have tools to make things? Can you find someone in the painting who is using a tool to measure? Can you find someone drilling a hole? There is a special tool called a level. Can you find one here? What does a level do? Can you find the tool called a plane? What does a plane do? What colors do you see in this picture? Red, white, and blue are also the colors in the American flag. The artist is an American who lives in Seattle, Washington. He uses opaque watercolors called gouache (gwash) and likes to paint shapes so that they appear flat. Lawrence grew up around carpenters and cabinetmakers in an area of New York called Harlem. When he was twenty years old, his work was shown for the first time in a neighborhood library. He painted this picture about fifty years ago as part of a series he calls The Builders. All through his life, he has painted pictures of black people doing everyday things. He especially likes to show them working with tools and has a collection of tools in his studio because they are beautiful, he says, 'like sculpture.' "

Questions for Closing a Portfolio Presentation

1. Which pictures show people doing things in another time or place that people still do today?

2. Which pictures show us exactly how some people looked and dressed?

3. Which picture do you think shows the greatest use of the artist's imagination?

4. Which picture would you like to make up a story about?

5. Compare the mood in Lawrence's *Cabinet Makers* with Seurat's *A Sunday on La Grande Jatte.*

6. Which picture has the deepest space? Which has the shallowest?

7. Which picture seems the most real to you? Why?

8. Act out a story with your classmates about one of the paintings.

9. Write a short poem about one of these paintings.

Grade 1
Artists Paint People Doing Things

Art Concepts and Skills

Artists show individual figures and several figures doing ordinary, everyday things in addition to showing figures engaged in those events that are special in our lives.
Students paste down small photographs of heads clipped from catalogs and then complete a drawing of themselves and their family or friends engaged in some activity that is important in their lives.

You'll need

catalogs (or magazines)
scissors and paste
white or manila paper
crayons

Here's how

1. Look through catalogs or magazines and find several heads: one that looks a little like yourself and others that look a little like the other people that will take part in the activity you will show. Cut them out.
2. Paste the heads on a piece of drawing paper.
3. With crayons, draw a picture of yourself and your family or friends, and show what you are doing, what you are wearing, and where you are.

Motivation

What do you and your mom, dad, brother, sister, or a friend like to do together? Perhaps you remember some favorite activity you have done with a grandparent. How about: fishing in a boat, playing ball, riding in a truck, going to the zoo, having a picnic, flying a kite, gardening, jogging, biking, shopping, having a story read to you, visiting an art museum. Maybe you remember a very special day, such as someone's wedding or birthday. How did you dress for the activity you choose to show? Where did it take place—indoors or out? What details will you need to include?

Vocabulary
activity
details

Table 5.1 Art Docent Program (Sample hands-on lesson to follow a portfolio presentation.)

EVALUATING STUDENT DEVELOPMENT IN ART PRODUCTION

As children become involved in regular and sequential lessons in art, their artistic production is expected to change. Classroom teachers need to look at the outcomes of a series of motivations and have some criteria for evaluating both the process and product. Four aspects of art production can be evaluated to assure and assist in the child's progress. Ideally, all four aspects work together and support each other, and all should be used in evaluating student development in making art.

The first of these is the child's degree of skill in handling materials, both during the time the child is working and within the finished artwork. The child should show increased motor control in using materials because without constantly improving material-handling skills, expression is held back. In a child's early years, highly developed motor control is not expected. However, an increasing capacity to master materials and a desire to develop skills are evidences suitable for evaluation.

The second aspect for evaluation deals with how the child has organized his or her artwork and made the different parts function—how the child has used colors, lines, shapes, and the other elements of art. It also refers to how the child has made use of repetition, balance, variety, and the other principles of art. When a child achieves unity in an artwork, he or she has made it look whole, harmonious, and complete.

The third aspect evaluates expressive or emotional content in the child's artwork. This has to do with feelings and moods as seen in choices of subject matter as well as in the selection of colors, use of lines and shapes, and so on.

The fourth focus for evaluation in the productive realm involves assessing the degree of creative imagination, independent thinking, and ingenuity used in making the artwork. This has to do with original ideas, making unusual connections by relating two or more usually unrelated ideas, using humorous or insightful approaches, or finding new ways to express an idea, solve a visual problem, or use a material. Technical skill and an aesthetically pleasing form may be present, yet imaginative aspects and fresh insight may be at a minimum.

The teacher's supportive and encouraging remarks bring out the best in all children. For the preschool and kindergarten child, an impromptu and informal discussion as the completed art products are being hung about the room is usually adequate. "Chang's painting makes me feel like a sunshiny day—happy and warm. Emily's drawing tells us how strong and furry her black dog is. Alec loves red and orange, and he has arranged them well. Lupe has repeated this yellow shape over and over, and it makes an interesting pattern. Mallory has found another new way to draw a tree."

There are three occasions when such encouragement can take place: during the initial motivation period, during the working process, and then later, while discussing the finished work. Specific comments are more meaningful and offer more opportunity for the child's growth: "Rafael, I am delighted to see how you repeated slanted lines in your picture. They show that the skier is moving down hill very fast," or "I am very pleased to see how much you enjoy painting with red and yellow," are more specific than "That's nice." Precise statements during the working period may refer to product as well as process: "Daniel, it makes me happy to see how much you enjoy making purple circles." Instead of a vapid "That's nice, Maria" or "Good work, Kim," the teacher should first look carefully at the work. Comments as to the length of time and amount of effort that the child has put into a work can provide opportunities for positive reinforcement: "Dean spent a long time on his picture. He has worked hard to show us his tree house."

Following are examples of appropriate remarks addressing the four aspects of evaluation:

1. *The child's improved skill and control of the medium:* "Laura painted her background color up very close to the house." "Juan really is doing a good job of making his crayon drawing dark and waxy." "Jan was very careful when she attached the legs to the body of her clay elephant." "Peter used just the right amount of paste when he pasted the paper in his zoo collage."

2. *The elements and principles of art that the child has used—the choices the child made and the ways that he or she has organized the composition:* "You have used red in several places, Rebecca, and my eyes move from one to the next." "I like the

blue and green colors that contrast with the big, orange sun, Dalijit." "You did a good job of repeating this shape, Noriko. It gives your picture a sense of rhythm." "These two small, bright spots of red on this side of your picture help to balance the large, dull blue spot on the other side." "Lori looked at the rabbit in the cage very carefully and showed us how soft its fur is and how long and pink its ears are."

3. *The expressive quality, the degree to which the child has injected feelings and emotions into the work:* "I feel happy when I see the warm colors in your painting, and I remember going to the circus last summer." "Your picture makes me remember a stormy night last October." "I can almost hear the circus music when I look at the bright colors and strong shapes in Cisco's clown picture."

4. *The inventiveness, ingenuity, and imagination shown in the child's work:* "Angela drew her horse different from anyone else's. I can tell that it's galloping fast." "Carlos found two new ways to show people jumping rope." "Anna used cut and torn tissue that she had crumpled to make the bird in her collage."

As children produce art at a more conscious, critical level, usually during the first grade, they may talk with the teacher in small groups or individually, verbalizing about their work and becoming more aware of the art elements and how to integrate them in their compositions. Occasional discussions after art production periods help the children deal more effectively and expressively with color, shape, line, contrast, rhythm, and allover composition. Future discouragement and frustration may be prevented. If teachers talk about the child's work in art terminology, the child develops an art language and awareness. A positive and constructive approach that does not single out one child's work as better than others can be achieved by asking such directed questions as "What is your favorite part of this painting?" "What shapes in Miyako's picture tell us about her boat ride?" "How did Joe make us feel the coldness of a snowy day in his picture?" "What shapes are repeated in Teruhisa's work, and how does this make us feel?"

Although displays of all the children's artwork should be ongoing throughout the year, paintings or drawings in which the child has placed much sincere effort should be attractively matted or mounted. This tells the child that he or she is important, and that his or her individual and unique achievements are respected and valued. A small label by the teacher may name and date the artwork and give an account of remarks made by the child when it was made. Art educators discourage showing personal preferences and comparing one child's work to another's, or using one child's work as an example for others to copy.

This does not mean, however, that a teacher should never choose one child's work for positive and directed comments that refer to the child's ingenuity, unique approaches and solutions, skillful use of materials, sensitive observations of things and events, empathy in the work, and so on. Such evaluative considerations are specific guideposts for young minds, opening the path for the child's artistic growth.

PROCESS AND PRODUCT: Reviewing and Reflecting

The questions that follow are helpful for small-group or class discussion after an art activity. Some questions review the working process to help children remember how they worked with materials and how they responded to the motivation as they worked. Other questions about the product itself help students reflect not only on how they arranged their compositions and used the elements and principles of art, but also on how they portrayed emotions and feelings and how they showed their imaginations.

Process

1. Can you use some new art words to tell about how you made your art?

2. Did you think about how you were going to draw or paint your idea before you started?

Following a discussion on depth and space, a kindergarten class first went outdoors to make preliminary sketches of landscapes and then returned to the classroom to lay out their final drawings. Here Jay begins to overlay colored tissue paper, selecting a variety of greens and other colors for his forest scene.

3. Did you try to imagine your idea on your paper before you started?

4. Did you take some careful looks at the real object (the horse, tree, person) that you were drawing and observe its edges, colors, textures, big and little shapes, and so on?

5. Did you act out any poses or movements so you understood them better?

6. Did you enjoy working with this medium?

7. Did you experiment and discover any new ways to work with your art material or tools?

8. Did you try to improve your skills in handling this medium?

9. Did you work hard and stay with the task longer than you usually do?

10. Did you stop working on your picture before you were finished and look at it to think about what you should do next?

11. Did you follow any step-by-step directions that were given?

12. Did you try to think of a new and different way to draw something that you have drawn before?

13. Did you try not to bother other students?

14. Did you cooperate in a give-and-take of ideas? (murals and group projects)

15. Did you clean up your work space and return materials to their storage places?

16. Would you like to repeat this art project?

A trip to a natural history museum motivated 5½-year-old Jeff to make this drawing of Native Americans. Notice the detail, including drums, campfires, and smoke. A child's experiences not only increase perceptual growth but stimulate memory and other cognitive powers.

17. Can you think of a different way you would draw this subject next time?

18. Do you know about a great artist who painted this same subject?

Product

1. Did you fill the paper with your picture, keeping in mind the size and shape of the paper, and let some objects touch the sides of the paper?

2. Did you make the figures or important shapes large enough for your idea?

3. Did you show the necessary action for the idea you were drawing?

4. Do you need to look more carefully or act out the motions or the pose yourself?

5. Is the idea you wanted to show clear and easy to see? Would this picture fit better on tall paper, larger paper, smaller paper?

6. Could you make the ground or sky more interesting in any way?

7. Did you show enough details to tell about your idea?

8. Did you include overlapping if it was necessary?

9. Did you make a focus or center of interest? How did you do this?

10. Did you use a variety of colors to give your picture the feeling you wanted?

11. Would you use the same colors next time?

b

a. A visit by a clown can provide strong motivation for subsequent drawing and painting activities.

b. Bold, black lines characterize this painting of a clown by a first-grade student.

a

12. Would using lighter or darker colors tell your idea better?

13. Did you use some large and some small shapes?

14. Does your composition seem balanced?

15. Did you use several patterns for variety or decorative purposes?

16. Did you show any contrasting things: colors, shapes, lines, sizes, textures?

17. Did you make several different kinds of lines: thick/thin, long/short, straight/curved, broken/continuous?

18. Did you make your negative spaces interesting?

19. Did you place distant objects higher up and make them smaller if you wanted to show deep space?

20. Do all the parts harmonize and give you a feeling of unity?

21. Did you make any of the parts of your picture (clay animal, puppet) in a new or different way?

22. If you could make this picture over again, what would you change?

23. Is the feeling or emotion that you were thinking about easy to see?

24. Would your idea have worked better if you had used a different medium?

Art has a body of knowledge, concepts, and skills. Art requires thoughtful effort, hard work, practice, and decision making. Art requires the child's best performances in the realms of understanding, thinking, feeling, perceiving, and expressing with precision and beauty. These do not happen by chance. Only through skillful teaching over the years can the very best performances in both art process and production be elicited from children.

Young children enjoy making their own books. Sonja, age six, used an autobiographical format to interweave real-life experiences with fantasy to create her book, *The Humongous, Hairy Monster.*

I found a telephone. Called 911.

Carlos is proud of his illustrated journal. His success at communication—both by word and picture—reinforces his positive attitude about himself and school.

TOPICS FOR DISCUSSION

1. What are the purposes of a motivation that precedes an art production?

2. What is the purpose of observation as it relates to the art experience?

An imaginative kindergartner comments on this drawing: "People are hanging in a dungeon. An elf is on top of the ladder, locking them up with a key. The girl doesn't know how to tie her shoes, and her dad (the big guy on the wall) won't do it for her. The elf's boss is at the bottom of the ladder."

3.   How does the child's verbal description assist perceptual awareness?

4.   Find reproductions of three works of art by different artists. The three works should all reflect a common subject or theme. Create sample questions like the ones in this chapter.

5.   Explore and list poems, stories, and objects that might be used as motivation for imaginative artwork.

6.   Apply the four aspects for evaluating children's art to an actual example of a child's artwork.

7.   At what point(s) of the art activity would encouraging remarks from the teacher be most appropriate and beneficial? Develop a list of possible encouraging remarks for each of these stages.

8.   Discuss the ways in which positive and directed comments about student artwork can eliminate feelings of competition.

9.   Develop two positive and directed comments for each of the four evaluation points described in this chapter.

10.   What are the characteristics of process and product? For each, develop additional questions for discussing a completed art activity.

NOTES

1.   Donald and Barbara Herberholz, *A Child's Pursuit of Art, 110 Motivations for Drawing, Painting, and Modeling* (Dubuque, Iowa: Brown & Benchmark Publishers).

2.   *Swassing-Barbe Learning Modality Index* (Columbus, Ohio: Zaner-Bioser Company, 612 North Park Street, 43215).

6

The Teacher as Facilitator

Although teachers vary in styles and techniques, each is responsible for involving a large number of children in a wide variety of learning activities. Teachers of all levels, including those in early childhood classrooms, are concerned with classroom management—organizing students and materials, planning the daily program, and establishing an environment conducive to learning. Meeting the needs of individual students while orchestrating the many strands of an educational program presents a challenge to all teachers, new and experienced, and at all levels, including those who work with children with exceptional talents or special needs. One of the teacher's primary goals is to motivate, encourage, and nurture the curiosity and enthusiasm that is characteristic of early childhood. Experiences in art provide motivation for young learners while challenging them to develop creative thought processes. Teachers must pay particular attention to developing strategies and organizing the time, space, and materials needed to provide an enriching environment.

THE TEACHER: A Key Person

The teacher is in charge of arranging and structuring children's experiences in producing and responding to artworks. As facilitator, the teacher must provide many avenues for students to develop their skills and refine their senses, which leads to concept formation and greater emotional awareness. Such arrangement and structure ensure the fullest development of each child's inherent and unique potential.

Research by Torrance indicates that a child's creativity peaks at the second-grade level and then tends to be stifled by demands and pressure to conform from curriculum, peers, and teachers.[1] Thus, a creative thinker is forced to adjust to the norm. Torrance also found that teachers tend to favor a child with a high IQ but low creativity. His study describes the creative child as one who seems to "play around" in school, who is engaged in manipulative and exploratory activities, who enjoys learning and fantasy, who is intuitive, imaginative, flexible, inventive, original, perceptive, and sensitive to problems. The creative student, Torrance believes, is often not identified as intellectually gifted.

Further evidence for the need for a supportive and stimulating early learning environment comes from research by the Goertzels.[2] They studied the lives of four hundred eminent people of this century and found that the childhood homes of almost all

Bright colors in *The Purple Robe* by Henri Matisse are enjoyed by kindergartners as they look at these small reproductions. If, in the discussion of artworks, children know that their comments and responses are accepted and valued, they are more likely to trust their perceptions and judgments.

"Circus" is the theme for opening day in this kindergarten class. Each month, this teacher totally transforms her classroom environment, using new and innovative ideas to capture the attention and to spark the imagination of her students.

these persons emphasized a love of learning and that a strong drive toward intellectual or creative achievement was present in one or both parents. A neutral and nondirective family attitude was practically nonexistent. Three out of five of these people had disliked school, but the teachers they liked the most had let them progress at their own pace, allowed them to work in one area of special interest, and had challenged them to think.

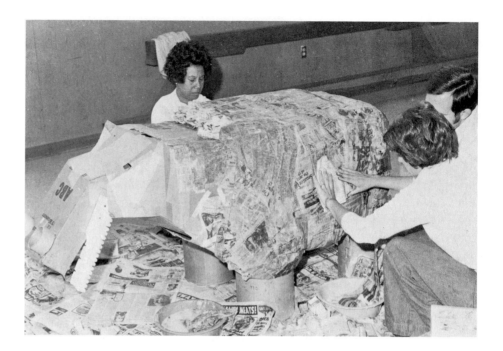

Early childhood teachers participate in an in-service class and learn how to cover boxes and cartons with wheat paste and newspapers to create life-sized animal forms.

The teacher is responsible for including in the plan for the year's program ample opportunities for children to make and respond to art—to use observation, memory, and imagination. The teacher is an important role model: If the teacher values children's originality and treasures the unique and sensitive responses that children make during encounters with art, the children will likewise place importance on these things. They will be more likely to resist stereotypes, to demonstrate flexibility, and to attain some measure of self-direction in producing art images with a variety of materials and in responding to many different kinds of art forms. If, in a discussion of artworks, children know that their comments and responses are accepted and valued, they are more likely to continue to engage in describing, analyzing, and interpreting strategies and to enjoy exploring their feelings and trusting their perceptions and judgments. The teacher must also arrange and plan for situations where children can reflect on, respond to, and discuss their own artworks as well as those of adult artists.

The teacher sets the stage for learning in the classroom as well as for the attitudes and tastes that the children are forming. The physical ambience of the room, with its exhibits, bulletin boards, and display corners, has an important visual impact. Items should be well chosen and displayed in such a way as to create an orderly, uncluttered, and warm and inviting atmosphere. Items displayed may be two- and three-dimensional objects from the natural world as well as artifacts of all kinds that are being used for art experiences and other areas of the curriculum. The extra time it takes to keep the room visually enhanced and appealing tells the children that the teacher values school and cares about each of the boys and girls.

A teacher's enthusiasm for learning can be contagious. By having a pleasant and positive attitude, the teacher can make the children feel relaxed and comfortable in the classroom situation. If a teacher shows excitement and curiosity about learning new things, the children follow suit. If the teacher encourages the children to work hard and to take pride in a job well done, the children begin forming work habits that will sustain them in later years. If teachers treasure and display beautiful things from the worlds of nature and art, children develop similar positive attitudes.

The students in this classroom integrate art and literature by creating shoe box dioramas of their favorite fairy tales.

THE TEACHER'S CONTACT WITH PARENTS

At the beginning of the school year, the teacher should find occasion to send a letter home to the parents or to meet with them in conference or back-to-school night and explain the goals and behaviors to be expected in the child's artistic growth. Visits to the school teach the parents the art program goals and how to help the child achieve them. Parents may be invited to serve as art aides.

Children's drawings and paintings need to be received by understanding and appreciative parents in order to reinforce the child's artistic development at school. Children will be acquiring an art vocabulary to discuss their own art and those of adult artists. It will be helpful and enriching if the home environment is supportive of these things and fosters a continuing dialogue. Following are suggestions and reminders to parents:

1. Art stimulates the imagination and makes the child think more inventively. Art provides a healthy, natural, and satisfying activity for the child now, and habits begun in early childhood can last and flourish throughout life. Children's artwork is an indication of their personality. Parents should respect their children's artwork and endeavor to see their children's point of view.

2. Originality and independence in art, rather than copying and imitative activities, should be praised. Encouraging children to be resourceful with materials develops the children's capacity to be inventive. The unique, the original, the novel solution to a problem, the unexpected, the humorous approach in expression—these qualities should be cherished and nourished. A parent's specific comments, rather than generalized ones, show the child that the parent has taken time to really look at the artwork and that it is valued. Coloring books and patterns tend to destroy children's abilities to think for themselves and to foster stereotyped and dependent responses. Comparing a child's work with that of a brother or sister also creates negative feelings and attitudes.

3. A place in the home that is supplied with art materials encourages the child to draw, model, construct, cut, and paint. A place to keep their collection of interesting objects sharpens children's visual and tactile sensitivities and nourishes their curiosity. Displaying children's artwork shows the family's interest, respect, and support.

Time, space, materials, and encouragement are the essential ingredients of a quality art experience for young children. Providing a safe environment where students are encouraged to experiment and to create should be a top priority for teachers in early childhood education. Jessica will be proud when her teacher pins her drawing on the bulletin board for the whole class to share.

4. When artwork is sent home from school, appropriate comments by the parents will build the child's self-esteem. A less than confident five-year-old told her teacher, "My mommy always says my art is wonderful—even the bad ones." Her teacher replied, "Let's look at some of your artwork and choose the ones you think are best to take home." As they collected the pieces, the teacher mentioned specific qualities in each of the chosen works and later told the child's parents of her accomplishments, both in using materials and in expressing her own ideas, so that the parents could look at their child's work and make specific comments rather than generalized ones.

5. Trips to galleries and museums establish a cultural habit that will endure throughout life. Small reproductions of favorite artworks are available in museum shops and can be hung in children's bedrooms. Trips to interesting places in the community give children experiences that will be reflected in their artwork.

6. Sharing books with children that have color reproductions of paintings, sculpture, and the like can be a rewarding experience for both parents and children. Children's books on artists make fine birthday gifts that are appreciated for years.

7. Special after-school and Saturday art classes are offered by universities, museums, and community programs. Children's participation should be encouraged.

TIME FOR ART: Regular and Frequent

State departments of education throughout the United States tend to recommend about one hundred minutes of time for art per week in the elementary classroom.[3] Preschool and kindergarten children need time for art every day. Often five or ten minutes is all the time required for these children to engage in drawing, modeling, cutting, or looking at and talking about a reproduction. As they grow older, children can work for longer

A classroom "art line" allows wet paintings or prints to hang safely out of the way while they dry.

periods of time. First graders should be expected to work twenty or thirty minutes on simple art tasks and longer periods on more complicated tasks that involve several steps. Kindergartners and first graders are ready to spend extended time periods working together on such art tasks as mural making and construction activities. In so doing, they learn to respect another's point of view and see their own production contribute to the whole. They also can begin to engage in longer discussions in which they compare several reproductions of artworks.

Art experiences with different media should be repeated to be educationally valuable because children gain more skills and insight with each experience. Teachers should keep a portfolio of each child's work, inserting dated drawings, paintings, cut-paper work, and so on that show progress, deviations, or regressions in the child's development. If the child has verbalized about or named an artwork, a notation can be attached to the drawing. Art is language for children, and this cataloging technique can reveal much about children's personalities and their perceptions and feelings about the world.

Since art production and art responding both involve alert and vigorous minds, teachers would do well to schedule art periods early in the day, when children's ability to attend and to remain on task is at a high level. Aesthetic sensitivity and media skills develop in the same way that skills in reading and mathematics progress—through frequent and regular scheduling.

ART MATERIALS: Suitable, Safe, and Varied

Small muscles in early childhood are developing motor control rapidly, and art materials that provide the child with experiences in cutting, joining, applying, brushing, twisting, forming, adding, squeezing, rolling, pressing, printing, taping, and drawing are basic. Materials and processes introduced and used in early childhood should require minimal assistance from the adult, while enabling children to gain feelings of confidence and competency on their own. Small children can learn to cut both paper and fabric if they are supplied with good scissors. Pens; soft-lead pencils; small-size crayons; marking pens; oil pastels; small, medium, and large stiff-bristle brushes; tempera paint; glue, glue sticks, and paste; tape; clay; salt ceramics; staples; blunt needles and yarn—all provide fertile soil in which the seeds of the young child's imagination can grow.

Young children's lack of mastery in handling materials may sometimes be due to the frequent introduction of new materials, which does not allow children time to gain skills and competency with any one material. This is not to say that variety in materials is not needed. After the initial exploratory and experimental period, children may find that a new material enables them to give form to a latent image. Children work with materials a number of times to learn which materials suit them best and what limitations and possibilities are characteristic of each.

Considerable attention has been given recently to toxicity and the potential hazards of using art materials incorrectly. Many states have enacted legislation that requires more thorough examination and certification of art materials used with children. During the child's period of maximum growth, when body metabolism is high, division and addition of cells in the body cause young children to be particularly susceptible to substances that may have little or no adverse effects on adults. For this reason, government and health agencies have conducted laboratory tests and developed standards to ensure that products are safe for classroom use.

Two nonprofit organizations that have a long history of testing and certifying products are the Art and Craft Materials Institute (ACMI) and the American Society for Testing Materials (ASTM). Manufacturers who meet the stringent requirements for certification developed by these two organizations are permitted to print safety seals on their product labels. These seals certify that the materials are not toxic and that they do not cause acute or chronic health problems. The first step in selecting art supplies and using them safely is to scan the product's label, looking for one of the safety seals shown. If the product is not labeled or if additional information seems necessary, the consumer can request a material safety data sheet from the manufacturer or supplier. Local chapters of such national health organizations as the American Lung Association are often able to provide additional information and resources.

Certain art products are prohibited for use with very young children but are acceptable if used by older students or adults. These materials are potentially hazardous unless precautions are taken to assure safe handling. High on the list of unsafe materials are products that contain certain solvents. A few solvents pose a particularly high risk and should be used with caution or not at all. According to Dr. David H. Garabrant from the University of Southern California School of Medicine, benzene and n-hexane, both solvents commonly used in rubber or paper cement, are particularly hazardous and should not be used in any art class under any circumstances.[4] Other products, such as spray fixative, contain solvents that are less harmful but should be used only when there is adequate ventilation and then only by adults. Dry products, such as powdered tempera or instant papier-mâché mix, should also be handled only by adults because the particles may become airborne; once in liquid form, these products are safe for student use.

Adults who work with young children in art activities must be informed about health and safety. Although there is no need to overreact, a few precautions and a sense of safety awareness will help teachers maintain a hazard-free environment for the students in their care.[5]

School stages and multipurpose rooms can provide large spaces needed for group art projects. Students here are making kites that will be flown and then displayed on the curtains backing the stage.

SPACE: The Classroom as Studio and Gallery

The self-contained classroom is one in which all children are in the same grade and the teacher is responsible for all the children's experiences. The school district is responsible for providing textbooks in art or other packaged, sequential programs for the classroom teacher, and for making available the services of an art consultant or resource person. Some districts provide a visiting art teacher. The open or nongraded classroom consists of a large number of children of several age groups, working at their own levels of accomplishment and regrouping for various subjects. Some schools have a special art room to which the children go at specified times during the week.

In preschool and kindergarten rooms, children may choose during activity periods to work in one of several spaces—one of which may be an art learning station as described in this chapter. At other times, art tasks may be structured with small groups or perhaps the entire class working together.

Easy access to and immediate availability of art materials are imperative to a good art program. When art supplies and work spaces are convenient and neatly organized, the teacher feels more relaxed and eager to provide a maximum number of art activities, and the children are more stimulated to innovate, experiment, and participate. Four kinds of space within the classroom should be considered:

1. Storage space for materials, tools, and supplies

2. Space for projects not completed

3. Space for displaying the children's finished work, both two- and three-dimensional

4. Space for displaying interesting art-related objects and reproductions

Access to paints and brushes is most convenient when they are stored in cabinets or on shelves near the sink. Several large cans are handy for storing brushes of various sizes. Brushes need to be cleaned before being put away and should be stored with bristles up. Storage of different sizes, colors, and kinds of paper should be on shelves or in drawers within reach of the small child. Shallow, plastic trays or dishpans with labels attached can

The traditional painting easel in the classroom (usually near a sink) promotes large paintings in the early years.

be used to store marking pens, chalk, oil pastels, crayons, colored pencils, scissors, glue sticks, and tape. Cardboard boxes, ice-cream cartons, or plastic dishpans can be labeled and filled with such materials as felt, fabric, yarn, feathers, and scrap materials.

In a classroom gallery, teachers need to display the work of the entire class or the work of small groups of children on a rotating basis that includes all children. When teachers only put up the "best" pictures, they are signifying a preference that might cause children to copy others or to become locked into repeating certain images to receive recognition. Children who are eager to please could easily become repetitious in their art expression. For children whose work is never selected, the message is clear, and they can become easily discouraged.

At some time during the year, after artwork has been collected in student portfolios, each child may select his or her favorite for an exhibit to be called Portfolio Favorites or Artists' Choices. This approach not only provides recognition but also involves students in a selection process. As an extension, students may name their works of art and tell why they selected a particular piece. Their comments can be written and included as part of the display.

There usually are opportunities for exhibiting student artwork outside the classroom. Prints, paintings, and drawings can be displayed in the principal's office or in the school office. Large art pieces show off best in such spaces as the auditorium or cafeteria. Libraries, airports, stores, and other public buildings frequently are interested in displaying children's art. Museums and galleries sometimes sponsor shows of student artwork, especially in March, which is National Youth Art Month. Classrooms, schools, or districts sometimes compile a collection of student drawings and creative writings for publication in a printed booklet. All such efforts to feature a child's work communicate value and respect.

Giant books are written and illustrated by students in this Palo Alto class. Displayed on easels around the room, the books are easily accessible to the kindergarten readers. Art can form an important connection for the young learner between mental images and the written word.

This bulletin board shows a math and art relationship in a hands-on experience. It was created by students at the Sacramento Country Day School.

IN MY WORLD

OF VINES

SONJA CALDWELL

"I've published three books," writes seven-year-old author Sonja Caldwell. Computers in the classroom facilitate her creative story writing. After her teacher has corrected the handwritten copy, Sonja enters her story into a computer. The cut and paste story is combined with original drawings to create the book.

ART LEARNING STATIONS

An art learning station is a small space that provides one or two students with a minienvironment for independent or semi-independent activity. With materials set up and visual or verbal instruction provided, children are able to work with minimal supervision, thereby gaining confidence in their ability to do things by themselves. Some children feel more comfortable and free to experiment, fantasize, and develop ideas and images in the quiet, private atmosphere that an art learning station provides. Learning stations also make it possible to organize and use materials that are too small, too few, or too awkward for an entire class of children to use at one time.

As in any art activity, the focus in an art learning station is on divergent and creative responses. At the same time, the child is learning to follow simple directions in producing a final product. The learning station is basically designed to reinforce or extend a skill or concept that has been introduced by the teacher. To function productively, an art learning station needs to meet the following requirements:

1. Be attractive and enticing, offering the child ways to explore, investigate, and manipulate

2. Have well-defined rules for its use, such as a limit on the number of students at the center at one time

3. Provide the supplies needed

4. Require few written directions for the primary child

Snowman Poem
There was a little snowman.
Who had a carrot nose.
Along came a bunny and
   What do you suppose?
The hungry little bunny.
Looking for his lunch
Ate that snowman's nose.
Nibble, nibble, crunch!

Simple directions, ample supplies, and a limit on the number of students using this learning station make it a comfortable space for independent activity.

5. Suggest several directions in which the student may work to develop, reinforce, or extend learning

6. Contain a wide variety of multilevel activities that can be adjusted to the needs and abilities of individual children

7. Have several ways of doing the activities, such as listening, reading, observing, manipulating

8. Include some self-correcting devices, such as color coding, matching numbers or shapes, or puzzle matching

9. Provide a place for finished and unfinished activities

10. Be changed at regular intervals to coincide with curriculum changes or student interests

Teachers must instruct students in the most effective use of an art learning station. As each new station is developed, the teacher should explain the new concept. Stations should be part of the daily program; they become an integral and effective part of curriculum planning as teachers recognize and utilize the variety of ways that learning can be reinforced.

A See and Touch art station may have natural objects and art objects for the children to investigate. The teacher can make up a game sheet on which numbered objects, such as a mounted owl, dried weeds, pressed flowers, the dried skull of an animal, feathers, butterflies, colored Indian corn, shells, or a bird's nest are described in such terms as rough and scratchy, crumbly, swirling, white, pointed, smooth, and so on, and the child must match the term with the object. This tactile station should sometimes have an arrangement of folk-art items, such as a pottery bird from Mexico, a puppet from India, a mask or a carved wooden lion from Africa, a piece of Eskimo soapstone sculpture, a Hopi Kachina, carded wool, brass bells, or stone beads. A magnifying glass provides an intriguing focus for visual perception.

Some particularly appropriate art production activities for learning centers include mixing colors with paint, lessons that reinforce basic clay techniques, working with templates, making potato prints, and so on. Sample activities dealing with great works of art

Color mixing using watercolor markers is the activity at this art learning station. This portable center is placed on desktops or tables for an art learning station session and is then stored easily when the teacher has scheduled activities that require a more traditional classroom arrangement.

include making a collage after seeing some of those created by Picasso or Braque, or making a painting of dots using cotton swabs after viewing works of the Impressionists. After the entire class has looked at portraits and self-portraits of great artists, two students can work at a learning station, each drawing the other's portrait; or students may use a mirror at the learning station and draw a self-portrait, further reinforcing the concepts introduced in the classroom setting.

Following are examples of art learning stations that lend themselves to self-contained areas of instruction and that assist the child in making an individualized response to an art motivation:

String Starters

Materials: String or yarn, scissors, glue, crayons, 9 × 12 inch paper
1. Glue a short piece of string to the paper.
2. What does the string make you think of? A jump rope? A fishing line? A clothesline? The tail of a fish? The back of a camel? The shoe of a giant?
3. Complete your picture with crayons.

Crayon Warming Tray

Materials: Warming tray, unwrapped wax crayons (soak in warm water to remove paper), paper, masking tape, mitt
1. Tape the paper to the edges of the tray.
2. Move the crayon slowly on the paper, letting the crayon melt as it moves. Press down hard.
3. Add more colors to cover the paper completely.
4. White, gold, or another color can be blended on top of a color.

Catalog Clips

Materials: Old catalog, scissors, glue stick or paste, 9 × 12 inch paper, crayons or markers
1. Cut out a face, shoes, pants, sweater, wheel, clock, or lamp from the catalog.
2. Paste it on the paper.
3. Draw the rest of your picture.

Grade-level art lessons are sequenced and color coded in this kit called "Creative Expressions." The art activities introduce vocabulary and concepts and can be used with an entire class or at learning stations.

Instructional Materials for Art Learning Stations

Teacher convenience is a primary consideration for the sequential art lessons presented in *Creative Expressions*.[6] Twenty art activities for each grade level are presented in color-coded folders. The standard-size folders easily fit in classroom file cabinets or portable file boxes. A blank on the front of each folder is for a student art example. The list of materials needed and simple directions are printed inside. Many illustrations make the directions easy to follow. Objectives, teacher hints and information, and evaluation questions are printed on the back of the folder, along with the art components to be emphasized in the lesson. Each grade level has sequential lessons in drawing, painting, printmaking, the elements of art, and three-dimensional experiences. Because extensions or additional activities are often listed in the teacher's section on the back of the folder, *Creative Expressions* is an excellent resource for setting up art learning stations to reinforce concepts, knowledge, and skills.

As Ralph Voight points out, the art learning station implies certain teacher characteristics or behaviors, an enlarged learning environment, greater learner independence, and revised physical arrangements in the classroom. He goes on to state that the learning center embodies the implementation of an idea that enables children to grow at their own rates, in their own styles, and to their uniquely personal potentials.[7]

TOPICS FOR DISCUSSION

1. Review the work conducted by the Goertzels and Paul Torrance. Describe the type of home and school environment that is most likely to encourage the creative student.

a

c

b

Set-ups for art learning stations provide space for intense, uninterrupted efforts for one or two children at a time.
a. "String Starters" aids divergent thinking.
b. Warming tray and crayons require student concentration while searching for image formation.
c. "Catalog Clips" sparks individual ideas for expression.

2. What are the advantages of maintaining an art portfolio for each child? How can these portfolios be used in conferences with parents? In evaluating student development as discussed in Chapter 5?

3. What messages are communicated to children when their artwork is attractively displayed at school and at home? How might a teacher display small groups of pictures so that all students feel involved?

4. What is the ideal length and frequency of art activities for young school-age children? How do you think this would vary from art schedules for preschool children?

5. Discuss variety versus mastery in the use of art materials. What would you consider a happy medium, and how would you determine this?

6. What are the advantages of learning stations? What would be a few of the reasons for having an art learning station in the classroom?

7. If you visited a classroom with many learning stations, what might you assume about the teacher and his or her expectations about learning?

8. How might thematic art activities be used in learning stations? Briefly outline the materials and processes needed for a theme that would interest a young child.

9. The See and Touch station described in the chapter would reinforce concepts about one of the elements of art—texture. Plan a learning station that would reinforce learning about two other elements.

10. If possible, interview a teacher who uses learning stations consistently, and discuss the advantages and disadvantages of learning stations as well as the scheduling and organization required for effective use.

NOTES

1. Robert F. Biehler, *Psychology Applied to Teaching* (Boston: Houghton Mifflin, 1971), 248.
2. Victor Goertzel and Mildred Goertzel, *Cradles of Eminence* (Boston: Little, Brown, 1962), 3–9.
3. Guy Hubbard, *Art in Action, Teacher's Manual* (Austin, Tex.: Holt, Rinehart & Winston, 1987), vii.
4. David H. Garabrant, "Art Hazards" (Paper prepared for a workshop cosponsored by the American Lung Association of Los Angeles County and the Santa Monica Unified School District, 1984).
5. Charles A. Qualley, *Safety in the Artroom* (Worcester, Mass.: Davis Publications, 1986).
6. Lee Hanson, *Creative Expressions* (Palo Alto, Calif.: Dale Seymour Publications, 1990).
7. Ralph Claude Voight, *Invitation to Learning: The Learning Center Handbook* (Washington, D.C.: Acropolis Books, 1973), 2.

7

Artistic Talent and Special Needs

●●●●●●●●●●●●●●●●●●●●●●●●●●●●●●●●●●●●●●●

When young children reveal developmental characteristics in their art products either earlier or later than would be expected, *or* when physical or mental disabilities interfere with artistic development, some adjustment in the art program is necessary so that these children will realize their fullest potential. If the art curriculum for early childhood has been formulated to provide a qualitative developmental sequence of lessons, it is fairly easy to ensure correct placement for those children who are progressing either more rapidly or more slowly through the general stages of growth. If art experiences are haphazard, of low quality, and not adequate to develop appropriate skills and knowledge at specific levels of development, then they have little to offer *any* child, let alone those with extraordinary talents, abilities, or special needs.

Very young children form mental images before they can form words. They enjoy capturing those mental images in art and are enthusiastic about sharing their unique artworks with others. It is the adult's responsibility to provide meaningful experiences that challenge the child's motor, perceptual, affective, cognitive, and aesthetic skills. In the case of high-ability or special-needs students, too often the early spark of enthusiasm dies because experiences are limited. If adults encourage coloring books, copying, and rigid, manipulative activities, children are not able to explore, discover, select, and communicate the rich visual imagery that is uniquely their own. Without supportive and nurturing environments for artistic growth, young children are unable to experience the satisfaction of accomplishment and the joy of personal expression. This is of particular importance when children feel isolated or "different," as high-ability students or students with special needs often do.

Quality art experiences can connect children to the real world as well as provide an opportunity for growth and communication through a personal language of nonverbal symbols. For the child of exceptional talents or of special needs, art becomes significantly important as a means of expression and as an avenue to understanding the thoughts, feelings, and perceptions of others. Although each of us is unique, we are more alike than different; art provides a common language, a means of connecting individuals to a larger community.

IDENTIFYING THE ARTISTICALLY TALENTED

Perhaps the single characteristic that most typifies the artistically talented student is rapid progression through the various stages of artistic development. When compared to other students their age, artistically talented students consistently demonstrate abilities at

Artistically talented students progress rapidly through the various stages of artistic development and display sophisticated perceptions at an early age. The two sets of drawings show "a person's face," "a person running," "a house," and "a television set." Set **a** is an example of the average expectations for a third grade student, whereas the drawings in set **b** show the advanced perceptions and skills of a talented third-grade artist.

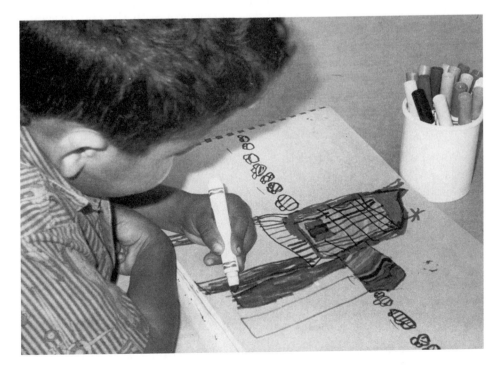

Ricardo completes a drawing of his home, which will be inserted in his "All About Me" booklet. As can be seen from his drawing, he has moved the objects in his drawing off the bottom edge of the paper and has developed a horizon line. His perception skills are well developed for a kindergarten student, and his art work is both detailed and elaborate. Ricardo is already recognized for his artistic ability by his teacher and classmates.

extraordinarily high levels. Adults familiar with the typical artwork of students at various grade levels frequently comment on the maturity or advanced ability of the exceptionally talented child.

The classroom teacher is sometimes the first adult to notice a student's unusual talents, although other students also are usually aware of the exceptional talent of a peer. As can be expected, however, identifying the exceptional and uniquely talented student is not an easy task unless there exists a basal art program for all students. There are no standardized tests for art ability, so the most reliable means of identification is by looking at the accumulated body of work created by a large group of children. If one becomes familiar with what is typical, the artwork of the exceptionally talented child becomes clearly evident.

In addition to advanced development in art production, highly talented students are very interested in art activities, take the activities seriously, and seem to find satisfaction in them. Frequently, talented students have accumulated a sizable amount of artwork, and they may spend a great deal of time and energy drawing (sometimes all over the pages of books, classwork, or any other available surface—much to the despair of teachers). Talented students display ease and dexterity in creating art products, and they frequently use visual representation to communicate their experiences, ideas, and deepest feelings.

CHALLENGING THE EXCEPTIONALLY TALENTED

The classroom teacher is usually also the first person to acknowledge a sense of inadequacy in providing challenging art experiences for talented children. Often the solution is to give the student paper and crayons and additional time for free drawing. While this is not harmful, neither is it stimulating nor does it help in developing the child's potential. The talented child needs some instruction in the use of new materials and moves rapidly beyond the manipulation of tools.

A conceptual approach to art experiences originates with an idea and requires that the student use materials merely as a means to solve a problem. Given encouragement, the talented student shows unusual and unique ideas and is highly fluent in generating a variety of solutions. When provided with an open-ended art problem to solve, talented students frequently exhibit widely divergent solutions and art products.

The teacher's role is to encourage, support, and challenge the talented student. Although this may appear to be an overwhelming task to an adult who perceives the child as "already knowing more than I do," the situation is similar to a coach who trains and challenges the world-class athlete. Maturity, experience, knowledge, and interest are the primary ingredients necessary to guide and support children with exceptional abilities and talents.

The talented young child is eager to participate in games or activities that have many solutions. *If* is a powerful word; teachers should develop long lists of "what if" and "what would things look like if . . ." questions, such as

1. What if cars were made of bricks?

2. What if it snowed on your birthday?

3. What if the sun were blue?

4. What if you had a monster for a pet?

5. What if people could walk on ceilings?

6. What if you lived in a circus?

7. What if you had a butterfly for a pet?

8. What if puppies grew on trees?

9. What would things look like if you could fly?

10. What would things look like if we were on another planet?

This drawing by Joel, age eight, demonstrates the advanced artistic development of an exceptionally talented student. The work of art, entitled "Scoot Over," shows a variety of imaginative characters riding in an elevator.

11. What would things look like if you were bigger than an elephant?

12. What would things look like if you planted magic seeds in your garden?

13. What would things look like if everyone walked on their hands?

14. What would things look like if we lived in houses made of candy?

15. What would things look like if people were taller than buildings?

Exploring the world of fantasy offers opportunities for talented young children to create personalized images that are both original and imaginative.

At times, talented students may repeat schemas, but with modifications, until they exhaust the theme and variation motif. Whatever the motivational topic, the talented student may try to incorporate his or her current set of images such as monsters, ballerinas, horses, cars, or outer space. Sometimes this occurs when students have received praise and recognition for specific pieces of artwork. It takes self-confidence for a child to take risks and to create original work. Eventually, the talented child will tire of the repetiveness or gain enough confidence to proceed to other images and ideas. Motivations (see Chapter 5) are essential in helping the talented child who is "stuck;" these motivations often help stimulate the original ideas and rich images that flow from the highly creative mind into the art products.

Exceptionally talented students are usually interested in other people's artwork—that of their peers and also of adults. Parents and teachers can enlarge the young child's experience by providing opportunities to see exhibitions of student art, to visit art galleries and museums, and to look at originals and art reproductions from a variety of

This series of drawings, by Emily at age six, shows a high degree of talent as indicated by the complexity and variations in figures overlapping, action, detail, and composition.

At times, talented students repeat a set of images—such as battle scenes—until they exhaust the subject. These drawings of tanks by one seven-year-old artist represent a series that lasted for a period of several months until he tired of the repetitiveness.

cultures, past and present. The combination of rich visual experiences and a supportive environment for creative exploration results in fluency, variety, and increased sophistication of imagery in the talented child's artwork.

THE CREATIVE ENVIRONMENT FOR EXCEPTIONAL TALENT

Just as there is an ideal environment for the growth and development of living things, there is an optimum environment in which children may best develop. Psychological safety and freedom are necessary if people are to behave creatively. All children, but especially those who exhibit high levels of artistic ability, have a need to experiment and seek out their own symbolic expression. According to E. Paul Torrance, a leading author in the field of creativity, children reveal their intimate imagining only if they feel loved and respected. This is the essence of what Torrance calls the creative relationship between a teacher and child.[1] For this reason, the classroom teacher is instrumental in developing the optimum environment for creative expression. With very young children, the teacher is a particularly strong influence and has the primary responsibility of providing a safe environment for exploration.

Artistically talented students are given the opportunity to work with professional artist Nancy Gordon in this Saturday morning class in Chula Vista, California. Providing opportunities to interact with professionals is one way to meet the needs of highly talented students.

When the significant adults in a child's life are highly critical and judgmental, when uncertainty is reinforced by disapproval, creative and original artwork diminishes. Limiting statements such as "dogs aren't green" or "don't be so messy" stifle originality. Students' self-confidence can also be undermined by constant exposure to art that utilizes patterns and prepared outlines. The message inherent in these activities is that the child is not able to create his or her own images, that the outcome must be predetermined by an adult.

Ann Wiseman states that parents and teachers hold the success of children in their tone of voice and generosity of understanding.[2] Children's creative potential is awakened by positive and honest acknowledgement of all artistic expression that shows sensitivity, uniqueness, and involvement. Encouragement and motivation form the basis of the environment that stimulates individuals to their highest potential.

OPPORTUNITIES FOR EXCEPTIONAL TALENT

Although all children need a creative environment for artistic expression, the highly talented student needs additional stimulation, opportunities that go beyond what is offered in the regular program. This can be partially provided by the classroom teacher. As a major influence in the child's life, the teacher need not be artistically talented but must be prepared to provide the open-ended art activities necessary to develop the student's abilities and to encourage discussions about the artwork of great artists. The exceptionally talented also need opportunities to interact with professional artists. The artist may be a visitor in the classroom or the student may visit the artist's studio. Either way, students can be impressed greatly by observing professionals at work.

Talented peers can also influence a student who shows a high degree of art ability. Students who are highly skilled, who have a great deal of natural talent, frequently feel alone. Interacting with peers of comparable talents not only alleviates the feeling of isolation but

Highly talented students need opportunities and recognition for their artwork. Kindergarten student Henry is shown here with his drawing of "people watching a parade" that was used by the California Art Education Association for a poster commemorating the state's Youth Art Month.

Two talented students discuss and compare their work as they experiment with clay, a new medium for them. Bringing students together so that they can interact and stimulate one another's creativity is one of the purposes of any program for highly talented students. Providing new materials also permits experimentation with techniques and ideas.

can stimulate ideas and a realistic sense of ability. For this reason, grouping students who are exceptionally talented can have positive results—in personal development as well as in artistic production.

A program designed to meet the needs of talented children should provide opportunities for students to work in one area in depth. Thus, a child who is interested in making pinch pots may be given the opportunity to create large ceramic animals or (with help from an adult) to experience the use of a potter's wheel. Another child might make a filmstrip by drawing a series of images on acetate, creating a pinhole camera, and developing contact prints. Many of these activities are beyond the scope of the regular classroom program, but after-school opportunities and Saturday morning classes can extend the range of the child's experience and compensate for the relatively limited challenge provided in the regular school program.

Acknowledging artwork that represents the highest degree of a child's potential is also a powerful influence on the child's development. When outlets and audiences are provided for the student's most creative work, when pieces of art are valued and exhibited, meaning is given in the real-life world. Even at a very young age, children are sensitive to the unspoken message communicated when their artwork is displayed for others to see. When value is given to their efforts, highly talented students respond with images that are richer and more elaborate and that consistently incorporate personal symbols depicting the enormous variety of experiences—both real and imagined—in these early years.

TALENTED *AND* GIFTED?

Several states have expanded their traditional programs for gifted students to include abilities other than intellectual or academic potential. One of these categories includes students who show exceptional talent in one or more of the visual or performing arts. What confuses some is the erroneous supposition that a talented child is also gifted in areas identified with high scores on IQ tests. While this may be the case, it need not be. Each individual is a blend of gifts and talents of varying degrees. A person with high mathematical aptitude is not necessarily someone with exceptional musical abilities. Students who demonstrate high creativity may or may not be successful academically. The child with extraordinary talent in art may or may not demonstrate equal levels of ability in other areas.

For many years, some states did not permit funds in gifted programs to be used for art books and materials. Art was not seen as being sufficiently academic to challenge the higher thinking skills of the intellectually gifted. Gradually, educators realized that the development of intellectual skills is fostered not only by convergent thinking but also by divergent activities that "extend awareness, rationality, and one's grasp of reality."[3] Quality art experiences extend and expand the mind of the gifted student. In some cases, the divergence inherent in problem-solving art activities provides an exceptional challenge to students who have been highly successful in providing the one right answer required in academic areas concentrating on convergent solutions. Introduction of art activities at a young age assists the gifted learner in acquiring the sophisticated skills needed for decision making and creative problem solving. Through early exploratory and manipulative experiences, the gifted learner develops concepts of investigating, selecting, planning, and evaluating—essential ingredients for the development of both cognitive and affective processes.

EVALUATING EXCEPTIONAL TALENT

Teachers are often concerned about evaluating the artwork of an exceptionally talented child. "What do I say when everything he does is better than anything I can do?" asked one teacher at a recent workshop. The use of process portfolio assessment (also known as authentic assessment or portfolio assessment) is particularly appropriate with highly talented children and can be modified even for very young students. It has the added advantage of individualizing assessment in classroom settings without singling out specific students.

Examples of drawings at ages seven, eight, nine, and ten show Victor's exceptional talent at various stages of his early artistic growth. Victor is self-taught and his work reveals his interest in exploring techniques and images. In addition to exceptional talent in art, Victor is one of those rare children who is also highly gifted in intellectual and academic abilities.

Assessment portfolios in art have two key characteristics: they measure a student's growth over a long period of time, and they involve students in the evaluation of their own development and artwork. This type of assessment is not oriented toward "best" product but is more concerned with process and growth.

A portfolio may contain everything the student has done (both complete and incomplete) over a semester or the school year. In one third grade classroom, the teacher has the entire class sketch five minutes every day, using actual objects arranged on desks. Two or three times a week, students write down ideas or observations about their art. A parent has built racks in the classroom to hold the children's art folders, so all student artwork is dated, collected, and placed in the folders along with their observations. At the end of the month, students reflect by recording their impressions through words and sketches, about their art—what they have learned and what they would do differently.

Many classroom teachers find portfolio storage unwieldy. Teachers with limited storage may choose one of two other approaches to assessment: portfolios with selected pieces (the teacher may make some selections but many are chosen by the student), or portfolios with assigned pieces (chronological samplings collected over a long period of time). In some classrooms, spiral-bound school notebooks become combination sketchbooks and journals. Whatever method is used, the portfolio always contains the student's own writing or dictated comments, recording thoughts on works that have been completed or are in process.

More than 100 elementary classroom teachers involved in the Visual Arts Portfolio Assessment Pilot Project in California reported on a variety of techniques for involving students in assessing their own work.[4] In one primary grade classroom, small groups of students (in rotation) selected pieces from their art folder to bring to the rug and discuss with their classmates. In another classroom, small groups of five or six students met with an adult for a monthly table talk. At first, they were asked to bring only the pieces they felt particularly pleased with; at a later session they brought artwork that showed something they had never done before. Another session focused on a series of pictures that were related to one another. Each meeting was led by an adult recorder (teacher, parent volunteer, aid) who presented discussion questions on charts and recorded the students' responses. Some possible categories and discussion questions for table talks follow:

Select the piece of artwork you like the best.
1. Why did you pick this piece?
2. What were you trying to accomplish?
3. What problems did you have while you were working on it?
4. Did anything happen that you hadn't planned?

Select a piece of artwork from last month and from this month.
1. How would you describe your artwork last month?
2. How would you describe your artwork this month?
3. Has your artwork changed? How?
4. What did you learn while you were making each?

Select a piece of artwork you thought was easy and one that was hard.
1. What was easy? What was hard?
2. Which one do you like better? Why?
3. What did you learn from the easy one?
4. What did you learn from doing the artwork that was hard?

As you can see, questions were limited, and meeting in small groups meant that the children all had an opportunity to discuss their work. Each student's response was jotted down (in phrases) and placed in his or her journal or attached to the artworks in the individual folios.

Involving talented students in process portfolio techniques is particularly helpful in developing awareness of their own abilities and achievements. The process portfolio provides a cumulative record of growth in perception as well as abilities in art production. At the same time, it provides both verbal and visual means to communicate ideas.

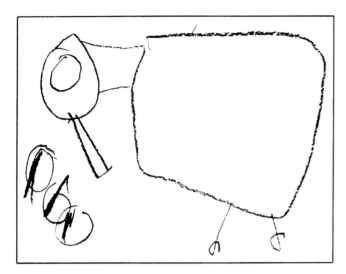

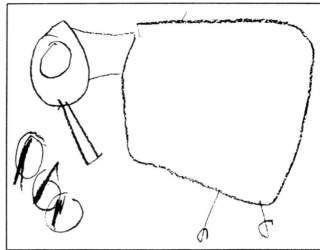

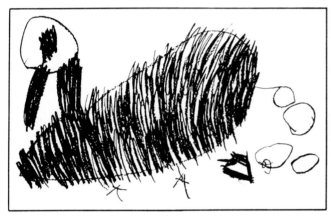

CHILDREN WITH DISABILITIES

Unlike highly talented students who advance rapidly through the various developmental stages, children with mental or physical disabilities have barriers that impede progression. School-age children with disabilities often encounter problems and frustrations in everyday life that other children never experience. Art activities can ease the frustrations of the disabled learner, provide a profoundly valuable form of emotional expression, and encourage improved muscular control, perceptual awareness, and a sense of personal achievement. As with all other children, the aesthetic experience for students with special needs should emphasize the development of the individual to his or her fullest potential. For this reason, if no other, the importance of art in the education of students with special needs cannot be overemphasized.

Federal legislation (Public Law 94–142) recently renamed the Individuals with Disabilities Education Act (IDEA), grants to the disabled child appropriate educational programs with particular emphasis on full inclusion. Part H of this legislation mandates early intervention services to infants and toddlers with disabilities.

This series of drawings of a bird and eggs was motivated by a nesting bird on the playground. The students, ages nine and ten, show remarkable awareness of their environment, despite limitations caused by their disabilities.

Drawing from the Ann Daly Center, Chula Vista, California

Enriching activities and a safe environment enable students to produce original artwork. Jimmy's drawing captures the popcorn experience enjoyed by his class.

The law also states that children with disabilities must be educated with nondisabled children to the extent possible. Ideally, the majority of students with disabilities would participate in the total school experience, while only children who are severely disabled would be placed in separate environments designed and staffed to meet their exceptional needs.

The Individualized Education Program (IEP) requires that persons most familiar with the disabled student's needs—as well as professionally qualified to select the most appropriate learning environment—meet to develop a plan for the individual child's education. The key element in the decision making focuses on placement where the child is most likely to experience success.

In most situations, disabled students are included in classrooms as often as possible so that they experience the social interaction that is a necessary part of every child's development. However, as art therapist Nancy Mayhew has pointed out, many children who are now integrated into regular classes for part of their day experience deep anxiety and are fearful of the reactions of others in their environment. These physical and mental barriers decrease these children's abilities to interact successfully with their environment, and cause social and emotional isolation. In working with these children, Mayhew has found that the art process performs a psychological service by promoting emotional and social growth, which, in turn, aids the learning process.[5] She sees art also benefiting four general areas of special importance for disabled children: language and communication skills, independent living skills, psychomotor development, and social-emotional growth.

Connie Dalke, a specialist in art, agrees with Mayhew's views and states that the combination of art and special education creates an exceptionally rich and effective learning environment. The fact that art experiences discourage copying actually promotes improved self-image. For example, children who are having visual perception problems are likely to have difficulty with reconstruction tasks such as handwriting or worksheets based on visual replication. In art, however, originality rather than copying correctly is rewarded. Therefore, concern about the correctness of the final product need not frustrate or hamper the potential creative urges of children with disabilities.[6]

Although Saul, age ten, is autistic and mentally disabled; he enjoys drawing and is willing to spend time and energy in creating detailed pictures. This drawing of his classmates is a unique statement about the world as he perceives it.

APPROPRIATE ART ACTIVITIES FOR SPECIAL EDUCATION

A discussion of appropriate creative activities for students in special education programs is difficult because the numerous types of disabilities offer a wide variety of potential obstacles to learning. However, the single factor that seems to be common to all disabilities is that most children who are physically or mentally challenged are identified as having difficulties in responding to outside stimuli. These difficulties often delay, distort, or limit development of the child's perceptual and expressive skills. Many students with disabilities can overcome these obstacles when introduced to creative activities that stimulate physical and mental abilities, increase awareness of the environment, and offer alternate ways of communication.

Using a Toy

A simple art activity for young students, one that can be adapted for use with children of differing disabilities, utilizes a favorite toy or stuffed animal. A beloved teddy bear, a toy truck, a tricycle, or a doll can offer unlimited possibilities for motivating sensory exploration and for stimulating perceptual awareness.

Media selected for this activity need to be suited to the individual child's abilities and limitations. Crayons may be awkward for children with severe physical disabilities because downward pressure is required, but colorful felt markers or sponges dipped in paints can provide flowing lines. Clay is a tactile medium that many children enjoy using. If students have difficulty kneading and manipulating it, however, the new synthetic modeling materials are much easier to control.

Before the actual art activity, children are encouraged to write letters or make up pictorial invitations asking their favorite toys to visit the classroom. When the toys and stuffed animals arrive, a number of activities are possible: Toys and children can participate in a parade to music; toys can be weighed and measured; the children can make a book of drawings, stories, and poems about their favorite toys. Some children might be willing to dictate stories to adults, to other children, or into tape recorders, and these stories can be a source of interest and entertainment for several days. After a drawing or painting experience in which the toys are used as models, the paintings and drawings as well as the actual toys can be exhibited. All these activities extend the art experience and make it more meaningful.

A bouquet of irises inspired a printmaking activity. After touching the leaves, stems, and flowers, visually impaired students used the edges of their hands and of cardboard strips to print irises. The use of tangible objects to motivate art activities is particularly successful in working with disabled students.

Using Themes

Thematic art activities are recommended for all students, but some subjects may be particularly suited to learners with special needs. Whereas some themes, such as "Clowns," "Umbrellas," "Shoes and Socks," "Pets," "Friends," "Playing," and "Families," might be appropriate for most children with mental or physical disabilities, other themes might not reflect the limited experiences of some children. The list that follows indicates some appropriate themes for use with young children in special education programs.

A is for Apple (letters)
Animal babies
Big bird, little bird
Birthday party
Blowing bubbles
Cars and buses
Clowns
Dinosaurs
Dogs, cats, hamsters
Families
Friends
Funny, fantastic faces
Games/people at play
Gardens, flowers, bugs
Happiness is . . .

Homes and houses
Jungle/jungle animals
Kites in the winds
Monsters and beasts
Parades
Parks and playgrounds
Popcorn's a-poppin'
Roots, stems, and leaves
Shadows
Shoes and socks
Things that fly
Tools I've used
Umbrellas in the rain
Z is for Zoo (animals)

Many other themes and topics will come to mind especially as they relate to activities involving the disabled learner. Participating in a parade, making popcorn, flying a kite, growing plants, holding an animal, blowing bubbles, having a clown visit the classroom, flying paper airplanes, taking a walk in the rain—all these experiences are enriching and both involve and intrigue children who vary widely in developmental levels.

Themes combined with looking and doing also provide opportunities to compare the many ways that artists have shown the same thing. Art reproductions that introduce subjects of interest to young children include Henri Matisse's *The Snail,* Marc Chagall's *The Flying Horse,* and Wayne Thiebaud's still life of ice-cream sundaes (called *Confections*). The boys playing in Winslow Homer's *Snap the Whip* and all the people in the snow in *Sugaring Off* by Grandma Moses make these two artworks popular. Artist Faith Ringgold has made a series of story quilts. One, *Tar Beach,* has a book written about it; after looking at art reproductions and seeing the book, children often enjoy making a paper quilt that tells a story. Teachers can combine artwork, themes, and activities by having the children wear crowns, discuss Georges Rouault's *The Old King,* and paint pictures of kings and queens. Young children, especially those with special needs, require the stimulation and enrichment found in an art developmental program that builds on personal experiences.

Preshaped Paper

Many art activities utilize paper cut in the shape of an object. Since precut paper defines the boundaries for students, it may be helpful for the visually impaired as well as for some students with learning or physical disabilities. However, shaped or precut paper should be used as a portion of an art activity that stimulates creative responses. For example, paper can be folded and cut in the general shape of a person. Students can then use colored markers, crayons, paints, or pieces of colored paper to show a Halloween costume on the front. Inside, they could do a self-portrait—the person behind the costume.

Another possibility is to cut paper to form a door that folds open. A second piece of paper is placed underneath and provides a surface for students to draw what they visualize when they open the door. If there is a goldfish bowl in the room, the teacher gives students paper cut in the shape of the bowl. Crayons or oil pastels are used to draw the goldfish, and a watercolor wash over the drawing results in a piece of artwork that not only records an actual experience but also has an expressive content. Preshaped paper can be used to enhance, rather than drain, an art activity of its potential for creative expression.

Chance Manipulation

Activities that enable the student to produce original work derived by chance manipulation of materials is another method frequently found to be successful when working with children with disabilities. Although these experiences fail to provide creative stimulation, they can be introduced periodically for variety and to promote increased awareness.

For example, a string dipped in black tempera paint and dragged across a piece of white paper provides the teacher with an opportunity to discuss such concepts as dark and light, lines and shapes, curved and straight. Spots of red, yellow, and blue paint (primary colors) can be painted on a piece of paper that is then folded along a midline and rubbed on the outside so that the paint inside smears and mingles. When opened, the accidental design is symmetrical, and some of the colors have mixed to produce new ones (secondary colors). These phenomena can be discussed and the mirror-image concept extended by holding a mirror up to an object so that half of it is mirrored or reflected in perfect symmetry.

The young child's awareness of his physical impairment is evident in this wire sculpture in which the left arm is shortened and bent. Art provides not only a creative outlet but also, sometimes, an emotional one for children with special needs.

"I am a Halloween ghost" was the theme for this shaped-paper lesson in a classroom for visually impaired students. The self-portrait drawing is revealed inside the folded-paper shape.

Process Rather Than Product

Some teachers of disabled children are tempted to provide activities that lead to more skillful-looking results. Dictated art presents little creative stimulation and does not provide the sense of fulfillment to be found in creating original art. Tracing, using patterns, and copying the work of others becomes manipulative busywork that fills the time but not the soul of the disabled child. Teachers concerned with the fundamental learning process and the needs of their students do not find satisfaction in methods of instruction that focus on the end product rather than on developing a child's abilities.

ADAPTIVE TOOLS AND AIDS

Myriads of adaptive tools are available for students with physical disabilities. Some, like double-handed scissors, are designed so that another child or adult can work the tool along with the disabled child. Many children with physical disabilities are able to squeeze objects, and spring scissors that automatically open. Although not labeled specifically for persons with physical disabilities, some commercial art materials are particularly appropriate: liquid gluesticks with sponge applicators, tempera-markers that apply paint by means of a slight squeeze on the self-dispensing bottle, and extra large crayons (over a half inch in diameter) or chunk crayons.

In addition, teachers have become very creative in finding ways to solve problems that might frustrate or limit the child with a physical disability. Rough-surfaced nonskid tape (the type found in hardware stores and used in bathtubs or on stairs to prevent slipping) can be cut and applied to pencils, crayons, markers, and paintbrushes to ensure a better grip. Velcro can be used in the same way and can be combined with gloves or mittens, if needed, to enable the child to grasp brushes and other art tools. Foam hair curlers can be slipped over brushes or pencils to help students with manual grasp difficulties. Stubby shaving brushes or sponge wedge brushes used for house painting also are worth trying as art tools.

Good organization is crucial in ensuring successful art projects for children with physical disabilities. Students who have difficulty picking crayons up from a flat surface appreciate having them in upright positions. The visually impaired child is often more secure using a large, shallow tray (often found in cafeterias) as a work surface. Water containers can be stabilized by setting them in the core of a roll of masking tape. Nonslip plastic sheeting is commercially available but is very expensive; nonskid tub strips may work just as well to stabilize materials on a slick surface.

In all cases, the adaptation of tools and materials to meet the needs of disabled children reduces frustration and increases the potential for success. With success comes a sense of accomplishment and heightened self-confidence.

MUSEUM VISITS FOR THE DISABLED CHILD

Young children with disabilities can enjoy a rich, visual world by viewing original art in galleries and museums. Many of the physical barriers that once existed in galleries and museums have been eliminated by the Americans with Disabilities Act of 1990. This legislation prohibits discrimination in the areas of public accommodations and services and states that disabled persons cannot be excluded from participation. Institutions like museums that receive federal funds must comply with regulations that ensure safe and convenient access. Wheelchair ramps have been installed, doors widened, and many other architectural features altered so that people with physical disabilities are able to move easily through public spaces. In addition, many museums have extended and adapted their programs so that children who are hearing or learning impaired can understand and interact with art. Some museums have a coordinator and docents whose primary responsibilities are assisting disabled visitors.

In preparing for a trip to the museum, teachers should use previsit activities in the classroom to inform young children about what they will experience. Art reproductions and improvisational techniques help students to experience an imaginary trip that introduces them to the purpose and function of a museum and also gives them a greater understanding of the art they will see.

Preparation for a museum visit also requires that the adult supervisors are thoroughly familiar with the physical accessibility of the building, the type of adaptive materials and equipment available, and the portions of the exhibitions that are most suitable for the young children participating in the visit. Some museums have lists of touchable

Creative art activities provide a means of expression while helping to improve muscular control and increase perception. Original drawing such as this one by Javier, age ten, demonstrates the potential that can be stimulated through art in special education classes.

art objects for visually impaired visitors. Special exhibitions or areas may be designated as touchable, and these are often of great interest to young children. If possible, a few postcards or small reproductions of artwork that the students see during their visit should be purchased. These can be used to motivate discussions about the art and the museum experience once the students have returned to the classroom. The postcards also can be attached to large pieces of paper and used as starters for a painting that shows the children viewing art during their museum visit. Pre- and postactivities reinforce the experience, increasing awareness and perceptual skills and forming a basis for appreciation.

INDIVIDUAL SUCCESSES

In a paper presented at an international conference, speaker Gay Chapman described many art activities that develop specific skills.[7] As Chapman pointed out, one of the great strengths of the art process is that the child with disabilities is able to set the learning pace and manipulate his or her own environment. This not only builds self-confidence but also leads to self-discovery. Art is one means of helping children with disabilites confront and adjust to the learning environment.

An innovative program in a Brooklyn school district integrates special education and gifted programs in Arts Partners classes. The students are combined into mixed groups that meet with a variety of artists over a ten-week period. Observers report that the gifted children learn spontaneity from the special education children, who express their ideas freely, unhampered by the need to find the one right answer. Both groups develop mutual appreciation and an understanding of individual differences as well as a sense of individual success.[8]

The art activities in the Arts Partners program illustrate that many methods and activities used in a regular art program are, to a large extent, also practical and effective when used with disabled children. Teachers introducing art activities to children with mental or physical disabilities may need to adapt some of the art experiences. However, it is essential that the abilities of the disabled child not be underestimated. In a set of six guidelines for teaching students with significant mental and physical disabilities, authors Blandy, Pancsofar, and Mockensturm point out that all students make a substantial contribution to the direction in which their art education proceeds.[9]

Teachers may find in working with disabled children that there is a need to simplify, repeat directions, demonstrate, provide cues, and divide the learning activity into manageable stages. Most of all, adults need to have the patience to step back and allow each student to experience his or her creative potential. The results, while possibly not highly representational, are the tangible products of a process that has involved decision making, problem solving, and the manipulation of the physical world so as to create unique and personal visual statements.

TOPICS FOR DISCUSSION

1. How may an art program be adjusted for children of exceptional talents or special needs? In what ways would meaningful experiences in art assist these children?

2. What are the characteristics of artistically talented children? What are some ways of identifying these children?

3. What type of program and experiences are best suited for talented students? What type of environment and what kind of opportunities are appropriate for children who are identified as gifted?

4. In your own words, describe the characteristics and purposes of the process portfolio and its appropriate use with highly talented students.

5. What are the benefits of appropriate art activities for children who are physically or mentally disabled? What would be the primary focus of these appropriate art activities?

6. Develop ten themes for art activities that could be added to the list on page 148 for use with young children in special education programs.

7. Locate and list sets of art reproductions that you think would be of particular interest to a group of young students with special needs. Develop appropriate questions to focus their attention and that would relate to their personal experiences.

8. What type of environment and what kind of art opportunities are appropriate for young children with physical or mental disabilities?

9. What problem is there in focusing on the end product rather than on the process in an art activity planned for children with special needs?

10. How have museums and other public places provided access to their programs so that children with physical disabilities can interact with art?

NOTES

1. E. Paul Torrance, *Creativity* (San Rafael, Calif.: Dimensions Publishers, 1969), 43.
2. Ann Wiseman, *Making Things: The Handbook of Creative Discovering* (Boston: Little, Brown, 1973), 3.
3. California State Department of Education, *Arts for the Gifted and Talented: Grades 1 through 6* (Sacramento, Calif.: California State Department of Education, 1981), vii.
4. California Art Eduction Association, *In the Process: A Visual Arts Portfolio Assessment Pilot Project,* (Carmichael, Calif.: 1991), 2.
5. Nancy Mayhew, "Expanding Horizons: The Practice of Art Therapy in a Special Education Setting" (Paper presented at the American Art Therapy Association's Ninth Annual Conference, Los Angeles, Calif., 1978), 5.
6. Connie Dalke, "There Are No Cows Here: Art and Special Education, Together at Last," *Art Education* 37 (November 1984): 6–9.
7. Gay Chapman, "Learning in a Friendly Environment: Art as an Instructor" (Paper presented at the Fifty-Fifth Annual International Convention of the Council for Exceptional Children, Atlanta, Ga., 1977), 3–4.
8. Kirsten Ives Haeny, "Learning Together Through the Arts," *Educational Leadership* 46 (March 1989): 34–36.
9. Doug Blandy, Ernest Pancsofar, and Tom Mockensturm, "Guidelines for Teaching Art to Children and Youth Experiencing Significant Mental/Physical Challenges," *Art Education* 41 (January 1988): 60–66.

Part 2

· · · · · · · · · · · · · ·

8

Drawing and Painting

● ●

Human beings have engaged in drawing activities since the first rock pictographs were made many thousands of years ago. Early people drew on cave walls and on clay pots. Egyptians used limestone tablets and sheets of papyrus. Artists in the Middle Ages drew on parchment made from goatskin or sheepskin.

Drawing is basic to art. Drawings can be valid works of art in themselves, or they can be used in planning other works of art. Drawings by the masters are treasured in museum collections. Many contemporary artists express themselves with sketches, figure and contour drawings, modeled renderings, and cartoons, using charcoal, chalk, pastels, Conte crayons (an exceptionally hard crayon, usually black, rust, or brown in color), pencils, markers, and pens and ink.

Throughout history, painting has been a mirror for our feelings and ideas about life. Artists, by recording the development of civilization all over the world, have left paintings that tell us about religion, national life, historic events, geography, and famous people.

THINKING EXTERNALLY

Many activities call on us to clarify and develop an idea with a sketch. Drawing and thinking are often an all-at-once phenomenon, making a graphic image an extension of the mental process and helping bring an idea into focus. Engineers, chemists, city planners, carpenters, surgeons, mechanics, and football coaches are but a few of the individuals who make useful and practical application of external thinking—that is, drawing.

Like other learned skills, drawing improves with practice. Many children and most adults believe that people are born knowing how to draw and that those who cannot draw instinctively never will learn. Some people probably do show a little more drawing aptitude in the beginning, but everyone's drawing skills increase with practice. Ten minutes of drawing every day results in improved drawing skills, and focusing on specific objects in the environment increases perception as well. People who do sit-ups every day get better at them; people who draw every day also improve.

Very young children approach drawing with great enthusiasm and spontaneity. Their marks are exciting to them. Directed observation is the key to refining their perception and heightening their awareness. Sometimes children and adults look superficially, without really seeing. Examination is fleeting and cursory while the individual merely names or identifies the object. By carefully examining lines, shapes, colors, dark and

Young children approach drawing with great enthusiasm and spontaneity. The more details they perceive, however, the more details they are likely to draw, and the more differentiated their visual configurations become.
"Matt's Circus," Matthew James, Grade Christian School, Medford, Oregon, Grade 3, age 8. Courtesy © 1991–92 Crayola® Dream Makers™

light areas, and textures, as well as relative proportions and sizes of figures and objects, children can develop their perceptions. The more details they perceive, the more details they are likely to draw and the more differentiated their visual images become.

DEVELOPING IMAGES

There are three ways to develop an image in drawing: from memory, from looking at objects in the real world, and from the imagination. Frequently, children are asked to draw or paint objects of which they have only dim memories, and the results are disappointing. When asked to draw a person or object that has greatly influenced a child's life, the results are usually more detailed and may show exaggeration that reveals some emotional significance to the young artist. A neighbor who is very frightening may appear large and menacing in the drawing, while the child's self-image is small and practically hidden. A friendly dog may appear to be all tongue, and a piano player may have dozens of fingers on each hand.

Drawing objects in the real world is one of the best ways to increase visual perception and discrimination. An adult can reinforce and direct children's observations of details. For example, a teacher may ask first-grade students to draw a leaf. Once the drawings are completed, the teacher can give each child several leaves and ask the children to rub each leaf between their fingers. Some leaves have smooth edges while others have serrated edges. Many leaves are different shades of green, and some are yellow, gold, or red. The children should look at each leaf's shape, veins, and stem. If asked to draw a leaf again, the children, because of their increased sensory interaction with their environment, will have greater awareness and be able to depict a leaf more realistically.

As children mature in the schematic stage of development, they need frequent opportunities to draw from direct observation. Visually interesting objects set close to small groups of students catch their interest and imagination. Interesting objects that have simple shapes and parts—toys of all sorts, fruits and vegetables, live pets, mounted birds and animals, costumed models dressed as a character in a favorite story—lend themselves to developing the habit of observing carefully while drawing. Teachers can call the students' attention to the contour lines, angles, and curves in the still life or figure, and help students compare relative sizes and proportions. Students can note the different textures, dark and light places, and colors before they begin to draw. More mature students can learn to use small paper viewfinders—a square of paper with a small rectangle cut from the center—to focus on the part of the object, figure, or landscape they are going to draw.

Although drawing real objects from direct observation increases perception and eye-hand coordination, sometimes an artist may want to go beyond reality to create images that do not exist in the real world. Artists may choose to exaggerate, distort, or use

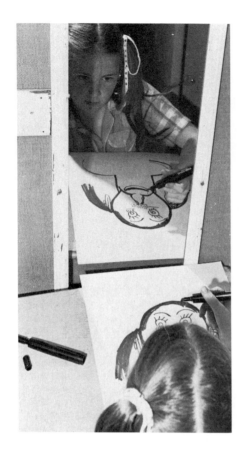

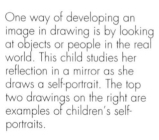

One way of developing an image in drawing is by looking at objects or people in the real world. This child studies her reflection in a mirror as she draws a self-portrait. The top two drawings on the right are examples of children's self-portraits.

Making a graphic image is an extension of the mental process and helps bring an idea into focus. This drawing by a six-year-old artist captures his impression of an eclipse.

Marking pens, crayons, and paints are now available in sets labeled "multicultural." These materials contain a variety of skin tone colors.

unreal colors to create a mood or feeling—for example, the bright yellow cow in Marc's painting in the Color Gallery. Children frequently follow the same course, either consciously or intuitively. Drawing from the imagination can result in delightful and highly original scenes, somewhat based on reality but that exist only in the child's mind.

WHEN CHILDREN DRAW

Children begin drawing very early in life when they first trace a finger through spilled oatmeal, move a stick on the surface of sand, or make a few crayon or chalk marks on a piece of paper. It is indeed exciting to discover that the kinetic activity of moving one's hand when it is holding a crayon can leave a mark on a paper.

To draw is to depict forms with lines; it is to pull or move a drawing instrument in a direction that causes the instrument to make marks. Young children can become more perceptive about visual details and more able to make distinctions and differentiations if they have drawing materials that encourage definite drawing activities. The best tools for children to use are markers, crayons, oil pastels, pens, chalk, and soft lead pencils. Most drawing instruments have small tips, and these almost always require a small piece of paper; conversely, thick chalk is an excellent medium for drawing large figures, animals, and houses on the sidewalk or on a large piece of paper.

Drawing plays an especially vital role in young children's artistic development because during early childhood children need to see very clearly the images and symbols that they are making and to feel that they have control of the material. If children work only with easel paint, they may experience some frustration and disappointment because the runny paint drips downward and smears easily into other colors. Children need drawing tools to make outlines and details; it is at this time that their perceptual explorations lead them toward finding and recording all sorts of things that are of fundamental importance in their development of concepts.

Crayons

Probably the most familiar medium for childhood art is the wax crayon, with its glowing vibrant colors. However, the waxy effect is not often realized when children only use it to make line drawings. They should be encouraged to bear down on the crayon, applying

A small piece of paper is taped to a warming tray, and a child creates a melted-crayon drawing by moving crayons slowly over the surface. The entire paper can be covered with crayons, or background areas can be brushed with india ink or watercolors.

sufficient pressure to achieve this medium's rich, waxy look. Having a thick pad of newspapers under the drawing paper is helpful; this surface is more conducive to crayon work than is the hard desk or tabletop.

Thick, round-topped crayons are often frustrating for small children to use. At a time when they are perceiving and refining visual forms and details, small crayons better suit their needs. A thick crayon in the hands of a five-year-old child is equivalent, in proportion, to a broomstick-size crayon in an adult's hand, making it difficult for the child to grasp and control its direction. Children find it much easier to draw small details such as fingernails, shoelaces, and teeth with slender crayons. These crayons tend to break more easily than thick ones, but children should never be made to feel intimidated and fearful about using them. The large crayon boxes provide a great assortment of colors, shades, tints, and dulled colors. Additionally, sets of multicultural crayons are now available that supply six different skin tone colors as well as black and white, which may be used for shading and highlighting.

First graders can be encouraged to explore different ways of using crayons and can be shown some of the rich possibilities that this medium provides. They may wish to draw their ideas lightly on white or manila paper with a yellow crayon, making changes and corrections as they desire, and then color in the areas solidly. Children should not use a pencil for a preliminary drawing when using crayons; with the pencil, they create small details that cannot be covered or colored with the blunt, softer tip of the wax crayon. Older children should be encouraged to imagine their entire drawing on the paper before they begin, thinking of background areas and spaces around the objects. Children may be reminded that repeating the same color, shape, or texture in several places will give their drawing unity, and that dark colors used next to light hues give the drawing contrast. Watercolor washes or diluted food color washes can be applied to white spaces left uncolored. This is called crayon resist, and will be discussed later in the chapter.

Accordion-pleated cardboard forms a holder for crayons or oil pastels so that they will not roll off the desk.

For hundreds of years artists have made images with melted colored wax, a method of painting called encaustic. In our century this medium has been used by several artists; Jasper Johns, for instance, used melted wax on crinkled newspapers stuck to canvas. For early childhood art classes, a warming tray used for serving food also can be used for making melted crayon drawings. Garage sales usually offer excellent buys on warming trays. The drawing paper should be taped to the tray so that the child does not need to hold it while drawing. Warming trays do not usually get hot enough to cause any burned fingers; however, the child may want to use a kitchen mitt to hold the paper in place. Two children can be at the warming tray at a time—one to observe and wait for the next turn and the other to work. Paper wrappings should be removed from crayons by soaking the crayons in warm water. Children can choose to draw directly on the paper, or they can make a drawing with a thick, black, marking pen and then add the color by pressing down firmly and moving the crayons slowly enough to allow for the flow-melting action that the heat causes. The results are rich and waxy. Colors can be placed next to each other and the entire surface of the paper covered. Two colors can be blended on top of one another. The use of white on top of a color makes the color lighter. Gold and silver crayons add exciting touches. If the entire surface of the white paper is not covered, watercolor or food color washes can be applied to the white areas.

Oil Pastels

Oil pastels offer a unique drawing experience for young children. Oil pastels are available in rich, glowing colors and are softer than wax crayons. They should be applied boldly, and children should press down hard enough to achieve the brilliant effect typical of this medium. Once again, a newspaper pad underneath the drawing paper provides a helpful cushion and makes it easier to apply the oil pastel strokes. Oil pastels are vibrant when applied to black or colored paper because, unlike crayons, they are opaque. They are somewhat like oil paints in that a lighter or darker color or white oil pastel can be applied on top of another color. Oil pastels are especially successful when used as a resist technique in which the child makes a drawing and then applies watercolors, a diluted food color wash, or india ink to the background areas.

Whereas drawing real objects increases perception, sometimes an artist may want to go beyond reality to create images that exist only in imagination.

"Dark Land," Tyson Schwarz, Westview Elementary School, North Vancouver, BC, Grade 2, age 7. Courtesy © 1991–92 Crayola® Dream Makers™

Markers

Washable markers, or marking pens, come in black and a wide range of light, regular, and bright colors. If the child holds the pen somewhat upright, a narrow line is made. If the marker is held at an angle, the child can make a broad mark. These broad marks may be placed side by side to fill in a large shape or area in the child's drawing. Children often use a black marker to make a line drawing and then add color either with colored markers or with some other drawing medium; crayons may be used in the traditional manner or with a warming tray as described above. Oil pastels with their rich vibrant tones and colored chalk with its soft fuzzy colors may also be used in combination with black markers.

Colored Chalk

Large areas of white, black, or colored paper can be covered easily with colored chalk. Young children respond readily to chalk's bright, vibrant tones. Chalk tends to be dusty and smudgy and can sometimes be frustrating for very young children to handle; the dipping suggestions that follow will facilitate and enhance its use. Also, chalk is not a safe material to use since the dust is considered harmful for young lungs. Both dipping methods described dry quickly, and the colors do not readily dust or rub off the finished pictures. Teachers need to use colored chalk that is designated for use on paper, not chalkboards. Colored chalk also is available in very thick sticks for children to use in drawing on sidewalks. Groups of children may choose to draw a street of houses, dinosaurs, giants, or so on on large outdoor expanses of cement.

Dipping Chalk in Starch

Colored chalk should first be dipped quickly in and out of water and drained on a paper towel. The tip of the chalk should then be dipped in liquid starch that has been poured into a jar lid or small container. The chalk can then be used to rub firmly on white or

This kindergartner enjoys seeing vibrant tones of starch-dipped chalk on her house/figure picture.

A second grader, inspired by a visit to a California mission church, drew a bride and groom in front of one on black paper, using colored chalk dipped in starch.

a

b

a and **b.** City buildings were drawn and colored with chalk/starch colors after much visual analysis of real and photographed city scenes.

c. Colored chalk dipped in white tempera makes dramatically toned marks on black paper.

c

colored paper. The tip of the chalk should be redipped in the starch as needed to keep the chalk marking and flowing in a smooth, velvety manner that almost looks like tempera paint. The colors lighten as they dry and will not rub or smudge as dry chalk does. The youngest children may want to draw directly onto the paper with the starch-dipped chalk, but first and second graders and older children may prefer drawing their ideas first with a piece of dry chalk or perhaps a thick, black marking pen and then applying the colors.

Dipping Chalk in White Tempera

The tip of the colored chalk should be dipped into about a tablespoon of thick, white tempera paint poured in a jar lid or small container. The children can practice making a variety of short marks—short, straight strokes; short, curving strokes; zigzags; little spirals and circles; up and down strokes—on a small piece of black or dark-colored paper. The marks they make should show the distinct color of the chalk, edged with white tempera, against the dark paper. The children should not scrub with the tempera-dipped chalk unless they want to create a mixed, blurry tint.

Resist Techniques

The basis for resist techniques is the incompatibility of two materials. The waxiness or oiliness of wax crayons or oil pastels applied to a surface resists the watercolor, food color, or india ink wash that is applied later.

Clear Wax Resist

An introductory experience in wax resist can utilize paraffin or white or yellow crayons to make a secret drawing for a classmate. Students make a coded message using clear or white marks on white paper or yellow marks on yellow paper. Once the drawings are completed, students can exchange them and brush on a coat of watercolor or thinned tempera paint. The drawing appears almost magically as contrasting colors of paint are applied.

Crayon Resist

Subsequent wax resist activities can involve the students in drawing with many colors of crayon and applying thin paint over the entire surface. Holiday themes lend themselves to this technique; a drawing of a haunted house becomes even more effective when a coat of black or dark blue paint is applied. Blue and green washes of paint over an underwater scene reinforce the illusion of the sea, and heavily patterned crayon designs increase in boldness and impact when paint is applied afterward. Children need to apply the crayon heavily; otherwise, the paint will cover the crayon drawing. The teacher must point out that it is the wax from the crayon that keeps the water and paint from coloring the paper. If there is not enough crayon, if the waxy surface is too thin and sparse, the paint soaks into the paper and hides the crayon marks. Several layers of newspaper or a piece of window screening beneath the paper help with the heavy application of crayon or wax. Oil pastels are more easily applied, and tempera, watercolors, or india ink applied as a last step make a particularly effective background for the finished artwork.

Tempera Resist

With the tempera resist technique, thick, creamy, tempera paint is used to make a picture on colored construction paper. When the paint is thoroughly dry, a coating of india ink is brushed over the entire surface of the picture. The ink blackens the area where the paper is exposed, but the painted lines and spaces prevent the ink from soaking into the paper. Temporarily, the ink blackens the outer surface of dried paint, and the original painting seems to disappear.

After the india ink is thoroughly dry, the entire artwork is gently washed with water. A cookie sheet or some other flat surface should be placed under the paper to act as a support and to prevent tearing. As the water soaks into the dried tempera, the paint partially dissolves, lifting away much of the pigment as well as most of the ink that dried on the painted surfaces. The result is an interesting, textured design, with the colors of the paper and paints combined in an antiqued effect against solid black.

A simplified version of this process uses only white paint or very light tints of colors on colored construction paper. The effect is bold and striking and is particularly suited for portraits of people, tropical fish, and birds.

A variation of the tempera resist technique begins with the students painting colorful pictures. Contrasting colors of crayon are then applied over each area of the dried painting. A wet sponge is applied to the surface until the underlying tempera paints begin to flake off. The result is a mottled, textural picture in which the residual crayon accents the seemingly weathered tempera tones that remain.

Designs created in glue provide a foundation for a multimedia work of art. Once dry, the white glue becomes transparent and forms a raised surface that adds interest to the drawing.

Drawing with Glue

A thick line of glue oozing from a spout and flowing onto paper has great appeal to children and provides an interesting challenge for them. In this activity, children draw lightly with a pencil first, until their pictures or designs are pleasing to them, and then trace over their lines with glue, holding the bottle upside down and gently squeezing so that the glue trails directly from the tip. A large, thick, primary pencil is probably best for the initial drawing because it discourages small details that may be difficult to draw with glue. Making a free-form design with glue directly on the paper is also an acceptable approach to this lesson.

White glue applied to black paper appears transparent when it is dry, thus creating raised black lines on black paper. Colored chalk may be applied to the areas within the shapes that the glue lines have made, using a fingertip to push the chalk into the spaces next to the lines. The chalk has a muted quality because the black paper dulls the colors. If the glue line drawing has been made on white paper, oil pastels, watercolors or diluted tempera paints can be used to complete the work.

A variation when drawing with glue is to add black india ink to the glue bottle. Three parts glue to one part ink is a good proportion. When used to make lines on white or colored paper, the glue stands out black and bold. Art reproductions of works by Rouault, Pollock, Klee, Calder, or Miró as well as examples of stained glass help students develop appreciation for the use of black lines in art and introduces them to the styles of several well-known artists.

Drawing with Sand

After making a drawing with a glue bottle, children can add colored sand while the glue is wet. Sand can be easily colored by adding water to dampen it, putting in a few drops of food coloring, shaking or stirring to blend the color, and then putting the sand on a flat surface to dry. The drying procedure can be speeded up by placing the sand in a warm oven. Once sand has been sprinkled over the wet glue lines, the design should be set aside until the glue has dried. Excess sand can be removed by tipping and shaking the design

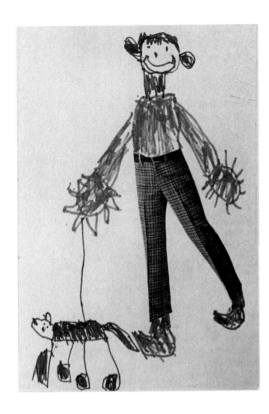

A pair of pants was the glued-on starter for a five-year-old boy's drawing of himself walking his dog.

over newspaper, and can be returned to the container for reuse. Soap powder, salt, or rice can be used in place of sand. This activity introduces texture in an artwork. Students should be encouraged to rub their fingers gently over their drawings and feel the lines and shapes with their eyes closed. The concept can be extended by having the students compare their sand drawings, which have actual texture that can be felt, to pictures in magazines, which contain visual texture that can be seen but not felt.

Idea Starters for Drawings

Most young children produce drawings frequently and with fluency, but a few children show little interest in drawing, probably due to a lack of confidence in their ability. All youngsters respond with enthusiasm to idea starters. This art task gives children a specific focal point and directs their thinking to the innovative possibilities upon which they may elaborate, enrich, and deviate from their schemas. The basic concept of idea starters is to paste one item to a piece of drawing paper and use that object as a visual point of departure in creating a picture.

Catalog Clips: Faces and Clothing

Faces or an item of clothing, such as a sweater, pants, shoes, or hat, that have been clipped from a magazine or catalog are especially conducive to developing the child's concept of the human figure. The teacher or the child should use a glue stick to attach the cutout to a piece of drawing paper. The subsequent discussion should deal with what the person is doing: running down a hill, walking a dog, playing ball, skiing, pulling a wagon, sweeping a floor, jumping rope, or painting a building. The motivation should then lead the child to think about where the figure might be—on the street, in a garden, at the zoo, on a mountain—and who else might be with the person. Next, the child uses crayons, pencils, markers, or oil pastels to complete the drawing.

Short pieces of yarn were shaped by one five-year-old child into swings for a group of performers. Others used the pieces for the roof of a house and for ocean waves near a lighthouse.

Pieces of Yarn

Each child is given a short length of yarn to place on a piece of paper in a curve, circle, zigzag, line, angle, and so on. The motivational discussion should cause children to wonder what the yarn suggests to them. Could it be the string of a kite? A fishing pole held by a man in a boat? The outline of an elephant's back? The top of a building? A clown's head? The peak of a mountain? A jump rope? The antennae of a butterfly? The children glue the yarn to the paper and complete their picture with drawing materials.

Seeds

Each child should have a paper with four or five flat beans or large seeds glued on it. The motivation focuses on roots, stems, and parts of plants. The teacher can bring in several flowers or weeds that have been pulled up so that the children can examine them closely and touch the roots, stem, leaves, flowers, and seed pods. The class talks about how the shapes of leaves and plants differ and about all the different colors of flowers. The children are then ready to design their own imaginary plants, drawing the roots below the ground, growing down from the glued-on seeds, and the stems, leaves, flowers, and seed pods growing upward above the ground from the seeds.

Flags

Small paper flags mounted on short wooden sticks can be purchased in craft stores. They are brightly colored and come in assorted designs. Class discussion should focus on where the children have seen flags flying and who carries flags. One child should demonstrate how a real flag is held—how the elbow is bent—and how the flag flies high above the head. The children can discuss where they have seen flags: on buildings, on boats, on flagpoles, at fairs, and carried by horseback riders in parades. Each flag should be glued to a piece of drawing paper and then the children can draw a picture with a flag in it, adding appropriate figures and environmental details.

Flags glued to drawing paper suggested soldiers to one kindergarten child and racing cars to another.

Children's Photographs

In the mural "There Was an Old Woman" shown in the photograph on the next page, first-grade children were given actual photographs, about 4 inches high, of their own faces. These photographs were cut out and glued to a 12 × 18 inch piece of drawing paper. Using markers and scraps of colored paper and fabric, the children drew or cut shapes of the rest of their bodies and clothing. The completed figures were cut from the drawing paper and assembled on a bulletin board, which in this case was covered with a piece of yellow felt. Several children painted and cut out a shoe house, a few flowers, and the title. Not only did the children's figure concepts become more detailed and elaborate, but the boys and girls also experienced a new awareness of drawing a person's body because their own faces were serving as the focal points. By grouping the finished figures around a central item and using a unifying theme, the whole group of children enjoyed working together on a class art project.

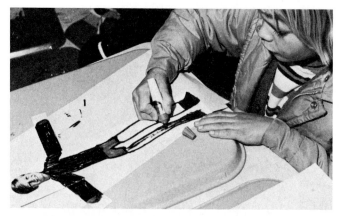

a

a. Photographs of heads clipped from a catalog were glued to twelve-inch strips of lightweight poster board, and shorter strips were added for arms. The children drew the bodies and clothing with felt pens.

b. Each child in the first grade had a photograph of his or her own face and was highly motivated to draw himself or herself in this assembled mural.

b

Related mural topics for a group of children to create—using either their own portraits or heads clipped from catalogs and magazines as idea starters—include

1. A castle filled with kings and queens

2. An office building where many people work

3. A super rocket with space travelers in compartments

4. An ocean liner with many tourists in the cabins

5. People walking through the jungle on trails

6. Children getting on the school bus

7. Children playing games on the playground

In all these topics, each child draws a figure and some of the environment that is needed for the completed mural. Each item is individually drawn and cut out, and then all of the parts are assembled on the background. For a permanent mural, the parts can be glued in place. Pins should be used if the children wish to disassemble the mural later and retain their individual work.

Opportunities for students to draw from direct observation should be numerous and frequent. Contour drawing, with model or object close to student-artist, emphasizes keeping one's eyes on the model or object while the pen is moving. Students may glance at the paper to reposition their pen. Students make a slow, continuous line, with their eyes on the model or object, and pretend that a sleepy ant is crawling along the edge of the image that they are drawing and that their pen is pushing it along.

WHEN CHILDREN PAINT WITH TEMPERA

Painting should play a constant and integral part of early childhood art programs. Tempera is the most functional and popular paint for young children to use. It should be purchased in liquid form in plastic containers with squeeze tops so that it may be easily dispensed. The squeeze top is convenient and also is economical in that only the amount to be used needs to be squeezed out at one time—usually about a spoonful of each color onto paper plates. If tempera paints are too thick, they can be thinned by stirring in a little water; however, tempera is opaque and should have a creamy consistency—too much water makes it transparent and runny. Paper for painting activities should be heavy enough so that it does not tear when it becomes wet with paint. Although long-handled brushes are the most common, short-handled stiff bristle brushes are easier for young artists to use. Flat and round stiff-bristle brushes in small, medium, and large sizes should be plentiful, because the exclusive use of big, wide brushes encourages the students to smear and stroke paint rather than make images and paint sensitive forms and details.

Children should each have a clean, moist sponge or paper towel for wiping their brushes clean between colors. This eliminates the necessity of water cans, which might spill and which need changing when dirty. Also, if a water-soaked brush is dipped into tempera, the water dilutes the tempera and makes it too thin and transparent; therefore it needs to be wiped dry with the sponge or paper towel before it is immersed in another color. Children should wear an old shirt worn backwards or a vinyl apron to protect clothing. A large plastic garbage bag with a hole cut for the child's head and two holes cut for the arms makes an excellent slip-on protective smock. Brushes should be washed in warm, sudsy water and rinsed at the end of the painting period and then stored, bristles up, in a large can or laid flat in a plastic container.

Tempera is also available in two other forms: tempera cakes or blocks, and tempera marker sets. The cakes are in a plastic palette, similar to water color trays, but the blocks are much larger and are opaque. The child uses a wet brush to stroke back and forth across the cake until the brush is loaded with paint. Colors may be mixed by taking the brush to another cake and loading it with a small amount of that color. Cleanup is accomplished by rinsing the cakes with a clean wet brush and wiping them with a paper towel,

Diagonal features and horizontal stripes create a sense of movement and emotion in this expressive portrait by a second-grade student.

or by holding the tray briefly under the faucet. Tempera cakes are extremely convenient for classroom use. Tempera markers come in sets of six colors in small unbreakable plastic containers. The specially designed tip allows small children to squeeze the bottle, holding it upright, and make large thick marks directly on the paper.

Teachers should set up many painting experiences to enhance the various approaches children may take. For instance, giving the children colored paper to paint on enables them to see new relationships between colors and the unifying effect of the background. Premixing colors occasionally for the children encourages them to try mixing colors themselves. Pastels, blended tones, grayed colors, gold, silver, magenta, peach, and lime are not frequently used colors, and their introduction arouses children's interest and causes them to think of new subject matter for picture making. Children should have opportunities to paint on both large and small paper. All sizes of brushes should be available so that the children can select those that best suit their needs. Some children may feel threatened and overpowered by large, blank sheets of paper or find themselves unable to manage, delineate, and control the wide strokes that a large brush forces them to make. Older children profit from having a piece of scrap paper handy to try out brush strokes, brush sizes, and color mixing. With the teacher's guidance, students can work together in planning, sketching, and executing a mural on a large piece of paper, with each child painting several items individually.

One of the most important design elements for the child is color because it incorporates and reflects both the cognitive and affective domains in the child's artistic growth. Children live in a world of color. They see it in flowers, in clothing, in cars, in rain puddles on oil-slick streets, in animals' fur and birds' feathers, in sunsets, in paintings, and in people's eyes and

Pour spouts on commercial paints and a cardboard carton that once held bottles of tonic water form a unit that is easily carried and distributed to students.

A serious look at a commercially produced color wheel can help children to understand primary and secondary colors.

hair. Color can make us feel happy or sad, warm or cool, and the colors children use in their paintings and drawings often reflect these qualities. We usually associate a color with familiar things, and as very young children begin to paint and draw, they slowly develop this color-object relationship. Fire is red and yellow, so these colors are thought of as warm. Sky and water are green, violet, and blue, and these are usually considered cool colors. Children like to have favorite colors, and they usually choose bright, intense hues. If children compare the green leaves of the budding willow tree with the green leaves of the oak, if they look at the blue summer sky mirrored in a lake and the blue-gray sky above city buildings, they develop a more refined awareness of color's delicate or intense tonal differences.

Color wheels may be purchased, or the students can make them. Children can draw around a paper plate and then use the curved edge of the plate as a guide to draw three

Easels attached to a fence form a convenient paint area that is both accessible to the classroom and easy to clean up. Paolo works on his multicolored painting of house and landscape in this Palo Alto schoolyard.

arcs, creating six sections in the circle. They apply the primary colors—red, yellow, and blue—to three of the sections and mix two primary colors at a time to make the three secondary colors—orange, green, purple—for painting the three remaining sections. These "beach balls" or "balloons" can then be cut out and mounted in a bright display on the bulletin board.

Children may choose two opposite colors on the color wheel to create a painting, adding black or white to each color for tints and shades, or mixing the two colors in varying amounts to achieve dulled tones. If given the complementary pair of colors red and green, the child might choose to paint an elephant in a green jungle with red blossoms on the trees. If given the complementary pair of colors blue and orange, the child might paint a mouse eating orange cheese off a blue plate. Only warm colors may be selected for painting a picture, or the child may use only cool colors. An entire painting based on a monochromatic color scheme can be made by using only one color and black and white.

Most preschools and kindergartens have several easels available for ongoing painting activities. Easels are convenient for children. However, because the paper hangs vertically on the easel, thin and watery paint tends to drip and run down. Children need to learn to put the brush back in the same color to avoid getting the brush or the paint supply muddy and also to wipe each side of the brush on the inside edge of the paint container to avoid dripping and having excess paint on the brush.

In addition to ongoing easel-painting opportunities, tabletop painting activities that focus more definitively on skill building can be set up and structured by making use of newspaper-covered desks and tables or even floor space. Small groups of children, perhaps

At age six, Jessica's paintings are colorful, bold, and detailed. This self-portrait was completed at the classroom easel after discussing and looking at reproductions of self-portraits by master artists.

two or three, should have a disposable palette, such as a paper plate, holding several spoonfuls of thick tempera paint. They also need another paper plate to use for mixing two or more colors together. (It is recommended that children use magenta, turquoise, and yellow to mix secondary colors as these colors, in tempera, create truer secondary colors.)

Painting Skills Expected of Young Children

After very young children have had a number of initial exploratory experiences with one or two colors of paint, they can learn how to handle brushes and paint. They should begin to know and demonstrate proficiency in

1. Using their fingers and not the fist to hold the brush, and holding the brush close to the ferrule

2. Using the tip and side of the brush, making thick and thin lines and strokes, and avoiding scrubbing with the brush

Even very young children are able to display their understanding of the components of various types of paintings. After discussing and looking at reproductions of landscapes, this kindergarten child clearly shows an understanding of the concept in this watercolor painting.

Many painting experiences and follow-up discussions on aesthetic concepts increase children's skills and self-judgment for future productions. This large mural was painted by second- and third-grade children for the Bryant Elementary School Library in San Francisco.

These two boys are using tempera tubes rather than brushes to paint their peek-through figure. Note the whimsical muscles on the figure's arms.

3. Using a large, flat brush for large areas and smaller, narrow brushes for details and for painting close to another painted area

4. Using chalk, occasionally, for preliminary sketching before applying paint

5. Painting large areas first and preventing smearing by letting a color dry on the paper before applying details either on top of the painted area or close to it

6. Mixing colors on their disposable paper plate palettes: adding a little bit of a color to white to make a tint; adding a little bit of black to a color to make a shade; mixing a little of the color's complement to a color to dull it

7. Wiping the brush clean on moist sponges or paper towels before using it for another color

8. Completing a painting by covering the entire surface of the paper with paint, giving consideration to composition, adding patterns, small details, and so on

9. Washing brushes in warm, sudsy water when finished and storing them in a designated container; cleaning up work area

Painting Peek-Through Figures

Appeal to children's sense of humor, and you have a ready-to-go motivation for painting the human figure. Cardboard panels with cutout peepholes for faces stimulate children's sense of the dramatic and illusory. Not only do the children delight in this comical art task, but they expand and enrich their cognitive awareness of the human form.

This project utilizes large pieces of corrugated cardboard, often discarded after mattresses and refrigerators have been shipped in them. A single, narrow panel is sufficient for one figure whereas a longer panel works well for a living mural. Small ovals just the size of a child's face should be cut very close to the top so that children can peep through them. Two smaller holes cut on both sides, either halfway up or near the top, can serve as

A girl uses a small brush to paint background near her figure's hair.

Some panels may have a half circle cut along the top edge, where the child may place his or her chin instead of looking through the oval-shaped hole.

openings for the children's hands. Placing hand holes up high requires children to extend the figure's arms up or bend its elbows to reach the opening. Children may wish to paint a flower or some object near the opening for the hand to pretend to hold as it projects through the opening.

The panels should be placed flat on the floor or on several tabletops while the children sketch their figures. Chalk enables children to draw freely without fear of making a mistake, because they may quickly rub off any area they wish to change. Chalk is closely related to brush strokes, and children are able to use it to draw details and decorative elements that are easily transposed to paint. The children should be reminded to paint the large areas first, using a large, flat brush. Smaller areas, edges, and details should be painted with a smaller, stiff, flat brush. Paint should be dry before a color is placed next to it or a detail painted on top of it. The children enjoy painting the background on the panel and adding suitable environmental details.

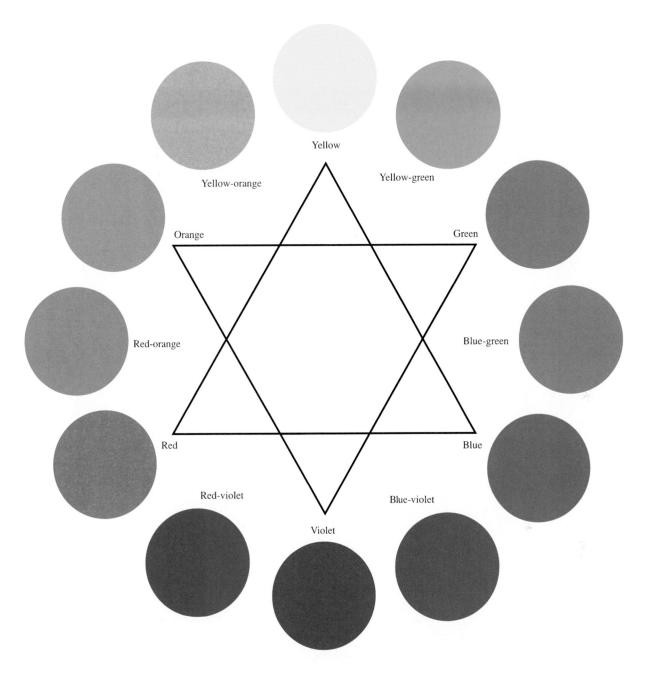

Plate 1 The Color Wheel

Plate 2 Frida Kahlo, *Fulang-Chang and Me,* 1937. Two-part ensemble (assembled after 1939). Part one: 1937, oil on composition board, 15¾ ×11 in. (40 × 27.9 cm.); painted mirror frame (added after 1939), 22¼ × 17⅜ × 1¾ in. (56.5 × 43.1 × 4.4 cm.). Part two: (after 1939) mirror with painted mirror frame, 25¼ × 19⅛ × 1¾ in. (64.1 × 48.3 × 4.4 cm.), including frame.

Collection, The Museum of Modern Art, New York. Mary Sklar Bequest.

Plate 3 Edgar Degas, *The Millinery Shop*, 1879–1884. Oil on canvas, 39 × 43½ in. (100 × 110.7 cm.).

Mr. and Mrs. Lewis L. Coburn Memorial Collection, 1933. 428. Photograph © The Art Institute of Chicago. All rights reserved.

Plate 4 André Derain, *London Bridge*, 1906. Oil on canvas, 26 × 39 in. (66 × 99.1 cm.).

The Museum of Modern Art, New York, Gift of Mr. and Mrs. Charles Zakok.

Plate 5 Mary Cassatt, *The Bath*, 1891–1892. Oil on canvas, 39½ × 26 in. (100.3 × 66 cm.).
Robert A. Waller Fund, 1910.2. Photograph © The Art Institute of Chicago. All rights reserved.

Plate 6 Li An-zhong, *Shrike and Bamboo*, Sung Dynasty, circa 1110. Colors and ink on silk, ht. 10 in. (25.4 cm.).

National Palace Museum, Taipei, Taiwan, Republic of China.

Plate 7 Marc Chagall, *Green Violinist*, 1923–1924. Oil on canvas, 78 × 42¾ in. (198.1 × 108.6 cm.).

Solomon R. Guggenheim Museum, Gift of Solomon R. Guggenheim, 1937. Photo: David Heald. (#37.466)/© Solomon R. Guggenheim Foundation, New York. © ARS, New York/ADAGP, Paris.

Plate 8 Simon Tookoome, *I Am Always Thinking about Animals*, 1973. Stonecut and stencil, 21½ × 30¾ in. (54.5 × 78.6 cm.).
Art Gallery of Ontario, Toronto. Gift of the Klamer family, 1978. Acc. no. 78/538. Photograph by Carlo Catenazzi.

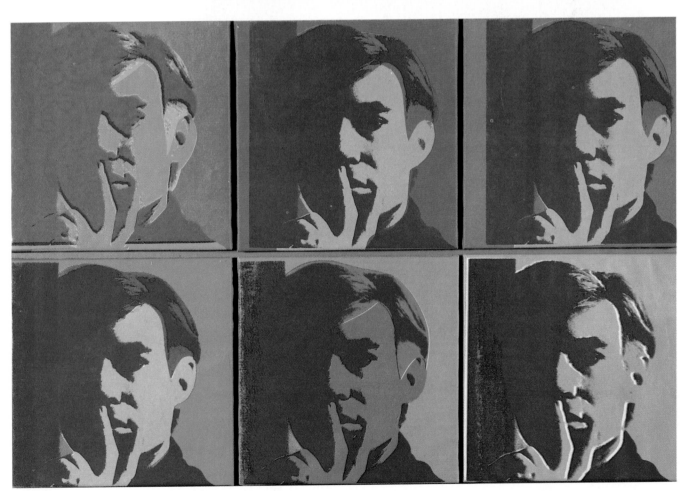

Plate 9 Andy Warhol, *A Set of Six Self-Portraits*, 1967. Oil and silk screen on canvas, each 22½ × 22½ in. (57.2 × 57.2 cm.).
San Francisco Museum of Modern Art, Gift of Michael D. Abrams. (no. 78. 196 A–F)

Realism

Plate 10 Grant Wood, *American Gothic*, 1930. Oil on beaverboard, 29¾ × 24¾ in. (76 × 63.3 cm.).

Friends of American Art Collection, 1930.934. Photograph © The Art Institute of Chicago. All rights reserved.

Plate 11 Piet Mondrian, *Composition, II,* 1929 (original date partly obliterated; mistakenly repainted '1925' by Mondrian when he restored the painting in 1942). Oil on canvas, 15⅞ × 12⅝ in. (40.3 × 32.1 cm.).

The Museum of Modern Art, New York, Gift of Philip Johnson.

Plate 12 Georges Seurat, *A Sunday on La Grande Jatte*, 1884–1886. Oil on canvas, 81½ × 121 in. (207.6 × 308 cm.).

Helen Birch Bartlett Memorial Collection, 1926.224. Photograph © The Art Institute of Chicago. All rights reserved.

Plate 13 Jacob Lawrence, *Cabinet Makers*, 1946. Gouache with pencil underdrawing on paper, 21¾ × 30 in. (55.2 × 76.2 cm.).

The Hirshhorn Museum and Sculpture Garden, Smithsonian Institution. Gift of Joseph H. Hirshhorn, 1966. Photo by Lee Stalsworth. © Jacob Lawrence.

Plate 14 Vasily Kandinsky,
Painting No. 198, 1914.
Oil on canvas, 64 × 36¼ in.
(162.6 × 92.1 cm.).

The Museum of Modern Art, New York,
Mrs. Simon Guggenheim Fund.

Plate 15 Henry Moore,
Reclining Figure, 1939. Carved
elm, 37 × 79 × 30 in. (94 ×
200.7 × 76.2 cm.).
The Detroit Institute of Arts, Gift of the
Dexter M. Ferry, Jr., Trustee Corporation.

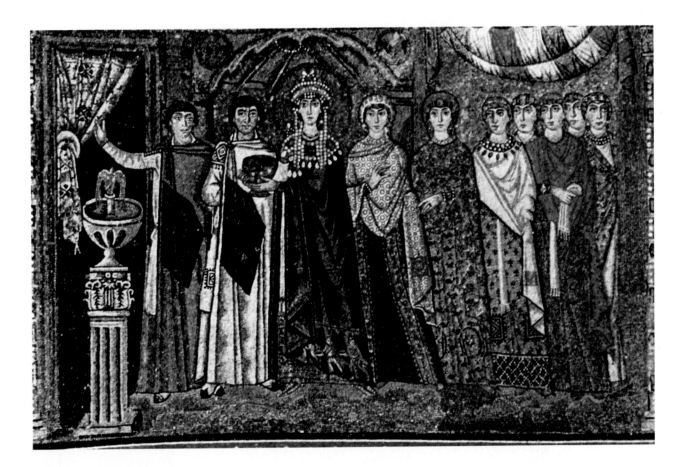

Plate 16 *Empress Theodora
and Retinue*, circa 547. Mosaic,
San Vitale, Ravenna.
American Archives of World Art, Inc.

Plate 17 Pablo Picasso, *Family of Saltimbanques*, 1905. Oil on canvas, 83¾ × 90⅜ in. (212.7 × 229.6 cm.).

National Gallery of Art, Washington, D.C. Chester Dale Collection, 1963.10.190. © ARS, New York/SPADEM, Paris.

Plate 18 Pablo Picasso, *Still Life*, 1918. Oil on canvas, 51¼ × 38¼ in. (97.2 × 130.2 cm.).

Chester Dale Collection, 1963.10.195. National Gallery of Art, Washington, D.C. © ARS, New York/SPADEM, Paris.

Plate 19 Vincent van Gogh, *The Bedroom*, 1888. Oil on canvas, 29 × 36 in. (73.6 × 92.3 cm.).

Helen Birch Bartlett Memorial Collection. 1926. 417. Photograph © The Art Institute of Chicago. All rights reserved.

Plate 20 Rufino Tamayo, *Animals*, 1941. Oil on canvas, 30⅛ × 40 in. (76.2 × 101.6 cm.).

The Museum of Modern Art, New York. Inter-American Fund.

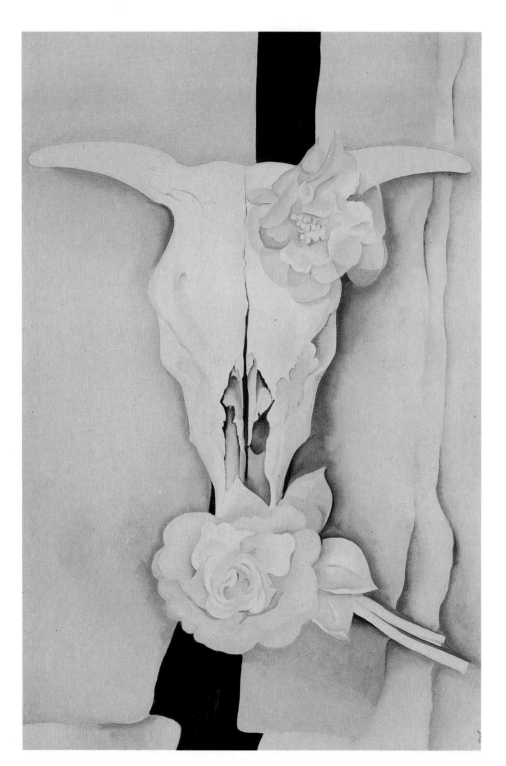

Plate 21 Georgia O'Keeffe, *Cow's Skull with Calico Roses*, 1932. Oil on canvas, 35¾ × 24 in. (91.2 × 61 cm.).

Gift of Georgia O'Keeffe, 1947.712. Photograph © The Art Institute of Chicago. All rights reserved. © Georgia O'Keeffe Foundation/ARS, New York.

Plate 22 Amedeo Modigliani, *Head of a Woman*, 1910– 1911. Limestone, 25¾ × 7½ × 9¾ in. (65.4 × 19 × 24.8 cm.).

National Gallery of Art, Washington, D.C. Chester Dale Collection.

Plate 23 Signed: work of Khemkaran, *Prince Riding an Elephant,* Mughal, period of Akbar, 1556–1605. Leaf from an album, gouache on paper.

Metropolitan Museum of Art, New York. Rogers Fund, 1925.68.4.

Plate 24 Henri Matisse, *The Wild Poppies* (center panel), 1953. Charcoal and gouache on paper, 31½ × 134⅝ in. (80 × 342 cm.).

The Detroit Institute of Arts, Founders Society Purchase, Robert H. Tannahill Foundation Fund, Friends of Modern Art Fund; Gift of Mrs. Allan Tannahill. © Succession H. Matisse/ARS, New York.

Plate 25 Franz Marc, *Yellow Cow*, 1911. Oil on canvas, 55⅜ × 74½ in. (140.5 × 189.2 cm.).

Solomon R. Guggenheim Museum, New York. Photo: Carmelo Guadagno. © Solomon R. Guggenheim Foundation (49.1210).

For an imaginative extension of peek-through figures, the children can use horizontal and vertical panels with cutout holes for animal paintings. The silly appeal of having one's face growling from a lion's body or perched atop a giraffe's neck irresistibly invites even the most timid young painter to become involved.

TOPICS FOR DRAWING AND PAINTING

How to provide situations that help children break through stereotyped expression and move on to less rigid and more sensitive realms is a challenge for teachers. Appropriate and stimulating motivations keep children's thinking dynamic, their schemas enriched, and their imagery varied and flexible. As described in Chapter 5, motivations open the door for a wide range of expressive topics for drawing and painting activities. Introducing topics that call on actual or imagined experiences encourages language development and enlivens the art lesson. These may be based on the child's experiences or may tap into imaginative and fantasy ideas. The topics used may spring from other areas in the curriculum such as science, social studies, literature, music, and so on. A live animal or a classmate dressed in an improvised costume and using a few props can ignite children's imagination and increase visual awareness. A vest, hat, umbrella, cane, cape, fan, bouquet of flowers, basket, doll, beads and jewelry, or cardboard crown are all possible ideas for costumes and props. When children draw or paint a subject that is similar to one painted by a great artist, they can better appreciate the variety of ways in which different artists depict the same subject matter. In this way, there is a natural flow from actual art production to art heritage and art appreciation.

Subjects that appeal to young children include

1. The animal I want for a pet
2. A caterpillar
3. Playing in the park
4. Trucks, trains, and planes
5. Forest friends; jungle beasts
6. Carousels and roller coasters
7. Walking in the rain: boots and umbrellas
8. My family, my home
9. Dressed up for Halloween
10. A trip to . . .
11. Birds, butterflies, fish
12. Clowns
13. Dancing the Hokey Pokey
14. Breaking the piñata
15. Flying Japanese kites
16. My favorite fairy tale
17. The scarecrow

A "from above" theme stimulates children to imagine themselves looking down from a hot air balloon and to paint the landscape, mixing colors for fields, rivers, trees, houses, and fences.

Introducing topics or themes enlivens the art lesson and helps children understand how great artists have depicted similar subject matter.

"Fish in the Sea," Anne Gabel, Huntley Project Elementary School, Worden, Montana, Grade 2, age 7. Courtesy © 1991–92 Crayola® Dream Makers™

a

b

a and b. Vigorous drawings of a train and a truck by five-year-old children are aesthetically adapted to long, narrow paper.

c and d. Tall apartment buildings and tall rockets were painted by kindergartners.

c

d

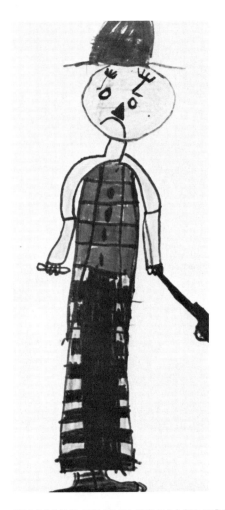

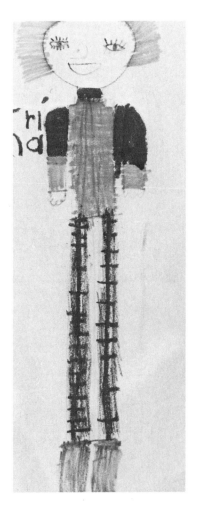

Drawing tall giants requires children to stretch their concept of the human figure to fit a long, narrow piece of paper.

CHANGING THE FORMAT FOR DRAWING AND PAINTING

Paper that departs from the usual 12 × 18 inch size challenges the child to make new visual configurations. If crayons, markers, or pencils are used, the paper should be fairly small: 6 × 9 inches, 6 × 6 inches, 9 × 3 inches. Either drawing media or painting materials may be used with larger pieces of paper. Several of the artworks in the Color Gallery have different compositional formats, within which artists made shapes that work harmoniously. The teacher may suggest topics that are adaptable to a particular shape of paper. Included here are some subjects that match unusual paper shapes.

Tall Paper

High-rise building with people looking out the windows, church with steeple, clowns on a ladder, tree full of squirrels, girl on a tree swing, castle tower and a princess, Jake the giant, spaceship with an astronaut, very tall man/woman with boots, umbrella, and hat, giraffe or ostrich, acrobats on a unicycle, raccoons climbing a tree, person on stilts, tall bird.

Long, Wide Paper

Inside a submarine, long train, bus full of people, boys and girls painting a fence, racehorses, dancers on a stage, chickens on a fence, alligator, the most beautiful caterpillar in the world, candy-making machine, floating on water, things that crawl, camel caravan, storefronts and houses on a street, playing tug-of-war.

Round paper from a dentist's office was used for these circular representations by kindergarten children.

Life-sized paintings greeted visitors to this kindergarten class. Here students display two of the self-portraits that filled the classroom for an open house. Perception and art skills are both developed when students are asked to search out and paint objects and people from the real world around them.

182

Round Paper

Children playing The Farmer in the Dell, swimming in a pool, fishing in a round lake, children playing jacks or marbles, butterfly, flying carpet, magic wheel, clown's face, mother cat nursing kittens, my friend the sun, coiled snake, circus ring, pond full of ducks.

Square Paper

Eating at a picnic table, inside a magic box or radio, mechanical snail, face of a growling lion, grasshopper or ant, sitting in a chair, bird in a cage, bug on a big flower, comet or shooting star, very fat clown, looking down on a city block, baseball game.

IN CONCLUSION

A successful drawing or painting lesson can be identified by the number of different interpretations of the assignment. Each child should have his or her unique set of mental images and experiences to bring to the activity, and this should be reflected in the diversity of the artwork. Another criterion in establishing the value of a drawing or painting lesson is how each child feels about his or her work of art and about himself or herself as a creative person.

While enjoying the physical sensations of painting or drawing, a very young child may not make an effort to create an image that looks realistic. Even when children have started to develop pictures of objects in their environment, they do not necessarily draw objects the way the objects look to adults; nor are the colors realistic. The art of young children has a distinct character and is dominated by the vision of the world as they feel it and understand it to be. Adults who are not familiar with young children's art frequently ask, on seeing a child's work, "What is it?" This question implies that art must look like something and that the child has failed in some way, when it is quite possible that the child was happily experimenting with lines or color or a material. Pictures reflect children's perceptions of important things in their world. In any case, the question "What is it?" creates a barrier between the child/artist and the adult/critic.

TOPICS FOR DISCUSSION

1. What is directed observation, and what are the expected outcomes of using this technique?

2. How would an adult reinforce and direct a child's observations without causing the child to feel inadequate? Give examples.

3. What role does drawing play in a young child's artistic development?

4. Review the three sources of image development, and use them in discussing possible sources of images in the Color Gallery.

5. Select one of the techniques described in the drawing or painting sections of this chapter. How would you explain or demonstrate it for young children?

6. Select a child's drawing or painting in this book. Focus on the four aspects of evaluation discussed in Chapter 5 and develop comments to use in evaluating the artwork.

7. What themes or topics lend themselves to using one of the resist techniques? In what way?

8. What are some factors that should be considered before, during, and after a drawing or painting activity?

9. Plan and discuss an experience for young children that would utilize premixed paint to reinforce a specific color concept.

10. What are the criteria for determining a successful art experience?

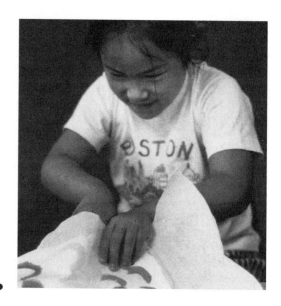

9

Cutting, Tearing, and Pasting

●●●●●●●●●●●●●●●●●●●●●●●●●●●●●●●●●●●●●●

Cutting, tearing, and pasting are difficult tasks for the very young to master, and children take tremendous enjoyment in developing these skills. Boys and girls who develop cutting, tearing, and pasting skills early in their lives will continue to enjoy creating with paper. Children who are in the scribbling stage will not cut or tear recognizable objects; rather, they are content to experiment and cut and tear for the sake of manipulating the material. This is good practice and should be encouraged. At first, these young children don't necessarily want to paste down what they have cut or torn. For them, it is enough to cut or tear little pieces of paper and arrange them on the tabletop. For these very young children, cutting and tearing paper helps develop motor skills in conjunction with visual perception. Gradually, after being involved in the playful approach of making random shapes, they gain some control, and are able to cut or tear the shapes they wish to make. This learning process may be impeded or harmed by asking children to cut out shapes that have been drawn by an adult.

By the time children are four or five years, cutting, tearing, and pasting become one activity, and a table with supplies may be set up in the classroom. A variety of materials should be placed at this center: at times colored paper may be available, at other times tissue paper, and sometimes patterned paper or fabrics may be added.

As children explore using cut and torn paper for making artworks, they will learn to combine and mix several other media with their cut and torn projects. They will enjoy seeing reproductions of the colorful collages created by Henri Matisse and Romare Bearden.

CUTTING PAPER

Children need good quality scissors to prevent their initial cutting experiences from becoming sources of frustration and failure. Without good scissors and lightweight paper, children's skills do not develop, and later, when they reach the symbol stage and are ready to depict the human figure, animals, plants, buildings, and such, a lack of cutting and pasting experiences impedes their ability to communicate visual images in cut paper.

Children need to practice using scissors. A number of boys and girls will need some initial help in learning the correct way to hold scissors and how to manipulate the paper as they cut, turning the paper rather than the scissors as they make longer and more continuous cuts. Very young boys and girls can first practice cutting skills by blowing a puff of air and pretending that they are cutting the air into little pieces. Preschool and

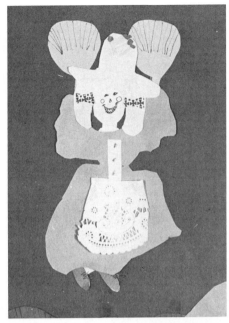

Body parts of figures were assembled in an action position, pasted down, and then dressed in colored paper clothing.

Mahito is cutting and constructing flowers to use as part of a spring mural in his kindergarten classroom. Thematic approaches connecting many parts of the curriculum are further enriched by art experiences in this culturally diverse school.

Children who begin cutting and pasting from their earliest school days and who continue to have frequent opportunities to practice arrive at third grade with highly developed skills, as demonstrated by these depictions of trains.

Folding, cutting, and pasting are skills that improve through practice. Young children willingly undertake difficult tasks that improve fine motor skills if they involve purposeful art projects. Jieun Lee concentrates intently as she makes a complex paper form to be displayed in her kindergarten classroom.

kindergarten children need to have the time, space, and supplies available on a daily basis to practice cutting and pasting. As a safety measure, they must be cautioned not to run with scissors in their hands and that they should walk holding the scissors tips down.

To develop some beginning skills in using scissors, children may be given small pieces of paper, about 6 × 6 inches. They should enter one side of the paper with their scissors and "take a walk," making straight cuts as they go until they exit from their "walk" on another side of the paper. With a second piece of paper, they can practice making only curving cuts, to take a "walk" in which they twist and turn the paper until they exit from another side of it. In a third skill-building exercise, the children fold a small piece of paper in half, hold the folded side in their left hand (if they are right-handed), and cut out a simple shape that unfolds to be symmetrical. This same procedure may be used to teach them how to cut an interior opening in a piece of paper. They should also learn that two or three light-weight pieces of paper or tissue paper can be cut at the same time to produce like shapes.

The teacher will want to encourage students to cut freely into paper without drawing any shape with a pencil ahead of time, which makes for tiny, cramped details that are difficult to cut out. The teacher can discuss the kinds of shapes the children are cutting, referring to them as straight, curved, thin, jagged, large, or small.

Older children who have mastered basic cutting skills can be introduced to simple paper sculpture techniques such as fringing, scoring, and curling paper. They can also learn to make slits and small tabs for joining two pieces of paper together, to roll a rectangle into a cylinder, and to roll a pie-shaped section from a circle to make a cone. Children will enjoy having the opportunity to use shiny paper, dull paper, and textured paper as well as fabric and felt.

TEARING PAPER

Torn-paper activities help young children develop motor skills along with visual perception. As they learn to control finger muscles through both cutting and tearing paper, they become more aware of shapes, sizes, and proportions.

Children will benefit from practice sessions in which they freely tear paper before starting actual art activities that focus on collage-making. Directions might include having the children use newspapers, old magazines, and phone books, first tearing the paper in half, then tearing a strip from one edge, tearing a big shape, tearing a little shape out of the middle of the big shape, tearing tiny bits, and tearing wide and narrow strips. Children can learn to control the torn edge by using the pinch-and-tear technique—that is, holding the forefingers and thumbs from both hands close together in a pinching position and moving bit by bit as they tear. Another technique is to place the forefinger on the paper and tear the paper by pulling it up and against the finger.

PASTING PAPER

When children are ready to paste one piece of paper to another, a glue stick is probably the easiest and most expedient adhesive. School paste is usually available, but, the teacher needs to stress the importance of not using too much paste. Many times, paste is applied in globs, and the result is a piece of paper that is curled and lumpy. Students must learn to apply paste evenly with their fingers to the backside of the paper shape that they have cut out. When the paste is applied to small bits and pieces of paper, it should be a thin, shiny coat that covers the entire surface. When paste is applied to large shapes, it need only be smoothed evenly around the edges.

Old magazines or phone books are useful paste-applying surfaces. When a clean surface is needed, the child simply turns a page. A damp sponge or paper towel nearby to wipe sticky fingers eliminates some of the frustration of handling small pieces of paper. When the children begin to cut realistic symbols, the teacher can introduce more advanced skills—for example, how to paste details and smaller pieces of paper on top of other shapes.

Oil pastels and marking pens were used to complete this drawing that began with a shape cut from a piece of newspaper classified ads.

The columns and printed lines found in the classified sections of the newspaper form natural cutting lines for geometric shapes found in cityscapes. This third-grade student's highly original scene is part of a unit on the community.

TWO-DIMENSIONAL PAPER ARTWORKS

Newspaper Creations

Children may use shapes that they have cut or torn from the classified ad sections of newspapers as starting points for picture-making. They begin by tearing or cutting various shapes from the paper—strips, ovals, squares, circles, triangles, or free-form shapes. After making several such shapes, the child examines them to see if one suggests the body or head of an animal, bird, insect, reptile, fish, or perhaps the child imagines the shape to be a spaceship, robot, or flower that will serve as an idea for the drawing. Or children begin with an idea in mind and cut or tear a piece of newspaper in the shape they will need to develop their idea. They paste the newspaper shape onto a piece of white or colored paper and draw the rest of their picture with a pencil, adding, for instance, the remainder of the animal's body as well as foreground items such as plants that will overlap the newspaper shape of the animal. They then go over their lines with a thick black marking pen. If they have chosen colored paper for their background sheet, they may use oil pastels for adding color since this medium is opaque. If crayons or marking pens are used, white paper should be utilized for the background because these two media are rather transparent and will not be suitably visible on colored paper. The newspaper shape and some of the background areas may be left uncolored.

Cut or Torn Paper People

Cut and torn paper activities can be designed to motivate and reinforce learning in other subject areas. For example, in studying the human body in science or in activities related to dance and physical education, children are able to understand that the body bends in certain places: the elbow, waist, wrist, knee, and ankle. Students can stand up, bend at the waist, bend the elbows and knees, and so on to observe and perceive kinesthetically the bending places in the body.

There are sixteen body parts: the head, neck, upper torso, lower torso, upper arms, lower arms, hands, upper legs, lower legs, feet, and neck. The teacher may have the class continue standing and make observations of their own necks, torso, upper arms, upper legs, and so on before they cut or tear sixteen pieces of paper to represent these body parts. They may make the following observations, for example, of the upper arm: it is joined to the body at the shoulder; the elbow reaches the waist; it is the same length as the upper leg; the lower arms are the same length as the upper arms; and so on. Children should start with the head, an oval shape, and make it about one or two inches high. The piece that represents the head determines the proportion of the other rounded strips and rectangles that make up the remainder of the human figure.

Once all the pieces have been cut or torn, the students arrange the pieces on another paper to show a person in action—for example, engaged in various sports, games, or work activities. The children will enjoy arranging the pieces several times to show different kinds of movement and action before pasting the pieces down and adding some details with marking pens or crayons. Older children are able to add a second person in another color. These additional paper people can be made in different sizes and placed higher or lower on the paper or so that they overlap and show depth. Students can all paste their paper people on one large background paper to form a mural about playground sports and games.

"Two People in Action" is the theme of this lesson, which uses torn construction paper pieces.

a. Cut paper shapes are arranged on a paper background as preparation for crayon rubbing.

b. A piece of typing paper is placed on the top and corners are taped to prevent sliding. The flat side of a black crayon is rubbed over the surface to bring out the impression of the paper shapes beneath.

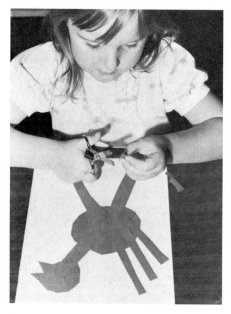

a

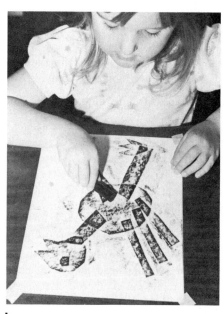

b

As a language arts extension, the children can tell what the paper person or people are saying. For older children, this lesson can enrich creative writing activities or introduce dialogue and quotation marks.

Cut Paper Rubbings

For many years people have enjoyed making brass rubbings on tombs in England and India. Children have amused themselves watching magical pictures appear when they place a piece of paper over a coin and rub it with a pencil. Crayon rubbings are made in somewhat the same manner, except that the children create original cutout designs or pictures prior to making the rubbing.

"Elephants at a Water Hole" is the title of this crayon rubbing by a third-grade student.

Necessary materials include several sheets of paper, scissors, paste or a glue stick, masking tape, and a black wax crayon, preferably thick and with the paper removed. Tagboard, index cards, or manila folders—all slightly stiff and heavier—are best for making the cut shapes. Typing, ditto, or white butcher paper should be used for the background and for the final rubbing because drawing paper is too heavy. The teacher should demonstrate the overall process so that the children understand that the rubbing and not the actual cut picture is the finished product. First, the children cut out simple shapes for their pictures or designs. They may choose to make their own portraits, cutting a large, oval shape for the face and then cutting the features separately and pasting them in place. Or they may make animals, birds, fish, cars, airplanes, buildings, or any other object, cutting all the parts separately; that is, the body of the dog, the legs, the neck, the tail, and the head are each cut as a separate piece and placed in proper positions. Cutout shapes may overlap. Making short snips in a shape and then folding the snips over—for instance, to create the tail feathers of a bird—produces an interesting result. Stripes may be placed on a tiger and polka dots on a clown. Children enjoy using a hole punch for a few accents and details. Paste should be used very sparingly, applying a tiny dot in a strategic position and smearing it thinly, because paste blobs are highly visible on the finished rubbing.

When the children have finished their cutout pictures, a piece of typing, ditto, or butcher paper should be placed on top of each cutout picture, making a sandwich of the bottom sheet, the cutout work, and the top sheet. Masking tape should be used to hold the two pieces of paper in place. A thick, folded section of newspaper used as a pad under the sandwich results in a better rubbing.

Children should stand up while making the rubbing. Using the black crayon flat on its side, the children rub softly at first, making short strokes on the surface of the paper until they find the cut picture with their crayon marks. When the edges of the cutout picture begin to show, the children begin rubbing harder and harder in the same short strokes, moving the crayon in one direction rather than rubbing back and forth. The finished rubbing should emphasize the edges and make the images stand out in contrast with the background.

Sometimes it is interesting to make the first rubbing of the cutout picture and then lift the top paper, move it over an inch or so, and make another rubbing that overlaps the first one. The second rubbing should be made lighter than the first rubbed figure,

A pipe-smoking funny man and a motorboat grew piece by piece as children each added to the arrangements in these pass-it-on pictures.

animal, or building because it will appear to be behind it. The image can be repeated several times to create a school of fish, flock of birds, fleet of ships, herd of cows, and so on. A wash made of diluted food colors can be applied over the rubbed shapes for added interest.

The class may decide to work together on a group project to create a mural on a long piece of butcher paper. For example, each child could cut and assemble a house for "Houses on Our Street." Other topics could be: "Circus Time," "Our Pets," "Our Trip to the Zoo," "Sea Full of Fish and Mermaids," "Our Faces," and "Cars and Trucks." The children might enjoy discussing Seurat's *A Sunday on La Grande Jatte* in the Color Gallery and then making a combined rubbed mural of themselves and their friends at the beach or park.

Pass-It-On Pictures

Gamelike in approach, pass-it-on pictures require children to be adaptable and quick in their thinking when cutting or tearing images freely from colored paper.

Each child should have a piece of white or black construction paper, 9 × 12 inches in size, and an assortment of colored papers and paste or gummed colored papers. Children must each cut or tear out one shape from the collection of small pieces of colored paper in front of them, paste it anywhere they choose on their background, and at a given signal—two minutes is usually sufficient—pass their background to the student on their right. Also at this signal, the children each receive a background paper from the neighbor on the left, and they must quickly decide what the shape reminds them of and how they can add to it to make the picture grow. This passing on continues for about ten turns, with each child adding a part to each picture for a composite finished arrangement.

The children are quick to find humor and suspense in observing what happens to the picture that each started and how their friends changed and enriched the picture as the game progressed. They may want to play the game several times and will find that practice increases their skill and ability to see novel configurations in shapes. They should let their imaginations dictate directions for unexpected and whimsical results. The children can conclude the activity by titling the finished pictures.

Snakes with Patterns

Snakes, water serpents, and lightning bolts have served as symbols in artworks of various Native American tribes. For instance, the Navajo believed that arrowsnakes or "racers" could fly and that feathered arrowsnakes would assist them through the skyhole. A similar shape, the zigzag, sometimes symbolizes lightning; it can refer to the power of the spirits and is either used alone or held by a figure. Children can become aware of the importance of such symbolism and at the same time learn how several cut paper shapes may be used in a repeat design to create a pattern. This activity may be coupled with a science unit.

Students start with a strip of colored construction paper that is 6×18 inches and fold it in half to create a 6×9 inch shape. They fold it in half again to create a $6 \times 4\frac{1}{2}$ inch shape. A ruler or straight edge is used to draw two lines diagonally as diagrammed on page 194. When straight cuts are made on these lines and the paper is unfolded, an 18 inch zigzag is created. A small triangle for the snake's head (or end of lightning bolt) should be glued to one end of the zigzag strip. If it is a snake, eyes are added and a fang may be attached. The children then use colored paper to cut out other multiple shapes—circles, half-circles, triangles, strips, rectangles, curving shapes—and use these to make a repeated pattern on the long zigzag body of the snake.

Paper Badges

Children can make cut paper badges that may be used as name tags, or cut paper medals that may be given as thank-yous or used to honor a special person. Students design these badges by folding and cutting three different pieces of colored paper. Each student needs a 6 inch square, a $4\frac{1}{2}$ inch square, and a 6×3 inch rectangle. The students fold the 6 inch square in half and then in half again. Curving and straight edges are cut on the open sides, eliminating the four corners, so that when the paper is unfolded, it is a circular design. The students then do the same with the $4\frac{1}{2}$ inch square, except that they vary the cut edges. The small circular design is pasted in the center of the large circular design. Decorations can be cut from the paper scraps and pasted on. The students use a black pen to write the person's name on the medal. The third piece of paper—the rectangle—is attached to the round shapes as a ribbon. The bottom of the ribbon can be cut diagonally, in a point, or in an inverted point design.

Tissue Paper Collages

Making collages with colored tissue paper provides young children with a good opportunity to improve their skills in tearing paper or cutting freely and boldly with their scissors. The many bright colors of tissue paper, and the wide range of tints and shades of one color, are visually stimulating.

Children should start with six small pieces of tissue to review specific tearing and cutting skills. Their first challenge is to take a piece of paper and try making large, curving cuts. The second piece of paper is used to make straight and jagged cuts. The third piece of tissue is folded in half and a large shape cut from it, thereby making two of the same shape. Another piece of paper is folded in half twice and four shapes cut all at once. Learning these multiple cuts will be useful later when students make such things as feathers for a bird or petals for flowers. The fifth piece of paper is folded and a symmetrical shape is cut. The last piece of paper is used to try tearing a shape. This is best accomplished when students hold their fingertips close together and remember to pinch and tear. Wrinkles in the tissue paper enhance the collage effect and provide textural interest.

After the children gain confidence in freely cutting, they are ready to make a collage. They should look through their practice cuts and see what images emerge from the scraps. They may suddenly discover an alligator's head, part of a rocket, or an elephant's trunk, and then be eager to complete the picture with more cut shapes. To assemble their

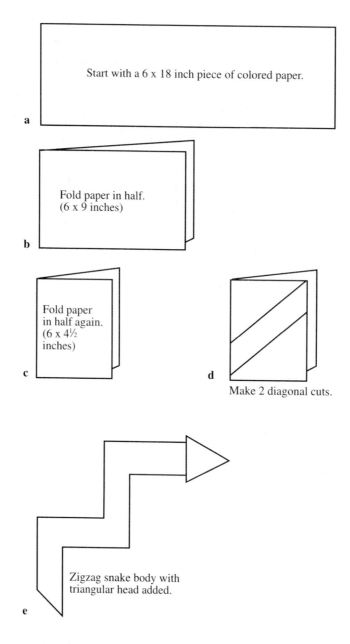

Start with a 6 x 18 inch piece of colored paper.

a

Fold paper in half.
(6 x 9 inches)

b

Fold paper
in half again.
(6 x 4½
inches)

c

Make 2 diagonal cuts.

d

Zigzag snake body with
triangular head added.

e

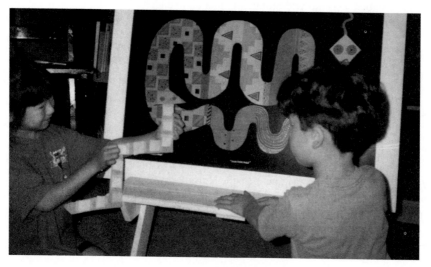

Children use repeated cut shapes to create colorful patterns on paper zigzag snakes. Artist Jeff Lowe's "Rattle, Rattle, Rattle" from his *Images of America* series provides visual elements for students to use in describing this brilliantly colored gold embossed print.

A brush is used with a half glue and half water solution to adhere colored tissue to white paper. Black lines can be added to the collage before or after for details.

collage, students dip a small, clean brush into a solution of white glue mixed in equal parts with water in a jar lid or other small container. They apply a small amount of the solution onto a piece of white drawing paper, and place a piece of tissue paper on top of it. A little more glue mixture needs to be brushed on top of the tissue. Some colors of tissue paper may bleed with the liquid mixture; keeping the brushing to a minimum reduces this effect. More pieces of paper are applied to the collage, and overlapping pieces achieve interesting differences in light and dark areas. The entire background can be quickly covered by cutting or tearing numerous small pieces of tissue and using them to fill it in in a mosaic-like manner. A brush wet with the glue solution can be used to pick up each small piece of tissue and position it on the paper.

The children may wish to draw their pictures first with a permanent black marking pen or a black crayon and then cover the paper with pieces of tissue in the approximate shapes made with the pen or crayon. No attempt is made to cut the tissue shapes exactly as in the drawing. If children have not made a drawing first, they may want to add some details with black pens after the collage is dry. The essence of collage making is a cut-and-torn-paper appearance along with the visual enhancement created by overlapping shapes. Collages can be ironed when they are dry to flatten the paper.

Texture Collages

"Hands off" and "Do not touch" are frequently heard admonitions that run counter to the natural human inclination to explore the world around us through our sense of touch. Smoothly polished wood, shining brass, bumpy fabric, soft fur, gritty sand—all invite the hands to feel, to sense differences, and to enjoy a multitude of tactile qualities. Children need to develop their capacity to differentiate between textures and to enjoy the sensory experiences of associating different textures and surfaces with different objects. When children draw, paint, model, and cut or tear out pictures, they are usually more involved with shapes, colors, and lines than they are with texture. When making texture collages, the young child learns to think in terms of physical feel or surface quality.

In making texture collages, children should have the opportunity to handle and compare a number of materials and to talk about whether the materials are soft, rough, smooth, spongy, shiny, slick, furry, and so on. After they have thought of things that the

This third-grade student adhered collage scarecrows made of fabric scraps to a background before adding the environment with oil pastels.

materials remind them of, they are ready to make touch pictures—texture collages. Velour surfaced paper may suggest kittens to children. Sheet sponge may suggest undersea plants; shiny foil paper may suggest flashing, colored fish. Sandpaper and felt may remind children of camping in a tent or a pleasant day on a sandy beach. Yarn and fabric may become clothing or hair. Corduroy could be the walls of a house. Leather scraps could be a horse or a cow. Before children paste down the various parts of their picture, they will want to try moving them around to discover the most pleasing arrangement. They may decide to repeat some shapes to give their pictures more unity or to add other textures to enrich the overall quality of the concepts they are trying to convey. They may want to use marking pens or crayons to draw some finishing details.

Zigzag Books

The pages of a zigzag book flow in a continuous progression from front to back. They tell a sequential story or they can be the focus for a cluster of connected concepts. The children choose a topic and make up their story line together, with each child cutting out one picture for the series of episodes that are needed to tell the tale.

A blank zigzag book is made of sturdy cardboard so that it can be folded and unfolded a number of times. Children enjoy looking at the pictures over and over, and may even give a visual and oral presentation to another class. Mat board is cut into 8 × 10 or 9 × 12 inch pieces for the pages. These pieces are fastened at the sides with tape on both front and back so that the pages fold up in an accordion-like manner from either end.

After the children have decided on a title and a story line, each child chooses an episode that he or she would like to depict. Fabric, felt, yarn, and various kinds of colored and textured paper are cut and combined for individual pictures. If the children arrange their cutouts on a piece of background paper the same size and shape as the pages in the zigzag book, they will find that their arrangement fits the page when they transfer the pieces to the book. After arranging their pictures, the children use paste or glue sticks to fasten down the cutout pieces. Several children may cut out letters to spell out the title.

a

Zigzag books are sturdy receptacles for composite group ideas. They promote sequential thinking about events, or they may unify many concepts having to do with a single theme.

b

Six-year-old children thought about what their life ambitions were and how they would look as adults and then made a zigzag book called "When We Grow Up."

This jumbo zigzag book resulted from a third-grade group's study of Martin Luther King's life and accomplishments.

Oral communication and creative writing skills can be integrated with the art task of making a zigzag book. The children will be proud of their individual contributions and will enjoy taking turns telling and retelling the stories and looking at their illustrations. The book that the children are holding in photograph A above tells the story of *Silly Dilly the Clown,* who had a dog named Billy. Each page of the book describes how Billy went searching at the circus for his lost master, first asking the balloon seller, then the thin

This bilingual mural from a Glendale, California, kindergarten class is arranged on a curved baseline, with thought given to the design of surrounding areas.

man, the popcorn seller, the bareback rider, and so on, if they had seen Silly Dilly. The dog, made of felt, traveled from page to page with the aid of the storyteller, creating the necessary suspense leading to a happy ending on the last page.

Suggested story lines for zigzag books include

1. The street where Tom lives

2. Things that are round

3. The crocodile who couldn't find his dinner

4. Rainbows and colors

5. Rockets and space people

6. Our families

7. Breaking our piñata

8. An airplane named Harry

9. Favorite nursery rhymes

10. Dinosaurs

Cut Paper Assembled Murals

Mural making with cut paper, using an assembled technique, is a highly stimulating activity for early childhood. Large pieces of colored banner paper or butcher paper provide the background. These papers come in rolls in several brilliant colors. They can be cut or torn to assemble the background areas. For instance, the ground area will be lowest and may have a torn edge along the top for a horizon and be placed against a contrasting color for the sky. The ocean might have torn edges where it meets the sand, or jagged mountain peaks could be cut. All the pieces are pasted together or attached on the backside with masking tape.

The background composition should be in keeping with the children's spatial concept development. That is, if children are beginning to draw on a baseline in their individual drawings, they will understand a mural background composed of a long piece of blue paper with a strip of green paper attached to the bottom. The baseline concept can be expanded to form a multiple baseline arrangement using several colors of banner paper. Baselines can be curved or bent. If the theme calls for a street, river, or road, the mixed plane and elevation concept will be understood as a spatial arrangement. That is, the

"Butterflies on the Wing" swoop upward together in this assembled mural created by first-grade children. Each butterfly was painted with tempera, cut out, and adhered to the background in the area above the painted flower garden.

street, river, or road can be depicted as if one is looking down on it, whereas the houses, trees, cars, and people may be perpendicular to it as if viewed at eye level. A small committee of children may help the teacher prepare the background ahead of time, deciding which areas will be sky, which will be ground, where the lake, ocean, streets, and mountains will be, and cutting and tearing the paper accordingly. The background for the mural is placed on a large table or on the floor so that, as the children finish items, they can place them on the mural and continue to rearrange them until the final pasting occurs. If the topic selected is "Our Neighborhood," for example, children name items that could be included, such as a grocery store, school, church, temple, barbershop, fire station, motel, trailer park, apartment house, police station, radio station, trucks, cars, bicyclists, stop signs, park and play equipment, lampposts, airplane, sun, helicopter, and so on. Children choose which items they will make, and there should be discussion as to relative sizes of the different objects. Generally speaking, the average cut paper mural requires that the children make items about the size of their own hands. A very large building or elephant may be two hands high, and a dog may be only as large as the palm of the child's hand.

The children each make their chosen item from cut paper, preparing all details and decorations with cut paper, not pencils. They need to have a choice of colors and kinds of paper. It may be useful to cut a number of small pieces of colored paper, 6 × 9 inches, 4 × 5 inches, or smaller, so the children can conveniently make their selections. Scrap boxes of paper come in handy, too. Children may wish to paste their animal or figure onto a small piece of tagboard and then cut out the finished figure. This extra stiffness enables the child to make the animal or figure stand out from the background by using small dots of soft foam with adhesive surfaces on both sides.

When the children finish, they bring their items to the prepared background and begin the assembly. The largest items are placed first, and efforts are made to have a center of interest, objects that overlap, eye-leading lines, and unifying positions, with colors and shapes repeated to create a cohesive and related arrangement. Items can be moved and shifted and additional shapes made, until the class agrees on a final composition. The items are then adhered to the background with glue sticks. Too much paste applied in untidy blobs makes for a messy finished mural.

Topics that are especially successful with cut paper murals are those that include a large number of people, animals, plants, and objects, such as "The Zoo," "Chinese New Year's Parade with Dragon," "The Circus," "Noah's Ark," "The Farm," "The Pied Piper," "Nursery Rhymes," "Fairy Tales," "On the Playground," "At the Seashore," "Dinosaurs and Dragons," "Paul Bunyan," and "The Parade."

First-grade students used cut paper—construction and tissue—in creating this enormous jungle mural on a long length of white butcher paper. Different sections of the mural show families of animals (lions are seen here), which lent a feeling of unity and order to the composition. Students learned about the effects of overlapping and repeating shapes.

A set of rubber alphabet stamps offers opportunities to foster language development along with the child's cut paper skills. A cut paper mural can be made and the rubber stamps used to print words or sentences about the objects featured. Members of a second-grade class made cut paper persons of themselves or a best friend doing what that person did best and then fastened them to the mural background and applied two or three stamped words. "Pat jumps rope," "Raphael rides horses," "Bob hits balls," and "Jim runs" were some of the phrases that were stamped around the figures. The words became a part of the design because they were combined to create an interesting arrangement.

THREE-DIMENSIONAL PAPER ARTWORKS

Whereas most cut paper activities are two-dimensional and thus flat, a few basic skills can expand children's experiences into making three-dimensional artworks with paper. Colored construction paper can be fringed, or curled by rolling it around a pencil. Small tabs can be cut on the edge of a piece of paper, paste applied, and then the piece attached to another piece. Or these tabs can be made and inserted into a slit in another piece of paper. A pie-shaped piece cut from a circle can be formed into a cone. A rectangle of paper can be rolled and taped to form a cylinder. Following are activities involving these skills and ways to combine paper with other media and scrap materials.

Fold-Over, Stand-Up Animals

American sculptor Alexander Calder formed large stabiles and mobiles from flat sheets of metal. He even made an entire miniature circus of whimsical animals and figures. In a similar manner, sheets of paper can be cut and pasted to form three-dimensional artworks in early childhood classrooms. A discovery-look at a number of photographs of different animals can lead to a discussion in which children describe what makes each animal look the way it does. Does a bull have a thick, powerful neck and a small head? How long are the legs of a hippo? What makes a pig look different from a lion? How many ways is a rabbit's shape different from a giraffe's? By comparing and contrasting distinguishing characteristics, students become more aware of shapes and comparative sizes and proportions. Each animal's important characteristics—the strength of a bull, the ferociousness of a lion, the graceful curves of a cat—can be exaggerated.

These preschool children are developing their cutting and gluing skills when they add both two- and three-dimensional decorations to their crowns.

Young children love to wear headpieces, and when they can make bright crowns all by themselves, they treasure them highly and wear them for all sorts of pretend play.

Students are provided a piece of 4½ × 6 inch colored construction paper to fold in half. They lightly draw with a piece of chalk or crayon the important outside edges of the animal of their choice, with the fold serving as the animal's back. They then cut the animal out and let it stand up on its feet. They may turn the paper inside out so that the chalk or crayon lines are inside and do not show. They add parts and details such as the neck and head, horns, ears, tail, and such. They may wish to use crayons, oil pastels, or marking pens for some of the finishing details. When students are finished, all the animals can be placed on a tabletop for a jungle, parade, zoo, or farm scene.

Cylinder Sculpture

By rolling a 9 × 4½ inch piece of colored construction paper into a short cylinder and securing it with clear tape, children can make all sorts of three-dimensional faces of people or animals. They can also use the cylinder as a base for a figure. They can attach noses that project, fringed eyelashes, ears that stand up or out, hats, curled hair, moustaches, beards, and so on.

Corrugated Paper Crowns

Very young children can be temporary kings or queens when they proudly wear a brightly colored and ornamented crown of their own making. Corrugated paper serves as a sturdy base for these headpieces, and on them the children can glue, tape, and staple all sorts of decorative materials. Corrugated paper comes in scalloped rolls in a variety of colors and is available from office and school supply houses. A strip about 21 inches long can be stapled to a wider piece of colored paper of the same length and then overlapped at the back and stapled to fit the individual child's head. The added piece of construction paper elevates the height of the crown, giving the child more space to decorate. Children may cut the tops of their crowns into points, curves, fringes, or whatever manner they choose.

With a plentiful supply of such things as discarded gift wrap ribbons, colored paper, and yarn, the children are ready to use scissors, glue, tape, and staplers. The children can create projecting decorations by adding feathers, soda straws, and pipe cleaners. They can make moving parts with fringed paper and crepe paper streamers. Foil paper, gold and silver stars, and alphabet stick-ons add sparkle and shine. Folding colored paper and cutting several shapes at the same time encourages the child to make a repeated motif. Buttons and beads with one side flat enough to hold a bit of glue add interesting design accents and serve as make-believe jewels. A pile of egg carton bumps may be painted with tempera and glued on for fake diamonds, emeralds, and rubies.

When they have finished, the new kings and queens may parade in a grand procession or rule their kingdoms seated on thrones. They may happily act out stories and imagine themselves in their new roles as grand monarchs.

Hidden Homes

After discussing with the children how some animals make their homes inside hollow trees and how some sleep inside caves, the teacher can show the children a variety of photographs of these creatures. This activity integrates science with art. The children become more aware of hibernating animals and how they sleep for long periods in safe, warm places. They learn that some birds and small animals build their nests and homes and find security and safety inside knotholes and hollow trees.

Homes in Caves

Each child needs two pieces of paper for this activity in which he or she creates an animal in its cave. An 8 × 12 inch piece of colored construction paper is used horizontally for the cave front. The children tear out an opening and then, on the sides of the opening, draw rocks, vines, shrubs, flowers, and trees with markers, crayons, or oil pastels. This paper is centered over the second piece of paper, which is the backing (a 9 × 12 inch piece of colored paper), and the cave opening is traced on the backing with a pencil. The front piece is now set aside. Cave dwellers such as bears, lions, and wolves are cut from small pieces of paper. It is easier if the students cut out the individual parts of an animal—head, body, legs, tail—separately and then paste the parts together. Paper tabs folded on the back of the completed animal make the animal stand out from the background. More animals, rocks, trees, and so on can be added to the backing. Details can be drawn with marking pens. To complete the stand-up cave sculpture, the cave front should be stapled to the backing with the right and left sides even. This makes the backing slightly bowed because it is an inch longer than the front piece, and the cave stands up on its own.

Homes in Tree Trunks

The children hold an 8 × 12 inch piece of manila paper over a rough surface and rub the side of a dark colored crayon over it to create a barklike texture. The paper is folded in half, and a knothole is made by tearing out a semicircle on the folded edge. If the shape isn't torn out entirely, there can be a flap that can be opened and closed at will. The knothole opening is then lightly traced onto the backing paper—a 9 × 12 inch piece of construction paper. Inside the marked space, the children can draw a nest of birds, an owl, or a squirrel or chipmunk eating acorns. With crayons, oil pastels, or marking pens, they can add insects and dangling spiders. The right and left sides of both papers are stapled together evenly, so the front piece serves as the simulated tree bark and the backing piece bows slightly. All the children's tree trunks can be stood up for a show of "Hidden Homes in Tree Trunks."

IN CONCLUSION

Frequent experiences in working with paper and paste give children the opportunity to master the skills that will enable them to express themselves with freedom and spontaneity. However, the child learns best when he or she is ready to attain such skills and feels a need for them. Using new materials and tools can be a frustrating experience. If a child is bothered by not being able to tear a strip of paper, the teacher and child may need to work together to accomplish the task: the teacher holds the paper on the table and uses a finger as the guide while the child actually tears the paper. Or the teacher may need to hold the paper for a child who is experiencing difficulty in holding the scissors and making cuts. As teachers assist boys and girls in gaining mastery, they should review the following questions:

1. Is each child using paper, scissors, and paste with increasing sureness? Some children will need additional help and more individual support while they work. Some children need to repeat an experience whereas other boys and girls need to work with a greater variety of materials or with more complex activities.

2. Does the work of each child show increasing skills in organizing his or her ideas in creative ways? Some children need additional assurance and encouragement to use their imagination.

3. Is the artwork of each child unique, and does it show a personal and distinctive way of using materials? A teacher who is supportive of those things that are unique in each child's art can help to build confidence.

TOPICS FOR DISCUSSION

1. What motivational topics are particularly suited for cut and torn paper art activities that incorporate texture and/or three-dimensional elements?

2. In addition to motor skills, what are two other skills that would be developed by involving young learners in mural making? What are possible connections to other subject areas in a mural-making project?

3. Create your own cut or torn paper still life. Make notations of appropriate terms to be introduced and questions to reinforce concepts about the elements and principles of art.

4. Compare your cut or torn paper still life to the painted still life by Picasso and the cut paper design by Matisse in the Color Gallery to find similarities and differences.

5. Display and discuss several cut or torn paper still life compositions. Consider the model for art criticism in Chapter 2 and formulate three appropriate questions for an artwork that is not your own.

6. What connections could be made to other subject areas using the zigzag book project?

7. To better understand the difficulty of learning to use materials, try cutting or tearing paper by reversing the materials so that your *nondominant* hand is doing the task. If you are right-handed, cut or tear with your left hand. Describe the experience. What problems did you have? What would make the task easier?

8. How might a teacher restructure a cut and paste activity for a child who is having difficulty in organizing the idea of what he or she wants to make?

9. What three questions should teachers ask themselves as they supervise and guide children in cut and torn paper activities?

10. Select an activity in the chapter that you think would provide an appropriate multicultural connection. Which of the purposes of art in Chapter 1 would you present if you were to introduce the activity to young children? How would you do it?

10

Printmaking

• •

Most children have had their first experience in printmaking when they pressed a finger on a stamp pad and made a fingerprint. If given a magnifying glass, they enjoyed examining the curving and swirling lines that they saw in the print and on their inked fingertip. Children can understand the printing process when they remember seeing the prints their shoes make in the sand or snow and the pattern of tread marks that a car tire leaves in the mud.

The first printmakers probably were early cave dwellers who found that the shape of a hand could be made on the stone walls of their homes. One of these ancient human beings placed his or her hand on the cave wall and then blew around it through a hollow reed with dry, powdered pigment that had been ground from earth. When the hand was removed, its shape remained, and so began the art of making stencils, a simple form of printmaking.

Prints have been made in many cultures, both as a means of producing fine art and as a way to embellish clothing and objects in the environment. Woodcuts or woodblock printing is one of the oldest ways of making prints, the first ones probably being made by the Chinese in the eighth century. The craft spread from China to Korea and Japan, where woodcut prints became a very important art form, with prints showing people engaged in many of life's activities. Although no woodcut prints dated earlier than the beginning of the fifteenth century exist today, it is believed that the technique was used before then for royal stamps and textile printing. The Japanese chop is a stamp that the artist prints on a finished artwork as his signature. Printing with stamps on fabric is found in Africa and other parts of the world. Intaglio, a type of printmaking that includes etching, engravings, and drypoint, originated in the Middle Ages when rubbings and prints were made from incised designs on shields and armor. The carryover of terminology that we use with printmaking reflects the history and traditions of printmaking. For instance, the flat surface that is used to transfer an image to paper or fabric is called a block or plate, even in cases when neither wood nor metal is being used.

Printing was widespread in China under the Tang Dynasty (AD 618–907). Movable characters made from fired clay were the invention of Bi Sheng in China in 1041, and cast-metal characters were being used in Korea by 1392. The modern printing press with its movable type was used in Europe beginning in the fifteenth century, and woodcuts became the method used to reproduce drawings for printed books. Artists such as Albrecht Dürer (1471–1528) designed many woodcut prints but left the actual cutting to a craftsman. Then, in the sixteenth century, metal engraving and etching became the important printmaking techniques in Europe, and for the next several hundred years, woodcut prints

Brazilian poet and artist José Francisco Borges taught himself to make woodcut prints for the covers of his booklets to provide graphic images for his folk stories.

José Francisco Borges/Collection of the authors.

were not very popular. In the middle of the nineteenth century, printers of beautiful books began to use woodcut prints again for illustrations. During this time, Japanese prints found their way to Europe and influenced the art production of several artists: Degas, Toulouse-Lautrec, van Gogh, Cassatt, and others. In the twentieth century, there has been a great deal of interest in woodcut prints. Prints made of several colors require that a different wood block be carved for each one.

Printing processes used by artists today include: engraving and etchings (which involve the scratching of fine lines into a sheet of metal, usually copper), lithography (by which images are made with wax or a greasy material on a flat piece of limestone and then processed before being covered with ink and a print made), woodcuts, lino prints (which are similar to woodcuts but softer and easier to carve), and silk screen prints (whereby a stenciled image on a stretched sheet of silk impedes ink from going through the silk when a squeegee rubs ink across it).

Printmaking is filled with surprises and suspense. One is never quite sure what the finished product will look like until the magic moment when the block is pressed or stamped on the paper. Children are intrigued with the step-by-step process leading up to the moment when their prints are completed. Equally fascinating is the rhythmical element inherent in repeating a single design many times to make allover patterns, as is sometimes done with gadget printing, potato printing, eraser printing, and other small relief prints.

A relief print is the result of applying ink or paint to a raised surface and then pressing that surface onto paper. Relief printmaking involves three steps, the first of which is the making of the relief image, whether it is cut on the flat surface of a potato half, or cut from wood or lino. Second, this block or plate is either inked with a brayer, pressed onto a paint-saturated pad, or brushed with paint. Third, the block is pressed, and thus printed, onto a piece of paper. Relief prints can be printed on all sorts of paper, white or colored. If printing ink is used, construction paper should not be used because of its high absorbency. Such papers as Fadeless paper (available from art supply sources) or Astrobright or Brighthue papers (available from printing supply sources) are recommended. Using colored water-soluble ink opens the door to a variety of printed effects. A white print on dark paper creates a very different effect than does one printed in black on light paper.

A print can be made singly and mounted or matted for display, or it can be repeated a number of times to create a patterned effect. By repeating their motif over and over, children begin to understand the meaning of the terms *repeat print, rhythm,* and *allover pattern.* Patterns resulting from printmaking can be used for covering boxes and cans and for notebook covers, bookbinding, and wrapping paper. Group projects include printing calendar illustrations, notepaper, greeting cards, program covers, and, of course, murals. For a group mural, children can each cut a block of a fish, car, or house, for instance, and then all the children can print their blocks onto a large piece of butcher paper, adding some objects cut from colored paper for environmental details. Suitable topics for mural-making include

1.   Insects, birds, and flowers in a garden

2.   Cars and trucks on a highway

3.   Groups of animals in a jungle, zoo, or farm

4.   Fish and sea life

5.   Astronauts and spaceships

6.   Rows of houses and stores

PRESS PRINTS

Children enjoy using markers to turn their own fingerprints into various animals and objects. By pressing their fingertip onto an office stamp pad and then onto a piece of paper, they have a basic shape that may be turned into any number of objects with a few lines added. For instance, students can use black stamp pads and black and orange markers at Halloween to create a picture with pumpkins, skeletons, black cats, and witches.

TRANSFER PRINTS

Transfer printing is the process of printing the shape and texture of an actual object onto paper. In this kind of printing, the design has already been made, usually by nature. For example, to print a leaf, it should be covered with ink and a piece of paper pressed down on top of it. The ink will transfer the leaf onto the paper, showing the leaf shape with all its lines, ridges, veins, and edges. Students can collect a variety of leaves—fern, geranium, ivy, and maple—and print the back sides of the leaves where the veins are most

Transferring the shape and texture of an object onto paper is one simple way to make a print. Gyotaku (fish printing) has its roots in ancient Japan. Colorful fish prints can be cut out and used in a classroom mural.

prominent. It may be possible to print a feather or a piece of old weathered wood. Anything that is firm and has texture will print. *Gyotaku* is the art of making transfer prints directly from fish. It was originally done as a form of recordkeeping in Japan. While training to be samurai warriors, men were required to record the fish they caught by inking them and pressing paper to the inked fish.

POTATO PRINTS

Potato prints provide several ways to explore printmaking. The oval or round shape that is created when a potato is cut in half can be used by the youngest child. Teachers should use a large, sharp knife when halving the potatoes to obtain a very flat, evenly cut surface. After the cut half has been placed on paper toweling for a few minutes to absorb moisture, it is pressed onto a paint-saturated pad. Then a potato print is made by pressing the cut half onto paper. A suitable pad may be made with six layers of paper towels that are moistened with water and placed on a paper plate. About a spoonful of liquid tempera is poured on the center of the pad and brushed evenly over an area about the size of the potato. Each time students make a print, they need to press the potato onto the pad. More paint will need to be added to the pad occasionally. Children may either print the potato shape a number of times randomly to create an irregular pattern or in rows to make a regular repeated pattern. When the paint is dry, the children may use another color of paint and stamp additional shapes on top of the first ones. Instead of using a paint-saturated stamp pad, students can apply tempera to the cut surface of the potato with a brush. They will need to apply more paint with the brush each time they make a print. White, black, or colored paper may be used when making prints with tempera since it is an opaque medium.

An alternative medium for potato prints is watercolors. A few drops of water on each color in the watercolor tray softens the pigments and makes them easier to use. The surface of the potato is brushed with the watercolors before making the print. Because watercolors are transparent, stamping several different colors of watercolors on top of each other after the color underneath is dry creates an interesting overlapping effect. It is advisable to use white paper with watercolors because of their transparency.

The children can also print several potato shapes and, after they dry, let the shapes suggest forms to use in drawing the rest of the picture; for example, the shapes may be heads of people. The children then draw the bodies with crayons, oil pastels, or marking pens. Or the shapes might be wheels on a car, centers for flowers, or the bodies of birds, turtles, or insects.

The oval shape of a potato print was impetus for these family portrait drawings, done with oil pastels. The final step was brushing thinned diluted food color wash on the background.

After students have mastered the basic printing process with potatoes, they can use a paper clip to carve out a design from the flat, cut surface of the potato half. A few gouges, lines, and simple shapes can result in a pleasing print. Design possibilities are further extended by trimming the sides of the potato half to create a square, triangle, rectangle, or other geometric shape. A few gouges with the paper clip can transform the shape into a design motif or a more realistic form such as a house, boat, or spaceship.

CLAY PRINTS

Either plasticine or water-based clay can be used to make a print. A chunk of moist clay is flattened on one side by hitting it against a flat desktop. A design is then carved out using a pencil point, plastic forks and knives, large nails, or the edge of a piece of cardboard. The decorated side can either be painted or pressed into a paint pad, as described earlier, and printed.

ERASER PRINTS

Small erasers are suitable for children to use in making patterns. They can be inked repeatedly on office stamp pads and pressed onto paper. Art gum erasers are so soft that children can carve a design easily with an unbent paper clip or their fingernails. The art gum eraser can then be pressed onto the stamp pad and printed on the paper in a random or regular repeated manner. If two or three such erasers and colored stamp pads are available, students can put math strategies to work by making simple patterning configurations, such as two red prints and then one black print in row after row of motifs.

GADGET PRINTS AND PAPER SHAPES

As a starting point and focus for this art task, the children need an assortment of circles, squares, rectangles, and long strips of colored paper. From these, they may choose one or more to glue down to a piece of paper. A long strip of paper may suggest the stem of a flower to one child or a tree trunk to another. A rectangular piece might remind them of

Printing with the edges of cardboard strips provides opportunities for students to experiment with line. In this lesson, gray paper forms the background for black and white lines.

A student puts the finishing touches on a group mural. After studying fish, students cut fish shapes out of tagboard, painted them, and printed the fish on a large piece of butcher paper. Sand and water were printed with pieces of sponge dipped in tempera. Detail lines were added with pieces of cardboard, whose edges were dipped in dark-colored paint.

the shape of a car, airplane, or wagon, the torso of a person, or the body of an animal or bird. A circle might help the children to focus on a plant design, a ladybug, a wheel, a clown's head, a turtle, or a sun face. Whatever the precut geometric shapes suggest is then ready to be embellished and completed with simple gadget prints.

Collected gadgets such as small blocks and sticks of wood, corks, erasers, forks, and jar lids are easy to handle and provide a variety of shapes for printing and completing the image or design. The children should gently press the gadget on a paper towel pad that is soaked with tempera and make a print on their paper. Children are free to repeat and combine these in all sorts of designs and images in combination with the colored paper shapes.

a

b

PRINTING WITH CARDBOARD STRIPS

A variety of short lengths of cardboard strips—2, 3, and 4 inches—can be cut by the teacher on the paper cutter beforehand from thick mat board and corrugated cardboard. A moist piece of sheet sponge or several thicknesses of paper towels should be placed on a paper plate and tempera poured down its middle length. Students press the edge of a cardboard strip into the paint and then onto a piece of construction paper to make a printed line. The student can repeatedly press the strip into the paint and then onto the paper to form designs, figures, and objects. Black paint on white or colored paper is suitable, as is white or light-colored paint on black or colored paper. When the paint dries, the student can add some color with oil pastels. A variation on this printing technique is to provide some simple cut paper shapes—circles, squares, and such. One or two of these can be pasted onto the background paper before the printing is done with the cardboard strips.

INSULATION TAPE PRINTS

Rolls of dense insulation tape with peel-off paper on the adhesive side are available at hardware stores. This product is about a quarter of an inch thick and is easily cut with a scissors. Small design motifs can be created by adhering small pieces of tape to a block of wood or a piece of corrugated cardboard. The interest span of the very youngest child can be maintained because the entire process takes but a few minutes. Office stamp pads should be liberally covered with stamp pad ink. A stamp pad in each color—black, red, blue, green, and purple—provides children with a wide range of design possibilities. Children press their block with the design on it onto the stamp pad and then onto their piece of paper. A very simple design made with only a few bits of tape takes on a new importance and assumes interesting relationships when it is repeated very close together a number of times, especially if a second design on another block is used alternately with a second color of ink. Children should be cautioned not to use their printing block on more than one color as the second stamp pad would become stained with ink from the first pad.

CARD PRINTS

Young children who have had plenty of experience cutting paper will have the skills they need to put together a card print. The children should use a 5 × 8 inch file card for the background and another file card, piece of tagboard, or manila folder from which to cut their designs. Parts of an animal, such as the ears, wings, and legs, can be cut separately

a. A child presses a block onto a well-inked office stamp pad each time before printing on paper.

b. Flocks of birds, schools of fish, crowds of people, and herds of animals are achieved by each child printing his or her design a number of times on a multicolored paper background. Pieces of insulation tape are attached to a piece of corrugated cardboard to make each design.

a

a. Cutting and designing skills as well as the know-how of printing are involved when young children make card prints.

b. Dark and light contrast sharply in card prints. The elephant and lion print was made by a five-year-old child.

b

Each child made a house, tree, or car for this "card print" mural. Pieces are printed separately, several times, on a long piece of butcher paper. A piece of waxed paper covers the inked card to keep the background and fingers clean while the print is being carefully pressed and rubbed on its backside. Or houses may be printed on a separate piece of paper, cut out, and pasted in place.

A brayer is used to roll ink evenly over the block or plate as the student prepares to pull a print.

and glued down on top of other pieces. Students need to be cautioned to use small amounts of paste or glue as big blobs will show up on the finished print. The edges of the cutout shapes create a white outline on the finished print. The printing ink is rolled onto the brayer from the inked tray or sheet, and the image is given a good coating of ink with the brayer before printing it on white paper or colored Astrobright paper.

For the sake of neatness, it is advisable to cut a stack of newspaper sheets in half. When the student rolls the brayer over the surface of the card print, the excess runover of the brayer goes onto the newspaper, which is then discarded. The card print is placed on the printing paper, turned over onto another piece of clean newspaper and rubbed on the paper side. This newspaper is then discarded and any ink left on the fingers wiped clean with a damp sponge before pulling the paper off the card.

A variation on making card prints does not use a rectangle for background. Rather, the bird, house, or fish is cut and pasted or glued together as an image complete in its own shape. It is then inked and printed. Each child may apply his or her print to a large piece of banner or butcher paper for a mural such as "A Sea Full of Fish," "A Tree with Many Birds," "The Houses on Our Street," etc.

FELT PRINTS

Scraps of felt can be used to create a relief block for printing. Older children will want to plan their design first by making sketches. Because younger children have less skill in controlling scissors, they may choose from precut felt scraps left from other projects. The felt pieces are arranged and glued to a piece of cardboard. Once the glued pieces have dried, ink is rolled on the surface with a brayer, paper placed on top, and the back of the paper rubbed gently with the fingertips.

POLYSTYRENE PRINTS

Making a print with a sheet of polystyrene, which is a sheet foam material, is an easy and pleasurable task for young children. They will want to repeat this activity a number of times, trying out new images and forms as their concepts expand. This printing material can be recycled from meat trays, but it is also available in art supply catalogs under such

a

c

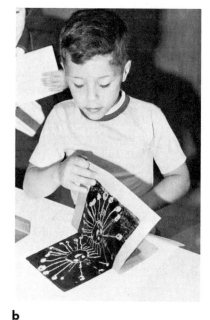

b

d

e

a. A kindergarten child rolls water-base ink on his printing plate with a brayer. The paper is carefully placed on top of the plate and rubbed with the fingers to assure an even printing.

b. The paper is pulled off the plate, and the print appears.

c, d, and **e.** Since they are mostly linear, these prints strongly appeal to the very young child. They offer avenues for the development of conceptual symbols.

names as Scratch-Foam and Poly Print. The 9 × 12 inch sheets in the commercial packages may be cut into quarters; if meat trays are used instead, their curved sides should be trimmed on a paper cutter before they are used by the child.

Children are first given a pencil and a piece of paper the same size as the polystyrene plate to work out ideas for their prints. The paper is taped to the plate and the lines of the drawing gone over again with the pencil. Students need to press down firmly with the pencil so that an imprint is made in the plate. They then remove the paper and go over the lines again to make sure they are deep enough. If the lines are not deep enough,

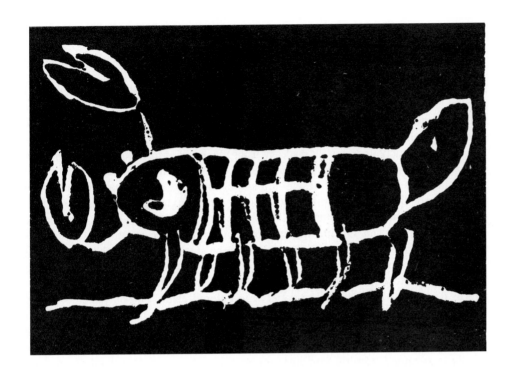

"Lobster in a Tank" is the result of one child's experience at a seafood market. Printed in bright red, the bold image became the front of an invitation to an open house.

they will fill with ink and not print properly. All areas left standing will print the color of the ink used. All the lines and shapes that are pushed down show up as the color of the paper on which the plate is printed.

Children should be encouraged to plan for a balance of light and dark areas and to be innovative with their pencils, using close-together lines and dots to create patterned areas. Thin lines, thick lines, and large and small shapes give variety to the print. Including letters and words should be discouraged unless the student understands that it is necessary to draw them on the printing plate in reverse; otherwise they will print backwards.

After the student has prepared the printing plate, it is ready to be inked and printed. Black or colored water-soluble inks can be rolled with a brayer onto a baking sheet or plastic tray. The child uses the brayer to cover the plate with ink. A piece of typing paper, Fadeless paper, or colored Astrobright paper cut a little larger than the plate should be placed carefully on top of it and gentle pressure applied with the fingers on the paper to assure an even printing. The paper is then pulled off the plate, and the finished print is left to dry before being matted for display. Construction paper is too absorbent for use with printing ink.

Any number of prints can be made from the plate; however, the plate will need to be reinked for each print. Children are interested in seeing the different effects they can create by changing the color of the ink as well as the color of the paper on which their prints are made. An unusual effect is created if a piece of paper of another color is cut and pasted onto the background paper before making the print. For instance, a strip of green paper could be pasted onto the lower portion of a print in which grass is important, or a circle of yellow could be placed in the area where the sun will appear in the print.

If children cut out the basic shape of a house, fish, or bird from the polystyrene, and add engraved lines for details, they may combine their products by printing them in a planned arrangement to create "A Hillside Covered with Houses," "Fishes in the Sea," "Birds in a Tree," and so on.

MONOPRINTS

When artists enter their original prints for a show, the rules may indicate that they cannot enter a monoprint because it is a print that can only be made one time. Some people, therefore, do not consider a monoprint a true print. Actually, most monoprint techniques are closer to drawing or painting than printmaking, but the ability to transfer pigment from one surface to another is a major element of printmaking, and in this respect, the monoprint qualifies.

A simple monoprint can be made by using finger paint to make a picture or a design on a piece of paper and pressing another piece of paper on top while the paint is still wet. Sometimes the picture or design is made in finger paints that have been applied evenly to a cookie sheet. After using fists, fingers, and palms to create a design so that the shiny surface of the pan shows through, the student lays a sheet of newsprint paper on the surface of the paint and smooths the back of the paper with clean palms. The design is transferred to the paper, and the finger paints can be smoothed out to make another design. The monoprint may be pressed with an iron when it dries to flatten it.

Another procedure for creating a monoprint requires carbon paper. After a picture or design has been drawn on paper with colored chalk, carbon paper is placed face down on the chalked surface. Rubbing a hand over the back of the carbon paper results in the chalk being transferred to the dark shiny surface. The teacher will need to spray the paper with a fixative to keep the print from smearing. Carbon paper can usually be obtained from the computer services department of the school district, because multiple copies are printed using carboned computer paper. It is advisable to try a sample piece of carbon paper to make sure the carbon releases before doing this activity with children.

A similar technique can be used to make a tempera print. Once a chalk design or drawing has been completed (the chalk must be applied heavily), another piece of paper is coated evenly with white tempera paint. While the tempera is still wet, the chalk drawing is placed face down in the paint. The child rubs the back of the paper with fingers and hand and separates the two papers before they dry. Two pictures result: the chalk will have merged with the paint on one paper and some chalk will be left on the original drawing. Although there are two pictures, only one is a print. As in other printing processes, the design on the print is reversed or backwards from the original. For this reason, children should be discouraged from using letters or numbers in this type of artwork.

A sheet of medium grit sandpaper as a printing plate introduces texture into the printing process. This process results in a monoprint unless the sandpaper image is colored again with crayon before making a second print. Children start by drawing on the sandpaper, bearing down on the crayon and filling in all the shapes with color. Paper is placed on top of the waxy image and an iron is used to transfer the image to the paper. It is suggested that when displaying the print, the sandpaper plate is mounted alongside the printed image; this illustrates the fact that printed images are reversed from the printing plate.

IN CONCLUSION

Throughout the year, children should make all kinds of prints. Each time, they will be intrigued with the surprise of viewing their final product, and will discover that the design possibilities in printmaking are unlimited.

Respect and appreciation for children's artwork is shown when the teacher mounts or mats and displays the finished products at the school. Likewise because prints lend themselves to making multiple images, they are especially suitable for communicating with parents. Invitations, note cards, and calendars made in multiples by the boys and girls may be sent home to encourage their parents to participate in building the child's confidence and self-esteem.

Multicultural symbols and motifs present connections that may serve as visual resources for printmaking. Children may study the symbols and motifs found in such crafts as adinkra cloth from Ghana, Japanese family crests and chops (used as stamped signatures), and pottery designs from the American Southwest.

TOPICS FOR DISCUSSION

1. How are the tools and techniques of printmaking different from other art forms?

2. What skills are developed in young learners through exploration of printmaking?

3. Printmaking provides a means for making multiple images. Discuss Andy Warhol's set of self-portraits in the Color Gallery. How do they reflect theme and variation through the serigraphs (silk screen prints)?

4. What are relief prints, and how are they appropriate as an art form for the young learner?

5. How do relief prints differ from rubbings? Make samples of both from the same plate.

6. Develop themes for art projects involving printmaking. Share and compile lists with others.

7. How could you use printmaking in a lesson combining art and another subject area of the curriculum?

8. List or diagram the steps in making a print and compile a list of vocabulary words. How would you introduce these to young learners?

9. Discuss printmaking in terms of repetition, pattern, and rhythm. How can these concepts be introduced into lessons?

10. How could you use printmaking as part of a multicultural art lesson?

11

Modeling and Constructing

• •

Sculpture and architecture are three-dimensional art forms that have figured significantly in people's lives for thousands of years. Prehistoric people believed that a carved object that looked like a person or animal must have special powers, and the earliest pieces of sculpture were probably made to help hunters. Later sculptures were made to represent gods. Ancient kings had their likenesses carved, probably in the hopes of making themselves immortal. Early Christians had sculptures of saints as well as demons and devils in their churches to remind people of the presence of good and evil, because many churchgoers could not read or write.

Enormous fountains that include sculptures are found in many modern cities, as are sculptured monuments that commemorate events and pay tribute to famous people. Many pieces of sculpture exist to be enjoyed for themselves, for the beauty of their forms, and for the colors and textures on their surfaces. In the Color Gallery, we see two examples of contemporary sculpture: Modigliani carved stone to create his elongated, expressive *Head of a Woman,* and Henry Moore carved his elmwood *Reclining Figure* with its curves and undulating forms that create an interplay of positive forms and negative spaces.

Sculptors work in many different media. When making assembled and constructed sculpture, the artist joins pieces of metal, wood, plastic, or even stuffed fabric forms to make a configuration. This type of sculpture was not widely practiced until the twentieth century and is called additive sculpture. Carved sculpture, usually made from a block of wood or stone, is called subtractive sculpture. Here, the artist removes pieces from the block with a knife or chisel until the desired form is achieved. When one works with clay, wax or other soft pliable materials, the process may be both additive and subtractive. Clay pieces can be fired in a kiln later to make them permanent, or the finished piece can be cast in metal or plaster. Sculpture may be in-the-round, or in bas-relief, in which images are set against a flat background. Coins and friezes on buildings are examples of low relief or bas-relief.

Architecture is the art of designing buildings. Buildings serve as shelter for people while we work, play, study, meet, or worship. Different periods in history are marked by different architectural styles that were suited for the lifestyles of the people who used the buildings. Architects have always been challenged and limited by the materials, sites, budgets, and engineering techniques available. To be a successful work of art, a building must fulfill practical requirements and be satisfying in appearance.

Students in a second/third-grade combination class had a robot parade after constructing unique robots from objects found at home.

The child lives, moves, and plays in a three-dimensional world. Consequently, the task of modeling and constructing is a natural channel through which the child's concepts of form become richer, more detailed, and interrelated. If only painting and drawing activities are experienced, the child faces the challenge of creating the illusion of three-dimensional space on a two-dimensional surface—translating roundness, depth, spatial relations, and texture into the limitations of a flat plane. A child's conceptual base of information about the three-dimensional world develops when he or she engages in modeling and constructing activities.

All children, and especially those who do not readily express their ideas with paint, crayons, or markers, can derive pleasure and valuable experience from repeated projects in modeling and constructing things. When children manipulate a pliable modeling medium, they feel the roundness, the depth, the overall wholeness of a figure, head, or animal, and through this tactile intake, they can refine, better understand, and communicate their knowledge of forms. By alternating two- and three-dimensional materials, the teacher activates the child's concepts in each media as well as cross-related ideas. This increasing knowledge of three-dimensional forms intermingles with the child's two-dimensional drawing skills to prevent rigid fixations of stereotyped schemas.

Children can work with many construction materials and find them challenging and interesting. They can learn to tape and glue. Preschoolers and kindergartners can learn to pound nails and saw small pieces of wood. Children can discover for themselves that such familiar objects as newspapers, boxes, tape, paste, wood scraps, and paint can be manipulated and combined to create all manner of three-dimensional objects. They need only a minimum of assistance in their work and often enjoy collaborating in pairs so that one child can hold while the other child tapes or glues.

Preschool and kindergarten children spend a good deal of time manipulating any modeling material they are given. They enjoy pounding, rolling, squeezing, making coils and balls, and imprinting objects into soft modeling materials. They should not be pushed into making recognizable objects until they are ready to do so naturally. However, if they have many opportunities to play with the clay and other modeling materials, their growth will proceed rapidly, and representative symbols will begin to emerge. When children are ready to make use of some actual techniques, the teacher can show them, for instance, how to moisten two bits of clay to make them stick together, how to roll out and cut

"Storyteller" by D. Trujillo of Cochiti Pueblo in New Mexico shows a seated figure holding several children. Such examples of folk art are enjoyed by adults and children for their simplicity and human appeal.

pieces with a dull, plastic knife or tongue depressor, and how to make textures by scraping or imprinting. First graders and older children enjoy the challenge of a specific motivation or topic after they have passed through the earlier experimental stage of manipulating a modeling material. They can work creatively within a given framework and benefit from new areas of exploration and expanded ideas.

CLAY

Clay modeling and constructing includes making objects, either functional or sculptural, by a combination of techniques—forming pinch pots, using slabs, winding coils into forms, and adding coils to slabs, pots, and other forms. Two kinds of clay are commonly used in schools: the water-based kind that hardens and is usually fired in a kiln, and the oil-based variety that is reusable and never dries out. The oil-based type is called plasticine and can be used over and over. The objects made with plasticine are generally tossed back into a container and are not kept by the children. However, plasticine's even consistency makes it a good material for manipulation and learning a few basic skills in modeling and forming.

Large, brown paper bags, pieces of canvas or denim, or the back side of vinyl all make excellent reusable work surfaces for activities involving water-based clay. Newspapers should not be used because the ink may be worked into the surface of the clay, and because the moisture of the clay causes the paper to tear and get mixed into the clay body.

Very young children need time to pound, pinch, mash, and roll clay. One way to make a small ball is to roll it between one hand and the tabletop.

Two clay animals made by kindergarten students from pinch pots are ready to be fired. Holes have been poked into the hollow balls to let the steam escape and to prevent the pieces from exploding in the kiln.

Very small children naturally spend much time pounding, pinching, mashing, and rolling clay. The teacher may introduce several methods of working with clay. For instance, the teacher can demonstrate the two ways of rolling a small ball of clay: one is by rolling the lump of clay between the palms, and the other is by rolling the clay between one palm and a tabletop. A pinch pot can be made from a round ball of clay about the size of a lemon by holding clay in one hand and inserting the thumb of the other hand into the center. As the ball is pinched and rotated, it slowly becomes rounded and hollow like a small pot. Care needs to be taken to make the sides an even thickness. The pinch pot can be left as a small pot or bowl or additional parts such as a handle or small legs can be added. Another introduction in manipulating clay is teaching students to make a coil.

Like the ball, it can be formed by rolling a lump of clay on a surface with the palm. Once the coil starts to lengthen, the palms of both hands can be used. Young children are often quite content to roll coils of clay for no particular purpose other than gaining the confident feeling of mastery.

A third technique to demonstrate is to roll clay out to make a slab. Doweling that is 1¼ to 2 inches in diameter and cut into 6 to 8 inch lengths can be used as small rolling pins. Again, the flat of the hand is used to roll the doweling over the clay until it is the desired thickness. To create a textured surface, the clay can be rolled between pieces of burlap. A flat piece of evergreen needles, a weed, or pieces of rice can be rolled into the surface, or various found objects can be stamped into the clay while it is soft. Once children can make a slab, it is easy for them to use a tongue depressor or plastic knife to cut the slab into pieces to make wind chimes, to fold a long slab in half and press the edges to make a pocket for dried flowers, or to square the slab off to make a tile or small box.

If pieces of clay are not carefully joined, problems may occur. Frequently, children merely press pieces together, and the pieces break apart when the project is dry. Although many ceramics books recommend scoring the parts to be joined and brushing them with slip—a solution of water and clay about the consistency of very thick cream—this is not the best approach to use when very young children are learning to work with clay. An old toothbrush dipped into water and rubbed on the surfaces of the clay pieces to be joined provides both a roughened surface and moisture. When two surfaces are treated in this way and joined together firmly, the resulting juncture keeps the pieces together through drying and firing.

Two pinch pots, with edges roughened and joined, form a hollow ball. The round shape can be preserved by placing a piece of crumpled newspaper inside before the two halves are put together. This hollow ball can be made into a person, an animal, a monster, or an imaginary creature. Legs, beaks, tentacles, wings, horns, heads, and other appendages can be added using the toothbrush technique. Texture can be created by imprinting the clay surface with a variety of tools such as combs, forks, nails, tongue depressors, patches of burlap, or wire screening. Anything combustible added to the clay, such as a wad of newspaper, rice, or dried weeds, will end up as a few ashes after the firing. A pencil or some other object must be used to make a hole in the side of the hollow ball created by two pinch pots. The air pressure both inside and outside the ball must be the same or the clay will explode in the kiln. A good rule of thumb is that anything bigger in diameter than an adult thumb should be hollowed out—a pencil can be inserted to make a hole in an extraordinarily thick coil, for example. Any solid piece or any hollowed form must have an escape path for air during firing.

To explore the possibilities of modeling a clay figure, children can look at photographs of sculpture by the British artist Henry Moore. Well-known for his seated and reclining figures, Moore was inspired by ancient African and pre-Columbian sculptures as well as by smoothly weathered wood and stones. To make a clay figure, children roll out a thick cylinder of clay about 6 or 7 inches long. Using a plastic knife or tongue depressor, they make a vertical cut about 2 inches or so on one end to separate the legs. A neck and head are squeezed from the other end. Two smaller cylinders are rolled out to serve as arms and are attached to the shoulders. A tongue depressor or finger is used to make a smooth join. The figure can now be bent and shaped into a position—kneeling, sitting, bending, reclining. The elbows, knees, and waist can be bent as needed. The head can be turned to one side, and feet and hands can be pinched from the clay or added with small pieces. When the pose of the figure is satisfactory, the surface of the clay should be smoothed evenly with a finger or the tip of a tongue depressor and allowed to dry. Small animals may also be made by starting with a cylinder base.

Clay pieces should be allowed to dry slowly. If the atmosphere is too hot and dry, they may crack. Plastic bags can be placed over drying clay pieces to slow down the process. Dampened paper towels are sometimes needed in very dry conditions.

Dry clay pieces are called greenware. As greenware, the pieces are very fragile. Once the greenware has been fired in a kiln, they are referred to as bisque and are much sturdier. After the bisque firing, a ceramic glaze can be applied. Glaze is a solution that

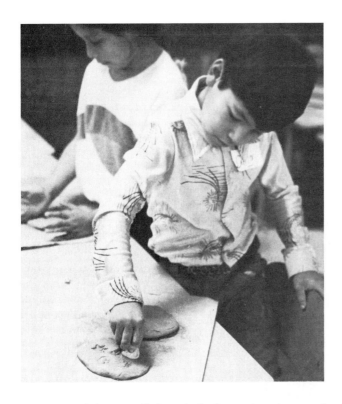

Two pieces of clay are rolled into balls, flattened, and stamped with fired clay stamps. A weed or flower holder is formed when the two pieces are joined.

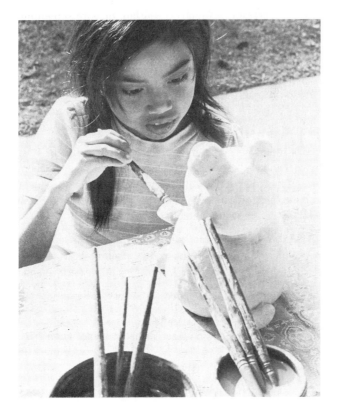

This student brushes glaze on a bisque-fired animal.

a

b

a. Preschool children develop manipulative dexterity in rolling balls of salt ceramic.

b. Beads are strung on soft yarn with a large-eyed needle.

looks somewhat like tempera, but it turns into a glassy surface with a shiny or flat color once the piece is fired again. Sample disks that have been painted with glaze and fired are useful in showing the children what colors are available. Once the glaze has been painted on, the bisqueware needs to be fired again. Alternate finishes for bisqueware that do not require a glaze firing include

1. Staining the bisque piece with thinned-down tempera—white or a color—and quickly rinsing off the excess paint until the desired stained effect is achieved. The colors are seen in the lower parts of the surface and create a pleasing effect.

2. Painting the bisque piece with acrylics or tempera and then covering it with acrylic spray.

3. Leaving the bisque piece its natural color but covering it with a clear matte or shiny acrylic spray.

4. Brushing a clear gloss glaze called Joli (available from art stores) over the stained, painted, or natural bisque surface.

ADDITIONAL MEDIA

Three additional media for modeling and construction activities can provide children with stimulating and pleasurable experiences. All are easy to use in the classroom and the necessary materials may be purchased from the grocery store.

Salt Ceramic

One batch of the recipe that follows makes a ball about the size of a large orange. Food color—either in liquid form or the highly concentrated paste food colors—or liquid tempera can be mixed into the water, or the batch can be left white. Salt is less expensive if it is purchased in large boxes rather than in one pound boxes.

> 1 cup of salt
> ½ cup of cornstarch
> ¾ cup of water, with one of the coloring agents listed above displacing the same amount of water

These three ingredients are cooked over medium heat and stirred constantly with a wooden spoon until the mixture thickens into a big blob. The mixture is removed from the heat and placed on a piece of foil. After it cools a bit, it is kneaded thoroughly and then stored in a plastic bag. If it must set a while before being used, it may need to be kneaded again to make it soft and pliable. Salt ceramic dries to a rock hardness without being baked in an oven. Toothpicks, cloves, feathers, and such can be embedded in salt ceramic while it is soft. Finished objects can be brushed with Joli or sprayed with a clear acrylic.

Baker's Clay

An optional ¼ cup of liquid tempera can be added to the following recipe for baker's clay:

> 1 cup of salt
> 4 cups of flour
> 1½ cups of water

These ingredients should be mixed thoroughly by hand, adding a little more water if necessary. The dough should be kneaded about five minutes until it is soft and pliable. This clay should not be mixed ahead of time because it loses its springiness and resiliency if stored and often becomes too sticky to use. Items made with colored dough are best left to air dry. Items made from uncolored plain dough can be baked an hour or two on foil-covered baking sheets in a 300- to 350-degree oven until nicely browned and hard all the way through. Thick, large pieces require a longer baking time than small, flat objects. A browner color can be achieved by increasing the oven temperature.

Beads and Pendants

Children begin very early to roll bits of any modeling material in the palms of their hands to make small balls. They also learn to coordinate hand and eye in stringing all sorts of beads. By combining these two manipulative skills, very young children can make necklaces from either salt ceramic or baker's clay. They will need blunt plastic needles with large eyes and a length of yarn or thick string about 18 inches long. The children pinch off pieces of colored salt ceramic or baker's clay, roll the pieces in balls, and push the needle and yarn gently through the centers. Some children are interested in the more advanced skill and challenge of alternating colors or sizes of beads—one red bead and then one yellow bead, or one large bead and then two small beads. Whatever planned or random combination is made, the necklaces are easy to make and attractive to wear. Making them holds the attention of very young children for some time.

The finished strings of beads should be placed on foil and dried thoroughly for several days. Periodically, they should be turned over gently to ensure that they dry evenly on all sides. When completely hard, they are ready to be worn.

Young children enjoy modeling salt ceramic or baker's clay to create yarn-hung pendants that they themselves wear or give to family and friends. To make a yarn-hung pendant, each child needs a 30 inch length of thick yarn, with a 2 inch strip of felt folded over and glued in the center of the yarn. The felt forms the base on which the children later glue their pendants. Four or five batches of salt ceramic or baker's clay in strongly contrasting colors are sufficient for an average class. If white salt ceramic or baker's clay is used, the pieces can be brush-painted with watercolor or tempera when they are dry. The children can roll coils and small balls and make pinched and formed shapes to place on the basic flat shape that they have pressed down on the felt tab. These small, decorative bits of salt ceramic or baker's clay may need to be lightly moistened to make them stay in place. If they fall off in drying, they can be glued back in place later. Pencils, toothpicks, tongue depressors, and other small tools are useful in creating small dots and pressed-in textures. Such simple forms as flowers, butterflies, turtles, elephants, airplanes, and faces make good motifs, or abstract designs can be created. The pendants dry hard in a few days. They should be turned frequently so that they dry thoroughly and evenly. A clear acrylic finish or Joli glaze adds shine to the finished pieces.

Salt Sculpture Figures

A small cardboard tube or an empty frozen juice container and a large lump of salt ceramic are the basic materials for salt sculpture figures. To keep the figure from being top-heavy, the tube itself should be filled with salt ceramic and the head modeled right on top of it. To avoid the disappointment of having the head break off later, a piece of dowel stick or a chop stick may be inserted through the top of the head and on down into the filled cylinder. The children each need a large lump of salt ceramic and several small pieces of other colors for adding facial features, unless they wish to paint the head when it is dry. If the children have used salt ceramic before, they probably need only be reminded of the necessity for kneading it before they begin work and of how to moisten rolls and balls of the material to adhere them as facial details. Toothpicks may be helpful in sticking added parts to the base. The teacher should point out that exaggerated or oversized features show up well from a distance. Pressing salt ceramic through a garlic press can create hair and beards.

After several days, when the salt heads and the salt ceramic inside the tubes or containers are dry, the figures are ready to be finished. Yarn, rope, or cotton can be glued on for hair and beards; felt, colored paper, and fabric for garments; pipe cleaners or sheet sponge for arms; and braid, feathers, and other scrap materials for other details.

Children should be encouraged to make a definite character, perhaps one from a favorite story or from a television show. The character can be real or make-believe, human or animal. Figures can also be used in dioramas.

Baker's Clay Murals

Baker's clay murals provide a rich bas-relief experience in early childhood classrooms. When finished, they are usually displayed in entrance halls and school offices. These murals are a group project, with each child in the class contributing at least one item to the composition. Many topics related to areas of the curriculum, such as science, social

a

b

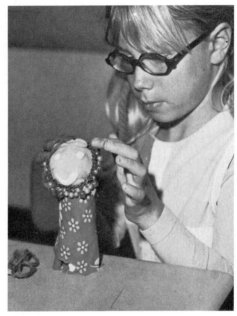

c

studies, and literature, are suitable for these large panels or murals. Any theme in which there are a number of items for the children to form and shape individually and then assemble on the prepared background is appropriate.

More than one thousand children participated in making a mural for the Department of Motor Vehicles building in Sacramento, California. Each of the twelve panels was 10 feet high and 2 feet wide. The general theme was "Highways and Byways of Sacramento," with each panel focusing on a specific scene, such as "Sutter's Fort," "Lake Folsom," "Airports," "Farm Life," "State Fair," "Gold Discovery Days," or "Fairy Tale Town." As each panel developed, the children came up with fresh, innovative ideas for additional items, and at the end of the project, the panels were filled with people, cars, buildings, hawks, sunbathers, fireworks, bikes, and blimps. A detail of the "Farm Life" panel is shown in the photographs on pages 228 and 229.

a. Six-year-old children showed much originality and diversity of form when they made these salt-head figures. Colored salt ceramic made it possible for the children to model contrasting facial features.

b and **c.** Young children enjoy the challenge of finding appropriate scraps of materials for adorning their figures after the salt heads are hardened. Glue and tape are suitable adhesives.

a

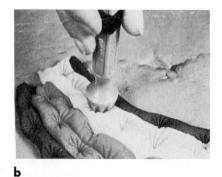

b

c

a. The title on a baker's clay mural can be made with balls and ropes of dough.

b. This baker's clay tool is pressed into a rainbow on a mural to add starlike imprints for textural accents.

c. Green baker's clay was pushed through a garlic press, and a toothpick was used to implant the "grass" to the mural background for a baseline effect.

d. "Farm Life" is the theme for this ten-foot-tall baker's clay panel. Orchards, barns, scarecrows, farmers, fields, and trucks are arranged on a textured, multicolored background.

d

Preparations must be made by the teacher, perhaps with some parental assistance, before the class begins work on the mural. A baker's clay mural requires a ¾ to ⅝ inch thick piece of particle board or plywood, covered with chicken wire, and with some thin, flat boards painted black and nailed on the sides for the frame. Finished murals are heavy; two sturdy screw eyes and a wire across the back enable the panel to be hung later.

Baker's clay is mixed in the desired colors for the background—yellow, for instance, for the ground area and turquoise for the sky. If a river, street, lake, or mountains are included, they need to be arranged at this time. The background clay should be slightly softer than the clay that will be used for modeling so that it can be rolled out easily with a rolling pin. The background is formed by breaking off small amounts of the clay and pressing it with fists and knuckles onto the board. When a large area is covered, it is rolled smooth with a rolling pin. One full batch of dough generally covers about 1 square foot of background. The clay should be rolled to a thickness of about ½ inch—enough to cover the chicken wire. If the dough on the background is too thin, many cracks will form as it dries. After the background is finished, the board is covered with a large sheet of plastic—a large garbage bag or one from the dry cleaner's—to keep the mural from becoming too dry before all of the children's modeled forms are put in place.

Usually, baker's clay used for modeling the mural figures can be mixed in half-batches to avoid wasteful leftovers. Plenty of liquid tempera must be put into the water when mixing the dough so that colors are bright and intense in the finished piece.

a

b

After a general discussion about the theme of the mural, what objects are to be made, and what sizes they should be, the children select what they wish to make. After choosing from the supply table small lumps of the baker's clay in as many colors as they need, the children work on a paper towel at their tables or desks, using a bit of water on their fingertip to adhere two parts of their animal or figure together. The finished form can be easily lifted from the paper towel and later put in place on the background. An assortment of plastic and wooden gadgets and tools for cutting, imprinting, and rolling the clay is useful.

The children who finish first should keep their items on the paper towel and cover them with a sheet of plastic to prevent them from drying out before they are placed on the background. It is best to delay assembling the mural until all the children have finished. This helps in planning where to place each item in relation to the other animals and figures. Generally speaking, the largest items should be placed first, with thought given to making a pleasing and cohesive composition that has one or more focal points. Consideration needs to be given to which shapes will direct the viewers' eyes toward objects of interest and lead them throughout the composition. Sometimes a street or path can be added to provide a baseline and unify scattered objects. A water-filled spray bottle serves as glue when assembly begins, with the background receiving a light spray of water before each item is placed on it. A garlic press with very small holes helps considerably at this point, since green clay of various shades can be pressed through and a toothpick used to cut off small clumps of grass. Placing the grass under the feet of each figure or at the bases of houses, trees, and animals tends to unite these items and prevents a floating-in-the-air appearance.

When the mural is finished, it should be left to dry in a warm dry room. It may take several weeks to become thoroughly dry, and during this time, the colors appear to fade and look very flat and unattractive. However, when the mural is absolutely hard and dry, any of several finishes can be applied and the colors will recover their previous brilliance. The best finish to use is a brush-on resin. Envirotex—or other brand of resin—works well. This product comes in a two-bottle package, the liquid in one of the bottles serving as a catalyst for the other. A small, equal amount of each liquid, about 1 or 2 ounces, is poured into a clean can and stirred about a minute, according to directions on the bottles. Then it is quickly brushed on the mural. One coat is sufficient, not only to bring back the colors but also to give the mural a high-gloss coat that is glasslike in appearance. Small pieces of the figures that have come loose in drying can be adhered when brushing on the

a. Assembly begins on a baker's clay covered panel as children complete small animals, human figures, and other objects needed for the theme.

b. The complete panel is displayed proudly. Each child contributed one or more figures related to Mother Goose.

Envirotex. Other finishes, such as spray-on clear acrylics, clear varnish, lacquer, and Joli glaze, bring back the color, but they require a number of coats to achieve sufficient and lasting shine or glaze.

Topics that work especially well for baker's clay murals are similar to those for cut paper murals: "Nursery Rhymes," "Fairy Tales," "Aesop's Fables," "Seasons," "Birds and Butterflies," "Our Town," "The Zoo," "Scarecrows and Farms," "The Factory We Visited," "Boat Harbor," "The Circus Parade," "Flower Garden," and "All about Us." A study of *Noah's Ark* or *The Peaceable Kingdom* by primitive artist Edward Hicks or a study of Seurat's *A Sunday on La Grand Jatte* can be a springboard for the children's own interpretation and version of these themes.

Edible Art

Bread dough and candy clay as modeling materials are probably used most appropriately at holiday times—those special occasions when children need outlets for expressing creatively the happiness of the season. Chapter 14 lists a number of topics for stimulating the children's thinking when they begin modeling and constructing with these food forms.

Bread Sculpture

Bread made from various grains and shaped in a variety of forms has long been a basic element in our diet. Who knows what adult or child first thought of shaping decorative forms while kneading, squeezing, or playing with soft, pliable, bread dough? It is debatable whether the Chinese or Egyptians were the first to make bread. Long, long ago, the Chinese knew about fermentation and steaming. Yet it is believed that, about five thousand years ago, a king's baker in Egypt made dough and forgot about it. Wild yeast cells settled on the dough, and when the dough was baked, it rose high and light. By luck, the baker saved part of the dough and used it to make more. Loaves of Egyptian bread baked thousands of years ago are now in museums. The Romans had their apprentices wear gloves and gauze masks to prevent sweat and bad breath from affecting the dough. They often baked bread in artistic shapes. If a poet was the guest of honor, the bread was baked in the shape of a lyre, and weddings called for bread shaped like joined rings.

People used to believe that bread rose by magic until 1859 when Louis Pasteur found that yeast was a live plant. Scientists tell us that four hundred tiny yeast cells can be placed on the head of a pin.

Bread has often been a part of symbolic rituals, and many a baker with an artist's sense of three-dimensional form and design has used the unbaked dough to model popular symbols—angels, teddy bears, and such. Small children respond immediately when handed lumps of soft bread dough. They sense its plasticity, and their hands respond to its tactile appeal.

Children can expand their multicultural understandings by modeling bread dough forms around holiday themes, such as Halloween, because parallels exist in several cultures. Every year in Mexico, for example, November 2 is celebrated as the Day of the Dead, and it is an occasion for making different kinds of food in the shapes of skulls, skeletons, and masks. A special bread called *pan de muertos,* or bread of the dead, is made in the belief that the souls of dead people return and enjoy eating it. The cemeteries at this time are places where families and friends meet, decorate the graves, and receive the blessings of the priests.

The ever-popular jack-o'-lantern is Irish and Scottish in origin. One legend tells that it was named after a man named Jack who was condemned to roam the earth with his lantern after he was barred from heaven for his stinginess and from hell for playing too many practical jokes on the devil. In the 1600s, the Irish peasants decided that October 31 would be a good date to celebrate the good works of St. Columba, a missionary who converted Scotland.

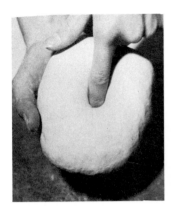

a

b

c

a. Bread dough should be kneaded until it is smooth and elastic. It should bounce back when a finger is pressed into it.

b and **c.** Bread dough is soft, pliable, and fun to form into skeletons, bats, cats, owls, and witches at Halloween. Any holiday would be an appropriate time to let children make their own interpretations of characteristic symbols in bread dough. The dough bakes quickly to a golden crust.

So they made the rounds, seeking donations to buy meat for a feast, prosperity being assured for generous donors and threats being made against stingy persons. Thus trick-or-treating was born. This type of historical and cultural information makes bread sculpture near the Halloween season an exciting and appropriate activity. Children can choose to model cats, skulls, bones, skeletons, mummies, jack-o'-lanterns, spiders, witches, broomsticks, pots of magic brew, ghosts, goblins, or bats from the soft dough.

Of course, bread sculpture need not be limited to Halloween. At other times of the year, children can make faces, suns, animals, birds, and people of various kinds from the soft, pliable dough. Edible puppets can also be made with bread dough. The form should be about the size of a child's hand, with all the features and decorations attached. A length

These youngsters can have their puppets and eat them, too. Made of edible bread dough, the puppets are brushed with an egg glaze and baked on a wooden stick.

of dowel stick or a sturdy meat skewer is inserted in the finished puppet before it goes into the oven. The child may choose to make just the head or face of a puppet, and a show can be staged when the bread puppets have cooled—before the children gobble them up.

One batch of the recipe that follows makes one large bread sculpture about the size of a baking sheet, or it can be divided into smaller portions for five or six children. After the children have washed their hands, they make their pieces directly on a lightly sprayed or greased baking sheet or on a piece of foil, because trying to lift and move the forms after they are completed is difficult. The dough is formed into sculpture by cutting, rolling coils, pinching, and squeezing. Bodies can be made in several separate parts and a tiny bit of water applied as glue if the child has used so much flour that the pieces of dough will not stick together. Children enjoy using almonds, pumpkin seeds, and sunflower seeds for eyes, noses, and other small decorative details. A shiny, golden glaze is obtained by beating an egg with two teaspoons of water and using a pastry brush to coat the modeled forms before placing them in a 400-degree oven. Scissors can be used to make a number of little snips after the glaze has been applied. This creates a texture that can be used for fish scales, sheep's wool, alligator skin, and similar surfaces. Poppy seeds and sesame seeds can be sprinkled over the egg glaze for accent areas. The odor of fresh bread baking, either in a classroom oven or one in the school kitchen, is a truly memorable one for the boys and girls.

Bread Recipe
1 cup of water
1 teaspoon of sugar or honey
1 tablespoon or 1 package of dry yeast
2 cups of flour
1 tablespoon of oil
1 teaspoon of salt

Let the first three ingredients stand in a bowl until the yeast softens—two or three minutes. Add 1 cup of flour and stir vigorously with a large spoon. Beat until smooth and then add 1 tablespoon of oil and 1 teaspoon of salt and 1 more cup of flour. Beating the batter thoroughly makes for a lighter and tastier loaf of bread. To have a dark dough that contrasts with the white dough, whole wheat flour, wheat germ, or bran can be substituted for a portion of the white flour. Pour the thick batter onto a floured board, and add more flour slowly as you knead the dough, keeping a coating of flour on the dough. To knead, fold the dough into a lump and push it firmly away from you with the heels of your hands. Knead for about five minutes, until the dough is smooth and elastic and no longer sticks to your hands. The kneading process is finished when the dough is smooth and satiny and when it

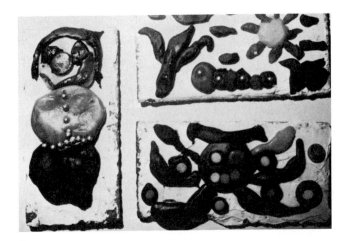
a

b

bounces back if a finger is poked into it. Adding too much flour results in a stiff, heavy dough. Place the dough in an oiled bowl, cover the bowl with a clean towel, and set the bowl in a warm place to let the dough rise for about forty-five minutes. Then punch the dough down and work it into a smooth ball. Divide the dough into portions for use in various parts of the bread sculpture or for five or six children to use. When sculptures are completed, let them rise in a warm place for about thirty minutes. Bake them for fifteen to twenty minutes in the lower third of a preheated 400-degree oven. Large forms may take longer. The bread should be golden brown and baked through. Let the bread cool on a rack.

a. Frosted graham crackers are decorated with candy clay.

b. Colored candy clay can be modeled in any number of decorative shapes and placed on top of frosted cupcakes.

Candy Clay

The pleasant task of modeling and shaping with candy clay enriches the child's concepts of making bas-relief forms. Animals, people, or plants that stand upright should not be made with candy clay. Paste food colors dye the candy clay to bright and irresistible hues, and each child should have marble-sized balls of several colors. The children should work with clean hands on freshly scoured desks on a piece of paper towel.

Candy clay designs can be placed on a plain graham cracker or one that has been covered with buttercream frosting. Children also enjoy decorating frosted cupcakes with candy clay for special occasions or working together to decorate a large sheet cake. The approach to decorating such a cake with candy clay is similar to that of making an assembled mural, with each child making one item about as tall as his or her finger and placing it on the frosted cake. Themes for cake murals might be: "Mary, Mary, How Does Your Garden Grow?," "Nursery Rhymes," "At the Circus," "Butterfly Land," "All of Us Standing in Rows," "A Favorite Story," "Silly Pets," or "Robots and Astronauts."

Candy clay can be mixed in the classroom by several of the students, or an adult or older child can mix it ahead of time and store it in plastic bags. Once mixed, it is not sticky to the hands. One batch is enough for a class of thirty students to each decorate a graham cracker or a cupcake. It is best not to choose a hot day to work with candy clay, as the butter tends to melt and make the clay too soft and sticky.

Candy Clay Recipe
⅓ cup of butter
⅓ cup of light corn syrup
½ teaspoon of salt
1 teaspoon of vanilla
1 pound box of powdered sugar
Food coloring

a

b

a. Stand-up characters are made from fruit, vegetables, and toothpicks.

b. Wooden chopsticks are inserted in a potato (left) and orange (right) to hold edible puppets. Toothpicks are used to secure raisins, slices of carrots, tiny marshmallows, parsley hair, and dried fruit.

Blend the first four ingredients, and then mix in the powdered sugar. Knead till smooth. Add more powdered sugar, if necessary, to make a nonsticky, pliable clay. Divide into small portions, and mix in food colors.

Buttercream Frosting Recipe
1 pound box of powdered sugar
¼ teaspoon of salt
¼ cup of milk
1 teaspoon of vanilla
⅓ cup of butter

Combine the ingredients and beat with an electric mixer until smooth and creamy. The mixture should spread very smoothly to make a neat surface on which to decorate with candy clay. If it is too stiff, beat in a few more spoonfuls of milk.

Edible Jewelry

Very young children can not only make necklaces, but they can eat them, too. Stringing the various items is good training in manipulative skills, and deciding the order for large/small, dark/light, and rough/smooth items calls for counting and decision making. A large-eyed needle and some lightweight crochet thread are needed for each child. Food items, such as any dry cereal that has a hole in the center, raisins, prunes, dried apricots or other dried fruit, beef jerky, or gum drops, are placed in bowls for the children to make their selections.

In the middle of the necklace, the children can place a pendant such as a tiny box of raisins, or they can make a pouch from a clear piece of vinyl purchased by the yard from variety stores. Masking tape is used to seal the sides of this little envelope, and then it is filled with sunflower seeds, nuts, raisins, and so on.

Fruit and Vegetable Assemblage

Materials for this nutritious art project can include such items as the following, plus any others that are in season or readily available: apples, oranges, potatoes, celery, carrots, lemons, lettuce, radishes, mushrooms, parsley, small squash, jicama, green beans, pumpkin seeds, nuts, lunch meat, cheese, grapes, cucumbers, pretzels, pickles, alfalfa sprouts, cloves, and tiny marshmallows. Some toothpicks and waxed paper or paper towels for each child's desk or table area are also necessary. The teacher should cut and slice the carrots, celery, or other items so that small separate bowls of each are ready for the children to select from and use. Small hors d'oeuvre or aspic cutters can be used to cut interesting shapes from slices of carrots, celery, turnips, and the like.

Whatever the assemblage project, children will learn about good foods and nutrition while learning about structure, design, and adhering separate parts—and at the same time have a tasty treat. For starters, the teacher can give each of the children a wooden meat skewer and let the children select and arrange cutup edibles on their skewers. The filled sticks are then placed into half a cabbage head for an attractive edible arrangement.

An edible puppet is fun for young children to make. The head is selected from the assembled items—potato, apple, lemon, carrot, and so on—and a wooden chopstick inserted inside it for the handle. Toothpicks are used to adhere the features—slices of carrots or raisins, for example—to the puppet's head.

Another construction project calls for the children to each have a small paper plate for creating a special arrangement. Using lettuce or greens of various sorts for a background, they can choose to make a face, perhaps with a halved pear serving as the foundation. Or they may want to make an attractive design of cheese cubes, halved grapes, and pretzel rings.

To make a stand-up construction, children may create animals, perhaps with a carrot section for the body, toothpick and grape legs, and a radish head. A racing car can be made from a zucchini with stuffed-olive headlights and carrot-slice wheels.

PAPIER MÂCHÉ

A stack of newspapers, a roll of masking tape, some corks, cut-up dowel sticks, cardboard tubes, and wheat paste are all that are needed to start making wadded paper creatures. The lumpy, bumpy creatures shown in the photographs on page 236 were all brought into being by six-year-old children. The materials are common and inexpensive, and the process provides channels for a wide range of responses by each child.

To make a mammal, bird, fish, or reptile, a large sheet of newspaper is wadded up by the child into an oblong, round, or egg shape. A few strips of masking tape are used to hold the wad firmly together. Corks, a short piece of wood, and cut-up pieces of cardboard tubes are taped in place for legs, ears, tails, heads, and horns.

Wheat paste should be mixed with water to a smooth, thick consistency by the teacher. To do this, pour 3 or 4 cups of water into a large bowl and use an eggbeater while gradually adding dry wheat paste. The final mixture should be smooth and creamy.

Several children can share a paper plate of paste into which they dip short paper strips. Strips of paper towels, newspapers, or brown paper bags are cut quickly beforehand on the paper cutter by the teacher into approximately 1-inch widths. The short strips are thoroughly soaked and covered on both sides with the paste. Excess paste is wiped off with the fingers before the strip is applied to the animal. Several strips are needed to cover up the wadded form completely. The final layer of strips should be school paper toweling or brown grocery store bags rather than newspapers. The children smooth out the strips with their fingers until the animal is neat and even on the surface. The animal is then left to dry thoroughly, usually for several days.

While the animal is drying, the children think about how they are going to decorate their creatures—what colors of paint they will use and what scrap materials they will choose to glue on, such as cotton, buttons, yarn, or feathers. Then, using tempera that is smooth and opaque, the children paint their animals with a base color. After this base coat is dry, they add features and decorative stripes, dots, and so on, with smaller brushes and cotton-tipped swabs. They can glue on a rope tail, button or thumbtack eyes, a yarn mane or hair, felt or sponge ears. If a shiny glaze is desired, the entire creature can be coated with a clear acrylic spray when it is dry.

a

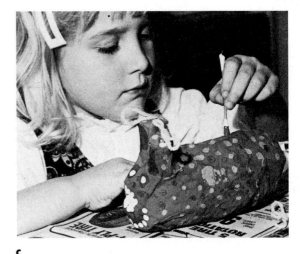

c

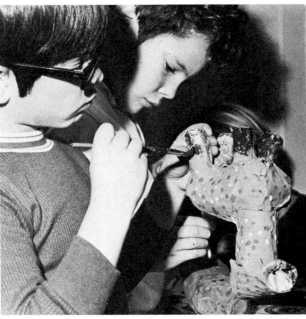

b

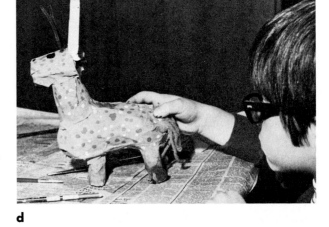

d

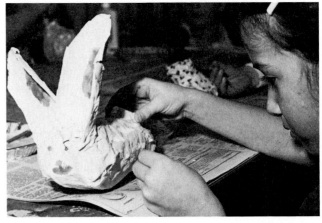

e

a. Children use masking tape to fasten corks and cardboard tubes to wadded-up newspapers before covering the entire form with strips of paper towels or brown paper bags that have been soaked in a wheat-paste mixture.

b. Contrasting colors are added for decoration when the base coat of paint is dry.

c. Cotton swabs dipped in paint are handy for making small dots.

d. Yarn, pipe cleaners, felt, feathers, and all sorts of scrap materials can be glued on the animal for final embellishment.

e. By cutting cardboard tubes in half lengthwise, a six-year-old girl fashioned tall ears for her wadded-paper rabbit.

a

b

c

d

Instead of wadded-up newspapers as a base, small boxes and cardboard tubes can be fastened together with masking tape. These adapt themselves well to constructing cars, fire engines, streetcars, trains, trucks, planes, boats, spaceships, robots, submarines, and the like. Cardboard tubes and thick dowel sticks can be cut up for wheels and smokestacks. Short sticks can be taped on for sailboat masts, propellers, and airplane wings. These small, boxlike conveyances appeal to young children because their forms are familiar and their size is such that children can cope with them. The concept is three-dimensional design, yet two-dimensional decorative elements also are involved.

When all the parts are securely taped in place, the entire form is covered with a layer of paper strips that have been dipped in wheat paste. This holds all the parts together and provides a smooth surface for the child to paint. When the construction dries, the children are ready to paint it with tempera. After a base coat of color has been applied and has dried, the children can add windows, doors, wheels, and contrasting trim of all sorts, using smaller brushes. Boats need portholes, cabins, and flags. Planes can have emblems and numbers painted or glued on, and photographs of faces clipped from magazines can be glued onto the windows.

A group project using large cardboard cartons, carpet tubes, and round ice cream cartons can result in large animals for the classroom. With these larger creations, the boxes are assembled and held together with wide strips of butcher tape. Wads of newspapers can be attached with strips of paper dipped in wheat paste. In this manner, rounded forms can be built up and the general contours of the animal formed. All the children can participate in this phase to develop a lion, bear, giraffe, or fat hippo. When the animal is completely dry, the children can paint it with tempera, or it can be spray painted outside. A coat of clear varnish or shellac gives it a finished look. Usually these animals, especially if a few pieces of lumber are included in their framework, are strong enough to hold a child on their backs. One teacher made a number of saddlebags for the hippo her

a and **b.** Kindergarten boy contemplates how he will paint his cars and plane after they have been covered with paste-soaked strips of paper towels.

c. Creamy smooth wheat paste is used to coat newspaper strips before covering the boxy conveyances.

d. Several colors of tempera and both large and small stiff brushes are needed to paint the boxy conveyances after the wheat paste has dried.

Kindergarten students inspect Tiddalick, the giant frog from an Australian aboriginal folk tale. The papier-mâché frog was used as part of a play that culminated a summer art camp.

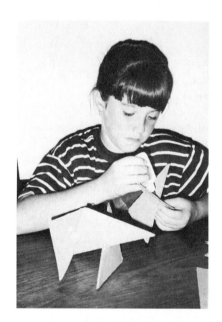

Stabiles made of corrugated cardboard that is precut in a variety of geometric shapes are notched and glued together by students. Pieces may be added in an informally balanced manner as the glue dries. Students enjoy seeing pictures of both stabiles and mobiles by Alexander Calder and then painting their own sculptures with bright colors.

class made and then filled them with task cards and books. No matter how the boxy beings are used in the classroom, making them and having them for use later are exciting experiences for young children.

CARDBOARD STABILES

A famous American sculptor of this century—Alexander Calder—is known for inventing new kinds of sculpture called stabiles and mobiles. His stabiles are stationary, whereas parts of the mobiles gently move. To make these sculptures, he cut large pieces of sheet metal into shapes and balanced them on rods so that they slowly moved in the breeze. He often painted the flat sheets of metal in bright colors. Sometimes his stabiles and mobiles remind us of real objects; other times, they are to be enjoyed for their shapes alone.

To make a cardboard stabile, the teacher cuts out a number of small geometric shapes—about 3 to 5 inches or so in size—from corrugated cardboard on the paper cutter. The children use scissors to cut a small notch in one of the sides of each of two pieces. They then push the two pieces together, notch to notch, and add a drop of white glue to make them stay together. The children then join another pair of cardboard pieces in this manner, and when the glue on both pairs of notched cardboard pieces has dried, join the pairs to each other in the same notching and gluing manner. They add on to their stabiles with more pieces of cardboard until they have created a rather large piece of sculpture. The children must be careful to keep their sculptures balanced or they will fall over. The sculptures can be painted later if desired. Students may also enjoy working in small groups and making large, freestanding, stabile sculptures in this manner.

MINIATURE HOUSES AND BUILDINGS

Children can use square pieces of white and colored construction paper and follow a basic folding process to create the base form for all sorts of small houses and buildings. Once the paper is folded, the building's back, front, and sides are determined. The paper can then be unfolded to lay flat on the tabletop or desk while the child adds doors, windows, shingles, bricks, and so on with markers, crayons, and oil pastels, or by using scissors and paste and colored paper. The house is refolded and pasted together for its final form. Another piece of paper pasted on the top forms an overhanging roof. Students can make a false front for one end of the building by cutting a storefront from another piece of paper, decorating it, and pasting it onto the folded house.

All the children's buildings can be assembled on a tabletop covered with butcher paper on which streets and sidewalks are drawn. Tree trunks can be made by rolling a 3×4 inch piece of paper into a cylinder and securing it with glue or tape. Half of a 6 inch circle rolls into a cone to glue on as a foliage top for the tree-trunk cylinder. Students find it challenging to invent other ways to make stand-up trees, people, cars, dogs, signs, and so on.

The basic form for the house or building is made by using a square piece of paper, 9×9 inches or so, and folding the paper in half in one direction. The paper is then unfolded, and each of the two sides that are parallel to the fold are folded in to the center fold. Then the paper is folded in half from the other direction, unfolded, and the other two sides folded in to the center fold. The square has now been divided into sixteen small squares. The dotted lines, as indicated in the diagram on page 240 are cut. This forms the four sides and roof of a house or other small building.

WOOD SCRAPS AND GLUE

Construction projects involving wood scraps offer children excellent three-dimensional experiences. If spread on the floor where small hands can sort, pick up, and handle them, wood scraps in a multitude of shapes and sizes cause young children to experiment and imagine, to relate and design, to think in terms of height, width, depth, and weight. Children will find in the scraps shapes that may suggest to them the body of a bird; the basic shape for a truck, boat, or plane; the legs or arms for a figure; the trunks for a grove of trees; or the parts for a building or an abstract composition.

Cabinet shops and construction companies discard odds and ends of wood scraps. If these pieces are too large for the children to handle easily, they should be cut into assorted smaller geometric and free-form shapes. A few flat boards and Masonite sheets are helpful to use as bases on which some of the children can glue their constructions.

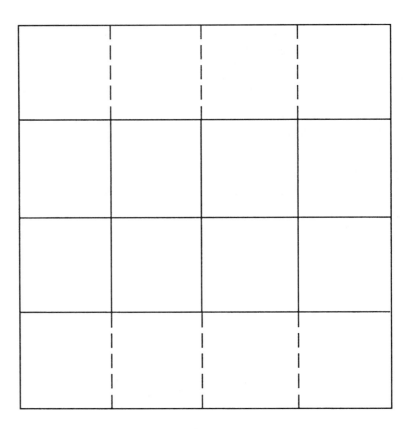

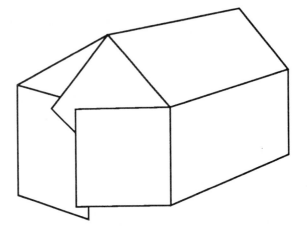

Fold paper in both directions as shown. Unfold, cut on the dotted lines, and refold to make a building.

The teacher needs to advise the children that, in adhering wood pieces, a small amount of glue will dry and hold two wood pieces together rather quickly, whereas a large puddle of glue will require a long time to dry. Masking tape holds the wood pieces in position while they are drying. When the objects are completed and the glue is dry, the children may wish to paint them and add various kinds of decorations. Bits of fabric, feathers, pipe cleaners, and photographs of faces clipped from magazines can be glued onto the constructions.

Bas-reliefs can be made with wood scraps, too. For this art task, a flat piece of Masonite or thin plywood is used for the background, and the wood pieces are glued down flat in an arrangement. The children could be presented with the problem of designing a "Funny Machine" or a "Mechanical Animal or Person." Thick yarn might be used along with the wood pieces if a linear element is needed, and the finished work can be painted with watercolors or tempera or sprayed all one color.

a

b

c

a. Children should see, feel, and study wood shapes carefully as they make selections for their glued-together constructions.

b. A piece of masking tape is helpful in holding several wood scraps in place until the glue dries.

d

c. A bird assembled by a kindergarten child is embellished with paint and feathers. The structure is glued to a Masonite base.

d. A boat by a kindergarten child has basic form and structure.

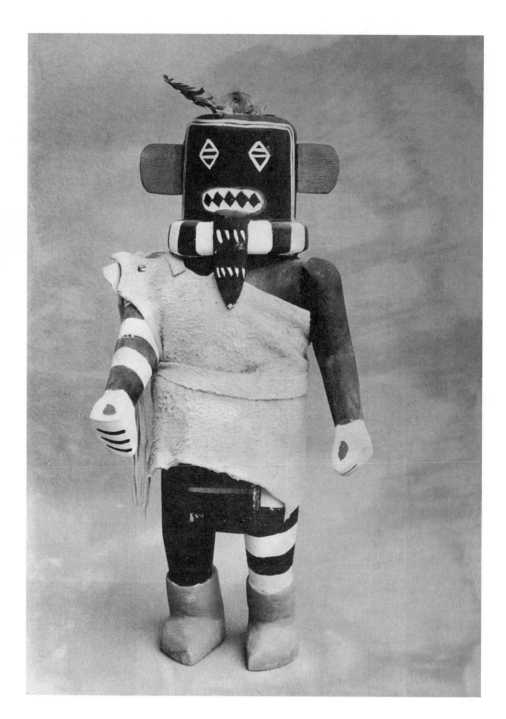

Children learn from seeing three-dimensional forms from many cultures. A kachina from the Southwest was constructed from wood and leather. Kachinas are used to teach Hopi children about the religious beliefs of the tribe.

IN CONCLUSION

Some children may be repetitive in their work with clay, perhaps making dozens of similar little forms; this gives them a certain sense of security in their own achievement. As children become secure in knowing that they can model and construct what they wish with any given material, they tend to explore other possibilities. Later, they may start to preplan some of their projects and yet let their work grow spontaneously.

Watching a child at work and taking a careful look at his or her finished products reveals much about the child's artistic growth and personality. Some timid children or those who have been overly cautioned at home about soiling clothing and hands may need special encouragement to work with clay and other three dimensional materials. Different media appeal to different children in various degrees of enthusiasm. Kinesthetic learners usually produce more creatively with materials that can be modeled and shaped.

Sending artworks home as mentioned in Chapter 6 is important. In preparing three-dimensional artwork for the trip, special care must be taken because these objects may get lost or broken on the homeward journey. Shoe boxes and other small containers may be used, with the clay objects and sculptures being packed carefully and the box tied or taped shut. When the teacher has the opportunity to communicate with parents, he or she may make some suggestions about the values of working with clay and other three-dimensional media.

TOPICS FOR DISCUSSION

1. Which of the elements of art are particularly applicable to sculptures?

2. Select a sculpture in your community. Apply three of the elements of art to it either in a discussion or short paper.

3. What are the similarities and differences between additive and subtractive sculpture? Between mobiles and stabiles?

4. Which age groups would respond more readily to working within a given framework? Develop specific motivations or topics for three-dimensional constructions and sculptures that would offer creative challenges to these children.

5. Compare the two sculptures shown in the Color Gallery—Modigliani's *Head of a Woman* and Moore's *Reclining Figure.* Utilize the model for art criticism in Chapter 2 to evaluate or critique the two artworks.

6. How can three-dimensional art experiences provide opportunities for learning that cannot be found in two-dimensional projects?

7. What are some possible motivating themes suitable for use in art projects that involve modeling and constructing?

8. List five concepts that can be taught when children are introduced to modeling and construction activities. Include appropriate vocabulary.

9. What positive and supportive statements could you make to a child as he or she is working in three-dimensional materials?

10. Review this chapter and Chapter 4. Write five informational statements that you would tell parents about the development of child art and learning that takes place as children explore materials.

12

Puppets and Masks

●●●●●●●●●●●●●●●●●●●●●●●●●●●●●

Creative drama is an excellent way to develop the imagination of young children. Boys and girls need no written lines to memorize or structured situations to imitate. What they do need is an interesting environment and motivating activities that allow them to experiment. Dramatic play is one of the best ways children have to express themselves. Here, they feel free to state their own thoughts and feelings. Adults often discover how children feel about themselves and others by listening to their dramatic play. The pretending involved in the experience—whether planned or spontaneous—is a necessary part of the child's development.

Many times creative drama begins in a section of the classroom where there are large play blocks. One child builds a "store," and soon others are joining in as customers and clerks. Speaking on toy telephones to friends is another way children become involved in dramatic play. A puppet show in which children make up a story as they go along is especially valuable. The use of simple props, costumes, masks, and puppets can enhance dramatic play because children delight in using imagination to create and embellish the situation.

Dramatic play is an important medium for language development because it helps children become fluent in expressing verbally their own thoughts and feelings. A child who is reluctant to speak in other situations is almost compelled to speak in order to be included in the puppet play. Even very shy children become more vocal when they feel their own persona is hidden behind a mask or their ideas spoken by the puppet they hold in their hand. Both puppets and masks offer a safe distance between the children and an audience that might otherwise be frightening.

PUPPETS AND PUPPET MAKING

The exact origin of puppets is unknown. Some believe that the Egyptians invented puppets, yet some of the first puppets were made along the Ganges River in India. Oriental countries have a long tradition of puppetry, and the ancient Greeks even had puppet theaters. Roman puppeteers held performances in homes and public places and traveled as road shows. Italy is well known for its puppetry, and in the Middle Ages, Italian puppeteers took their portable theaters to France, Spain, Germany, and England. When young children make puppets, they are not only enjoying a playful art activity but are also joining in a long historical line of make-believe, laughter, and adventure.

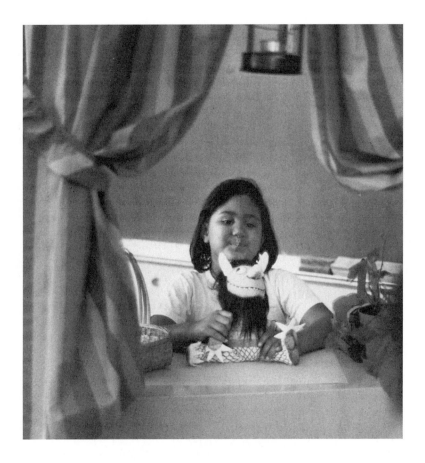

Any simple opening can be transformed into a puppet stage by adding a few feet of material for stage curtains. Creative dramatics stimulates the imagination of young students, and simple materials can be transformed into colorful and charming puppets.

Puppets are three-dimensional, small-scale representations of people and animals. They are directly controlled by children's hands, both when the children design them and later when the children make them talk and move as animated creatures. They may even be extensions of the child's own personality, disguised somewhat in paper, paint, and cloth. Children delight in playing with puppets, and they especially enjoy making puppets.

Flat-Stick Puppets

Probably the simplest puppet for the very young child to make is the flat-stick puppet. Children who are drawing figures and animals can make a flat-stick puppet by simply cutting out their drawing and gluing or stapling it to a tongue depressor or flat stick of wood. They may find it fun to glue on bits of fabric, felt, and yarn for items of clothing. By sitting below the level of a tabletop or behind an improvised puppet stage made from a cardboard carton or large blocks, the children can hold onto the sticks and make their puppets move and talk.

Lollipop Puppets

From an assortment of cardboard pieces—rectangles, circles, and ovals—the children select one shape that they staple to a short, flat stick, such as a tongue depressor. Then the children make selections from an assortment of yarn, buttons, macaroni, colored paper, felt, and paint, and create a face, gluing on hair, a nose, and other features. The children enjoy naming their brightly colored puppets and creating impromptu dialogues among each other's puppets.

a

b

a. This kindergartner draws a schema with felt pens on stiff paper and cuts it out to make a stick puppet.

b. A variety of symbols for people is evidenced in these stick puppets as kindergartners position themselves behind an improvised stage made of building blocks.

Paper-Plate Puppets

Paper plates are inexpensive and are available in white and a variety of colors. Thin paper plates can be folded in half to form the mouth of a simple puppet. A hand strap needs to be stapled or glued onto the top half of the plate. The puppet is manipulated by placing the hand through the strap and the thumb under the bottom of the plate. The child may use paper and scrap materials to create teeth, eyes, whiskers, nose, hair, and other details, which may be added with glue or by stapling.

Another type of paper-plate puppet is very versatile in that it can double as a mask if holes for the eyes are cut at the proper places. A short, flat stick of wood is stapled or glued to the back side of the plate. If the stick is attached between two plates that are glued together, a two-faced puppet is possible. The puppet can be either human or animal in form. A tableful of interesting supplies and scrap materials, such as yarn, feathers, buttons, stick-on dots, tape, colored or metallic papers, egg carton bumps, paint, cloth, scraps of felt or fur, and corrugated paper, is a necessity. If the group has just enjoyed a favorite fairy story or folk tale, the children may wish to create characters to act out the story.

a

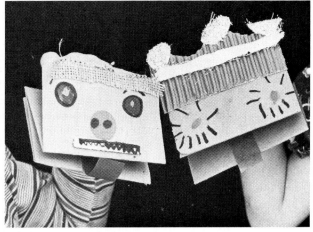

b

c

a. Heads bob up and down on fold-over puppets.

b. M-fold puppets offer many channels for the resourceful use of scrap materials.

c. Moving, dangling, and projecting parts aid these puppets in being viewed and manipulated.

Folded-Paper Puppets

The next three puppet forms are all made by folding colored construction paper in basic shapes and adding features and clothing. They involve skills in folding, stapling, cutting, gluing, attaching, and overall designing. The puppets are completed quickly and do not cause frustration for young children. In a few minutes, the children are ready to move into the world of fantasy and relate to their new talking friends. The techniques can be repeated often, with children making a different kind of puppet each time.

Fold-Over Puppets

The fold-over puppet is made by folding a piece of 9 × 12 inch colored construction paper vertically, and then stapling the top and open side. The top is folded over about 3 or 4 inches down, and the child's hand is inserted in the long open end of the tube. The children use cut paper, yarn, felt pens, gummed paper, stick-on dots, or whatever they choose to create the face and body of their puppets. They may add some hair, ears, and decorative details to the back side of the puppet also.

A simplified fold-over puppet can be made from small paper lunch sacks: The bottom of the sack becomes the puppet's face, and the natural fold of the sack forms the puppet's mouth.

a

b

a. Kindergarten children learn to handle glue, scissors, and all sorts of scrap materials when they make stuffed-bag puppets.

b. Simple materials make for a success-oriented art task. Thick yarn, stick-on dots, and meat trays are easy for young hands to handle.

c. Paper-bowl hat covers this puppet's yarn-covered head.

d. Masking tape wrapped around a scrap of fabric at the neck holds the puppet's garment in place.

c

d

M-Fold Puppets

M-fold puppets are also made from a folded piece of 9 × 12 inch colored paper. The paper is folded vertically and the long, open side stapled. Then it is folded in half horizontally and the two ends folded back again in an M-shape. The fingers and thumb are then inserted in the pockets in the back side, and the puppet's mouth opens and closes as the hand moves. Colored-paper eyes, teeth, ears, whiskers, tongue, and so on are glued, taped, and stapled in place.

Cootie-Catcher Puppets

To make cootie-catcher puppets, the children start with a 9 or 12 inch square of paper. This is folded diagonally twice to find the center, and each corner is folded to the center. The entire piece is turned over and the corners on the back side are folded to the center point. The piece is then folded in half from both directions, horizontally and vertically. By inserting the fingers in the back openings, the child opens and closes the puppet's mouth. The talking mouth can be stapled together to keep it from splitting as the child opens and closes it. Eyes, ears, eyelashes, tongue, teeth, and beards can be attached.

Stuffed Paper Bag Puppets

Stuffing a very small paper bag with a wad of newspaper and turning it into a delightful puppet by using bits of discarded materials and paint gives young children new pretend "friends" to play with and talk to, while also rewarding them with positive feelings of personal accomplishment. A scrap box filled with yarns, fabrics, felt, feathers, pipe cleaners, buttons, and the like proves to be a valuable aid in generating ideas and approaches in design. Paint, brushes, tape, glue, and staplers should be accessible.

Number-1-size paper bags are available at hardware and variety stores. Their small size makes them easier for little hands to handle. First, a piece of newspaper is wadded around the end of a short, wooden stick and pieces of masking tape wrapped around the wad to hold it firmly in place on the stick. This wad is inserted into a paper bag, and a piece of masking tape is wound around the base of the bag at the puppet's neck. Before children begin to work, they should discuss differences in facial features and the great variety of shapes that they can use to create eyes, eyebrows, lashes, noses, mouths, teeth, ears, beards, and such. Hair, hats, crowns, horns, simple clothing, and arms can be cut from colored paper, yarn, and scrap materials. A piece of fabric, tissue, or crepe paper can be gathered up and taped around the stick at the base of the bag to serve as a garment. Arms and legs can be attached to the garment with a stapler. Egg carton bumps, fringed paper, and stick-on dots help the child to think in terms of exaggerating and projecting the features and making use of decorative details. Adding objects that move, bounce, sparkle, and shine make the puppet easily seen from a distance.

PUPPETS FROM SCRAP MATERIALS

Sock Puppets

Every household usually ends up with a few odd or mismatched socks that can be used as the foundation for a sock puppet. The sock is pulled over the hand, with the heel over the thumb to form a mouth. By making a fist and moving their fingers, children make the puppet talk. Ears are formed by shaping and pulling part of the sock out from the side or top of the puppet head; the ears will need to have rubber bands or elastic hair bands wrapped around the base to hold them in place. Rickrack, yarn, lace, buttons, beads, felt, or rug scraps can be glued on to decorate the puppet.

Box Puppets

Basically, a box-puppet foundation consists of two small boxes taped together with gummed paper or masking tape. Individual cereal boxes or half-pint milk cartons are the right sizes for these puppets. The boxes are arranged so that when they are opened out, using the tape as a hinge, the sides rest together and the open ends of the boxes both face in the same direction. The boxes form the jaws of the puppet, and children insert their hands into the open ends to manipulate the puppet's mouth.

Although each box puppet begins with the same basic shape, imaginative decorations give each one an individual personality. Cardboard ears, wire or twine whiskers, candy cups cut and used for eyelashes, eyes formed from the cups of egg cartons, and features and designs created from yarn, string, paint, or felt markers all work well in adding details. Teeth, tongues, and fangs can be cut or torn from paper and added to the mouth formed by the two boxes. A handkerchief or scrap of cloth can be wrapped around the wrist and hand when the puppet maker is manipulating the puppet.

Glove Puppets

Tiny puppets can be made out of fingers cut off fabric gardening gloves, ski gloves, or children's knitted gloves. The children can decorate them by sewing or gluing on thread, yarn, buttons, feathers, felt, or fur to make facial features, hair, beak, whiskers, mane, topknot, hat, or crown.

Finger puppets are charming and adaptable to all sorts of play activity.

a. Ball of instant papier-mâché is formed over the child's finger into a tiny puppet head. Chin, nose, and eyebrows project in an exaggerated manner.

b. Feather is embedded in salt-ceramic bird's head when it is being modeled. Paint is brushed over the entire head after it is hardened.

c. Yarn is glued on this painted head to complete the finger puppet's decoration.

d. Circle of cloth is poked up inside the puppet's head to cover the child's hand.

e. The smallness of finger puppets appeals to children, and they enjoy seeing those made by others. These woven puppets were made in Ecuador.

a

b

c

d

e

MODELED PUPPETS

Finger Puppets

Finger puppets are particularly appealing to the very young child. They are tiny, charming, and adaptable to all sorts of play activities. The two materials that work best for small, modeled, finger-puppet heads are baker's clay and salt ceramic, the recipes for which are in Chapter 11. The children take a small wad of either of these pliable materials and stick a finger inside it to create a hole. This opening enables the child to hold the completed puppet on a finger and should be made a little larger than the child's finger, since the puppet's cloth garment will be glued inside it.

Boys and girls should model a simple face, pinching out a nose, ears, chin, and such, or adding tiny lumps of the material for these features. They can use a pencil or small tool to impress and imprint details. If the salt ceramic or baker's clay is colored, the finished head does not need to be painted. However, children may enjoy using paint for accents. Yarn, felt, cotton, wool, or other materials can be glued on for hair, hats, beards, and the like.

The puppet's garment is made from a small circle of cloth on which the child can draw designs with markers and then glue on rickrack, buttons, pom-poms, beads, and ribbons. When the garment and head are both complete, a bit of glue is dropped in the opening of the puppet's head and the center of the garment poked into it.

Clay also can be used to make finger puppets. Plasticine is temporary but provides many colors, whereas water-based clay needs to be fired but is more permanent. The clay

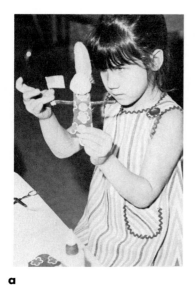

a

b

c

d

e

a. This kindergartner adds a flag to the pipe-cleaner arm of her tongue-depressor puppet.

b, c, and **d.** Tongue-depressor puppets are as different as the five-year-old children who create them.

e. Baker's clay gives crusty, wrinkled faces to these two witches. Children add clothing and wool hair after the puppets are baked in an oven.

can be squeezed around the finger and the features, hair, and clothing can be pinched out or scratched into the surface. This technique of pulling the details out of the clay prevents problems with joining two pieces of clay because poorly attached pieces fall off as they dry. Even very young children are able to squeeze and pinch a few details in their finger puppets.

Puppets on Sticks

Modeled puppets pushed on the end of tongue depressors are particularly suitable for very young children to make. Either baker's clay or salt ceramic may be used by the children to form small puppet heads and attach them to wooden sticks. The recipes for these two media are found in Chapter 11.

If uncolored baker's clay is used, the finished puppet head must be covered with plastic wrap until it is baked because the salt in the baker's clay tends to dry rapidly, making cracks and leaving a rather unattractive surface. The puppet head on the stick can be baked in a 350-degree oven until it is thoroughly hard and lightly browned. If colored baker's clay is used, the finished puppet may be left to air dry, but it will need to be given a shiny clear glaze when dry. To achieve this finish, it may be sprayed with a clear acrylic spray, or it may be brushed with Joli, a clear liquid that resembles clear nail polish and that is available in craft supply stores.

a

b

a. Salt-ceramic heads are modeled on top of a short stick.

b. Tape is used for attaching wraparound garments on stick puppets.

c. Contrasting colors of salt ceramic were added by this six-year-old girl to accent the features on her puppet's face.

d. Projecting features make for interesting profiles on these two puppets.

c

d

If salt ceramic is used for making puppet heads, several colors of this modeling material are needed so that the child can create facial features of contrasting colors. A bit of water may be brushed on the puppet head to secure the eyes, lips, and other features.

When the puppet heads are made from air dried material such as baker's dough or salt ceramic, the children can add feathers, peppercorns, cloves, or bits of macaroni for eyes and teeth. Hair, hats, and ears can be attached with a bit of glue after the heads are either dry or baked. For a garment, a circle of fabric with a tiny slit in the center can be slipped onto the tongue depressor and attached at the neck. Offering an assortment of scrap materials for clothing details and head coverings makes for unique creations.

Thick long sticks permit the child to make salt-ceramic puppets with large heads. Each child needs a small lump of salt ceramic about the size of a lemon for the basic head shape and several small pieces of other colors for details. For instance, the basic head shape might be green, and the child could add a yellow nose, red eyes, and a white beard. Although salt ceramic can be painted when it is dry, using brightly colored dough eliminates the need for this step. One recipe of the salt-ceramic mixture makes enough modeling material for three to four children. To make it pliable and plastic, the dough should be kneaded for a few minutes before using. The teacher should demonstrate how to make a ball of the salt ceramic and then push it down on top of a 9 or 10 inch stick of wood. The children pinch it, roll it in coils or into small balls, and use pencils and small gadgets to imprint textures. Bits of the salt-ceramic dough may be pushed through a garlic press and the clump of strings added to create a beard or hair. Parts adhere better if a bit of water is used as glue or if bits of toothpicks are used as nails.

Contrived and assembled stages for puppet and marionette shows can be made from corrugated cardboard or plywood. They should be sturdy and large enough to accommodate several children at one time. Youngsters enjoy decorating the stages and making backdrops. A table turned on its side can be used as a makeshift puppet stage.

For added details and decorative elements, feathers, toothpicks, pipe cleaners, macaroni, buttons, brass fasteners, and other articles can be placed in the dough while it is pliable, and rope, yarn, and fabric can be glued to the dried piece. Several days are required for the heads to dry thoroughly. A shiny glaze may then be applied. A square of fabric can be gathered or pleated and attached to the neck of the puppet with masking tape or colored plastic tape. Braid, lace, rickrack, felt scraps, or ruffles can be attached to the garment with glue or needle and thread.

Puppet Situations

Once the artistic creation is complete, a child's creativity and imagination can continue to be stimulated with activities that develop language skills and cognitive ability. A successful puppet-making experience results in a diversity of colorful and interesting characters, each with a unique personality. Along with the puppet's head and facial features, the addition of fangs, horns, beaks, pigtails, and other interesting details can emphasize the puppet's character. Props such as caps, hats, helmets, crowns, shawls, or even miniature masks can be added for interest. Children should have many opportunities to play with their puppets, either through plays or speech-making activities. While in front of a mirror, they can practice opening their puppet's mouth on selected important words or syllables and also determine the best angle at which to hold the hand controlling the puppet. Children can make their puppets talk and move about while performing in an impromptu show, whether the story line they use is taken from a popular story or nursery rhyme or is one of their own invention. Possible situations for the children to act out with their puppets include

1. A parent scolding a misbehaving child
2. Space people arriving on earth
3. A grandmother calling on the telephone
4. A shopkeeper and customer
5. A sleepy animal in the zoo
6. A spider spinning a web
7. A caterpillar about to make a cocoon
8. A puppy waiting for its dinner
9. A bird building a nest
10. An argument on the playground
11. Getting ready for a birthday party
12. Being late for school

First graders paint fruits and vegetables on this puppet stage for a dramatization on nutrition.

Diverse designs and materials are the result of different cultural beliefs and different tribal uses for masks in various areas of the world.

MASKS AND MASK MAKING

Children today most commonly associate making and wearing masks with Halloween. The tradition of wearing masks on the last day of October began long ago in ancient Gaul and Britain. The druids and priests thought that witches, demons, and the spirits of dead people came back to earth for this one night of the year. The druids lit bonfires to drive the bad spirits away, and they protected themselves by offering the bad spirits good things to eat and by disguising themselves with masks that made them look like evil spirits.

These animal masks, part of a kindergarten play, are attached to strips of tagboard stapled together to form a cap. In this way, the wearer's face is left uncovered but the persona of the mask is established.

Evidence of mask making has been found in oral and written history and among the artifacts of nearly every known culture. Masks have served numerous diverse purposes. For example, masks have been used to cure disease in Ceylon and Burma and by the American Iroquois tribe. In parts of New Guinea, large masks have been used to increase the authority of judges as they mete out justice. Protection is another reason for wearing masks, and some cultures have also used them to scare away intruders, to appease their gods, or for momentarily being another personality. In many cultures, masks are worn in rituals and in ceremonial dances. Contemporary tribes in the Southwest and Mexico use masks as part of their religious dances and celebrations. In Japan, actors in Kabuki theater use masks as an integral part of the drama.

Many ceremonial masks have exaggerated features and repetitive design elements, and make use of such decorative materials as paint or dyes, feathers, beads, bones, shells, hair, and fur. Tribal masks are usually symmetrical and often emphasize a mood or capture the personality of a spiritual creature through exaggerated and distorted parts. Mask makers often heighten the overall effect by using repeated lines and shapes to make dominant features stand out. Authentic folk art masks of other cultures are frequently found in museums and are particularly interesting to young children. Photographs, reference books, and videos are useful ways to bring masks into the classroom if real masks are not available.

Although we usually think of masks as dramatic and part of some celebration, modern-day masks are frequently utilitarian and are most often used for protection. Examples of useful masks include those of the deep-sea diver, the baseball catcher, the beekeeper, the surgeon, the astronaut, the welder, the goalie, the fire fighter, and the skier.

Paper Masks

Half or full face masks can be cut from a piece of colored construction paper that has been folded in half. Slits and tucks may be cut, overlapped, and stapled or taped to help the mask fit around the face. Side bands of paper can be attached above each ear to hold the mask in place. Paper can be cut, curled, torn, and pasted into place to add interesting features. Paper plates can also be used for paper masks, with features and decorations being glued, painted, or drawn on the surface.

Bird masks of construction paper may be made after students have looked at photographs of birds and examined the different shapes and sizes of heads and the different kinds of beaks, colors of feathers, sizes of eyes, topknots, crests, and so on. In so doing, children are developing concepts of what makes one bird different from another. To make bird masks, students fold a 9 × 12 inch piece of colored paper or colored tagboard in half so that they have the fold on the 9 inch side. To locate the eyes, the children use chalk to draw a small circle near the upper portion, about an inch in from the fold, on each side. The circles should be about as large as their own eyes. They also use a piece of chalk or crayon to draw the beak, starting with its point near the bottom of the folded paper and angling upward toward the eye and then outward to the edges of the paper. On the edges opposite the fold, they mark an inch or two for tabs for attaching yarn. This leaves about 8 or 9 inches for the mask across the eyeline when the mask is unfolded. Leaving the paper folded, the children cut out the mask in a symmetrical shape, unfold it, and cut out the eye shapes. They then make decorations by overlapping pieces of colored paper cut in feather shapes, curling strips to project and dangle, making fringe, and so on. They can also use crayons, oil pastels, or markers to add patterns and details. When the masks are finished, yarn is attached to the sides with tape. The students can wear the masks for creative movement activities—swooping, flying, gliding—as birds would do.

A blotted symmetrical paper mask can be constructed by folding a piece of paper in half and cutting it into an oval the size of the child's face. The students then paint half a face on one side of the fold line—there should be one eye, one eyebrow, half a nose, and half a mouth. When the paper is refolded and blotted, the painted features transfer to the other side, making a mirror image of the original painted features. This process of paint and blot may be done more than once if additional elements are needed to make a finished mask. Students may want to add other lines and decorations with oil pastels, markers, or crayons.

Papier-Mâché Masks

A metal bowl turned upside down can be used to form the mask. Students can also use heavy aluminum foil that has been pressed and molded to their own faces; the basic facial form can be preserved by placing wads of newspaper beneath the foil so that it will keep its shape while the strips of paper are applied. Strips of paper dipped in a glue-water solution or a wheat paste solution are used to build up layers for a papier-mâché mask. Three or four layers of paper strips should be used. The paper should be torn into pieces or strips less than an inch wide. For the best results, the layers should alternate in direction. The last layer of papier-mâché should be strips of school paper toweling or paper bags. Once dry, the mask can be painted with thick, creamy tempera. When completely dry, clear spray, polymer gloss medium, or shellac can be applied for a shiny finish.

Found-Object Masks

In most cultures, people used materials from their environment to create masks. For that reason we find masks made of many diverse materials. Some masks are made of wood, some are made of woven fibers, and some are made of clay or metal. Decorative items for the masks also vary from region to region, depending on the objects found in the environment.

To reinforce this concept, the teacher provides each child with an oval piece of cardboard that is scored down the center and folded back to better fit the face. The cardboard also has eye holes so that the child can see through it. The children collect things from their environment that they can use to make an interesting mask. The collection period lasts several days or a week.

On mask-making day, children select from their collections of found objects which ones they want to use to decorate their masks. Found-object masks often are decorated with such things as shells, bottle caps, beans, parts of pine cones, paper clips, keys, leaves, seeds, pebbles, plastic utensils, feathers, cloth, buttons, lace or rickrack, yarn, nails or screws, bolts, and wire. These objects are glued into place for facial

These students in a special education class enjoy their sack costumes. Their teacher made the oversized sacks out of various colors of butcher paper, and the students added facial features and other details with marking pens.

features as well as for patterns and textures. A discussion follows to determine which object or material was most frequently used, which was the most unusual, and which was the most imaginative.

Brown Paper Bag Masks

Large, brown, paper bags can form the base of masks that cover not only the face but the entire head. Large eye holes, a flap for the nose, and sections cut out on the sides for the shoulders relieve children's feelings of claustrophobia. Five-gallon ice cream containers also make good foundations for masks that cover the entire head.

Paper-cutting or tempera-paint techniques can be used for decorating or embellishing the sack masks. This particular lesson can also introduce or reinforce knowledge about color, line, and texture. Students can be encouraged to use limited colors (only two or three colors), warm colors (red, yellow, orange), cool colors (blue, green, purple), or neutral colors (brown, beige, black, gray). Lines can be thick, thin, curved, straight, long, short, or broken. Actual texture is added by gluing found objects to the surface, including various kinds of yarn and other fibers for hair. Patterns may be created with numerous small repeated lines or shapes, either painted on or cut from colored paper.

Paper-sculpture techniques are used in making this mask from torn, cut, scored, and curled paper. The base of the mask is part of a stocking that has been stretched over a frame made of cardboard and wire from a coat hanger.

A simple mask is formed from folded paper. Half of the face is painted on one side of the fold and transferred to the other half while the paint is still wet.

Corrugated paper forms the foundation of this simple mask, with yarn and construction paper used to represent hair and facial features.

This Tlingit mask was carved from wood and painted, reminding the viewer of a family memory, a myth, a dream, or perhaps a dance.

Stretched Stocking Masks

Nylon stockings can be stretched over a wire frame to form the foundation of a mask that is easy to see through and offers great flexibility for decoration. The wire frame is made by older children or adults from a wire clothes hanger that has a cardboard tube at the base. The tube is removed, and the wire is straightened and formed into an oval. The ends are stuck into the cardboard tube to form a handle. Knee-high nylon stockings are a perfect length to stretch over the wire frame, but other stockings or pantyhose can be cut in lengths and tied off. Once the frame is assembled, the children can use yarn, torn or cut paper, plastic tape, buttons, and other sewing materials to create features, hair, hats or crowns, collars, and jewelry. Possible themes include characters from favorite books, someone in uniform, a person from history, or birds and beasts. After the masks have been completed, children can participate in a "Who am I?" session in which they wear their masks and give clues; other children can ask "yes" or "no" questions in an attempt to guess who each mask represents.

IN CONCLUSION

Masks and puppets offer opportunities for young children to develop and express themselves creatively in two ways: first is the experience of making a puppet or mask, followed by the challenge of making the personality embodied in the object come alive.

Organized dramatic play in the classroom is structured in terms of materials and directions given by the adult. Here are a few simple guidelines for motivating dramatic play:

1. Select a simple story or theme that is part of the children's experience.

2. Motivate with pictures and discussion.

3. Do not overplan or overstructure.

4. Keep the activity short.

5. Encourage but do not force a child to participate.

In creating the situation for dramatic activities, most children utilize one of three themes: *domestic scenes* (role playing about home and the activities that occur there); *rescue* (someone is sick or there is some problem that has to be solved); and *sudden threat* (monsters or mean animals emerge that chase them). As they become older, children create more complicated roles and characters that help them act out their fears and relieve their aggressions.

Dramatic play occurs daily in the lives of young children and is their way of understanding and dealing with the world. Children are fascinated by puppets and masks because these objects permit them to enter into fantasy so easily. A simple puppet or mask used in dramatic play is a sure way of stimulating creative storytelling and providing children with a means of expressing their ideas and feelings.

TOPICS FOR DISCUSSION

1. What role does dramatic play have in the lives of young children?

2. What are the advantages of using puppets and masks with dramatic play?

3. Formulate at least five additional puppet situations to add to the list in the chapter. Share your lists and ideas.

4. How are puppets different from and similar to masks?

5. How would you adapt a puppet or mask idea for use with one of the groups of special needs students discussed in Chapter 7?

6. What are some other subject areas that have connections to a puppetry project in art? Plan drama activities using puppets that would motivate learning in one of these subjects.

7. What abilities of young learners are stimulated in creating original puppets? Adapt the process and product questions in Chapter 5 to puppet-making activities.

8. What have been the purposes of masks in cultures past and present? Which contemporary masks still serve these purposes?

9. Compile a list of themes for dramatic activities involving masks.

10. Using the five guidelines for stimulating dramatic play, plan an activity in which children would use a mask or puppet.

13

Fabric and Fiber

$\textbf{W}$orking with fabric and fiber encourages spontaneity and fosters skills in cutting, gluing, stitching, weaving, and designing—whether the children are making pictures or craft objects.

Fabric is an exciting, tactile material for young children to see, touch, and handle. It comes in an endless variety of colors, prints, and textures and lends itself well to both individual and group projects. Fabric and felt should be collected and stored in a number of labeled cardboard boxes, cartons, or plastic containers. Pieces can be sorted by color to make it easier for the children to find the scraps they need. Pressing the fabric before the children begin cutting makes it easier for the children to work with it. Good scissors are imperative when working with fabric and felt. Ordinary classroom scissors usually used for paper are not adequate for cutting cloth and may lead to a frustrating experience for the child; for this reason high quality scissors are needed for cutting fibers.

In becoming acquainted with yarn, children develop a basic vocabulary and understanding of the process of weaving and are able to make simple objects using several elementary techniques that involve looms and various fibers. Yarn should be wound loosely into balls from the skeins and kept sorted by color in boxes or cartons.

BANNERS

Banners as well as flags add richness and meaning to various occasions. Banners and wall hangings were very popular during the Middle Ages, having originated in Rome during the period of military conquest. They were carried into battle to differentiate military groups. Heraldic flags helped to identify friend or foe because the metal helmet and armor made recognition impossible. Standards were the personal flags of rulers, and small streamers and long, ribbonlike flags were carried by troops. During the Crusades, flags and banners were used by nobles and kings. Standards were used even earlier in Egypt and the Near East. Merchant and craft guilds in the Middle Ages used banners to identify themselves. Today we frequently see colorful banners in museums and galleries, in street displays, in churches, and at fairs.

In the classroom, banners can be a culmination of a group's thoughts and feelings about an idea or an activity; they can convey a message, an emotion, or a story. A banner should present its message clearly and effectively because it is viewed from a distance. When a group of students cooperatively work on a banner, each child participates in designing, cutting, pinning, and attaching the parts to the background. Whereas first and

Permanent markers were used to make drawings on squares of muslin, and the squares were sewn together to make a quilt. The theme for this project was "Groups I Belong To," which the students were studying in social studies.

second graders are able to pin their designs together and use a simple running stitch to hold the pieces in place, preschoolers and kindergartners may use fabric glue. Patchwork banners are recommended for group projects. Each child makes one square for the allover configuration, and all the squares are stitched together or adhered to a large felt or fabric backing. If regular fabric is used, it can be hemmed or bound with tape. Felt does not need hemming. These banners may hang in the room or school office for a number of weeks and then be dismantled in such a way that each child can retain his or her individual section.

Banners can be made from many kinds of fabrics—in solid colors, stripes, and prints. Buttons, beads, lace, rickrack, braid, tiny mirrors, and mylar can be added to the designs. Yarn is sometimes used for linear details and for writing words. Both sides of felt banners can be used for designs.

As young children begin cutting fabric, they may need a demonstration of specific techniques required for cutting fabric with scissors—for example, how to hold the scissors, how to fold the fabric to cut out a small opening for an eye or similar small spot, how to snip fringe, and how to fold and cut a symmetrical shape. They will find it easier to create figures in parts rather than making them in one piece—cutting the body, legs, arms, hair, hands, and boots out of separate pieces of fabric. Children may wish to draw their designs with a piece of chalk before cutting.

The top of the banner can be attached to a wooden stick or a metal rod by adding short straps of felt or fabric or by folding over several inches of the top and stitching it in place, leaving a narrow opening for the rod to slip through. Wooden balls or screw-on finials add adornment to the ends of this supporting pole. The bottom of the banner can have lead weights attached to make the banner hang evenly. Some banners have a rod or

a

b

c

a. This small, individual banner made by a five-year-old child is hung by felt tabs from a short dowel stick.

b. Kindergartners made a "Santa and His Helpers" banner, using felt on felt and a bit of fake fur for textural emphasis. The banner was later disassembled so that the children could retain their individual panels.

c. Colorful appliqué banners from Africa are living history books in that they tell of heroic deeds of a powerful dynasty of eleven kings who ruled for many years in what is now Dahomey. The banners appeal to the viewer through their simplicity and boldness.

stick inserted through a hem in the bottom. Lightweight banners may need lining, although this is seldom necessary. The lower edge of a felt banner can be cut in a scallop or other decorative manner, with fringe, tassels, or ribbons attached. Banners can hang flat against the wall, hang from a ceiling or beam, or be placed in a freestanding holder on the floor. Swinging wall brackets hold banners out from the wall, and, of course, banners can be carried in a procession or parade.

a

a. Appliqué banner made by first-grade children is made of red, yellow, and orange squares. Cutouts were adhered quickly with fabric adhesive.

b. Sixteen third-grade children combined efforts for this large, lined, patchwork banner. Children attached their cutout shapes with running stitches. Each square represents a favorite book.

b

An electric frying pan with several layers of heavy aluminum foil can be safely used to melt paraffin for batiking. The thermostat on the pan maintains the wax at an even temperature, well below the burning point, and the foil protects the pan's surface and also provides insulation between the heat source and the cans of wax.

Older children enjoy the challenge of designing a room flag or a school flag that perhaps features the class motto, the team emblem, the initials or name of the school, or some other simple motif. Heavy canvas is a good backing for outdoor flags, but the edges should be hemmed before the flag is placed on a pole or holder.

Occasions for making banners and flags are endless. They may be created to welcome parents and friends to an open house, to say thank you to the PTA for some project given to the school, to celebrate a special event or a change of season, to make a school picnic or musical performance more festive, or to wave in the wind at a school athletic event.

BATIK

For centuries batiks have been made in India, Indonesia, Japan, Africa, and other parts of the world. The batik process uses wax and resist-dye techniques to create allover patterns and pictures. Basically, batik is a process whereby wax or paste is applied to fabric in a decorative manner for the purpose of resisting the dye that is applied later. The wax or paste is removed after the fabric is dry. One of the main characteristics of batik is the spiderweb effect achieved when the wax hardens and cracks and the dye penetrates into the fibers in thin lines. In more complicated batiks, the fabric is waxed and dyed several times, creating lovely color and design patterns due to overlapping and color blending.

In adapting the rather complex batik process for use with young children, teachers will find the techniques described here to be filled with possibilities, yet simple and safe enough to be used in the classroom. All the necessary materials can be purchased in local stores.

Paste Batik

The paste method of batik does not use wax and the fabric is not dipped in a dye bath. It is related to a Japanese dye process called *sarasa*. It is also somewhat like an African resist technique called *adire eleko,* in which the design is applied on the cloth with a starch called *lafun,* which is made from cassava flour. In this African process, the starch is flaked off the cloth when the fabric is dry, and the fabric is dipped in the dye again to reduce the contrast.

These Japanese and African techniques can be simplified for young children by using a paste mixture made of ordinary store ingredients. This paste is used instead of melted wax to protect the fabric from the dye that is applied later. Wherever the paste is

a

a. Paste flows smoothly from a squeeze bottle as the child makes a drawing on a taped-down piece of cotton muslin.

b. Food dye solution contrasts sharply with the white areas that were protected by the paste. Intense watercolor washes can be used in place of the food colors.

b

squeezed onto the cloth, the fabric will be white when the piece is finished. The paste should be mixed in a blender until there are no lumps. The following recipe should be doubled or tripled for use with large groups of children:

½ cup of flour
½ cup of water
2 teaspoons of alum (in the spice rack at the grocery store)

Each child needs a small piece—about 8 × 10 inches—of 100 percent cotton muslin, bleached or unbleached, that has not been laundered or treated with permanent press. This fabric should be taped down on a piece of corrugated cardboard.

The paste is placed in several plastic squeeze bottles such as those used for dispensing mustard and ketchup. The children draw their pictures by holding the bottle perpendicular to the fabric and squeezing it to create and maintain a smooth flow of paste onto the fabric. They may make lines, dots, and solid masses, and then leave it to dry overnight. The next day, food color washes are brushed over the picture. The dried paste resists the color and leaves the fabric beneath it white.

Paste food colors, available from cake-decorating supply stores, are mixed with water in clean shallow cans or plastic containers that do not tip over easily. A small amount of this very intense dye is mixed with water to make a wash; once on the fabric the colors dry lighter than they appear to be when they are wet. Several colors can be brushed into separate areas of the same picture—red for a roof, brown for a tree trunk, yellow for a flower, and blue for the background. The fabric is left to dry thoroughly, and then removed from the cardboard backing. The paste is chipped and rubbed off with the fingers, revealing the white picture underneath. The fabric is ironed and the edges are trimmed before mounting or matting the finished product. Greeting cards can be created by gluing a small paste batik picture to a folded piece of colored paper.

For a group project, a length of muslin is taped to a large piece of corrugated cardboard, perhaps 3 × 5 feet. Each child draws a figure or animal with the paste bottle, placing them on several baselines that have been applied beforehand.

Drawn Batik

In this batik variation, the child draws a picture or design with a thick black water-soluble marking pen on Dippity Dye paper, a paper made of synthetic fibers and available from art supply catalogs. Colored markers can also be used. The paper is placed on a piece of white butcher paper. Melted wax is applied with a small, natural-bristle brush to cover all the lines in the drawing. The wax should be melted and kept at 250 degrees in a deep-fat fryer, at a depth of about one inch, or in a can standing in a foil-lined electric pan. For safety's sake, the wax should not be melted over an open flame or electric element or in a pan of hot water. Children dip the brush into the melted wax and quickly apply it to the lines on the Dippity Dye paper, working rapidly to prevent the wax from cooling on the brush; if the wax is too cool, it will not penetrate the paper and thus the marking pen lines will not be protected from the color washes. The wax will cover a broader space than the black lines, leaving a white outline on either side of the lines after the dye is applied.

After the children have completely covered all the black lines in their pictures with wax, washes made of diluted paste food colors are brushed onto the unwaxed areas of the paper. The wax protects the lines made with the marking pen. After the paper is thoroughly dry, it is placed on newspaper, ironed to remove the wax, and lifted up quickly from the white butcher paper on which it was originally placed. For display purposes, the finished batik may be mounted on a piece of white paper to allow the richness of the colors to show brightly.

Crumpled Crayon Batik

After children have completed a drawing on butcher paper with many colors of crayons, the paper is soaked in water and crumpled into a ball. After uncrumpling, the students flatten it and blot off excess water. With a wet brush, each child applies watercolors or diluted tempera over the surface. Because the color is more intense in the creased areas of the paper where the fibers have been broken down, the finished drawing has the cracked effect of a wax batik.

a

b

c

d

a. A child draws on fabric or Dippity Dye paper with water-soluble felt pens before applying wax.

b. Wax melts in a can that stands in a foil-covered electric pan. Here, a boy covers his felt-pen drawing with wax before he brushes the dye on the unwaxed portions of the fabric.

c. Diluted food coloring is brushed over the entire picture.

d. When the wax is removed by ironing, the drawn batik is finished.

Tempera Batik

Students use applicator squeeze bottles filled with white tempera to draw a picture on unbleached muslin. The paint must be allowed to dry thoroughly, overnight or longer. Thinned acrylic paints are then used by the students to brush into the shapes and over the tempera lines. Again, the fabric is allowed to dry thoroughly. As the final step, students immerse their pieces of fabric in water and work the dried tempera paint so that it lifts away. The original drawing will show through as white lines and shapes. This project lends itself especially well to underwater themes.

FABRIC CRAYONS

With fabric crayons, children make a drawing on a piece of ditto or typing paper. The paper is placed, crayoned side down, on a piece of 100 percent polyester fabric or Pellon. A piece of ditto or typing paper is placed on top of the drawing while it is being ironed, with the iron set at cotton. The top paper protects the fabric from the high heat necessary to transfer the crayon.

"Undersea Scenes" is a particularly appropriate topic for this acrylic batik lesson. The white-line drawing resists the watery washes of paint.

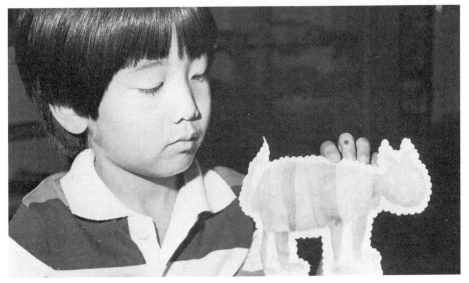

Fabric crayons were used on paper and the design ironed onto synthetic fabric to create this stuffed animal. Edges were trimmed with a scalloping scissors after stitching and stuffing.

A large wall hanging can be prepared by having each child draw a small building, figure, flower, animal, or whatever is needed for the topic, and then ironing the drawings onto the fabric in a pleasing and unified arrangement. Fabric crayons are useful for making stuffed items: the fabric with the transferred drawing can be sewn to a piece of felt or other fabric to provide a backing, stuffing placed inside, and the edges pinked, scalloped, or just cut with a plain scissors. Individual projects include fabric pictures, pincushions, tree ornaments, and pillows. Also, small squares of fabric can be mounted on heavy paper

a

b

a. Each child's drawing, done with special fabric crayons, is cut out and ironed onto synthetic fabric.

b. The drawing is lifted from the fabric after being ironed.

c. Kindergartners display the group project after all the drawings have been transferred to fabric.

c

for greeting cards. Since fabric crayon marks are permanent when applied to polyester fabric, teachers may enjoy making a garment for themselves, with each child drawing a small design and transferring it to the material before it is sewn together.

STUFFED STUFF

Drawing with marking pens on fabric or Dippity Dye paper takes on an added dimension when the figures are stitched to a backing and stuffed. The result is a type of soft sculpture that can be an individual production or an assembled group mural. When the three-dimensional mural is disassembled, the individual parts may be reclaimed by each child. Cotton muslin and Dippity Dye paper are inexpensive and provide a good base for the children to draw on. If marking pens are used, the children should have an old magazine or several thicknesses of newspapers under the fabric or paper to protect the table or desk from ink stains.

After the children complete their drawings on fabric, the figures are placed on another piece of fabric and the two pieces stitched together on the sewing machine, with a few inches left open on one edge. Older children can be taught a simple running stitch to use in sewing up the openings, or a sewing machine can be used by the teacher or a

a

b

c

d

e

a. A caterpillar is made of individual circles of fabric that are colored with oil pastels. Each child designed one section.

b. In this "Balloon Parade," kindergarten children introduced themselves for an open house by drawing figures with felt pens and assembling the stuffed forms with name balloons on a colored-paper background.

c. A butterfly tree was made by first-grade children, using felt pens on white fabric. When the tree was disassembled, each child retained his or her own contribution.

d. This six-year-old girl draws a butterfly freely on fabric and fills in areas with felt pens.

e. This city skyline is 7 feet long and epitomizes a study of urban architecture. Buildings show great diversity of shape and exterior ornamentation. Car, plane, sun, and clouds unify allover design.

parent. It is easier to sew the two pieces together on the right side and trim the raw edges with a pinking shears than it is to sew them on the wrong side and turn them inside out. The forms look neater if they are pressed before being stuffed. Polyester—available in pound bags—old nylon stockings, fine sawdust, or plastic bags are suitable stuffing materials. Objects made on Dippity Dye paper can be stapled, glued, or stitched before stuffing.

The children should work with a fairly small piece of fabric or paper. For the caterpillar shown on page 271, each child was given a circle approximately 7 inches in diameter, except for one child who received a 10 inch circle for the head. The children decided to add pointed pieces of felt to each segment. Pipe cleaners and feathers were added to the face for antennae.

The first-grade children who drew themselves for the "Balloon Parade" had their choice of several sizes of fabric pieces. They were urged to use the entire height of the material for their figures. The stuffed figures were assembled on colored paper, and then a bit of bright yarn with a name balloon was attached to the hand of each figure. The "Butterfly Tree" was done by a group of six-year-old children using marking pens. The variety in the allover designs and colors used is seen in each child's unique shapes and decorative details. The children perched their stuffed butterflies in a colorful swarm on a many-branched tree. The "City Skyline" mural was drawn and assembled by seven-year-old children who had just completed a unit on city neighborhoods and who had studied the many kinds of buildings that make up a city. They had looked in detail at the shapes, sizes, and kinds of architecture—churches, factories, schools, apartment buildings, offices, and so on.

Soft sculpture offers a rich potential of creative tasks for young children. Backgrounds for murals can be made from paper, burlap, or felt. With each child drawing one or two elements for the total concept, the entire class feels the pride of group effort, yet individual expression is paramount within the whole configuration. Children enjoy exploring the following topics for stuffed murals:

1. Birds in a bush
2. An airport
3. A boat harbor
4. Houses on a hill
5. On our playground
6. Witches and goblins
7. Dancing around the maypole
8. Children flying kites
9. Below the waves
10. Zoo parade
11. Birds, bees, butterflies, and blossoms
12. Burrowing animals below the earth

STITCHERY

Learning to express ideas in media other than crayons and paint is an important part of artistic growth in early childhood. Stitchery can be introduced by giving each child a 10 or 12 inch square of natural or colored burlap, some yarn, and a large-eyed, blunt needle. The teacher should pull threads in the burlap to assure straightness when cutting it and should fold masking tape around all four sides to prevent the burlap from unraveling. Burlap is best sprayed with starch and ironed before the child uses it. An embroidery hoop or a wooden stretcher frame helps young children to control their stitches, although one is not necessary. Blunt needles cannot be used for piercing fabric and felt, but they easily penetrate the loosely woven burlap. Children will want new pieces of yarn frequently, especially when they are just beginning stitchery, and therefore the teacher should have plenty of small pieces cut and available.

The first stitches of preschoolers are usually straight ones arranged in a random fashion. The size and number of stitches will vary because the child's attention span is quite short. Gradually, children become aware that they can consciously make their needles go up and down, right and left. They are not sewing a recognizable object at this stage. It is enough that they are learning to control their fingers. By age four, they may

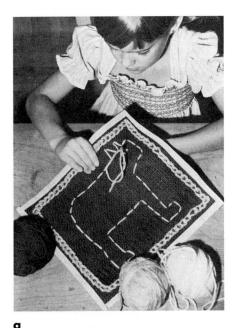

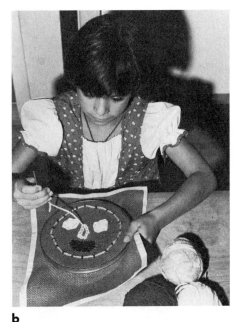

a

b

a. Masking tape keeps the edges from fraying while a child works on burlap. Here, a chain stitch is used for a border, while the animal is outlined with a running stitch. The child completes a French knot for an eye.

b. Couching is used as an outline for the face, with felt eyes and mouth attached with a running stitch, and a chain-stitched nose is added. Some children prefer embroidery hoops or a wooden stretcher frame to hold their fabric while they work.

c

d

begin naming what they have stitched, either before or after they have made it. Five-year-olds are eager to gain more skill with the needle, and this is a good time to extend their vocabulary with color and texture words. Beginners may simply enjoy pretending that their needle is taking a walk as it pulls the yarn along a straight, curving, or zigzag path.

Six-, seven-, and eight-year-olds are ready to learn more about specific stitches if they have had previous experiences with needle and thread. A sample of a few basic stitches made by the teacher and mounted in a display area encourages children. Children can also invent their own stitches or variations of the basic ones. Here are the four basic stitches:

1. The *running stitch* is a basic in-and-out movement with the needle and yarn. The stitches on the top surface of the burlap can be tiny and the ones underneath long, or vice versa, or the stitches can all be somewhat the same size. Several rows of running stitches can be placed close together to create a special effect.

c. This chain-stitched picture made by a Peruvian child is examined by a kindergartner.

d. A stitchery from Colombia embodies symbols for houses, trees, and spatial concepts that are comprehensible to young children.

RUNNING

Plain

COUCHING

Single

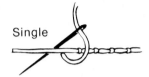

CHAIN

Plain

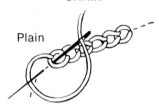

CROSS

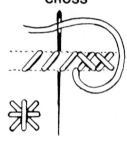

Basic stitches

Diagrams courtesy Lily Mills, Shelby, North Carolina.

A large burlap mural can be a group project, incorporating felt appliqué and four basic stitches.

2. The *couching stitch* is good for outlining and making borders. A piece of yarn is positioned on the burlap and secured with a few pins. Another piece of yarn or embroidery floss is used to stitch it down.

3. The *chain stitch* is useful for filling areas. Children may choose chaining to make a border entirely around the perimeters of their burlap.

4. The *cross stitch* is made by placing two stitches on top of each other in an X arrangement.

Perfection in stitches should not be the primary aim in early childhood. The process should be relaxing and pleasurable, with the emphasis on spontaneity, inventiveness, and stimulating the child to want to continue developing stitchery skills. Once started, a stitchery is something that the children can work on during their free time.

Although the children's technical needs during stitchery may seem cumbersome, problems can be solved by working with small groups of children at one time rather than with the entire class. Several parents or older children can help with threading needles and securing the end of the yarn when the child finishes. Children often enjoy helping each other when a new stitch is introduced. Fabric size should be small so that the child can finish the project before losing interest or patience.

Some children like to stitch spontaneously directly on the cloth. Such children proceed in a doodling manner and let a design evolve, or else they have a preconceived idea of just what it is they want to create. Sometimes children wish to make a preliminary drawing with crayons or cut paper. They cut out their main shapes and secure them to the burlap with pins. They stitch around the shapes, remove their patterns, and fill in details with additional colors and stitches of yarn. Some children choose to make their drawing in chalk on the burlap before they begin to stitch. It is also prudent to save some of the children's drawings and have them use the drawings as ideas for their stitcheries.

Weaving provides opportunities for using colors and textures. The weft strips are left loose at the end of each row to add decorative interest and to prevent the "hourglass" tightening that often occurs when students pull their weaving threads too tight.

Subject matter for stitcheries can include flowers, insects, animals, trees, butterflies, favorite stories, the sun, rockets, special holidays, poems, songs, and so on. An entire class can make alphabet squares, with each child selecting an alphabet letter and making an object to illustrate that letter. Later, all the squares can be stitched together for a wall hanging.

For a group stitchery, a piece of burlap about 3 × 6 feet can be securely stapled to a wooden frame, and the children take turns adding both appliqué and stitchery to represent houses, trees, people, and so on, perhaps on a multiple baseline background. The fabric edges for appliqué need not be turned under by young children; rather, they can simply be fastened to the background with a bit of glue or a running stitch.

WEAVING

Weaving is the process by which fibers—yarn, string, and thread—are interlaced. Civilizations, both ancient and contemporary, have created fabrics using a variety of materials and techniques. Weaving is most assuredly one of the oldest crafts in the world. As long as thirty thousand years ago, cave dwellers wove simple baskets with straw, reed, and other natural materials. Perhaps their inspiration came from observing birds building nests. Later, these prehistoric people wove with fibers and made cloth. The earliest woven fabrics were probably not made on a loom. People twined and looped natural fibers in many different ways to obtain results; gradually inventive weavers began lashing branches together to make a simple frame to hold the fibers taut. By observing samples of woven artifacts of other times and cultures as well as the works of contemporary crafts-people, young children come to value woven forms as genuine creative expressions.

Today many types of looms are available both to children and adults, and range from very simple looms to highly complex models. Young children have many ways to create woven items for both utilitarian and decorative purposes. They find the over-and-under process fascinating and are delighted with their new skills. Even the youngest children are able to learn the terminology of weaving: warps, wefts, and tabby. Their finger muscles develop dexterity and control as they use various colors and textures to make a woven piece.

Paper Weaving

Very young children find paper weaving easy to do and understand. Each child needs a weaving unit made from construction paper. The base is a piece of 12×18 inch construction paper or tagboard. Four 3×18 inch paper strips, two light-colored and two dark-colored, are stapled to the base at one end so that they alternate: one dark, one light, one dark, one light. These long strips become the warp of the weaving.

Each child has a weaving unit and eight strips of 2×12 inch black paper. To operate the weaving unit, the children first pick up both the dark-colored strips in one hand. They then push in a black strip—the weft—with the other hand. Once the black strip is in place, the children drop the dark-colored strips, pick up the two light-colored strips, and push in a new black strip. This is repeated until all eight of the black weft strips have been used, and the weaving is complete. The outside two warp strips should be stapled to the last weft strip and to the base piece. Other loose ends can be pasted by the children.

This weaving method can be used to teach the alphabet, numbers, or color families. For example, the vertical strips—warps—could all be white and marked with letters or names of colors or numbers (Arabic or Roman). Children are directed to pick up numbers one and three, or two and four. Or a child could be asked to pick up the strips that have the words *red* and *purple,* or *blue* and *orange* on them.

More warp strips could be added by making the strips only two inches wide. This would allow six strips to be stapled to the 12 inch base piece. Strips that are color related can be used so that children first pick up all the warm colors, then all the cool colors. Older children could number the strips and weave using the odd-numbered and then the even-numbered strips.

One paper weaving variation uses a magazine picture or a piece of wallpaper sample, with a piece of construction paper for a base. This woven magazine picture creates an interesting effect in the completed weaving. Pictures cut from magazines like *National Geographic* are particularly good for this project because the pictures are colorful and the paper is sturdy. The size will vary according to the size of the magazine picture or piece of wallpaper. The picture or wallpaper needs to be trimmed so that it is a square or rect-angle. The construction paper should be the same width as the picture but needs to be 4 or 5 inches longer.

To prepare the construction paper warps, the children start at the bottom and make several cuts to within $1\frac{1}{2}$ inches of the top; a light pencil line drawn across the paper at the $1\frac{1}{2}$-inch spot helps children remember to stop. The width of the strips being cut from the magazine picture or wallpaper can vary according to the children's age, ability, and dexterity. The weaving is most effective if the strips are less than a half-inch wide, but this is only possible with older students. When the children are ready to weave, they should cut one crosswise horizontal strip from the top of their magazine picture or wall-paper and weave the strip before cutting the next one. This eliminates confusion. The

a

b

a. A cardboard loom is strung with warp, and short pieces of yarn are woven back and forth with the fingers.

b. Striped mats were made on cardboard looms by eight-year-old children and stitched together for a wall hanging.

picture or wallpaper strip is woven over and under the construction paper strips. After a second strip is cut from the top of the picture, it is woven the opposite of the first one; that is, every place that the first strip went over the construction paper, the second one should go under. The reverse is also true: where the first strip went under the construction paper, the second strip should go over it. This over/under/over pattern is, of course, the foundation of all weaving and is called tabby.

Weaving on Cardboard Looms

A cardboard loom can be made by cutting ¼ to ½ inch notches along the upper and lower ends of an 8 × 10 inch piece of corrugated cardboard. Inexpensive chipboard looms with slits already cut are available from art supply catalogs.

Remember, the warps are the fibers placed up and down on the loom; they support the wefts, which are the fibers that go from side to side over and under the warps. Any kind of nonstretchy yarn or string can be used to warp the loom. The end of the warping string or yarn is attached to the back of the loom with a piece of masking tape. The warp is then wound around and around the loom, fitting the string into each top and bottom notch. When all the notches are covered, the end of the warp string is tied to the end of the string that was taped to the back of the loom at the beginning. The youngest children should be given precut lengths of yarn for wefts. This enables them to put each piece of yarn over and under the warps separately; they will not have to go back and forth with a long, single weft string. The lengths should be cut about 3 or 4 inches wider than the width of the loom, and the loose ends project or hang down the sides.

Mistakes on a cardboard loom are easy to correct by simply pulling out the weft. After the children have mastered the over/under process, they can thread a longer length of yarn on a large-eyed blunt needle or a paper clip and use this as a shuttle to take the yarn over and under, back and forth, in alternating rows across the warp strings. Different colors, textures, and thicknesses of yarn enable the children to create their own designs in their woven piece. They can arrange thick and thin stripes and alternate rows of different colors. The weft can be pulled up between each set of warp strings to create raised loops, adding a variety in height. The weft can be placed across the warps in a curved line and the spaces can be filled in with different colors of yarn. The children may choose not to weave all the way across the warps each time; rather, they may weave a column of eight or ten warp strings with one color and another column of four or five strings with a different color, thereby giving them more latitude in designing their woven pieces.

Probably the greatest problem that children encounter in weaving on a cardboard loom is how to avoid the hourglass effect; that is, the woven piece of fabric becomes pulled in and narrow in the middle because the weft yarn is being pulled too tightly as the children go back and forth with it. The teacher should demonstrate a preventive technique by showing the children how to weave a piece of yarn across the loom several times, leaving a small loop of yarn on either side before going back with it across the warp strings.

A pickup stick can be used to speed up the weaving process. A pickup stick is a flat stick of wood, perhaps a ruler, that is woven in and out across the warp strings and left in place. Then, each time the weaver desires to go from left to right with the needle and yarn, the stick is lifted upright. This creates a shed in which every other warp string is lifted. The pickup stick on a simple cardboard loom can only be used when going in one direction. When returning in the other direction, children must use the over/under process with the blunt needle. The pickup stick is also useful for packing the weft tightly in place. Generally speaking, the wefts completely cover the warp strings in the finished woven piece. When the piece is finished, the warps across the back of the loom are cut. The warp strings are tied together at the top and bottom of the piece to keep the weaving from coming unraveled. Additional clumps of yarn can be tied to the bottom of the woven piece to make fringes. The top can be mounted by stapling it onto a stick of wood. In addition to wall hangings, woven pieces can also be made into mats and purses.

An attractive holder for dried flowers or pencils can be made from a flat piece of weaving after it has been cut off the cardboard loom. The two sides of the flat piece should be brought together to form a hollow cylinder and stitched up. The bottom warps can all be tied together in a single overhand knot, or they can all be threaded through a large bead. The top warps can each be threaded on a needle and woven back inside the piece. After a loop has been attached to the top, the little tube can be hung on the wall and filled with dried flowers or pencils.

Weaving on a Large Frame Loom

An entire class of young students can participate in making a woven wall hanging or table mat with a sturdy wooden loom about 14 × 24 inches or 18 × 30 inches. Finishing nails are placed about ½ inch apart on both ends of the loom. String is then wrapped back and forth to form the warps.

Individual wefts are cut the width of the loom plus about 10 or 12 inches. The variety of materials that can be used for wefts is broad: ribbons; strips of felt and other fabrics, including terry cloth, satin, muslin, and calico; long pieces of straw and reeds; tissue paper, crepe paper, and newspaper twisted into strips; lichen; and, of course, thick roving.

A box of precut wefts that are all either warm or cool colors enables the children to choose colors and textures that are harmonious, varied, and compatible. Students can take turns choosing several wefts and weaving over and under the warp strings, pushing each weft up snugly in place against the one above it. The ends of each weft extend beyond the sides of the loom and form fringe in the finished wall hanging or mat. Older children can control the over-and-under, back-and-forth process more skillfully than can very young children and, using wefts that are several yards long, could weave back and forth several times with one piece, rather than dropping the ends on either side of

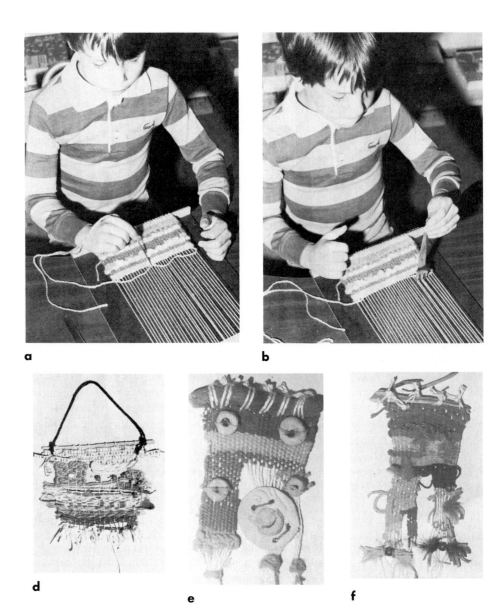

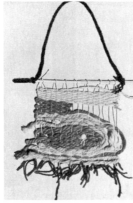

a and **b.** Weft yarn is woven over and under across warps and then "bubbled" downward in several places with a needle (a) before being packed neatly with a comb or fork (b). This helps to prevent an "hourglass" or pulled-in effect on the sides of the finished piece.

c and **d.** Straw, braid, and lichen, as well as yarn, were woven into the warp strings on cardboard looms by six-year-old children. Fringe tied on the bottom and a dowel through the top added finishing details.

e and **f.** Baker's clay beads, feathers, and other decorative objects can be added to a finished woven piece in a balanced or asymmetrical arrangement.

the loom. When the wall hanging is completely filled from top to bottom with wefts, the warps are eased off the loom and the piece is finished. A metal rod across the top makes a good hanging device.

Soda-Straw Weaving

One of the simplest techniques for teaching young weavers requires only a few soda straws and yarn. The finished product is a band or strap that can be used for belts, headbands, hatbands, purse straps, and so on. It can also be made into an attractive pencil or dried flower holder or napkin ring. The long bands made on this simple loom can be compared to the narrow woven bands traditionally made on more complex looms by men in West Africa.

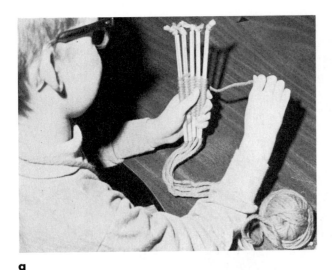

a

b

a. Yarn is moved in and out around soda straws, back and forth, and the woven area is then moved downward gradually onto the yarn that is extending down through the bottom of the straws.

b. The completed pouch for dried flowers is made by folding soda-straw weaving over, stitching up the sides, and adding a loop at the top for hanging.

Each child needs five large plastic soda straws, with about an inch snipped from each one. Next, the desired length of the finished product needs to be determined, with 12 inches added for tying, and five pieces of yarn are cut to this length, one for each straw. It is best to use rather heavy yarn for threading through the straws; this gives more body to the finished item. One piece of yarn is threaded through each straw and about an inch of the end of the yarn is attached to the top of the straw with masking tape to keep the yarn from pulling down into the straw. The other ends of the yarn, extending out the bottom ends of the straws, are tied together in one overhand knot.

A ball of yarn is used for the weft. A slipknot is tied to the middle of one of the straws. Then the straws are fanned out—like a deck of cards—with one hand, and the weft yarn is moved in and out around the straws, going back and forth. When several inches of the straws are covered with the woven yarn, some of the woven part is pushed gently downward on the straws and weaving continued. As the straws continue to fill and the woven part is pushed downward, the woven band is transferred onto the warp yarn that is hanging out of the lower ends of the straws. Weaving is continued until the desired length is obtained. Then the masking tape is removed from the tops of the straws, and the straws are pulled carefully upward and out. The warp strings can be tied one to another at both top and bottom. The weft yarn is cut, leaving a piece about 6 inches long. This "tail" should be threaded onto a large-eyed needle and inserted up inside the woven piece so that it does not come unraveled.

Finished bands made on soda-straw looms have many uses. A short woven piece—about 6 to 8 inches in length—may serve as the head and body of a figure. The child cuts four felt strips and attaches them for arms and legs. Buttons serve as eyes, and a mouth may be cut from a scrap of felt to complete the "floppy figure." A child might also sew the ends of a band together to form a napkin ring. A pouch for pencils or dried flowers can be made by weaving a band about 12 inches long, folding the bottom up not quite to the top, and sewing up the sides with a matching piece of yarn. The small flap that is left at the top can be used for attaching a loop for hanging the pouch on the wall. Another project involves several children working together to create a pillow top for the reading center. Each child weaves a band about 12 inches in length, and half the bands themselves serve as warps over which the other half of the woven bands, serving as wefts, may be woven.

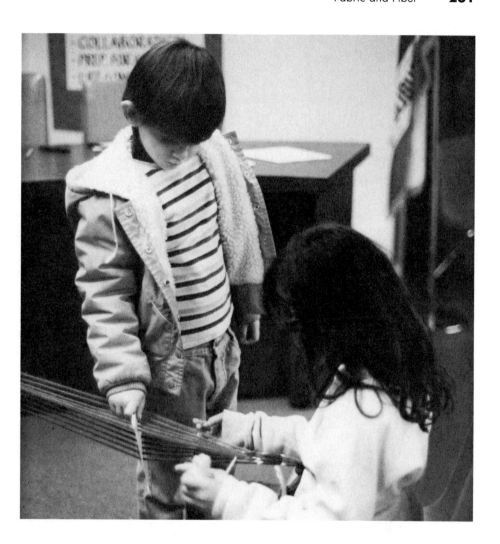

YARN PICTURES ON CANVAS MESH

Making a picture by looping yarn into a canvas mesh with a needle or latch hook requires a minimum of space and equipment, yet the results are beautiful and the process quickly learned. A large picture takes a class a number of weeks to complete. Several children may work on it at one time, and children enjoy seeing their efforts add to the color patterns appearing in the cut pile. Canvas mesh or scrim for the backing can be purchased in most craft or yarn shops. It comes in widths of about 36 inches and should have 3½ or 4 holes to the inch. A practical length to buy for a class project is about three-fourths of a yard. The cut edges should be covered with masking tape to keep them from coming undone as the work progresses. Orlon, acrylic, or rayon-cotton blended rug yarns can be used for rug pictures; they are inexpensive and available in a wide range of colors. The skeins should be loosely wound in balls to prevent them from becoming tangled.

 As the children work on design ideas for a group project picture, the teacher should point out that, due to the nature of the yarn and pile, the motif should be bold and simple, without too many small details. Two techniques are recommended for transferring the

A heddle made of wooden tongue depressors makes weaving easy for these two kindergarten weavers. Students work in pairs, weaving long strips on simplified backstrap looms. Through this activity, they come to appreciate this simple weaving device and learn how it has been used in past and present cultures throughout the world.

a

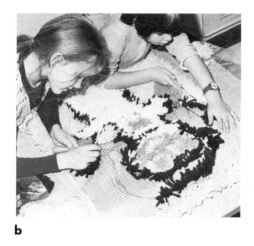

b

c

a. Canvas mesh can be placed on top of a child's drawing or painting and the picture drawn on the mesh with felt pens.

b. These six-year-old children enjoy the challenge of latch-hooking and delight in seeing their individual work contribute to the group production.

c. The entire class of first-grade children worked on this two-by-three-foot rug picture.

d

e

f

d. For the rya knot, cut a length of yarn about two feet long and thread it through the eye of the needle. Poke the needle down through a hole in the mesh, leaving a one-inch tail of yarn sticking up. A short piece of inch-wide cardboard is helpful in measuring the length of this tail.

e. Holding onto this tail with one hand, poke the needle back through the mesh immediately to the right of the hole where the tail is sticking out. Pull the yarn up. Then poke the needle down in the hole immediately to the left of the hole where the tail is, leaving a loop about as big as your finger.

f. Now poke the needle up through the same hole where the tail is, coming out below that loop you just left. Pull both tails to the same one-inch length as measured against the cardboard, and snip them with a scissors.

g

g. These six-year-old youngsters are justifiably proud of their rya-knotted rug picture.

a

b

c

d

e

a. Fold a piece of cut yarn in half behind the latch. Push the hook down through the first hole, under the horizontal threads of the canvas, and up through the hole directly above. The hinged latch will fall open.

b. Then, holding both ends of the yarn in the fingers, pull them around in front of the latch under the hook. Pull the hook toward you until the latch closes. Let go of the loose ends.

c. Continue pulling the hook until the loose ends have passed through the looped yarn, thus completing the knot.

d. Give the ends of the yarn a tug to tighten the knot.

e. When all the squares are completed, they can be whipped together on the reverse side to make a large patchwork-rug picture.

children's design to the canvas backing. In the first, each child paints a picture with tempera on paper the same size and shape as the canvas. The class votes on its choice, and the picture is then placed on a table with the mesh on top of it. Next, several children redraw the painting on the mesh with marking pens of matching colors. The areas colored by the marking pens will show the children where to hook or tie knots with the different colors of yarn.

The second method for transferring a design to canvas is to have each child make a small drawing. These drawings are placed one at a time in an opaque projector and viewed on a piece of white paper that is the exact size of the piece of canvas mesh. By moving the projector back and forth, the teacher can reduce or enlarge the image as desired to fit the shape of the paper. The students decide which design to use, or perhaps they select parts of several different drawings to combine within one composition. The mesh is taped over the paper, and several children can draw the design on the mesh with marking pens, being careful not to stand in the beam of light coming from the projector.

There are two ways of filling in the areas with pile. Small groups can be instructed in either how to use the latch hook or how to tie rya knots. These children can, in turn, teach their peers, until all the class has learned the technique. Hooking and knotting are no more complicated for young children to learn than shoelace tying.

When children are encouraged to use fabric and fibers in creative ways, they understand that, in previous ages, people crafted functional items and embellished these items with their own individual styles. Here, nontoxic textile paints were used to paint scenes representing various continents. The T-shirts were designed, painted, and worn as part of a summer art camp.

A latch hook is a small tool with a hinged latch that opens and closes to hold and pull the yarn before releasing it in a neat knot. Latch hooks can be purchased in craft stores or yarn shops. The yarn is cut before it is used, and the cut length determines the height of the pile. Usually, about 2½ inches is a workable length of yarn for a finished pile that is about 1 inch high. Most craft shops sell precut yarn for latch hooking, or it can be cut by wrapping it a number of times, without stretching it, around a piece of cardboard 2½ inches wide. A rubber band is wrapped around the middle of the cardboard to hold the yarn in place, and the top and bottom of the yarn is snipped with a scissors. These short pieces should be kept sorted by color in boxes or plastic bags. The children work on a table and try to hook across the canvas, starting at the bottom and working up, so that the pile falls evenly and in the same direction. However, they may enjoy filling in areas of the rug solidly in one color and completing the background later.

The rya knot is formed like the Ghiordes knot that is used in Oriental rugs, and the resulting short pile that it makes is called *flossa,* which is Scandinavian in origin. The rya knot is tied with a large-eyed needle. When a row of knots is completed, the row above it should be tied in alternating holes to the knots of the preceding row. It is better to work from the bottom up so that the knots are all tied in the same direction and the pile falls evenly.

When the yarn picture is finished, a narrow, flat piece of wood can be attached to the top to make it easy to hang. A class might like to present the finished work to the school office for all the children and teachers to enjoy.

IN CONCLUSION

It is important to encourage children who are working with fibers to make creative choices as they select and arrange their textures, shapes, and colors. Working with fabric and fiber improves children's skills in cutting, gluing, stitching, weaving, and patterning.

Examples of woven and stitched items from diverse world cultures can enrich the child's understanding of the important role that these crafts serve. Baskets, clothing, quilts, masks, and floor and wall coverings may be examined and their rich patterns, colors, textures, and decorative designs discussed. Children will come to understand that people through all times and places have chosen to not just make a functional and serviceable item, but to enrich and embellish it in genuinely creative and distinctive ways.

TOPICS FOR DISCUSSION

1. What was the purpose of banners in the past? How are they utilized in contemporary times?

2. Create your own banner, either as a sketch or from cut paper. Which of the elements and principles of art did you stress in your design?

3. How does weaving lend itself to invention and exploration? In what ways can a teacher make connections to history and other cultures when introducing weaving to young children?

4. Which of the elements of art are particularly applicable in discussions about fiber art? If possible, bring in an actual weaving or banner and formulate appropriate questions for evaluation.

5. Working with fabric and fibers encourages growth in what areas?

6. What motivational strategies would you use to evoke images and designs for batik activities?

7. List five themes that could be used for a batik activity.

8. Compile a list of local artists and craftspeople who work in fibers and who would be willing to demonstrate their art form to young children. Plan questions to ask that would focus the young learners' attention on such valuable concepts as color, texture, line, shape, and the ways the artist uses these in creating a design.

9. Make a list of vocabulary words for weaving and batik; how would you introduce them to young children?

10. Which of the four styles of art is best for designing yarn pictures in the early childhood classroom: realistic, abstract, expressive, fantasy?

14

Celebrations

●●●●●●●●●●●●●●●●●●●●●●●●●●●●●●●●●●●

Seasons and holidays from diverse world cultures offer exciting art opportunities for young children throughout the year. The human need to celebrate and make an event festive is universal. It has been perpetuated and fostered by both young and old throughout history. Celebrations can provide opportunities for children to engage in a variety of creative activities. Their feelings about celebrations and their awareness of each holiday's meanings and symbols can be proclaimed when they draw, paint, cut, model, and construct with art materials.

However, the art educational value of special holidays and events should not be abused by using celebrations as an incentive to decorate the classroom with thirty look-alike turkeys, Santa Clauses, or bunnies. Patterns and copy work rob children of the chance to express their own feelings and thoughts about a special day in unique ways. Such activities become obstacles to developing self-confidence, destroying a child's ability to respond imaginatively, joyously, and creatively in a new situation. This chapter suggests several ways to encourage children to celebrate special days with original and unique art expression, utilizing art activities described in Chapters 8 through 13.

Resource materials from the library can provide information about the origins of holidays and the meanings behind traditional symbols—background that children need and upon which they can base fresh and insightful approaches in their image making. The description that follows tells how Valentine's Day came to be, and a number of motivations for art tasks are suggested. People long ago thought and felt about things much the same as we do today, and children find it easy to identify with these emotions and to make their own visual responses.

It is believed that Valentine's Day had its beginnings in a Roman festival called Lupercalia when the men wore hearts pinned to their sleeves on which were written the names of women who would be their partners during the celebration. Sometimes, the couple exchanged presents—gloves or jewelry. In later times, a day honoring Saint Valentine preserved some of the old customs. Seventeenth-century maidens ate hard-boiled eggs and pinned five bay leaves to their pillows before going to sleep on Valentine's Eve in the belief that this would make them dream of their future husbands.

In 1415, the Duke of Orleans was imprisoned in the Tower of London. He wrote love poems or "valentines" to his wife in France, which are believed to be the first valentines. Sweethearts in the seventeenth and eighteenth centuries exchanged handmade cards trimmed with paper hearts and real lace. During the Civil War, valentine cards became popular in the United States. Satin ribbons, mother-of-pearl ornaments, and spun glass trimmed these elaborate cards.

Artwork by Jasper Johns has been included in Flag Day activities. Students learn that artists use symbols and ideas that relate to celebrations and events.

A valentine theme using "The King or Queen of Hearts" was combined with a lesson on the artist Georges Rouault. This portrait of royalty was drawn with black tempera paint and allowed to dry; the next day, jewel-like colors were painted into the spaces.

The following topics for drawing and painting about Valentine's Day stimulate original and personal art productions that incorporate historical and sometimes whimsical comments about February 14th:

1. Wearing a heart on my sleeve
2. My head on a pillow, dreaming
3. The Duke of Orleans imprisoned in the Tower of London
4. Soldier giving a valentine to a sweetheart
5. Cupid using a bow to shoot heart-tipped arrows
6. Mermaid or lion with a loving heart
7. House made of hearts and flowers
8. Automobile with heart-shaped tires
9. Valentine birds, bugs, and butterflies in a flower garden
10. The Queen or King of Hearts

This kindergarten class participates in a Lion Dance in celebration of the Chinese New Year.

FESTIVALS AND PARADES

Preparing for and participating in a special festival or parade has much meaning and enjoyment for the children. Folk festivals are characterized by ritual and tradition. Such occasions as harvest, seasonal changes, or the reenactment of historical or religious events are celebrated. There is such an innate human need that is satisfied by folk festivals and parades that they are found the world over. Sweden's Midsummer Eve festivities, Belgium's Procession of Penitents, Japan's Shinto Festival, China's New Year festivities, Munich, Germany's Oktoberfest, the Mummer's Parade in Philadelphia, Pennsylvania, the Pueblo Indians' Corn Dance, and the Rose Bowl Parade in Pasadena, California, are examples.

Children's spirits and imaginations are stirred by parades. Children love parades—big ones, small ones, serious ones, and funny ones. They love the music, the color, and the costumes, and they especially love to be in a parade at school. A parade can be structured around almost any event. It can be small, casual, and impromptu, such as marching to a drumbeat to visit another classroom with all the children wearing their newly finished paper crowns or carrying paper-plate puppets on sticks. A parade can help the children to appreciate and remember a special event; for example, on Space Day, the children can have a parade as they wear helmets made of boxes or ice cream cartons. The children may wish to carry decorated balloons and to make banners on brightly colored pieces of paper and then move in a procession to celebrate the lives of Jacob Grimm and Hans Christian Andersen, tellers of fairy tales. All parades must have some central theme, some organization, pattern, or arrangement, some aspect of rhythm, and certainly color and spectacle.

THE COMING OF SPRING

The celebration of the coming of spring can be made a very special occasion by the combined participation and efforts of several grade levels. A procession on the playground or in the multipurpose room, along with a short program signaled by flags and banners and accented with simple costumes, masks, and headgear can involve the children in the visual arts while music, dances, poems, and dramatic play can encompass all the arts.

In keeping with the spirit of spring, the children can embellish long cardboard tubes for make-believe horns and trumpets. Paper plates can be painted and mounted on sticks,

Diego Rivera's painting of a child was the inspiration for this life-size look-through figure, which served as a photographic opportunity at a school festival.

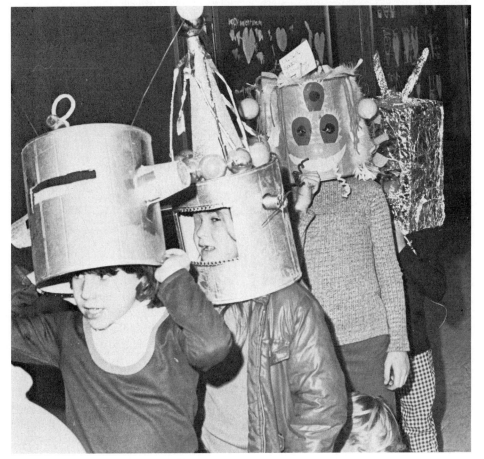

"Space Day" was celebrated by all the second-grade classes after they had studied the planetary system and human explorations into space. A special space-food luncheon was prepared, and each child created his or her own helmet for the afternoon parade held to honor the first space explorers.

These kindergartners used cardboard boxes to design a many-legged caterpillar representing the concept of new life in the springtime.

Pennants, crowns, and a maypole made colorful additions to the "Coming of Spring" festivities in which preschoolers through third graders participated.

with crepe-paper streamers attached to trail in the breeze. Short cardboard tubes with waxed paper wrapped around the ends become kazoos for the children to decorate and hum into. Aluminum pie pans taped together with pebbles inside make a satisfying rattling noise. Narrow strips of fabric or crepe paper tied to the ends of sticks serve as streamers to wave. Large, felt banners to celebrate the three spring months can be mounted and carried on poles, and can incorporate symbols and words associated with the customs and historical proclamations of this special season.

A maypole dance can be staged around a tether pole or around a long stick embedded in a bucket of sand. Long crepe-paper or fabric streamers are attached to the top of the pole, with each child grasping the end of one strip. Each child then faces another child, and they

a

c

b

a and **b.** Mirrors and clown makeup are used as students prepare for commemorating Barnum's first circus performance in 1873.

c. This kindergartner's painting of a clown was made more detailed and aesthetically whole by the child's experience of applying makeup to his own face.

walk around the pole, going over and under and carrying their streamers in what becomes a woven wrapping at the top of the pole. Very young children enjoy the simpler version—holding a streamer and walking around and around the pole in follow-the-leader fashion.

Large paper bags can be quickly converted into costumes for celebrations and imaginative play activities. At the same time, they provide young children with an opportunity to develop their painting and designing skills. A large hole is cut in the bottom of the bag for the head opening and small holes are cut in the sides for the arms to go through. The edges of these holes should be reinforced with masking tape to prevent them from tearing when the children put on or remove their costumes. Designs and pictures are applied with paint and brushes. The children should be encouraged to make designs on the sides and backs of their costumes after the paint is dry on the front. Older children enjoy gluing on paper fringe, egg carton bumps, and shiny and textured materials in combination with their painted designs.

Folded paper hats and crowns, crepe-paper headbands, and colorful sashes can be made and worn for the procession. The children can sing a few songs about spring and perhaps hear a poem

Five-year-old children showed great diversity of form concept when they drew witches using precut hats as visual starters. Felt pens, yarn, and fabric scraps were used to complete the drawings.

written by several of the older children in honor of the first day of spring. The children are, of course, eager to eat the cookies, candy, or bread that they have made in forms reminiscent of spring: flowers, butterflies, and birds.

CELEBRATIONS THROUGHOUT THE YEAR

Special days from our diverse cultures provide vehicles for creative and significant festivities. A story about some historical first or important event gives children ideas for all sorts of art tasks: mural making, painting, making dioramas, making kites or banners, assembling a zigzag book, and creating puppet shows. Birthdays of famous people can be solemnized or celebrated at school so that children learn about and come to appreciate those men and women who made important contributions to our lives.

The following is a sampling of noteworthy birthdays, events, and special days from our diverse cultures:

Jan.	4	Louis Braille's birthday (created alphabet for blind people)
Jan.	5	George Washington Carver Day (African-American who created numerous products from peanuts, soybeans, and sweet potatoes)
Jan.	9	First balloon flight in America, 1793
Jan.	12	Charles Perrault's birthday (wrote *Tales of Mother Goose*)
Jan.	15	Martin Luther King Day
Jan.	26	India's Republic Day, begun in 1950
Feb.	15	Susan B. Anthony Day
Feb.	26	Buffalo Bill's birthday
Mar.	6	Michelangelo's birthday
Mar.	8	International Women's Day
Mar.	10	Harriet Tubman Day (African-American who led more than 300 slaves to freedom and worked for women's suffrage)
Mar.	13	Uncle Sam Day (date of first cartoon showing our national symbol)

Mar. 22	Marcel Marceau's birthday (world's best-known mime)
Mar. 30	van Gogh's birthday
Apr. 2	International Children's Book Day
Apr. 4	Kite Day (Kazuhiko Asaba flew 1050 kites at once in Japan, setting a record in 1976)
Apr. 8	Flower Festival (Hana Matsukri) in Japan, Buddha's birthday
Apr. 26	John James Audubon's birthday
May 1	May Day, Lei Day in Hawaii
May 2	Leonardo da Vinci's birthday
May 3	Solar energy day, "Sun Day"
May 5	Children's Day in Japan (Feast of Flags or Banners)
May 5	Cinco de Mayo, Mexican holiday
May 23	Mary Cassatt's birthday
May 25	African Freedom Day
June 2	Martha Washington's birthday
June 5	World Environment Day
June 27	Helen Keller's birthday
July 1	Dominion Day, provinces united in Canada, 1867
July 6	Beatrix Potter's birthday
Aug. 2	Friendship Day (begun in 1919 by man who founded Hallmark Cards)
Aug. 9	Jesse Owens won his 4th Olympic gold medal (for running)
Sep. 10	Rosh Hashanah celebration, Jewish New Year
Sep. __	Native American Day, 4th Friday of September
Sep. 16	Mexican Independence Day
Sep. 26	Johnny Appleseed's birthday
Oct. 2	Gandhi's birthday (peaceful leader who helped free India from British rule)
Oct. 3	Universal Children's Day Celebration (write to U.S. Committee for UNICEF, 331 E. 38th St., New York, NY 10016)
Oct. 20	Circus Day (Barnum Circus opened in 1873)
Oct. 25	Picasso's birthday
Nov. 2	Day of the Dead in Mexico
Nov. 6	Basketball Day (game invented by James Naismith in 1891)
Nov. 9	Smokey Bear Day
Nov. 24	Carlo Collodi's birthday (wrote *The Adventures of Pinocchio*)
Dec. 25	Christmas
Dec. __	Festival of Lights (25th day of Hebrew month Kislev), Chanukah celebration lasting 8 days
Dec. 12	Feast of Our Lady of Guadalupe, patron saint of Mexico
Dec. 16	Beethoven's birthday
Dec. 27	Kwanza, African-American celebration, lasting 7 days

CELEBRATING WITH GIFTS

Throughout the school year, there are several celebrations when children want to give a present to a relative or friend. Unfortunately, holidays and gifts are frequently excuses for dictated art. Holiday arts and crafts books often feature projects with patterns and finished products that can only be made one way, following step-by-step directions given by the adult. Little creativity or personal involvement is required, and children involved in this sort of activity develop the feeling that what they do on their own is inadequate.

The finest gift that a child can give is what truly comes from within. For this reason, art activities that require creativity and imagination, not all-just-alike products, are best. It is essential that children not become secondary to the product or gift they make.

It is educationally advisable to use as gifts some of the artwork that the child has produced during the regular instructional lessons. If the teacher has been collecting children's artworks, paintings, drawings, prints, and cut paper pictures can be selected

a. These tiny pincushions with felt pen designs drawn on them make attractive and unique gifts.

b. A small funnel is helpful in filling the pincushions with fine sawdust. The side opening is then stitched closed, and the pincushion is finished.

a

b

Drawings and paintings not only make excellent gifts themselves, but they can be used to make calendars or sets of notecards. This spontaneous and whimsical drawing of a joker would be delightful as the front of a greeting card.

and attractively mounted as gifts. Interesting parts of drawings can be cut to fit the fronts of note paper. Greeting cards can be drawn, painted, or printed. Arrangements of dried flowers can be placed in a child's pinch pot. Fabric projects, such as batiks, stitchery, or fabric crayon designs, can be made into pillows, stuffed animals, or pincushions. Children can paint or draw self-portraits as gifts for parents or grandparents. They can decorate and bake cookies as a class project. They can create a collage of materials related to the holiday. Children can make mosaics out of holiday-related materials, such as pumpkin seeds or colored eggshells, or herbs and spices associated with holiday cooking.

The art production activities that follow are suggested for gift time. All result in a final product that is conceived and designed by the children, incorporating their skills of drawing, modeling, cutting, and assembling.

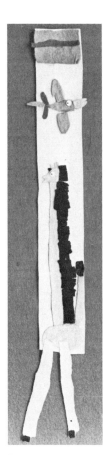

a

b

c

Calendars

Drawings, paintings, prints, or cut paper pictures that the children have made and of which they are particularly proud or, perhaps, artwork that they especially create for the occasion can be mounted and made into an attractive and useful calendar. Such calendars are a suitable gift project for preschoolers as well as older children because the artwork itself depends entirely on the imagination and maturity of the individual child.

A child's drawing or painting looks even more special and attractive when it is attached to a piece of construction paper, tagboard, or poster board of a contrasting color. Small, printed calendars are available in stationery stores and variety shops. They are inexpensive and have a gummed backing, making it easy for the young child to fasten it to the bottom of the mounting paper or poster board.

During the year, children may wish to replace the picture they have put on their gift calendar, changing it to one that fits the season or that tells about an event that month. To do this, the teacher stacks eleven sheets of paper of the same size under the top picture and staples them all to the backing so that, as the months pass, the child can create a new picture on each of the remaining eleven sheets. By putting the child's art on year-round display, adults show that they value and appreciate the child's ideas. Because the artwork is original with each child, no two gift calendars are ever alike.

Bookmarks

Making bookmarks involves drawing, or cutting and gluing, with paper, felt, or burlap stripping, which can be purchased by the yard in hobby and craft stores. Paper or felt bookmarks should be cut in strips that are 2 or 3 inches wide and 7 or 8 inches long.

a. A giraffe with fringed mane and a beady-eyed bird were designed by a six-year-old child to fit a long, narrow, felt bookmark.

b. These bookmarks were made by four- and five-year-old children who cut out felt shapes and glued then to burlap strips.

c. Fabric interfacing and felt pens were used for these drawn bookmarks.

a

b

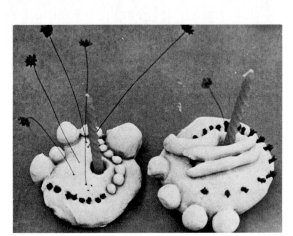

c

a. A preschooler finds it intriguing to embed dried flower stems into baker's clay. Very young children enjoy participating in this art activity and are proud of the products.

b and **c.** Small balls and coils of clay, as well as cloves, candles, and strawflowers, are combined by young children for these attractive table ornaments.

Children can snip out designs from assorted scraps of paper for a paper bookmark, or from felt scraps for a felt or burlap bookmark. Paste or glue sticks should be used for paper bookmarks, whereas glue is best for attaching pieces to burlap or felt strips. The children may choose to make a realistic representation or a simple design. Before they begin cutting, the children should be encouraged to think about adapting their design motif to the shape, making tall, long, or thin things that fit the narrow shape of a bookmark. Examples are a long-necked bird, a clown on stilts, an alligator, a fish, a mermaid, a tall building, a train, a tall man or woman, a girl jumping rope, or a figure holding a balloon or kite. The bottom of the bookmark can be cut diagonally, pointed, curved, fringed, or finished in whatever manner the child chooses. A hole punch can be used to make openings in burlap stripping to attach yarn loops for fringe.

Dried Flower and Candle Holders

Young children love to work with salt ceramic or baker's clay, rolling it into balls and coils, squeezing, poking, and imprinting it with any small gadget that is handy. A natural outgrowth of this play activity is to make dried weed and candle holders. Children can gather small, dried weeds on a nature walk, or straw flowers can be purchased.

Children should model and work with their baker's clay on a small piece of aluminum foil. This makes it easy to lift the finished piece onto a baking sheet and place it in the oven. If they are using salt ceramic, which air dries, a paper towel may be used. Cloves are handy for the young child to embed in the baker's clay or salt ceramic for decoration. The candles and the stems of the dried flowers are stuck into the clay while it is being modeled, removed for the baking process, and then glued in place after the clay is baked. If salt ceramic is used, the items are embedded and remain in place while the ceramic dries.

Plastic plates with the child's own drawing permanently applied make excellent creative gifts.

The lump of baker's clay or salt ceramic that the children use for their holders should be about the size of a lemon. Baker's clay requires several hours of baking at 300 or 325 degrees before it is thoroughly hard and dry. Both modeling materials may be used with or without color added to the batch. If colored baker's clay is used, it should be left to air dry; it can then be finished with a clear acrylic spray. The recipes for baker's clay and salt ceramic are in Chapter 11.

Plastic Plates and Mugs

Durable plastic plates can be made directly from children's drawings. The process requires a package of round paper blanks the exact size of the finished plate. These are available in art supply catalogs. The children work out the ideas for their plates on another piece of round paper first. The children draw on the round paper with water-soluble felt pens. By carefully placing the round paper blank on top of the original drawing and securing it with masking tape in several places around the edges, they can redraw their design. The manufacturer stresses the importance of keeping the paper free of grit, oily hands, and dirt. The finished circles are sent in to the manufacturer, who transfers the designs to sturdy plastic plates that are nonbreakable and dishwasher proof.

Using markers, crayons, colored pencils, or any other medium, students make pictures and designs for a plastic mug on die-cut drawing papers, also available from art supply catalogs. The drawings are then returned to the company who seals them inside plastic mugs.

DECORATING PAPER FOR GIFT WRAPS

Very young children are captivated by the old Japanese technique of folding and dipping paper in dye. They like to make several sheets of this decorative wrapping paper because no two ever come out of the dye baths looking exactly alike. Two and three

a

b

c

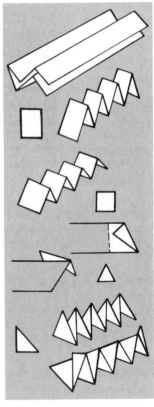
d

a. A preschooler folds Dippity Dye paper in triangular accordion folds prior to dipping it in diluted food color.

b. Corners or entire sides of the folded paper can be immersed in the dye and removed when the desired amount of color has been absorbed.

c. The magic moment comes when the child unfolds the paper and discovers the lovely pattern he or she has created.

d. The paper can be folded in several ways before dipping and redipping it in dye baths.

dips in the dye baths create the merged and blended tones, whereas the pleasing repetition of colored shapes results from the way in which the paper was folded before it was dipped in the dye.

The paper is folded in an accordion-like manner as illustrated above. The resulting packet should not be too thick, or the dyes cannot penetrate to the center. A paper folded very small produces small patterns, whereas a larger fold creates larger patterns. A special absorbent paper called Dippity Dye is available from art supply catalogs. Dye baths can be made from paste food colors because these colors come in a large

a

b

assortment of hues, are nontoxic, and are highly concentrated. The food color paste is mixed with a small amount of water in a small bowl or low can. The color should be intense because the wet paper dries to a lighter tint.

The folded packet of paper is dipped in the dye bath, one corner or side at a time, and lifted out when the desired amount of color has been absorbed by the paper. Children quickly learn how to control the spread of the color by the length of time they leave it in the dye. The dyed packet is squeezed with the fingers, which lets the excess color drip back into the dye and forces the color evenly through the layers of paper. The packet is then dipped in another color—darker than the first—either by dunking a corner or side that was not dipped before or by redipping a dyed corner or edge and removing it before the dye completely covers the first color. After the packet is again squeezed thoroughly, it is carefully unfolded and placed on newspapers to dry. The brightly patterned paper is pressed with an iron after it is dry and used for gift wraps, stationery trims, program covers, or greeting cards, or for covering cartons, boxes, cans, books, or notebooks.

MAKING PAPER FOR GREETING CARDS

What would the world be like without paper? What would art be like if there were no paper? A man named Ts'ai Lun invented papermaking in 105 A.D. in China. The process was kept secret for many years but the knowledge eventually spread to Arabia. The paper industry was flourishing in Baghdad around the year 800 A.D. It was finally introduced into Europe in the twelfth century by people returning from the Crusades, and by the fifteenth century, paper making was widely known. The first paper mill in the United States was started in Philadelphia in 1690, but until the 1850s, most paper was made by hand.

Paper is made from cellulose, which comes only from plant or vegetable fibers. Today, most paper is made of wood pulp in large mills, but old newspapers, wrapping paper, typing paper, paper towels, magazine pages, and advertising flyers can be broken down into pulp again and remade into clean new sheets of paper to be used for craft projects, greeting cards, or other types of artwork.

Children are better able to appreciate Ts'ai Lun's original invention in the second century if they experience making their own paper for a special greeting card. The papermaking process, greatly simplified, can be duplicated in the classroom.

A food blender is needed to make the pulp for paper. The blender container should be about two-thirds full of water, and to this is slowly added about one cup of paper that has been torn in half-inch pieces. The mixture must be blended thoroughly. Separate colored sections of newspapers, comic sections, or any of the types of paper already mentioned can be used.

a. Slurry is poured through a screen, leaving the fibers in a layer on top, as the first step in making paper.

b. A cloth wipe is placed on top of the screen, and the child exerts gentle pressure to squeeze out the excess water.

Fibers such as grass clippings, corn husks, dried leaves, rose petals, onion skins, feathers, or any stringy vegetable matter finely cut up can be added to the torn paper and water mixture. Lint from a clothes dryer is another good material to use as long as it contains no fibers that might wrap around the blades of the blender. All this is blended until there is a pulpy mush which is called slurry. Jars of different colors of slurry can be made by making pulp from different colors of paper.

A small piece of fine screening material is needed to make a sheet of paper from slurry. The screen, about 8 × 10 inches, is attached to a wood frame. The children hold the screen, screen side up, frame side down, over an empty plastic dishpan and use a plastic cup to dip out the slurry and pour it over the screen, distributing it as evenly as possible. Children may choose to use only one color of pulp, or they may pour, for instance, yellow pulp in one area and blue in another. At this time, the children can take bits of yarn, ferns, jute, flower petals, and so on and place them on top of the slurry on the screen.

The slurry need not be poured in a regular rectangular shape on the screen. Children may enjoy making a face or animal with different colors of slurry; the shape of the face or animal becomes the outside shape of the paper. When the child is done pouring pulp through the screen, a Handiwipe is placed on top of the screen and the water squeezed out gently, pressing from the center out. The screen is turned over onto a stack of newspapers, with the Handiwipe on the bottom. The screen is carefully lifted off, leaving the Handiwipe on top of the newspapers. The handmade paper is ironed until it is as dry as possible and then peeled off the Handiwipe. Printing and drawing techniques can be used to illustrate the card, or tissue paper collage designs can be adhered with a liquid glue and water solution.

TOPICS FOR DISCUSSION

1. Research the origins of holidays, celebrations, and events that occur during one particular month. Be sure to include celebrations in the local community.

2. Plan a parade or celebration to commemorate the birthday of a favorite artist. List appropriate activities, such as painting, puppets, mural making, and designing hats and costumes.

3. Sketch or describe an idea for a cut paper mural or a zigzag book as described in Chapter 9 that will celebrate an event or person important to young children.

4. Select one of the gift projects suggested in the chapter and plan ways to guide the responses of a group of young children as they explain how their projects are different and how they are alike.

5. Select one of the projects in the chapter and plan ways to reinforce vocabulary and concepts presented in earlier chapters of the book. Discuss your approach and give reasons for your emphasis.

6. Create a learning station that utilizes one of the celebration ideas presented in this chapter.

7. Design a bulletin board that features papermaking. What concepts and vocabulary words would you introduce?

8. Research holidays or celebrations in a past or present culture other than your own. Select one and write a description of how you would introduce this to young children.

9. Select a project from a previous chapter and adapt it so it is suitable for a local holiday or celebration.

10. Review the Content of Art Instruction in Chapter 1. How would you incorporate at least one of the three other content areas—in addition to production—in an art lesson that focuses on celebrations?

References

Chapter 1

Battin, Margaret P.; Fisher, John; Moore, Ronald; and Silvers, Anita. *Puzzles about Art, An Aesthetics Casebook.* New York: St. Martin's Press, 1989.

Cromer, Jim. *History, Theory and Practice of Art Criticism in Art Education.* Reston, Va: National Art Education Association, 1990.

Eisner, Elliot. *Educating Artistic Vision.* New York: Macmillan, 1972.

Gardner, Howard. *Art, Mind and Brain: A Cognitive Approach to Creativity.* New York: Basic Books, 1982.

Gardner, Howard. *Frames of Mind: The Theory of Multiple Intelligences.* New York: Basic Books, 1983.

Getty Center for Education in the Arts. *Issues in Discipline-Based Art Education: Strengthening the Stance, Extending the Vision.* Los Angeles: J. P. Getty Trust, 1987.

Herberholz, Donald and Barbara. *Artworks for Elementary Teachers,* 7th ed. Dubuque, Iowa: Brown & Benchmark Publishers, 1994.

Hurwitz, Al, and Day, Michael. *Children and Their Art: Methods for the Elementary School,* 5th ed., San Diego: Harcourt Brace Jovanovich, 1992.

Hymen, Ray. "Creativity and the Prepared Mind," Research Monograph #3. Reston, Va.: National Art Education Association, 1980.

Lankford, F. Louis. *Aesthetics: Issues and Inquiry.* Reston, Va.: National Art Education Association, 1992.

Maquet, Jacques. *The Aesthetic Experience: An Anthropologist Looks at the Visual Arts.* New Haven: Yale University Press, 1986.

Chapter 2

Anderson, Richard L. *Calliope's Sisters.* Englewood Cliffs, N.J.: Prentice Hall, 1990.

Bachtel, Ann. "Teaching Aesthetic Perception in the Elementary School." *Art Education,* Sept. 1985, 6–11.

Batterberry, Ariane R. *Pantheon Story of Art for Young Children.* New York: Pantheon, 1975.

Brommer, Gerald F. *Discovering Art History,* 2nd ed. Worcester, Mass.: Davis Publications, 1988.

Canaday, John. *What Is Art? An Introduction to Painting, Sculpture and Architecture.* New York: Alfred A. Knopf, 1980.

Cooper, J. C. *An Illustrated Encyclopedia of Traditional Symbols.* New York: Thames and Hudson, 1988.

Dissanayake, Ellen. *What Is Art For?* Seattle: University of Washington Press, 1988.

Feldman, Edmund Burke. *Varieties of Visual Experience,* 4th ed. New York: Harry N. Abrams, 1992.

Fichner-Rathus, Lois. *Understanding Art.* Englewood Cliffs, N.J.: Prentice Hall, 1986.

Frayling, Christopher and Helen; and van Der Meer, Ron. *The Art Pack.* New York: Alfred A. Knopf, 1992.

Goldstein, Ernest, et al. *Understanding and Creating Art, Books 1 and 2.* Dallas, Tex.: Garrard, 1986.

Heller, Nancy G. *Women Artists, An Illustrated History,* rev. and exp. ed. New York: Abbeville Press, 1987.

Highwater, Jamaica. *The Sweet Grass Lives On.* New York: Lippincott & Crowell, 1984.

Hobbs, Jack A. *Art in Context.* 3rd ed. New York: Harcourt Brace Jovanovich, 1985.

Horowitz, Frederick A. *More Than You See, A Guide to Art,* 2nd ed. New York: Harcourt Brace Jovanovich, 1992.

Hughes, Robert. *Nothing If Not Critical.* New York: Alfred A. Knopf, 1991.

Janson, H. W. and A. F., with Samuel Cauman. *History of Art for Young People.* New York: Harry N. Abrams, 1992.

Janson, H. W. and Janson, Dora Jane. *The Story of Painting from Cave Painting to Modern Times.* New York: Harry N. Abrams, 1977.

John, Arthur F. *Introduction to Art.* New York: HarperCollins, 1992.
Kampf, Avram. *Chagall to Kitaj: Jewish Experience in Twentieth Century Art.* Westport, Conn.: Praeger/Greenwood Publishing Group, 1991.
Lahti, N. E. *Plain Talk About Art.* Brooklyn: York Books, 1989.
Lippard, Lucy R. *Mixed Blessings, New Art in a Multicultural America.* New York: Pantheon Books, 1990.
McCarter, William, and Gilbert, Rita. *Living with Art.* New York: Alfred A. Knopf, 1985.
Mittler, Gene A. *Art in Focus.* Mission Hills, Calif.: Glencoe, 1989.
Munro, Eleanor. *Originals: American Women Artists.* New York: Simon & Schuster, 1979.
Ocvirk, Otto G., et al. *Art Fundamentals: Theory and Practice,* 7th ed. Dubuque, Iowa: Brown & Benchmark Publishers, 1994.
Ragans, Rosalind. *ArtTalk.* Mission Hills, Calif.: Glencoe, 1988.
Random House Library of Painting and Sculpture, vols. 1–4. New York: Random House, 1981.
Richardson, John A. *Art: The Way It Is,* 3rd ed. Englewood Cliffs, N.J.: Prentice Hall, 1986.
Rosenberg, Harold. *Art and Other Serious Matters.* Chicago: University of Chicago Press, 1985.
Roskill, Mark. *The Interpretation of Pictures.* Amhearst, Mass.: University of Massachusetts Press, 1989.
Russell, Stella Pandell. *Art in the World,* 2nd ed. San Francisco: Holt, Rinehart and Winston, 1984.
Selden, Rodman. *Artists in Tune with Their World.* New York: Simon & Shuster, 1982.
Sewell, Darrel; Mosby, Dewey; and Minter, R. A. *Henry Ossawa Tanner.* New York: Rizzoli, 1991.
Slatkin, Wendy. *Women Artists in History: From Antiquity to the 20th Century,* 2nd ed. Englewood Cliffs, N.J.: Prentice Hall, 1990.
Sporre, Dennis J. *Perceiving the Arts: An Introduction to the Humanities.* Englewood Cliffs, N.J.: Prentice Hall, 1985.
Steves, Rick, and Openshaw, Gene. *Mona Winks.* Santa Fe, N. Mex.: John Muir, 1988.
Steves, Rick, and Openshaw, Gene. *Europe 101,* 4th ed. Santa Fe, N. Mex.: John Muir, 1990.
Strickland, Carol. *The Annotated Mona Lisa.* Kansas City: Universal Press Syndicate, 1992.
Sullivan, Charles, ed. *Children of Promise, African-American Literature and Art for Young People.* New York: Harry N. Abrams, 1991.
Vasari, Giorgio. *The Great Masters.* New York: Park Lane, 1986.
Young, B., ed. *Art, Culture, and Ethnicity.* Reston, Va.: National Art Education Association, 1990.

Chapter 3

Finn, David. *How to Visit a Museum.* New York: Harry N. Abrams, 1985.
Glassie, Henry. *Spirit of Folk Art, The Girard Collection at the Museum of International Folk Art.* New York: Harry N. Abrams, 1989.
Herberholz, Barbara. *Art in Action Enrichment Programs, Levels I and II.* Austin, Tex.: Harcourt, Brace, Jovanovich, 1987.
Johnson, A. *Art Education: Elementary.* Reston, Va.: National Art Education Association, 1992.
Lipman, Jean, and Armstrong, Tom. *American Folk Painters of Three Centuries.* Arch Cape Press, N.Y., in association with the Whitney Museum of American Art, 1980.
Phipps, Richard, and Wink, Richard. *Invitation to the Gallery: An Introduction to Art.* Dubuque, Iowa: Brown & Benchmark Publishers, 1987.
Waterfall, Milde, and Grusin, Sarah. *Where's the Me in Museum, Going to Museums with Children.* Arlington, Va.: Vandamere Press, 1989.
Yenawine, Philip. *How to Look at Modern Art.* New York: Harry N. Abrams, 1991.

Chapter 4

Chapman, Laura. *Approaches to Art Education.* New York: Harcourt Brace Jovanovich, 1978.
Gardner, Howard. *Artful Scribbles: The Significance of Children's Drawings.* New York: Basic Books, 1980.
Gardner, Howard. *Art Education and Human Development.* Los Angeles: Getty Center for Education in the Arts, 1990.
Gessell, A. L.; Ames, L. A.; and Ilg, F. L. *The Child from Five to Ten.* New York: Harper and Row, 1977.
Goldstein, Ernest, et al. *Understanding and Creating Art, Books 1 and 2.* Dallas, Tex.: Garrard, 1986.
Gordon, Ann Miles. *Beginnings and Beyond: Foundations in Early Childhood Education,* 2d ed. Albany, New York: Delmar, 1989.
Kellog, Rhoda. *Analyzing Children's Art.* Palo Alto, Calif.: National Press Books, 1969.
Lanier, Vincent. *The Arts We See: A Simplified Introduction to the Visual Arts.* New York: Teachers College Press, 1982.
Lansing, Kenneth. *Art, Artists, and Art Education.* New York: McGraw-Hill, 1969.
Lowenfeld, Viktor, and Brittain, Lambert. *Creative and Mental Growth,* 8th ed. New York: Macmillan, 1987.
Parson, Michael. *How We Understand Art: A Cognitive Development Account of Aesthetic Experience.* New York: Cambridge University Press, 1987.
Peppin, Anthea. *The Usborne Story of Painting.* Tulsa, Okla.: Hayes Books, 1985.
Schirrmacher, Robert. "Talking with Young Children about Their Art." *Young Children,* vol. 41, no. 5, July, 1986.
Schirrmacher, Robert. *Art and Creative Development for Young Children.* Albany, New York: Delmar, 1988.

Tomlinson-Keasly, Carol. *A Child's Eye View—A New Way of Understanding the Development and Behavior of Children.* New York: St. Martin's Press, 1980.

Winner, Ellen. *Invented Worlds: The Psychology of the Arts.* Cambridge, Mass.: Harvard University Press, 1982.

Chapter 5

Stubbs, Charles; Winters, Nathan; and Cornia, Ivan. *Art Is Elementary, Teaching Visual Thinking through Art Concepts.* Layton, Utah: Gibbs Smith, 1983.

Szekely, G. *From Play to Art.* Portsmouth, N.H.: Heinemann Education Books, 1991.

Chapter 6

Qualley, Charles. *Safety in the Artroom.* Worcester, Mass.: Davis, 1986.

Spandorfer, Merle; Curtiss, Deborah; and Snyder, Jack. *Making Art Safely.* New York: Van Nostrand Reinhold, 1992.

Wachowiak, Frank. *Emphasis Art.* 4th ed. New York: Harper and Row, 1985.

Chapter 7

Arnheim, Rudolph. *Visual Thinking.* Berkeley: University of California Press, 1969.

Boston, N. E. *Determining Giftedness in Elementary Visual Art Students.* South Bend: Indiana University South Bend, ERIC Document Reproduction Service Number 301 025, 1987.

California Art Education Association. *In the Process: A Visual Arts Portfolio Assessment Pilot Project.* Sacramento: California Art Education Association, 1991.

California State Department of Education. *Arts for the Gifted and Talented: Grades 1 through 6.* Sacramento: California State Department of Education, 1981.

Chetelat, F. J. "Visual Arts Education for the Gifted Elementary Level Art Student." *Gifted Child Quarterly,* vol. 25, 1981.

Gardner, Howard. *Frames of Mind: The Theory of Multiple Intelligences.* New York: Basic Books, 1983.

Hunter, Madeline. *Mastery Teaching.* El Segundo, Calif.: Tip Publications, 1982.

Karnes, Merle B. *Creative Art for Learning.* Reston, Va.: Council for Exceptional Children, 1979.

Milgram, Roberta M., ed. *Counseling Gifted and Talented Children: A Guide for Teachers, Counselors, and Parents.* Norwood, N.J.: Ablex, 1991.

Morreau, Lanny, and Anderson, Frances E. "Individualized Education Programs in Art: Benefit or Burden?" *Art Education,* vol. 37, no. 6, November 1984.

Rodriguez, Susan. *The Special Artist's Handbook.* Palo Alto, Calif.: Dale Seymour Publications, 1984.

Smilansky, Sara. *Clay in the Classroom: Helping Children Develop Cognitive and Affective Skills in Learning.* Baltimore, Md.: Peter Lang, 1988.

Swann, Annette C., and Bickley-Green, Cynthia. "Basic Uses of Portfolios in Art Education Assessment." *NAEA Advisory,* Summer, 1993.

Uhlin, Donald M. *Art for Exceptional Children.* Dubuque, Iowa: Brown & Benchmark Publishers, 1982.

Uphoff, J. K. *Portfolio Development and Use: The Why's, How's, and What's.* Dayton, Ohio: Wright State University Department of Teacher Education, 1989.

Wakefield, John F. *Creative Thinking: Problem Solving Skills and the Arts Orientation.* Norwood, N.J.: Ablex, 1991.

Wehman, Paul. "Transition for Young People with Disabilities: Challenges for the 1990's." *Education and Training in Mental Retardation,* vol. 27, no. 2, 1992. (Special conference issue, ERIC Number ED 348810)

Chapter 8

Brookes, Mona. *Drawing with Children.* Los Angeles: Jeremy P. Tarcher, 1986.

Coles, Robert. *Their Eyes Meeting the World: The Drawings and Paintings of Children.* Boston: Houghton Mifflin, 1992.

Dean, Wayne. *The Incredible, Spreadable, Magic Drawing Book: A Course in Drawing for Young People.* Palo Alto, Calif.: Dale Seymour Publications, 1983.

Dvorak, R. Rafaello. *Drawing without Fear.* Palo Alto, Calif.: Dale Seymour Publications, 1987.

Edwards, Betty. *Drawing on the Right Side of the Brain.* Los Angeles: Jeremy P. Tarcher, 1979.

Johnson, Mia. *Teach Your Child to Draw.* Los Angeles: Lowell House, 1990.

Linderman, Marlene. *Art in the Elementary School: Drawing, Painting, and Creating for the Classroom,* 4th ed. Dubuque, Iowa: Brown & Benchmark Publishers, 1990.

Smith, N. R. *Experiences and Art: Teaching Children to Paint.* New York: Teachers College Press, 1983.

Topal, Cathy Weisman. *Children and Painting.* Worcester, Mass.: Davis, 1992.

Wilson, Brent; Hurwitz, Al; and Wilson, Marjorie. *Teaching Drawing from Art.* Worcester, Mass.: Davis, 1987.

Zhensun, Zheng, and Low, Alice. *A Young Painter: The Life and Paintings of Wang Yani—China's Extraordinary Young Artist.* New York: Scholastic, 1991.

Chapter 9

Bar, Marilyn. *Paper Crafts.* Palo Alto, Calif.: Monday Morning Books, 1989.

Brown, Charlene, and Davis, Carolyn. *Paper Art Fun.* Tustin, Calif.: Walter Foster, 1988.

Brown, Jerome C. *Mother Goose Papercrafts.* Carthage, Ill.: Fearon Teaching Aids, 1982.

Brown, Jerome C. *Classic Papercrafts.* Carthage, Ill.: Fearon Teaching Aids, 1991.

Grater, Michael. *Make It In Paper: Creative Three-Dimensional Paper Projects.* New York: Dover, 1983.

Grater, Michael. *Papercraft Projects with One Piece of Paper.* New York: Dover, 1987.

Hawcock, David. *Paper Dinosaurs.* New York: Sterling, 1988.

Lancaster, John. *Paper Sculpture.* New York: Franklin Watts, 1989.

Weiss, Harvey. *Working with Cardboard and Paper.* Reading, Mass.: Addison Wesley, 1978.

Chapter 10

Bolognese, Don, and Raphael, Don. *Printmaking.* New York: Franklin Watts, 1987.

Cross, Jeanne. *Simple Printmaking Methods.* New York: S. G. Phillips, 1972.

Meyesky, Mary. "Two Dimensional Activities: Printmaking." *Creative Activities for Young Children.* Albany, N.Y.: Delmar, 1990.

Solga, Kim. *Make Prints!* Cincinnati, Ohio: North Light Books, 1991.

Strose, Susanne. *Potato Printing.* New York: Sterling, 1968.

Chapter 11

Bawden, Juliet. *The Art and Craft of Papier Mâché.* New York: Grove Weidenfeld, 1990.

Chernoff, Goldie T. *Clay-Dough, Play Dough.* New York: Walker, 1974.

Hull, Jeannie. *Clay.* New York: Franklin Watts, 1989.

Jarvey, Paulette, *Let's Dough It Again.* Canby, Oreg.: Hot Off the Press, 1982.

Kanai, Tomoko. *Fun with Clay.* New York: Harper and Row, 1984.

Roussel, Mike. *Clay.* Vero Beach, Fla.: Rourke, 1990.

Solga, Kim. *Make Sculptures!* Cincinnati, Ohio: North Light Books, 1992.

Topal, Cathy. *Children, Clay and Sculpture.* Worcester, Mass.: Davis, 1983.

Wankelman, Willard F., and Wigg, Philip. *A Handbook of Arts and Crafts,* 5th ed. Dubuque, Iowa: Brown & Benchmark Publishers, 1982.

Chapter 12

Champlin, Connie, and Renfro, Nancy. *Storytelling with Puppets.* Chicago: American Library Association, 1985.

Feller, Ron and Marsha. *Paper Masks and Puppets for Stories, Songs, and Plays.* Seattle, Wash.: Arts Factory, 1985.

Grater, Michael. *Complete Book of Paper Maskmaking.* New York: Dover, 1984.

Hunt, Tamara, and Renfro, Nancy. *Pocketful of Puppets: Mother Goose.* Austin, Tex.: Nancy Renfro Studios, 1982.

Mayesky, Mary. "Dramatic Play and Puppetry," Unit 15. *Creative Activities for Young Children.* Albany, New York: Delmar, 1990.

Robson, Denny. *Masks and Funny Faces.* New York: Franklin Watts, 1992.

Sierra, Judy, and Kaminski, Robert. *Multicultural Folktales: Stories to Tell Young Children.* Phoenix, Ariz.: Oryx Press, 1992.

Sivin, Carole. *Maskmaking.* Worcester, Mass.: Davis, 1986.

Van Schuyrer, Jan. *Puppet Handbook: Introducing Stories to the Young Child.* Phoenix, Ariz.: Oryx Press, 1983.

Watson, Nancy Cameron. *The Little Pigs' Puppet Book.* Boston: Little, Brown, 1990.

Wright, Lyndie. *Masks.* New York: Franklin Watts, 1990.

Chapter 13

Alexander, Marthann. *Weaving on Cardboard: Simple Looms to Make and Use.* New York: Taplinger, 1972.

Belfer, Nancy. *Designing in Batik and Tie-Dye.* Englewood Cliffs, N.J.: Prentice Hall, 1977.

Enthoven, Jacqueline. *Stitchery for Children.* New York: Van Nostrand Reinhold, 1968.

Hecht, Ann. *The Art of the Loom: Weaving, Spinning and Dyeing Across the World.* New York: Rizzoli, 1989.

Kornerup, Ann-Mari. *Embroidery for Children.* New York: Van Norstrand Reinhold, 1969.

Meilach, Dona. *Creating Art From Fibers and Fabrics.* Chicago: Regnery Press, 1972.

Singer, Margo, and Spyirou, Mary. *Textile Arts; Multicultural Traditions.* Radnor, Pa.: Chilton, 1990.

Chapter 14

Burnett, Bernice. *The First Book of Holidays.* New York: Franklin Watts, 1974.

Dawson, Sophie. *The Art and Craft of Papermaking.* Philadelphia: Running Press, 1992.

Fowley, Virginia. *Folk Arts around the World and How to Make Them.* Englewood Cliffs, N.J.: Prentice Hall, 1981.

Gomez, Aurelia. *Crafts of Many Cultures, 30 Authentic Craft Projects from around the World.* New York: Scholastic, 1992.

Grummer, Arnold E. *Paper by Kids.* New York: Macmillan, 1990.

Grummer, Arnold E. *Tin-Can Papermaking: Recycle for Earth and Art.* Appleton, Wis.: Gregory Marekim, 1992.

Macdonald, Margaret Read, ed. *The Folklore of World Holidays.* Detroit: Gale Research, 1992.

Schuman, Jo Miles. *Art from Many Hands: Multicultural Art Projects for Home and School.* Englewood Cliffs, N.J.: Prentice Hall, 1980.

Shannon, Faith. *Paper Pleasures: The Creative Guide to Papercrafts.* New York: Grow Weidenfeld in association with I. Pariro, 1987.

Terzian, Alexandra M. *The Kids' Multicultural Art Book.* Charlotte, Vt.: Williamson, 1993.

Valentine, Malcolm, and Dace, Rosalind. *How to Make Your Own Recycled Paper.* Tunbridge Wells, Kent, England: Market Ecology/Search Press, 1993.

Glossary

● ●

abstract   A work or style that emphasizes design and a simplified presentation of shapes or forms. The subject matter may be recognizable but is transformed to emphasize colors, lines, textures, or shape/form.

Abstract Expressionism   A 20th century painting style that features large-scale works and the expression of feelings through spontaneous, active brushstrokes.

ACMI   Art and Craft Materials Institute, which certifies materials for safety according to stringent standards.

actual texture   Characteristic tactile quality of the surface of an artwork resulting from the way in which the materials were used.

adaptive tools   Regular or specially manufactured art tools that have been adapted for use by disabled persons to reduce frustration and provide better opportunities for success.

additive sculpture   A three-dimensional work of art in which the parts have been made separately and added (often refers to clay).

aesthetic perception   A designation for a specific aspect of art education that refers to learning to see the world metaphorically (through symbols) as well as directly (through the senses), in order to understand the expressive significance of an image, its import of message as aesthetically expressed.

aesthetics   The study of the qualities perceived in works of art; also the branch of philosophy dealing with concepts such as "beauty," on which criticism or judgments of artworks are based.

allegory   An imaginative device whereby a work contains a secondary meaning conveyed by symbols and illusions in addition to its literal content.

analogous colors   Colors that are closely related. For example, blue, blue-violet, and violet have the hue of blue in common. Families of analogous colors include the warm colors (red, orange, and yellow) and the cool colors (blue, green, and violet). Analogous colors are found next to one another on the color wheel.

appliqué   A textile technique in which separate pieces of material are sewn or otherwise attached to a larger piece of fabric. The entire work is also called an appliqué.

assemblage   A three-dimensional work of art composed of fragments of objects or materials (often found objects), which were originally intended for other purposes; the combining of unrelated materials into a new creation.

ASTM   American Society for Testing Materials, a nonprofit organization that issues certification seals on nontoxic art products.

asymmetrical balance   Having the type of balance in which the two sides of an object are not exactly alike but are in a state of equilibrium.

atmospheric perspective   An illusion of space in a two-dimensional work of art purposely created by progressive fainter and cooler (or bluer) hues to represent more distant objects (also called aerial perspective).

background   Parts of an artwork that are in the distance. The background is located behind the foreground and middle ground.

balance   The organization or arrangement of the elements in a work of art so that there appears to be a visual equilibrium or equality. There are three kinds of balance: symmetrical (formal), asymmetrical (informal), and radial.

bas-relief   Artwork in which parts project from the background to form actual depth and no part is entirely detached.

batik   A coloring or dyeing process that uses wax to protect design areas from coloration during the dyeing of the cloth or paper.

bisque   The first firing of a ceramic piece before it is glazed and fired again at a higher temperature.

blend   To mix colors together; also to progress smoothly from one color to another without making a line.

brayer A small roller used for inking a printing block or plate.

calligraphic drawing A kind of drawing made up of flowing lines and simple, curving shapes much like those used in calligraphy.

center of interest The visual focal point of a work of art; the area toward which all visual movement is directed.

ceramic An object made from clay that has been fired in a kiln.

charcoal A soft black material used to make drawings; also an artwork made with charcoal.

cityscape A two-dimensional work of art showing a whole or partial view of a city.

closed shape Space that is completely enclosed by a line. For example, a triangle is a closed geometric shape.

coil To wind into rings, one above the other. Also the technique of forming a pottery vessel by building up a series of clay "ropes" coiled one on top of the other on a flat clay base. Much of the pottery of primitive cultures was made by the coil method.

collage A pictorial composition created by attaching paper, fabrics, and other materials to a panel or paper; may be combined with painting or other techniques. When three-dimensional objects dominate, the work is called an "assemblage."

color An element in art that identifies the hue of natural and manufactured objects. Color is perceived as a response to the stimulus of radiant energy of certain wavelengths acting on the eye's sensors.

color scheme The colors an artist uses; also the way colors are combined in an artwork.

color wheel A system of showing the relationships among colors in the form of a circle. Colors that are next to one another on the wheel are called analogous colors; colors opposite one another on the wheel are called complementary colors.

complementary colors Colors that are opposites on the color wheel and contrast with one another. When complementary colors are mixed together, they tend to subdue the intensities and produce grayed hues. When placed next to one another, they produce optical vibrations. Examples of pairs of complementary colors are blue and orange, red and green, and yellow and violet.

composition The arrangement of the elements of art (line, color, value, texture, space, shape/form) in an artwork according to organizational principles, in order to create a unified, balanced artwork. The term is also used to refer to any work of art.

construction A work of art that is put together out of different pieces (rather than cast, modeled, or carved). An assemblage is one type of construction.

contour A single line or lines that define the outer and inner edges and surfaces of objects or figures.

contour drawing A drawing of an object using lines to show the outer and inner edges of an object.

contrast A principle of design that refers to using differences in values, colors, textures, and other elements to achieve emphasis and interest.

converge Inclined toward one another or come together at a point on the horizon line; converging lines in a two-dimensional work of art give the illusion of depth or space.

cool colors The family of related or analogous colors that ranges from violet through the blues and greens. Cool colors are so-called because they remind people of cool places, objects, or feelings.

creative Having the quality of originality in thought and expression.

cutout In art, a piece of paper cut into a shape and often arranged with other cutouts to form designs and pictures.

decorative Used as an embellishment or ornamentation.

depth In a work of art, the real or apparent distance from front to back or from near to far. Techniques of perspective are used to create the illusion of depth in two-dimensional artworks.

design The selection and arrangement of the elements in a work of art. Also, an organized, creative arrangement of the elements of an artwork (the lines, colors, textures, spaces, values, shapes/forms).

detail The distinctive feature of an object or composition that can be seen most clearly close up. Also, a small part of a work of art enlarged to show a close-up of its features.

diagonal Having an oblique direction; a line that extends either from upper right to lower left or lower right to upper left. Diagonal lines suggest motion and activity.

distort To stretch or change something out of its normal shape; change in an image (usually through exaggeration of proportions or space) purposefully made by an artist to make the work more interesting or expressive.

dominant The part of the composition that is the most important, powerful, or has the most influence; the most prevalent element (a certain color can be dominant, as can a line, shape, etc.)

egg tempera A type of tempera paint consisting of pigments mixed with pure egg yolk.

elements of art The visual parts of an artwork, such as color, value, line, space, texture, and shape/form; the "building blocks" an artist uses to create an original work of art.

embellish To adorn or enhance with additions; to elaborate or decorate.

emphasis A principle of art by which the artist organizes the elements in order to place greater attention on certain areas, objects, or feelings in the artwork.

empty shape An enclosed space that is left bare (instead of filled with pattern, color, texture); *see* filled shape.

engraving The process of incising lines into a surface to create an image; also a print created by this method.

etching   A technique in which a metal plate is incised by acid through scratches in a waxed coating; the metal plate is then inked and printed on paper; also a print made by this process.

exaggeration   Magnification or enlargement of parts of an object or artwork.

expressive   Emotion, feelings, or mood shown in such a way that others can see and identify it.

filled shape   An enclosed space that contains solid areas of texture, color, values, or patterns of repeated lines, colors, shapes, and values.

fixative   A liquid binder sprayed over artworks that are made with pastels, charcoals, and other materials to prevent smudging.

focal point   The central or principal point of activity or attention.

folk art   Traditional art made by people who have had no formal art training and who practice art styles and techniques handed down through generations.

foreground   The part of a work of art that appears to be in front, nearest the viewer. In a two-dimensional composition, the objects that are in the lower part of a picture appear to be in the foreground.

form   An object that has depth as well as length and width. For example, a circle is two-dimensional and is a shape; a sphere is three-dimensional and is a form. Also, the style or manner in which artists present their subject matter—the product of artistic organization, design, and composition.

formal balance   *See* symmetrical balance.

free-form   Not organized according to regulations or conventional rules; spontaneous.

fresco   (*"fresh" in Italian*) A painting technique for making murals in which water-based paint is used on wet plaster surfaces.

gallery   A space devoted to the exhibition of works of art.

genre   Paintings showing common people involved in ordinary scenes of everyday life, such as a domestic interior or a rural or village scene.

geometric   Employing simple rectilinear or curvilinear lines or figures used in geometry such as the circle, square, and rectangle.

glaze   In ceramics, a thin coating that is fused to a ceramic piece by firing in a kiln; a glaze may be applied by dipping, pouring, or brushing before the ware is fired. A glaze in painting is a thin film of transparent color laid over a dried underpainting.

gradation   A gradual, smooth change from light to dark, rough to smooth, or from one color to another.

hard-edged   A technique in which shapes are clearly and sharply defined, often in a simple application in which values and colors are even and flat in appearance.

harmonious colors   Colors that are perceived as going together because they are analogous, complementary, or otherwise related.

hatching   Use of parallel lines to create shading. When lines are overlapped at right angles to one another, the technique is called "cross-hatching."

high key   Dominated by light, bright, or pale colors.

horizon   A horizontal line where water or land seems to end and the sky begins.

horizontal line   A line that is straight across, parallel to the horizon or level ground. Horizontal lines in an artwork give the feeling of quiet and calm.

hue   The name of a color (such as "blue," "green," "yellow," "orange," "red," or "violet"); hue is another word for color.

illusion   False mental image. A common illusion in a work of art occurs when an artist uses perspective techniques to create the appearance of three-dimensional depth on a two-dimensional surface.

illustrate   To create designs and pictures for books or magazines in order to make clear or explain the text or to show what happens in a story.

image   A likeness or representation of objects and lifeforms used as the subject matter in a work of art. Also, a mental picture of something that is not in existence.

image banks   Observations of the visual world stored in memory; these stored images serve as a resource from which the mind can create realistic or imaginative images in works of art.

imagination   The power of recombining experiences or memories to create new images and ideas.

implied lines   The illusion of a line that does not exist in reality. Implied lines are created (1) when a visual series leads the eye from one point to another, or (2) when a change in surface suggests an edge to a shape or form.

informal balance   *See* asymmetrical balance.

intaglio   (in-*tahl*-ee-oh) A printmaking technique that transfers ink from areas (etched, engraved, or scratched) beneath the surface of a plate onto paper thus forming a type of two-dimensional art called a "print."

intensity   The brightness, strength, or purity of a hue or color. For example, a pure blue is very intense or bright; when its complement (orange) is added, it becomes dull or less intense. The intensity of a color can also be changed by adding neutrals (black, gray, white).

intermediate colors   Any of the six colors that are located between the primary and secondary colors on the color wheel; hues created by mixing primary colors with their adjacent secondary colors.

irregular shapes   Shapes that are not geometric or predictable (also called "free-form" or "natural"). Many shapes in nature are "irregular" or "natural."

landscape   A work of art that shows the features of the natural environment (trees, lakes, mountains). Although figures and manmade objects may be included in a landscape, they are of secondary importance.

latch hook   A hand tool with a hinged closure that holds a strand of yarn as it is pulled through backing; the hinge opens and releases the yarn to make a knot, and the yarn ends become part of the pile in a rug or wall hanging.

line A continuous mark or stroke with length and direction, created by a tool such as a pencil or pen that leaves a mark as it moves across a surface. A line can vary in length, width, direction, curvature, and even in color; it can be two-dimensional (a mark on paper) or three-dimensional (string or wire), or even implied. Line can refer to the boundary or external/internal edges of a shape or object.

linear perspective A system of drawing or painting that gives the illusion of depth on a flat surface. All horizontal lines that are parallel in nature converge on the horizon line at one or more imaginary vanishing points.

line drawing A picture composed only of lines, having no shading or areas of color.

lithography A printmaking process in which a flat stone, previously marked with a greasy substance (suspended either in liquid or a special crayon) that will retain the printing ink, is processed, inked, and run through a printing press along with paper. The print that results is called a "lithograph."

loom A frame or device in which yarns or other fibers are woven into fabric by crossing threads (called "weft") over and under stationary warp threads.

low key Dominated by dark or subdued colors.

medium A material used by an artist; often implies the technique of using that material. Plural is "media."

middle ground Parts of an artwork that appear to be between objects in the foreground and those objects in the distance (background).

mobile A balanced construction with moving parts, which is suspended from a single point above and which moves freely in the air currents; invented by Alexander Calder in 1932.

model A person who poses for an artist; an object that represents something; to shape, form, or build up with a pliable material such as clay.

modeled Using light and dark values on a two-dimensional surface to give the illusion of light falling in a three-dimensional form, delineating its form by means of shadow and light.

monochromatic One color; refers to colors formed by changing the values of a single hue by adding the neutrals (black, gray, white).

mood The feeling created through a work of art.

mosaic A picture made with small tiles, stones, pieces of paper, or other materials.

motif In design, the recurrent configuration repeated in a pattern. Also the main subject or idea of a work of art (such as "landscape" or "still life").

movement The arrangement of parts in a work of art to create a sense of motion by leading the viewer's eye through the work. Also a style or type of artistic practice (such as the Impressionist movement).

mural A painting on a wall, usually large in format; may also be a large piece designed to attach to a wall.

museum A building or place where works of art are kept and displayed.

negative shape (also called "negative space") The area around objects; called background in a painting or drawing. Can also exist as interior spaces in artworks such as open areas and shapes within a sculpture.

neutral A color not associated with a hue. Neutral colors include black, white, gray, brown, and tan.

nonobjective art Art that has no recognizable subject matter; the focus may be on color or the composition of the work itself. Also called "nonrepresentational art."

nontoxic Substances that are not harmful; nonpoisonous, safe.

observation The act of attentive viewing for a special purpose.

oil paint Opaque mixture of pigments dissolved in linseed oil, using turpentine as a solvent; used as paint applied to a panel or stretched fabric.

one-point perspective The representation of three-dimensional objects and space on a flat surface; horizontal lines that are parallel with each other appear to come closer together in the distance until they merge as a single, imaginary vanishing point on the horizon.

opaque Not allowing light to pass through; not transparent.

open shape Space that is partially enclosed by a line; in many cases, the viewer's eye will optically close the gap and perceive the implied shape.

optical Pertaining to the eye or what is seen.

original Inventive or creative; new, fresh, never before seen.

outline The line by which an object is defined or bounded; a line that represents the edges of a shape or form (sometimes called the "contour").

overlapping Covering or extending over part or all of an object.

palette A board or flat surface on which a painter places and mixes the paint to be used. Also, the typical group of colors that a particular artist (or group of artists) uses.

pastel A colored, chalky drawing stick; when pigment and oil are mixed and formed into a drawing stick, it is called an "oil pastel." Also, a tint of a color (such as pink).

pattern A design in which the elements (such as lines, colors, shapes) are repeated in either a regular or irregular manner.

perception Gaining of knowledge and insight about the visual and tactile qualities of the world by means of the senses and the mind.

perspective The representation of three-dimensional objects and space on a flat surface to produce the same illusion of distance and relative size as that received by the human eye.

pigment A dry substance that supplies the coloring agent for paint, crayons, chalk, inks, and dyes.

pointillism A method in which the principle of optical mixture or broken color is the foundation for applying colored pigment in tiny dots or small, isolated strokes. When viewed from a distance, the points of color appear to blend.

portrait An image of a person's face made with any two-dimensional medium or sculptural material.

positive shape   The area that makes up an object; the objects themselves as opposed to the background or space around the objects.

primary colors   The hues from which all other spectrum colors can theoretically be made: red, yellow, and blue are the three paint primaries. The three beam-of-light primaries are red, blue, and green.

primitive   Early or less sophisticated; also used to describe the art produced by untrained or self-taught artists.

principles of art   Refers to the way that artists organize and arrange the elements of art to create a painting, sculpture, piece of architecture, or craft objects. The principles of art are balance, emphasis, variety, proportion, movement, rhythm/repetition/pattern, variety, and unity.

prints   Multiple impressions made from a master plate or block by an artist.

process   A series of progressive and interdependent actions and thoughts directed toward specific learning, and often products, as part of meaningful art experiences.

product   A work of art; the end result of the art process.

profile   The outline of an object, especially the human face or head as viewed from one side; also a picture of the human profile.

progressive pattern   A pattern that develops step by step, as from larger to smaller or from smaller to larger.

proportion   A comparative size relationship between several objects or between parts of a single object or person. In art works, proportion may be seen as realistic, or it may be distorted and exaggerated for expressive or decorative purposes.

purpose   The reason for which a work of art was created by the artist.

radial balance   A design based on a circle with features radiating from a central point.

realistic   Art in which the subject matter is true to life without stylization or idealization.

relief prints   All those printing processes in which all nonprinting areas of a block or plate are carved, engraved, or etched away, leaving on the original plane surface only those lines and areas to be printed.

repetition   Motifs or elements shown over and over in a work of art; often creates movement and rhythm in an artwork.

representational   Any artistic style in which objects or figures are easily identified.

reproduction   A copy or duplicate of an original work of art.

resist   Process in which lines or surfaces are made with wax- or oil-based materials so that pigments suspended in water will not penetrate.

rhythm   Movement in an artwork or design, often developed by repeated shapes, lines, or colors.

rubbing   A handmade replica of an incised or carved surface made by laying a piece of paper over the surface and rubbing it with a crayon (also called a "frottage").

rya knot   Fibers tied tightly in a handwoven rug to form a thick pile, usually with a strong, colorful design (originated in Rya, Sweden).

schema   Organized set of marks forming recognizable images (symbols) in drawings and paintings.

sculpture   A three-dimensional work of art; a type of artwork seen in the round.

seascape   A work of art that shows part of the sea as the major image.

secondary colors   Orange, green, and violet; hues produced by mixing adjacent primary colors.

self-portrait   A drawing, painting, or other representation of the artist, made by him or herself.

serigraphy   Creative silk screen printmaking in which the artist designs, makes, and prints the stencils to create an original work of art.

shade   Black added to a color to make it darker; shades are dark in value.

shape   An element of art that is an enclosed space, having only two-dimensions. Shapes can be geometric (triangles, squares, circles, rectangles) or free-form (organic) with curving and irregular outlines.

silhouette   A black or dark shape with no interior details that represents the outline of an object, often a person's profile.

silk screen   *See* serigraphy.

sketch   A quick drawing that catches the immediate impression of a person, place, or situation.

slab   A manual technique of forming a ceramic object from clay that has been rolled and flattened.

slip   In ceramics, a very fluid mixture of clay and water used as a clay glue.

space   An element of art that indicates open areas in an artwork; also the illusion of depth in a two-dimensional work of art.

spectrum   The full range of pure colors; bands of colored light created when white light passes through a prism.

stabile   Similar to a mobile but is rigid and stationary rather than flexible and suspended; invented and named by Alexander Calder.

stencil   A method of producing images by cutting openings in a mask of paper or other material so that paint or dye may go through the openings to the material beneath.

still life   A drawing or painting of an arranged group of inanimate objects; usually, a still life is set indoors and contains objects such as vases, bowls, bottles, fruits, vegetables, flowers, etc.

stipple   To make small dots with the point of a brush by tapping with repeated staccato touches.

studio   The workroom of an artist.

style   Distinctive characteristics contained in the works of art of a person, a period of time, or a geographic location.

subtractive sculpture   Sculpture formed by cutting away excess material from a block to leave the finished work.

Surrealism   A style of art in which artists combine normally unrelated objects and situations. Surrealist artists utilize the subconscious, as well as dreams and fantasy as sources of inspiration.

symbol   A form, image, sign, or object representing a meaning other than the outward appearance.

symmetrical balance   Having the type of balance in which the two sides of a composition or object are mirror images of one another (also called "formal balance").

tactile   Pertaining to the sense of touch.

technical properties   Qualities of an artwork resulting from the use of materials, tools, and processes.

technique   The manipulative skill an artist employs in use and mastery of materials; also the artist's general knowledge of the mechanical details of the art form.

tempera   A water-based paint using opaque pigments.

texture   The element of art that refers to the quality of a surface, both tactile and visual.

theme   Images related to a common idea or subject and used in an artwork. An example would be art that shows "family" or "animals."

three-dimensional   Having length, width, and depth. An example of a three-dimensional artwork would be a sculpture.

tint   A light value of a hue, made by adding white to the original color.

toxic   Substances that are harmful or poisonous.

transparent   Having the property of allowing light to pass through so that objects underneath can be seen; the opposite of opaque. Watercolor paints are transparent.

two-dimensional   Having length and width; flat. An example of a two-dimensional artwork is a painting.

unity   A principle of art in which the elements are organized or combined with one another so that they form a harmonious whole.

value   An element of art that relates to the lightness or darkness of a color.

value scale   A series of tints and shades of one color ranging from the lightest at one end and gradually changing into the darkest shade at the other end.

vanishing point   In linear perspective, an imaginary point or points on the horizon line at which lines that are parallel and horizontal in nature will appear to converge.

variation   A change in color, size, or shape that makes an object different from the others it resembles.

variety   Being varied or diverse; changed to add interest to an artwork.

vertical   Perpendicular to the horizon; upright or going up and down.

viewfinder   A frame that shows a portion of the environment; used to find an image for use in an artwork.

viewpoint   A position from which an object or scene can be observed.

visualize   To form a mental picture; to see in the "mind's eye."

visual literacy   The ability to perceive and differentiate the sensory and expressive qualities in the visual world and to decode the symbols or messages that are aesthetically contained in artworks and the environment.

visual memory   The ability to remember the appearance of objects or scenes when they are no longer available for viewing.

visual texture   The appearance of texture in surfaces that actually have none. A photograph of tree bark would be an example.

warm colors   The family of related or analogous colors that ranges from yellow through the oranges and reds. Warm colors are so-called because they remind people of warm places, objects, or feelings.

warp   The set of yarns placed lengthwise in the loom, crossed by and interlaced with the weft to form a woven fabric.

wash   A thin, transparent layer of paint.

watercolor   Any paint that uses water as a medium, including acrylic, tempera, and transparent watercolor. Also an artwork made with transparent watercolor paints.

weaving   A pattern or method for interlacing yarns or other fibers to create fabric.

weft   The yarn or fibers that create the texture, color, and design of a textile; the filler or set of yarns placed crosswise to and interlaced with the warp.

woodcut   A relief printing technique in which the printing surface is carved from a block of wood. Also an original print made by this method.

Children's Books on Art

Learning About Colors, Shapes, Lines, and Textures

Art Concept Books (series) by Sharon Lerner (Minneapolis, Minn.: Lerner, 1974). *Square Is a Shape, Orange Is A Color, Straight Is A Line.*

The Color Box, ill. by Giles Laroche (Boston: Little, Brown, 1992).

Color Dance by Ann Jonas (New York: Greenwillow Books, 1990).

The Color Wizard by Barbara Brenner (New York: Bantam Doubleday Dell, 1989).

A Fishy Color Story: Learning About Colors by Joanne and David Wylie (Chicago: Childrens Press, 1983).

A Fishy Shape Story: Learning About Shapes by Joanne and David Wylie (Chicago: Childrens Press, 1984).

Hailstones and Halibut Bones by Mary O'Neill (New York: Doubleday, 1989).

How the Animals Got Their Colors by Michael Rosen, ill. by John Clementson (New York: Harcourt Brace Jovanovich, 1992).

I Am an Artist by Pat Lowery Collins (Brookfield, Conn: Millbrook Press, 1992).

Little Mouse's Painting by Diane Wolkstein, ill. by Maryjane Begin (New York: Wm. Morrow, 1992).

Mouse Paint by Ellen Stoll Walsh (New York: Harcourt Brace Jovanovich, 1992).

Museum Colors, Museum Numbers, Museum Shapes (Boston: Museum of Fine Arts, 1993).

Planting a Rainbow by Lois Ehlert (New York: Harcourt Brace Jovanovich, 1988).

The Real Color Book by Barbara and Donald Herberholz (Gold River, Calif.: 1905 Studebaker Pl., 1985).

The Shapes Game, verse by Paul Rogers, pictures by Sian Tucker (New York: Henry Holt, 1990).

Shapes, Lines, Colors, Stories (series) by Philip Yenawine (New York: Bantam Doubleday Dell, 1991).

Spirals, Curves, Fanshapes & Lines by Tana Hoban (New York: Greenwillow Books, 1992).

Square Triangle Round Skinny (four books in a box) by Eugenia and Vladimir Radunsky (New York: Henry Holt, 1993).

Thinking about Colors by Jessica Jenkins (New York: Dutton Children's Books, 1992).

Learning About Artists and Their Artworks

ABC, The Museum of Fine Arts by Florence Mayers (Boston: Museum of Fine Arts, 1986).

Alphabet Animals by Charles Sullivan (New York: Rizzoli, 1991).

Art for Children (series) by Jacqueline Loumaye (New York: Chelsea House, 1994). *Brueghel, Chagall, da Vinci, Degas, Gauguin, The Impressionists, Matisse, Miró, Picasso, The Renaissance, Rousseau, van Gogh.*

Art for Children (series) by Ernest Raboff (New York: J. B. Lippincott, 1987–88). *Marc Chagall, Leonardo da Vinci, Albrecht Dürer, Paul Gauguin, Paul Klee, Henri Matisse, Michelangelo, Pablo Picasso, Rembrandt van Rijn, Frederic Remington, Pierre-Auguste Renoir, Henri Rousseau, Henri de Toulouse-Lautrec, Vincent van Gogh, Diego de Silva y Velasquez.*

An Artist Grows Up In Mexico by Leah Brenner (Albuquerque, New Mex.: Univ of New Mexico Press, 1987).

Artists by Susan and John Edeen (Palo Alto, Calif.: Dale Seymour Publications, 1988).

The Art Lesson by Tomie de Paola (New York: Putnam & Grosset, 1989).

Art of _____ (series) by Shirley Glubok (New York: Macmillan, 1988). *Colonial America, New American Nation, Old West, Southwest Indians, Northwest Coast Indians, North American Indians, Plains Indians, Spanish in the U.S. and Puerto Rico, China, India, Japan, Africa, America in the Gilded Age, Photography, Ancient Peru, Ancient Rome, Etruscans, Vikings,* etc.

The _____ in Art, (series) by Sharon Lerner (Minneapolis, Minn.: Lerner, 1970). *Self-portrait, Kings and Queens, Warrior, Farms and Farmers, Portraits, Circus and Fairs,* etc.

Behind the Scenes (series) by Andrew Pekarick (New York: Hyperion Books for Children, 1992). *Painting Behind the Scenes, Sculpture Behind the Scenes.*

The Blue Faience Hippopotamus by Joan Grant, ill. by Alexandra Day (La Jolla, Calif.: Green Tiger Press, 1984).

Bonjour, Mr. Satie by Tomie de Paola (New York: Putnam & Grosset, 1991).

Buffalo Hunt by Russell Freedman (New York: Holiday House, 1988).

Cathedral, the Story of Its Constructions; also Castles, and others by David Macaulay (New York: Doubleday, 1973).

Children in Art, The Story in a Picture by Robin Richmond (Nashville, Tenn.: Ideals Children's Books, 1992).

A Child's Story of Vincent van Gogh by Laurin Luchner and George Kaye (Morristown, N.J.: Silver Burdett, not in print).

Come Look With Me (series) by Gladys S. Blizzard (Charlottesville, Va.: Thomasson-Grant, 1991,92). *Enjoying Art with Children, Exploring Landscape Art with Children, Animals in Art.*

Crocodile's Masterpiece by Max Velihuijs (New York: Farrar, Strauss & Giroux, 1992).

Diego by Jeanette Winter, text by Jonah Winter (New York: Alfred A. Knopf, 1991).

Enchanted World: Pictures to Grow Up With by Bryan Holme (New York: Oxford University Press, 1979).

Family Pictures, Cuadros de familia by Carmen Lomas Garza (San Francisco: Children's Book Press, 1990).

Famous Children (series) by Tony Hart (Hauppange, New York: Barron's, 1994) *Leonardo da Vinci, Michelangelo, Toulouse, Lautrec, Picasso.*

First Words by Ivan Chermayeff and Jane Clark Chermayeff (New York: Harry N. Abrams, 1990).

Getting to Know the World's Greatest Artists (series) by Mike Venezia (Chicago: Childrens Press, 1988). 13 titles: *Botticelli, da Vinci, Edward Hopper, Francisco Goya, Gauguin, Mary Cassatt, Michelangelo, Monet, Paul Klee, Picasso, Rembrandt, van Gogh, Pieter Bruegel.*

The Girl with a Watering Can by Ewa Zadrzynska (New York: Chameleon Books, 1989).

Go In and Out the Window, An Illustrated Songbook for Young People by Claude Marks, music edited by Dan Fox (New York: Henry Holt, 1987).

Grandma Moses, Painter of Rural America by Zibby Oneal (New York: Puffin, 1986).

Great Painters by Piero Ventura (New York: Putnam, 1987).

Harriet and the Promised Land by Jacob Lawrence (New York: Simon & Schuster Books for Young Readers, 1993).

History of Women Artists for Children by Vivian Epstein (Denver, Colo.: VSE Publishers, 1987).

Houses and Homes by Ann Morris, photos by Ken Heyman (New York: Greenwillow Books, 1992).

How to Show Grown-ups the Museum by Philip Yenawine (New York: Museum of Modern Art, 1985).

I Know That Building: Discovering Architecture with Activities and Games by Jane D'Alelio (Washington, DC: The Preservation Press, 1989).

An Illustrated Treasury of Songs National Gallery of Art, Washington, D.C., (New York: Rizzoli, 1991).

Introducing Michelangelo by Robin Richmond (Boston: Little, Brown, 1991).

I Spy: An Alphabet in Art by Lucy Micklethwait (New York: Greenwillow Books, 1992).

Just Imagine: Ideas in Painting by Robert Cumming (Middlesex, England: Kestrel Books, 1982).

Just Look: A Book about Paintings by Robert Cumming (New York: Charles Scribner's Sons, 1979).

Katie's Picture Show by James Mayhew (New York: Bantam Books, 1989).

Leonardo da Vinci by A. and M. Provensen (New York: Viking Press, 1984).

Leonardo da Vinci by Ibi Lepscky (Woodbury, N. Y.: Barron's, 1984).

Let's Go to the Art Museum by Virginia K. Levy (Pompano Beach, Fla.: Veejay, 1983).

Li'l Sis and Uncle Willie by Gwen Everett (New York: Rizzoli, 1992).

Linnea in Monet's Garden by Christina Bjork, ill. by Lena Anderson (New York: R & S Books, 1985).

Looking at Paintings by Frances Kennet & Terry Measham (New York: Van Nostrand Reinhold, 1979).

Looking at Paintings (series) by Peggy Roalf (New York: Hyperion Books for Children, 1992). *Dancers, Landscapes, Families.*

Looking for Vincent by Thea Dubelaar and Ruud Bruijn (New York: Checkerboard Press, 1992).

Marc Chagall, Painter of Dreams by Natalie S. Bober (Philadelphia and New York: The Jewish Publication Society, 1991).

Meet Edgar Degas by Anne Newlands (Toronto: Kids Can Press, 1988).

Meet Matisse by Nelly Munthe (Boston: Little, Brown, 1983).

The Metropolitan Museum of Art Activity Book by Osa Brown (New York: Harry N. Abrams, 1990).

Michelangelo's World by Piero Ventura (Kirkwood, N. Y.: Putnam, 1989).

Miro for Children by Helene Lamarche (Montreal, Canada: Montreal Museum of Fine Arts, 1986).

Mommy, It's a Renoir! by Aline D. Wolf (Altoona, Pa.: Parent Child Press, 1984). Also available as an accompaniment is *Childsize Masterpieces* by Aline D. Wolf (Altoona, Pa: Parent Child Press, 1987), a book of 36 color reproductions to use in making the games.

Move Over, Picasso! A Young Painter's Primer by Ruth Aukerman, published in _____ with the National Gallery of Art, Washington, D.C., (New Windsor, Md.: Pat Depke Books, 1994).

Numbers at Play: A Counting Book by Charles Sullivan (New York: Rizzoli, 1992).

Pablo Picasso by Ibi Lepscky, translated by H. R. MacLean (Woodbury, N. Y.: Barron's, 1984).

The Peaceable Kingdom by Ewa Zadrzynska (New York: M. M. Art Books, Inc., 1993).

Picture This: A First Introduction to Paintings by Felicity Woolf (New York: Doubleday, 1989).

Picture This Century by Felicity Woolf (New York: Bantam Doubleday Dell, 1993).

Pish, Posh, Said Hieronyumus Bosch by Nancy Willard (New York: Harcourt Brace Jovanovich, 1992). The fantasic imagery of this fifteenth century painter is explored.

A Potter by Douglas Florian (New York: Wm. Morrow, 1991).

The Private World of Tasha Tudor by Tasha Tudor (Boston: Little, Brown, 1992).

Pyramid by David Macaulay (Boston: Houghton Mifflin, 1975).

Rembrandt's Beret by Johnny Alcorn (New York: Wm. Morrow, 1991).

Rembrandt Takes a Walk by Mark Strand (New York: Clarkson N. Potter, 1987).

Round Buildings, Square Buildings & Buildings That Wiggle Like a Fish by Philip Isaacson (New York: Alfred Knopf, 1990).

A Russian ABC by Florence C. Mayers (New York: Harry N. Abrams, 1992).

The Seven Ancient Wonders of the World, a Pop-up Book by Celia King (San Francisco: Chronicle Books, 1990).

A Short Walk Around the Pyramids Through the World of Art by Philip M. Isaacson (New York: Alfred A. Knopf, 1933).

Smart Art, Learning to Classify and Critique Art by Patricia and Stephen Hollingsworth (Tucson, Ariz.: Zephyr Press, 1989).

Smudge by Mike Dickinson (New York: Abbeville Press, 1987).

Songs of the Wild West, commentary by Alan Axelrod, arrangements by Dan Fox (New York: Metropolitan Museum of Art, 1991).

Talking to the Sun: An Illustrated Anthology of Poems for Young People, selected and introduced by Kenneth Koch and Kate Farerell (New York: Henry Holt, 1985).

Tar Beach by Faith Ringgold (New York: Crown, 1991).

Visiting the Art Museum by Laurene K. Brown and Marc Brown (New York: EP Dutton, 1986).

A Visit to the Art Galaxy by Annie Reiner (New York: Green Tiger Press, 1991).

The Weaver's Horse by Jill and Robert Creighton (Toronto: Annick Press, 1991).

A Weekend with _____ (series) (New York: Skira/Rizzoli, 1991). *Degas* by Rosabianca Skira-Venturi; *Picasso* by Florian Rodari; *Rembrandt* by Pascal Bonafoux; *Renoir* by Rosabianca Skira-Venturi.

What It Feels Like to Be a Building by Forrest Wilson (Washington, DC: The Preservation Press, 1988).

What Makes a Degas a Degas? by Richard Mühlberger (New York: Metropolitan Museum of Art, Viking, 1994). Also *Monet, Bruegel, Raphael, Rembrandt,* and *van Gogh.*

Who Has Seen the Wind? ed. by Kathryn Sky-Peck (New York: Rizzoli, 1991).

Women Artists by Susan and John Edeen and Kay Alexander (Palo Alto, Calif.: Dale Seymour Publications, 1988).

N. C. Wyeth's Pilgrims by Robert San Souci (New York: Harry N. Abrams, 1992).

Learning About Multicultural Art

Annie and the Old One by Miska Miles, ill. by Peter Parnall (Boston: Little, Brown, 1985).

Aztec Indians by Patricia McKissack (Chicago: Childrens Press, 1985).

Chancay and the Secret of Fire by Donald Charles (Kirkwood, N. Y.: Putnam & Grosset, 1992).

Children of Promise, ed. by Charles Sullivan (New York: Harry N. Abrams, 1991).

Children's Atlas of Native Americans (New York: Rand McNally, 1992).

Don't Tell Anybody but . . . There Are Anasazi in Canyon de Chelly by Michael Fillerup (Chinle, Ariz.: Navajo Curriculum Development & Production Center, 1990).

Emperor and the Nightingale (book and cassette) by Hans Christian Anderson, read by Glenn Close, music by Mark Isham (Saxonville, Mass.: Rabbit Ears Storybook Classics, 1988).

A Fish That's a Box by M. M. Esterman (Arlington, Va: Great Ocean Publishers, 1990).

Flyaway Girl by Ann Grifalconi (Boston: Little, Brown, 1992).

The Folk Art Counting Book by Amy Watson and staff, Abby Aldrich Rockefeller Folk Art Center (New York: Harry N. Abrams, 1992).

The Girl Who Loved Caterpillars by Jean Merrill (Kirkwood, N. Y.: Putnam & Grosset, 1992).

The Goat in the Rug by Charles L. Blood and Martin Link (New York: Four Wings Press, 1990).

Indian How Book by Arthur Park (New York: Dover, 1975).

Land of the Long White Cloud: Maori Myths, Tales and Legends by Kiri Te Kanawa, ill. by Michael Foreman (Boston: Little, Brown, 1990).

The Legend of the Indian Paintbrush by Tomie de Paola (New York: Putnam & Grosset, 1991).

Liang and the Magic Paintbrush by Demi (New York: Henry Holt, 1980).

The Magic Vase by Fiona French (New York: Oxford University Press, 1991).

Moon Rope, Un Lazo a la Luna, written and ill. by Lois Ehlert, translated into Spanish by Amy Prince (San Diego/New York: Harcourt Brace Jovanovich, 1992).

Northern Lullaby by Nancy W. Carlstrom, ill. by Leo and Diane Dillon (New York: Philomel Books, 1992).

Pancho's Piñata by Stefan Czernecki and Timothy Rhodes (New York: Hyperion Books for Children, 1992).

Papagayo the Mischief Maker, written and ill. by Gerald McDermott (San Diego/New York: Harcourt Brace Jovanovich, 1992).

Pyramid of the Sun, Pyramid of the Moon by Leonard Fisher (New York: Macmillan, 1988).

Shadow, translated and ill. by Marcia Brown (New York: Charles Scribner's Sons, 1991).

Shaka, King of the Zulus by Diane Stanley and Peter Vennema, ill. by Diane Stanley (New York: Morrow Junior Books, 1988).

South, North, East and West, ed. by Michael Rosen, intro. by Whoopi Goldberg (Cambridge, Mass.: Candlewick Press, 1992).

Sundiata by David Wisniewski (New York: Clarion Books, 1992).

Sunrise Island, A Story of Japan and Its Arts by C. Alden (New York: Parents' Magazine Press, 1971).

Ten Little Rabbits by Virginia Grossman and Sylvia Long (San Francisco, Chronicle Books, 1991).

Turquoise Boy, A Navajo Legend by Terri Cohlene, ill. by Charles Reasoner (Mahwah, New Mex.: Watermill Press, 1990).

When Clay Sings by Byrd Baylor, ill. by Tom Bahti (New York: Charles Scribner's Sons, 1987).

Why the Sky Is Far Away, retold by Mary-Joan Gerson, ill. by C. Golembe (Boston: Little, Brown, 1992).

Zomo the Rabbit, written and ill. by Gerald McDermott (San Diego/New York: Harcourt Brace Jovanovich, 1992).

Resources for Art Education
Preschool Through Grade 3

● ●

Suppliers for Student Textbooks, Packaged Programs, and Videos (catalogs available)

Art Image Publications, Inc., PO Box 568, Champlain, NY 12919–0568 (800–361–2598). "Mini-Kits," sets containing thirty small laminated reproductions along with booklet on their use; "Imagine and Me" for kindergarten, kit with teacher's guide, audio cassettes for teacher and student, student book, and other assorted items; "Art: First Nations," kit of large art prints of North American Indian art along with teacher's guide.

Art Media, Etc., 1905 Studebaker Place, Gold River, CA 95670. "Art Docent Program," manual with portfolio and hands-on lessons to be used with sets of mounted reproductions.

Crizmac Art and Cultural Education Materials, 3316 North Chapel Ave., Tucson, AZ 85716. Native American reproductions; "Gente del Sol"—"Native Arts of Mexico and Guatemala" audiovisual program; "Whimsical Art of Paul Klee" print package; thirty modern art posters; art games.

Crystal Productions, Box 2159, Glenview, IL 60025. (800–255–8629). Ceramics prints; videos: "The Art Teacher Series," "Let's Create Series"; numerous videos on individual artists; "Take 5 Art Prints" series; "Multicultural Art Print" series copublished with Getty Center for Education in the Arts and the J. Paul Getty Museum: Mexican American Art, Selected American Indian Artifacts, African American Art, and Pacific Asian Art; world folk art video and prints; multicultural prints on art from China, India, Japan, and Islam; videos and prints on "Masks from Many Cultures" and "Masks and Face Coverings"; sets of prints on "Three-Dimensional Art," "20th Century Art," "Architecture," "Latin America," "African-American Painters," and various individual artists; "Clear, Elementary Art Skills" set 1 for K–3.

Dale Seymour, PO Box 10888, Palo Alto, CA 94303–0879 (800–872–1100). "Learning to Look and Create: The Spectra Program" containing prints, slides and teacher's manuals for K–8; "Creative Expressions," an art curriculum containing twenty lessons on cards for each grade level, K–6.

Davis Publications, Worcester, MA 01608. *Discover Art* textbooks for grades 1–8; *Discover Art Kindergarten;* sets of reproductions to accompany texts; teaching art 1–3 kits; various videos/videodiscs; children's fine art puzzles.

Harcourt Brace Jovanovich, Orlando, FL 32887 (800–782–4479). *Art in Action* textbooks, Guy Hubbard, for grades 1–8.

Knowledge Unlimited, Inc., PO Box 52, Madison, WI 53701–0052. Set of eight posters along with teacher manual on African American artists from the past 100 years.

Wilton Programs, Reading and O'Reilly, PO Box 541, Wilton, CT 06897. Series 100, six videos or filmstrips on "Color," "Elements of Design," "Artist at Work," "Art Around Us," "Many Ways of Seeing," and "Art Adventure"; Series 200, six videos or filmstrips on "People Doing Things," "Animals," "Portraits," "Still Lifes," "Landscapes," and "More People"; videos on "African American Art: Past and Present" and the "Life and Art of William H. Johnson."

W. S. Benson and Co., Austin, TX. *Through Their Eyes,* Brooks et al., textbooks for grades 1–3.

Suppliers for Reproductions of Artworks (catalogs available)

Art Extension Press, Box 389, Westport, CT 06881.
Austin Reproductions, Inc., 815 Grundy Ave., Holbrook, NY 11741. Sculpture replicas.
Haddad's Fine Arts, PO Box 849, Atwood, CA 92601.
Harcourt Brace Jovanovich, Orlando, FL 32887 (800–782–4479). "Art in Action Enrichment Programs, I and II."
Imaginus Inc., 51 Harpswell St., Brunswick, ME 04011.
New York Graphic Society, Ltd., PO Box 1469, Greenwich, CT 06482.
Shorewood Reproductions, 27 Glen Rd., Sandy Hook, CT 06482.
Starry Night Distributors, Inc., 19 North St., Rutland, VT 05701 (800–255–0818).
Universal Color Slide Co., 8450 South Tamiami Trail, Sarasota, FL 34238.
University Prints, 21 East St., Winchester, MA 02890.

Museum Resources (catalogs available)

Metropolitan Museum of Art, Special Services Office, Middle Village, NY 11381–0001.
Museum of Fine Arts, PO Box 1044, Boston, MA 02120–0900 (800–225–5592).
Museum of Modern Art, 11 West 53rd St., New York, NY 10019–5401.
National Gallery of Art, Mail Order Dept., 2000 B. South Club Dr., Landover, MD 20785.
National Museum of African Art, Dept. of Education, 950 Independence Ave. SW, Washington, DC 20560.

Whitney Museum of American Art, 945 Madison Ave., New York, NY 10021.

Magazines (by subscription)

Arts and Activities, 591 Camino de la Reina, Suite #200, San Diego, CA 92108 (for teachers).
Scholastic Art, Scholastic, Inc., 2931 East McCarty St., PO Box 3710, Jefferson City, MO 65102–3710 (for upper grades and teachers).
School Arts, 50 Portland St., Worcester, MA 01608 (for teachers).
Spark! Creative Fun for Kids, PO Box 5028, Harlan, IA 51593 (for children).

Art Supplies (catalogs available)

Beckley Cardy, One East First St., Duluth, MN 55802 (800–227–1178).
Chaselle, Inc., 9645 Gerwig Lane, Columbia, MD 21046 (800–242–7355).
Dick Blick, Dept. A, PO Box 1267, Galesburg, IL 61401.
Nasco, 901 Janesville Ave., Fort Atkinson, WI 53538; also 1524 Princeton Ave., Modesto, CA 95352 (800–588–9595).
Sax Arts and Crafts, PO Box 51710, New Berlin, WI 53151 (800–558–6696).

Index